# A HISTORY OF LUTHERANISM
# IN THE ANDHRA DESA

## (The Telugu Territory of India)

# 1842-1920

A THESIS By Martin Luther Dolbeer, Jr.
Submitted to the Faculty of THE HART-
FORD THEOLOGICAL SEMINARY in partial
fulfillment of the requirements for the
degree of DOCTOR OF THEOLOGY.

Published by the
BOARD OF FOREIGN MISSIONS
THE UNITED LUTHERAN CHURCH IN AMERICA
231 Madison Ave.
New York, N.Y.
1959

# VITA

Martin Luther Dolbeer, Jr., the son of Martin Luther Dolbeer and Jennie Clifton Dolbeer, was born July 1, 1921, in North Baltimore, Ohio. At the age of three months he accompanied his parents to Narasaravupet, Madras Presidency, South India (in the Andhra Desa), where they began their first term as missionaries of the United Lutheran Church Mission. Narasaravupet was the author's home for the next sixteen years. Telugu was the first language he spoke; he did not use English until he entered first grade. As a boy, he accompanied his father on evangelistic tours, inspections of schools and visitations to congregations.

The author received his education at the Highclerc School, Kodaikanal, South India, through the sophomore year in high school. He also spent a semester in Andhra Christian College, Guntur, taking courses in chemistry, physics and Latin. He was graduated from the Springfield, Ohio, high school in 1939. He took an English major at Gettysburg College, Gettysburg, Pennsylvania, and was graduated in 1943 with the degree of B.A., cum laude. He prepared for the ministry at Hamma Divinity School, Wittenberg College, Springfield, Ohio, receiving a B.D. degree in 1945 and being ordained by the Synod of Ohio that same year.

He served as assistant pastor, Kountze Memorial Lutheran Church, Omaha, Nebraska (1945-1948); pastor, First Lutheran Church, Southington, Connecticut (1949-1956); and pastor, Trinity Lutheran Church, Rochester, New York (1956-    ). He is a member of the Committee on Foreign Missions of the United Lutheran Synod of New York and New England, and served as chairman of the corresponding committee of the New England Conference of the Synod. He is a candidate for the Th.D. degree at the Hartford Theological Seminary, Hartford Seminary Foundation, in the field of Church History, including History of Missions, and Systematic Theology.

PREFACE

This <u>History</u> was planned originally by the author to be a
contribution to the historical records of the Lutheran Church.
It proved to be a far more difficult task than ever anticipated.
Much of the literature written by the missionary or the Home
Board of a Church is of little value historically.  It is written
to interest the reader in the cause of foreign missions.  To
ferret out truth and fact from exaggeration and distortion, to
arrive at the correct figure from statistical lists at variance
with each other, to determine the real meaning behind veiled
implications -- all of this and much more faced the author at
each turn of the road.

And then to come across a gold mine of unprinted documents
of whose existence you had no knowledge and find it hand-written
in old German script, material which took nearly a year in itself to translate and evaluate, such an obstacle turned the road
into a steep mountain climb.  It was an interesting but exhaust-
ing journey.

The attempt was made in this thesis to arrange the historical development so that it did not become a mere chronological
recitation of facts.  This was a difficult task for several
reasons.  Although each of the Missions under consideration had
very similar experiences in its historical development, there

v

is a wide variation of time involved.  A span of forty years
stretches between the founding of the first and the last of the
Mission Fields.

Under certain headings it was possible to discuss the Missions as a group; under others it was necessary to take one Mission at a time.  To bring unity out of confusion and relate the
historical development of one particular Mission so that it could
be followed throughout the thesis demanded a certain amount of
repetition and an abundance of references to other sections of the
thesis.

The matter of spelling in English the towns and places in
India is an interesting study in itself.  The same author or
source material would often spell the same place in two or three
different ways.  We have attempted some unity by using the spelling generally used by the Andhra or South Andhra Churches today.
For other places we have referred to the Directory of Churches
and Missions in India and Pakistan, 1951, and the Survey of India
Map Catalogue, 1945.

Translations from the German have been made only with veri-
fication by German students at Hartford Seminary Foundation or
Wittenberg College.

The author wishes to acknowledge the abundance of assistance
he received in gathering the material and preparing the thesis.
A word of appreciation goes to Hamma Divinity School and its

Dean, the Rev. Dr. E. E. Flack, for the Victor Tressler University Scholarship; to the Rev. Dr. J. Russell Fink for his coaching in the Telugu language; to Heinz Oelze for his help in securing source material from Hermannsburg, Hanover, in Germany; to the Philadelphia and Gettysburg Lutheran Seminary Library staffs for their assistance in using the archives, especially at times when classes were not in session; to the Foreign Mission Boards of the American and United Lutheran Churches for their willingness to permit the author to delve into their files, libraries and archives; to the Rev. Henry E. Horn for the use of the unpublished manuscript of H. E. Jacobs; to the Rev. Dr. J. Roy Strock for the use of his personal files of materials on the U.L.C. Mission and Andhra Christian College; to Mr. Howard Fischer and the Art Print Shop of Rochester for their invaluable assistance in preparing the map of the Andhra Desa; to my father, the Rev. Dr. Martin L. Dolbeer, Sr., for securing source materials from India and providing valuable suggestions through correspondence; to the Rev. Dr. Malcolm Pitt of the Kennedy School of Missions for his pertinent suggestions and many hours of helpful consultation on, and clarification of, Indian missions and customs. And finally to the ordinarius, the Rev. Dr. Matthew Spinka, and his Committee, I wish to add a word of thanks for interest and patience.

# TABLE OF CONTENTS

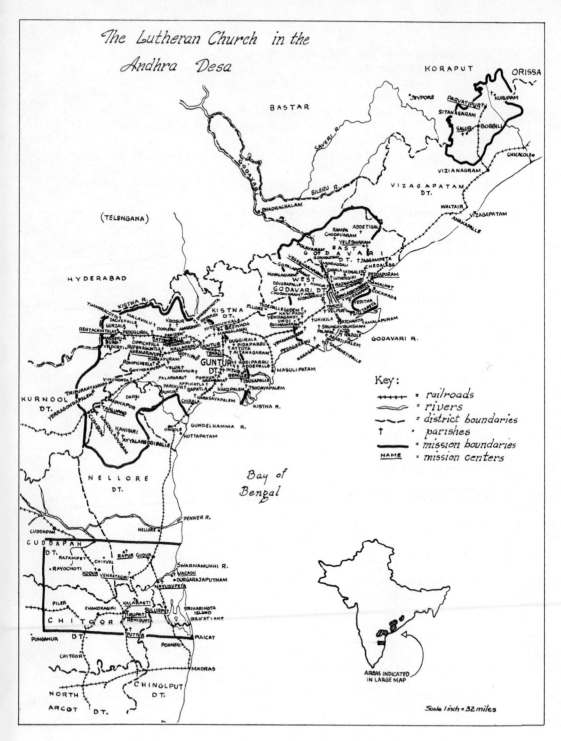

The Lutheran Church in the
Andhra Desa

CHAPTER I

THE LUTHERAN CHURCH AND THE 19TH CENTURY MISSIONARY MOVEMENT

A. Introduction

The Lutheran Church, so active in the early efforts of the missionary movement in the 17th and 18th centuries,[1] was slow to awake to its responsibilities in the modern era of missions. This may seem strange until it becomes apparent that the leading spirit behind the earlier movement came from Pietistic circles, which were strongly opposed by the majority of the Church.[2]

Protestantism generally was lacking in the missionary idea for a century following the Reformation. It is true that there was little opportunity for the expression of the missionary conception among the early Reformers, who were completely engrossed in the struggle against Roman Catholicism, the development of their theological positions and the controversies which followed, and the establishment of Protestantism throughout the areas opening up to them. Moreover, among the Protestant lands, especially Germany, there was practically no contact with nations outside Europe, and consequently little interest aroused.[3]

But, rather than be concerned over these difficulties in their way, the Reformers indicated by their theological arguments that they considered the call of Christ's Great Commission completed by the Apostles. Since the end of the world was fast ap-

1

proaching, there was no time to spread the Gospel throughout the whole world.  Although conscious of the Turks and Islam, the immediate task was to preach to the heathen or Gentiles, that is, the 'paganized Christian church', all around them in Germany and Europe.  Then from Europe it would spread spontaneously into other parts through travelers and prisoners.  Many considered it the special duty of the rulers to spread Christianity in their lands, but these in turned showed little concern.  All in all, it must be admitted that early Protestantism neither felt the duty nor the privilege of establishing missionary organizations and sending out volunteers.[4]  This was true in spite of the missionary idea inherent in Protestantism's restoration of the apostolic preaching of the Gospel, rather than the forcing of one's faith upon another by the sword.

This position was maintained until the rise of Pietism.  Missionary ideas and appeals appeared from time to time, mostly to remind the civil authorities of their responsibilities.  Leaders of orthodoxy bitterly opposed any attempt to present theological arguments in favor of the Christian's duty to "go into all the world" with the Gospel message.  Actual attempts to establish missions also were made.  When the Netherlands government provided the East India Company with a charter in 1602, provisions were made for the planting of the church and the conversion of the heathen.  As had been true for centuries, there was no thought of

2

the separation of church and state. This was considered a natural facet of colonial government and did not come from any true missionary spirit among the people or churches. Certain individuals were thoroughly aroused, however, and many offered sacrificial service. Preaching in the language of the people, Bible translation and education of natives to help in schools and churches were carried on at first. But where Dutch rule came to an end, the work vanished almost as quickly, mostly because of the superficial spiritual care by too few missionaries and the mass baptisms after negligible instruction. Where Dutch rule was maintained, a nucleus remained, however, upon which to base the great expansion of Christianity in the 19th and 20th centuries.[5]

Of greater interest to the Lutheran Church is the effort of John Campanius Holm, Swedish pastor working in "New Sweden" on the banks of the Deleware River in America, who initiated work among the Virginia Indians and translated Luther's Small Catechism into their language in 1648. This work lasted more than one hundred years.[6] Much more important in influencing later missionary developments and interest were the life and writings of Baron Justinian von Weltz. This Austrian nobleman was filled with concern because of the lukewarm Christianity evident in his day. He felt that vital Christian living and the study of the Bible naturally led to the desire to express one's faith "by the extension of the Gospel in the non-Christian world. ... That is a point of great significance, that for him missions and living Christianity stand in

3

innermost connection."[7]  In several appeals to rulers, nobles,
professional men, students and all 'Jesus-loving' Christians, von
Weltz called for the establishment of a society, supported by  voluntary gifts, which would work for the extension of Christ's Kingdom everywhere.  The plan included the formation of a "collegium
de propaganda fide," where young men would be prepared as missionaries.  He also advised the missionaries to make a thorough study
of the country to which they were called to serve -- its people,
religion and language -- and work diligently in translating, the
gathering of congregations and the preparation of home reports.

When, despite his urgent appeals, von Weltz's efforts met
with ridicule and concerted opposition, he showed that he believed
what he had been impelling on others by going forth as a missionary to Dutch Guiana in South America, where all too soon he gave
up his life.  It is not known how much influence he had on suc-
ceeding developments, but it is certain that from this time on the
mission imperative aroused increasing discussion and concern.  The
combination of vital Christian living and the mission spirit in
von Weltz indicates his close affinity to Pietism.[8]

Pietism was a reaction, to some extent, to the other extreme,
from the formalism and deadness of seventeeth century Protestantism.
The leaders of this movement in Germany, Philip Jacob Spener and
August Hermann Francke, gave the first real impetus to modern Protestant missions.  Although not primarily a missionary movement,

Pietism naturally led to the acceptance of the missionary idea. From the house meetings, called 'collegia pietatis', which Spener and Francke conducted for the study of the Bible and the exchanging of personal religious experiences, came forth young men inspired with "absolute devotion to divine service, ... ready to go anywhere where there was need of them."[9]  Deep, loving concern for others and their conversion led 'narrow-minded' Pietists to include the whole world in their thoughts and works of love.  They thus led Protestantism in the field of Inner or social missions as well as foreign.  Under the tutelage of Francke two of them, Plutschau and Ziegenbalg, were well prepared to answer the appeal of King Frederick IV of Denmark for missionaries to serve in the Danish colony in India.  None could be found elsewhere; and thus it developed that German Pietists manned the Missions established and financed by the Danes and English through the 18th century. It is of significance that the Protestant world now is celebrating the 250th anniversary of the establishment of this work in Tranquebar.

Francke also kept these early missions and the missionary spirit at home alive through his articles and reports.  He developed individual concern for such work until the Church through organized societies took the responsibility for its continuance and financial support -- a duty formerly left up to rulers.[10]

Following in the footsteps of the Pietists, but with even greater devotion and dedication, the Moravians and others who formed the 'Unitas Fratrum' under Count Zinzendorf gave themselves in the most amazing fashion to establish missions in many corners of the world. Because they kept separate from others, they were able to maintain their missionary spirit throughout the eighteenth century in the face of Rationalism, which proved so devastating to the spiritual fervor of German Pietism and the rest of Protestantism. The Moravian Brethren served mostly as poorly-educated laymen, but they made it clear that the work of missions is the responsibility of the whole Church. This was a basic contribution to the development of future missionary efforts, in addition to the emphases of individual conversion, personal religious experience and necessity of organization inherited from the Pietists.[11]

The influence of the Moravians and the Pietists did not stop there, however. John Wesley and George Whitefield, the great leaders of the revival which brought the Church back from its rationalistic lethargy, were led to spiritual zeal and understanding through contact with them.[12] The repercussions of the Wesleyan revival were felt far beyond the shores of England, playing a key part in the Great Awakening in the American colonies and putting new life-blood into the veins of European Churches, drugged by rationalism. It did not in itself lead immediately to foreign mission work, since its prime purpose was evangelism and the

6

spiritual renewal of Christendom; but it prepared the way and made possible the establishment of missionary societies and the development of leadership for the surge of missionary effort at the turn of the century.

## B. In Germany

We have noted how the Pietistic and Moravian movements of Germany contributed toward the rise of the evangelical and missionary spirit in England. The fresh missionary movements in England, in turn, put life back into what seemed nearly a dead cause on the continent. Indifference and rationalism had well-nigh closed the famous East India Missionary Institute at Halle by the end of the eighteenth century; and it was only because the Church of the Brethren had insulated itself from general Church life in Germany that it too had not become infected by the spirit of the times. The impact of William Carey and the Baptist Missionary Society formed in 1792 not only influenced circles in the Church of England, but spread to the United States and the European continent.

In Berlin there stood a lone figure struggling valiantly for the Gospel in the midst of little faith -- Pastor John Jaenicke, leader and pastor of the Bohemian Protestant refugees. Concern for the missionary effort was a prominent part of his ministry, both because of his earlier contact with the Church of the Breth-

ren and because of a missionary brother connected with the Danish-
Halle mission in India. But it was the inspiration of a pious
layman, von Schirnding, who had come in contact with the London
Missionary Society and had been appointed a director of that Society in Germany, which led "Father" Jaenicke to establish a missionary school, the first Protestant institution whose object was
primarily the direct training of missionaries.[13] From 1800 until
Jaenicke's death in 1827 some eighty missionaries went forth to
serve mostly under the London Missionary Society, the Church Missionary Society and the Netherlands Missionary Society. Financial
assistance for the school came from England and various areas of
Germany. Rhenius and Gutzlaff were two of the students of that
famous school who need to be mentioned not only for their great
work as missionaries, but also because of the important role they
performed in bringing Lutherans in the United States into the
missionary task.[14] Although this school did not continue too long
after Jaenicke's death, it led to the establishment of the Berlin
Missionary Society in 1824.

The English influence was even greater in Basel where a "German Society for the Promotion of Pure Doctrine and True Godliness"
established in 1780 by Augustus Urlsperger, Dean of Augsburg, became deeply interested, among other things, in the new English
missionary enterprises and spread information about them through
its literary magazine. This area had many former friends of the

old Danish-Halle Mission, and so it was not long before much enthusiasm was aroused and the Basel Missionary Institute established in 1815. Immediate cause of the starting of this seminary came
from gratitude on the part of the people of Basel when almost certain destruction was averted in 1815 as the city was being bom-
barded from Hueningen.[15] During seven years the institute sent
forth eighty-eight students to serve the Church Missionary Society. But in 1822 it began to send missionaries to its own fields.
Quite a number of regional and local societies came into existence in Germany to support the Basel Society. And some of these in
turn later became independent with their own foreign missions, such
as the Rhenish Society in 1828, the Dresden Society in 1836 and
the North German Society in 1836.

The opposition of the Lutheran Church toward missions had
changed to such an extent by 1823 that when ten prominent theologians, jurists and officers made an appeal for contributions to
help evangelical missions, response was immediate. Soon the Berlin Missionary Society was established with royal sanction. When
the effort to combine this society with Jaenicke's school proved
unsuccessful, an independent seminary was started in 1830 with the
first missionaries going to South Africa in 1834. Its confessional position within the United Church was Lutheran.

Confessional reasons led to the establishment of a number of
the societies. Both Basel and the Rhenish Societies are a combin-

9

ation of Lutheran and Reformed groups without any definite confessional character. In 1836 seven of the North German missionary associations connected with Basel formed their own society in Hamburg, opening up a missionary school in 1837. As many as 39 other societies were connected with this North German Missionary Society from time to time, including the "Mission Society of the Mustard Seed", which had been established in 1802 in East Frisia under the guidance of the Church of the Brethren and the London Missionary Society.[16] But continual confessional discord hindered this potentially great Society from developing any large work. A large portion broke off to join the Lutheran Leipzig Missionary Society; still another group helped to form the Hermannsburg Society, a distinctively conservative Lutheran group under the guidance of Louis Harms. An attempt to start work in the Telugu area of India, of which mention shall be made later,[17] proved to be beyond the financial ability of the Society and was transferred to Lutherans in America. Dissension finally ceased when the Society, under new management, moved its headquarters to Bremen. Having closed its school, the North German Missionary Society obtained its missionaries from Basel for its sacrificial work in West Africa.

As Lutheran confessional consciousness developed in Saxony, such societies as that of Dresden, formed in 1819, found their position incompatible with that of Basel despite the latter's will-

ingness to have pupils from Saxony ordained according to the
Lutheran ritual.  A school preparing missionaries was started in
1832; this was followed by a regular missionary seminary in 1836
and an independent Lutheran missionary society.  Under the leadership of Karl Graul, who became the director in 1844, strong effort
was made to develop this Society into the main organization for
missionary work of the Lutheran Church throughout the world, with
only partial success.  He moved the Institute to Leipzig, established the Society on a solid and thorough theological and ecclesiastical basis, maintained that only theologians of university
training should be sent out to the mission field, and diligently
investigated the best policies for mission work.  In 1840 the
Leipzig Society took over the remnants of the old Danish-Halle
Mission among the Tamils in India, except for that portion absorbed by the English Societies.

Not only were these missionary societies organized by groups
of zealous men and women, but also at times by individuals of such
outstanding ability that they dominated the character and development of the societies they organized.  This was true of John Evangelist Gossner, originally a Roman Catholic priest banished from
Bavaria for his unorthodox preaching and writing.  Dissatisfied
with the growing confessional emphasis of the Berlin Society as
well as its insistence on the scientific education of missionaries, at the age of 63 he started a mission of his own in 1836.

Privately he prepared artisans for missionary work, instructing
them only in Scripture and developing their spiritual life. His
idea was that they should support themselves by the work of their
own hands and thus provide for their maintenance as St. Paul had.
In ten years he prepared 80 missionaries for various missionary
societies. But in 1844 he started his own work among the Kols of
central India, and it was there that the Gossner Missionary Society had its greatest success. It was not until his death in 1858
that the Society was put on a sound basis under a Board of Administration and an appointive inspector. Gossner's peculiar ideas
were abandoned one by one.

The Hermannsburg Missionary Society was started in 1849 under
the leadership of Louis Harms, who had brought about a revival in
his village congregation at Hermannsburg. Earlier he had worked
with the North German Missionary Society and had been urged by that
society to teach in its school. His strong Lutheran confessional
position as well as his attitude that Christianity could best be
spread by sending out colonies of missionaries who would support
themselves and also encourage each other and the natives about
them, by setting an example of Christian behavior in all walks of
life, led him to separate from the North German Society. His enthusiasm was so contagious that his congregation made all sorts of
sacrifices, and quite a number of young sons of the peasantry offered themselves to him for missionary service. With such support

and also the urging of others interested in a strong confessional Mission, he opened an Institute in 1849. In four years twelve pupils together with eight colonists sailed forth on their own missionary ship "Candace" for East Africa. More will be said later of their work in the Telugu territory of India.

Thus, within the short period of thirty-five years, the influence of the missionary revival in England, the continuing success and example of the Church of the Brethren, and the growing reaction to rationalism since the time of Schleiermacher together with a renewed interest and study of the Bible, led to the practical expression of religious life in the establishment of these seven Missionary Societies. The growing interest of Church leaders in this movement helped to keep the Societies from becoming too separatist and narrow in outlook. Each of them developed a group of loyal people upon whom it depended for support and interest. Associations and mission festivals sprang up everywhere; information was disseminated through these and the publications of each Society. Outside of a few Women's Associations organized to support the education of women and help the neglected women of the East and Far-East, no new societies were organized for over twenty years. Gustav Warneck questions whether those societies that were formed toward the end of the nineteenth century in Germany were really necessary or contributed much to the missionary cause that could not have been accomplished by the expansion and rich experience of the older societies.[18]

Mention, however, should be made of one more Society, organized in 1876, of importance because of its establishment of mission work in the northern section of the Andhra Desa. It was the inspiration of a devoted Pastor, Christian Jensen, who had been active in providing, through a theological seminary in Breklum, over 200 pastors for America to care for emigrants there. He also was deeply interested in establishing Christian schools in Germany and publishing Christian books and tracts to counteract the godless and secular trends. He urged using deacons and lay preachers for the whole 'Landeskirche', and combining home and foreign missions under the sponsorship of the same society. Interest in missions in the Breklum area had been kept alive in the past through the old Danish-Halle Mission and the influence of Claus Harms; but until Pastor Jensen was able to hold a great Mission Festival September 19, 1876, which led to the organization of the Schleswig-Holstein Missionary Society, all funds and men had gone to other missions.[19]

New impetus was given missionary efforts as Germany established colonies in Africa. Some efforts were made to force the societies to abandon all their work except in the new German colonies, especially by those who had no real interest in missions other than that they serve national and commercial purposes. But the situation was gradually clarified. Within the short period of ten years both the old and newly-formed Societies began a great

14

deal of work in the colonies.

Other factors helping to increase missionary interest in Germany were the formation of a series of Provincial Missionary Conferences where mission workers at home were introduced to the knowledge and understanding of missions and the work that could be done in the congregation to increase interest and support. These conferences were also excellent for bringing the friends of the different missionary societies together and fostering ecumenical concern for the total work.

Perhaps as much as for anything else in the field of missions Germany is known for its great service in the field of scientific study of missions and the promotion of missionary literature. Best known in the 19th century was the historian, Doctor Gustav Warneck, who occupied for many years at the University of Halle "the only academic chair in Christendom then devoted to the teaching and study of missions, and who prepared monumental volumes discussing his beloved theme. To his study and to that of other German scholars the Lutheran Church owes much of that sobriety and thoroughness with which its mission work has been done."[20] His writings also had a profound effect upon the policy of missions throughout the whole world.

If the number of its missionaries and the total of its income for missions is considered, it must be admitted that Germany trailed far behind England and America in the missionary effort of

the nineteenth century. Yet certainly the quality and thoroughness of its work had no equal, especially in Africa. By the end
of the century there was a definite upsurge in the total work.
Warneck gives the total number of German missionaries as 880, of
baptized native Christians 380,000; and an income of about
$1,200,000. Exclusive of 100 Kaiserswerth sisters serving in the
East, German missions had 96 unmarried missionary women and 9 medical missionaries.[21]

## C. In the United States

From the earliest colonial days the Protestant Church in America was faced with a great missionary task. Efforts were made to
reach the American Indian as well as follow the westward movement
of migration into the interior. The amazing work of John Eliot
and the Mayhews among the Indians, added to the inspiring news
through Francke concerning the Danish-Halle mission in India, brought
forth the first missionary efforts of organization and support in
England. And when the work among the Indians practically disappeared with the scattering of the Indian tribes through warfare and
the spreading of colonists westward, more and more attention was
given to providing spiritual aid for the thousands of immigrants
from all sections of Europe. Until the Revolution most of the
clergymen and the financial help came from Europe. Work also was
started among Negro slaves.[22]

Again it was the Pietistic movement in Germany, coupled with the rising missionary spirit in England, which affected the Lutheran Church in America in its development of missionary interest. The thousands of Germans who poured into William Penn's land usually came for several reasons: warfare and unfavorable economic conditions in Europe as compared to the news of great economic opportunities in America; the desire to escape religious persecution, and the news of a land where one could worship in peace as he desired; the seemingly hopeless future in the midst of tyranny, poverty and crowded conditions, as contrasted to the exciting advertisements of the Frankfurt Land Company and others telling of the American paradise. Many of the early immigrants from Germany were Pietists and religious refugees from the Rhenish Palatinate.[23] There were ministers among them, but far too few for the thousands who came and spread throughout New York, Pennsylvania and New Jersey. The settlers often fell prey to dubious persons posing as pastors who took advantage of the great desire of these people to have religious services and schools for their children. Too late they found out that many were only interested in financial gain or represented one of the many sects springing up in the fertile soil of American revivalism. Calls for help went to Germany and England. Finally a delegation consisting of a pastor and two laymen was sent by the Philadelphia congregations to secure ministers and teachers and to campaign for funds to build churches

17

**and** school houses. The appeal was made to Pastor Frederick Michael Ziegenhagen, court preacher for the German King, George II, at London, and Professor A. G. Francke, son of August Hermann Francke, of Halle.

But it was some years later, when Zinzendorf made an effort to unite all the German religious groups, including Lutheran churches, that Dr. Francke moved quickly to meet the situation and found an able spiritual leader in the person of Henry Melchoir Muhlenberg. Muhlenberg, trained at the University of Goettingen and having taught some time in the Halle Orphanage, had originally planned to go to India as a missionary to a newly-opened field in Bengal. Meanwhile he received a pressing call to labor in a country church in Saxony, until Francke prevailed upon him to go as a missionary to the dispersed Lutherans in America. From the moment he arrived in 1742, he revealed his leadership, tactfulness and ability to organize. He traveled in every direction gathering the scattered people into congregations. His reports to Halle aroused the interest of many in Germany and Lutherans in England with the result that clergymen, teachers and funds began to arrive. By 1748 a Synod was organized and a common liturgy drawn up. Upon all his activities Muhlenberg left the stamp of strong Lutheran convictions mixed with deep pietism. He also was influenced by the great religious awakening of this period; George Whitefield preached for him and addressed the assembled Ministerium in Philadelphia in 1763 and took part in the service.[24] His missionary fervor is indicated not only by the enthusiasm with which he searched out Lutherans everywhere, keeping ever for his motto, "Ecclesia plantanda", but also by his continued interest in the first field of labor which he had selected. Knowing many of the missionaries in India from his days at Halle, Muhlenberg frequently introduced the subject of missions in the pastoral conferences.[25] The overwhelming task facing so few pastors together with the extreme poverty of the Germans in America forestalled anything more than this discussion and continued interest.

After Muhlenberg's death, efforts were made to reach the American Indian, but proved unsuccessful. A little was accomplished by the Salzburgers of the Ebenezer colony in Georgia. But the tide of immigration, which forced Indians into more remote regions, proved too much for those who made a sincere effort to convert them. Another factor was the growing and natural distrust arising from the unfair and cruel methods used to obtain control of the Indian's land. This finally led to the break of all communication between the Indian and the Lutheran pastors.[26]

By the time of the Revolution, it was apparent that the Lutheran Church could no longer depend upon the supply of pastors from Europe to care for the spreading frontiers. Nor were they too eager to have such pastors, who were more and more infected by the rationalism rampant in Europe. Many of the pastors already had been influenced by German rationalism and were publishing un-Lutheran hymnals and liturgies and substitutes for Luther's catechism. From this same spirit arose various efforts to unite the Lutheran Church with other bodies, such as the Episcopal Church[27] or other German groups.[28] A still further problem was the struggle between those who realized that English must be introduced into many of the churches -- Muhlenberg had preached in whatever language was necessary to reach the people -- and those who maintained that the Lutheran Church must remain a German Church. The latter believed that much of the unionistic and rationalistic spirit had come from too close contact with English-speaking denominations.[29]

With such internal problems it becomes apparent why the Lutheran Church was slow in responding to the missionary movement growing by leaps and bounds in other American Churches following the Second Great Awakening.[30] Suspicions of revivalism, unionism, rationalism and the use of the English language kept the majority of pastors and their churches out of contact with the movement. Only a few of the younger leaders, trained in America under the tutelage of prominent pastors[31] and conscious of the growing need for English in the churches, kept in contact with the missionary developments in America. In the meantime the Lutheran Church, to preserve itself, turned to the effort of establishing seminaries[32] and organizing a general body.[33] In spite of much opposition and suspicion[34] the organizing convention of the General Synod was held at Hagerstown, Maryland, October 22, 1820; and by the fall of the next year three out of the four synods had ratified the constitution and the first regular convention was held. The Synod was "authorized to devise plans for seminaries of education and missionary institutions,"[35] but the matter was deferred for several years until 1825 when definite plans were put into effect.

The Seminary, established at Gettysburg, Pennsylvania, in 1826, soon felt the impulse of the religious revival and missionary spirit dominating the many new seminaries established [36] since the opening of the Andover Theological Seminary in 1808. As in the other schools, a "Society of Inquiry on Missions" was started shortly and it maintained correspondence with other societies as well as with mission institutions abroad. "Thus early was the promotion of the cause of foreign missions due to students -- harbinger of the day when toward the end of the century the Student Volunteer and the Student Christian organizations gave to the cause of missions one of its most pronounced forward movements."[37] So active was this group that in 1835 they voted to "educate a pious young man of color for the intellectual, moral, and social elevation of the free colored people in this country."[38]

As the Halle Reports had kept many in America informed on foreign missions, so the first periodicals of the Lutheran Church in America contained much from these reports and other sources concerning the efforts of the Lutheran churches of Europe. This

21

was true of the first German Lutheran periodical, the Evangelisches Magazin (1811-17), and the first English Lutheran periodical,
the Evangelical Lutheran Intelligencer (1826-31). Many were deeply concerned that the "German" churches in America were so slow in
responding to the missionary movement.[39]

> "It was in order to furnish information that the Lutheran
> Intelligencer as early as 1826-29 published serially a his-
> tory of the first Protestant Mission at Tranquebar. In that
> same report it was recommended that on the first Monday of
> each month an hour's concerted prayer for missions be made
> by congregations; also that each minister preach one mission
> sermon a year to his people. Thus mission work among Luther-
> ans in America, as elsewhere from apostolic times to the
> present, began with a call to prayer."[40]

Sufficient interest had been aroused that by 1833 a Committee was appointed at the Baltimore convention of the General Synod
to prepare a report on missions which was to be brought back to the
next convention at York, Pa., in June 1835. This report was favorably received and aroused such interest that a convention of
Lutheran ministers[41] at Mechanicsburg, Pa., in October, 1835, organized the Central Missionary Society. Its first efforts were to
serve the scattered members of the Lutheran Church on the western
frontiers, but it also was emphasized that, as soon as possible,
missionaries were to be sent to "heathen" lands.[42]

About a year later appeals for help came from Charles F. A.
Gutzlaff,[43] who was making efforts to enter China, and Charles
T. E. Rhenius of India; this brought the concern about foreign
missions to fever-high pitch.[44] Rhenius, little known today and

yet considered by many to be India's greatest missionary next to
Christian Frederick Schwartz,[45] after twenty-one years of devoted
and effective service with the Church Missionary Society in Madras
and Tinnevelly, found it necessary to start an independent Lutheran Mission because of irreconcilable differences between the developing high-church attitude of the Society he served and his own
Lutheran position on ordination.[46]  Without any source of income,
Rhenius appealed to the Lutheran Church in all parts of the world
as well as to his many friends in India.  This spurred on the
movement in America, and a convention was called, in connection
with the meeting of the General Synod, to be held at Hagerstown,
Md., May 27, 1837.  The 44 delegates resolved to organize "The
Foreign Missionary Society of the Evangelical German Churches in
the United States."  Rhenius had appealed to all the Germans, and
this title was used with the hope of drawing the Reformed as well
as Lutheran into the Society.  First of all, three hundred dollars
immediately was appropriated for the India Mission, and semi-annual payments of one thousand dollars each were promised.  Authorization was given the Rev. Charles Philip Krauth, D.D., to write
requesting Rhenius if "he would be willing to be employed as the
missionary of the society to labor among the Tamils in India."[47]

Rhenius' diary for April 18, 1838, reports:[48]

"Today received a letter from Mr. Henry Hill, Treasurer of
the American Board of Commissioners for Foreign Missions,
Boston, dated Sept. 8th, 1837, transmitting 640 dollars for

our mission. This is an answer to a letter I wrote to Dr.
Schmucker more than two years ago. Thanks be to God!"

Immediately, on April 20, Rhenius wrote in answer to Dr. Schmucker's letter of July 10, 1837, that he would be happy to receive
financial support and missionary recruits, but he made no mention
of turning the Mission over to the direction of the German Foreign Missionary Society.[49] By the 9th of May Rhenius was entering
his last illness and died June 5, 1838. The news of his death led
the Society in 1839 to decide to establish its own mission. The
Rev. J. C. F. Heyer, a leading Home Missionary of the Central
Missionary Society, was selected as the most suitable person to be
the first foreign missionary,[50] and Dr. Krauth wrote to him concerning his acceptance of such a call as well as suggestions for
the best place to begin such work. Heyer replied that he would be
willing to go anywhere the Lord directed him, but thought that the
most suitable place to commence was on the Coromandel coast, perhaps in the Tinnevelly district, where the Rev. J. J. Mueller,
Rhenius' son-in-law, was still maintaining work alone.

Another letter was sent to Mueller, offering to take him with
all his catechists and congregations under the Society's control,
and to furnish him the money and missionaries to carry on the work.
This letter arrived just one month after Mueller had made the decision to return to the Church Missionary Society and thus precluded the entrance of American Lutherans into the work in the

24

Tinnevelly District.[51] The American Board of Commissioners, upon consultation, recommended the Telugu country as an almost untouched area; and thus, when the German Foreign Missionary Society met on Tuesday, May 11, 1841, in Baltimore, Md., the unanimous recommendation was to appoint the Rev. J. C. F. Heyer as a foreign missionary to the Telugu land. Also adopted was a plan of cooperation with the American Board; but this proved unsatisfactory to some present,[52] especially Heyer himself, who resigned and immediately offered himself to "The Society of the Synod of Pennsylvania for the Propagation of the Gospel."[53] The German Society changed its name at this time to "The Foreign Missionary Society of the Evangelical Lutheran Church in the United States," realizing that cooperation of all Germans in America was no longer practicable.

Heyer's action, which took many by surprise, seems to have been based on a sincere desire to make the Lutheran Church feel its own responsibility for Foreign Missions rather than any prejudice against working with other church bodies. He felt that the congregations would not develop a true love for the cause unless it was "their own independent, individual mission."[54] Since the convention of the Pennsylvania Synod, which had withdrawn from the General Synod in 1823, was to be held just one month after the General Synod, Heyer addressed a letter to their Missionary Society, appealing to them as their agent to the heathen to send him wherever the Society wished, and even offering to invest $1,000 of his own money in the cause.[55] The committee to which his letter was referred reported back to the Society that without the certainty of help from other Lutheran synods, there were not sufficient funds to establish and uphold a foreign mission effort. Fortunately, men of wider vision offered resolutions that were adopted on June 9, 1841, calling the Rev. J. C. F. Heyer to be their missionary to India and sending out appeals to the different missionary societies to cooperate in this effort.[56] Many congregations in the General Synod did respond to this appeal,[57] and the General Synod Foreign Missionary Society sent its first missionary to assist Heyer in 1843, later accepting full responsibility for the Mission.

Further developments in the missionary movement in the Lutheran Church will be brought out later. Other Lutheran bodies in America until recent date contributed to foreign missions primarily through other groups, especially to the societies of the churches on the continent of Europe to which they were related. Of importance to the Telugu area in India are the American Lutheran Church and the Augustana Lutheran Church. The former contributed comparatively large sums to the foreign mission work of the Hermannsburg Society. Sufficient interest had arisen by the time of the first World War to take over some of the stations of its India Mission and later the entire Mission. At the time (1869) the Augustana (Swedish) Synod belonged to the General Council,[58]

it became

> "part owner of the Rajahmundry Mission[59] and took its first
> step in organized missionary responsibility. It is also to
> be noted that from 1869 to 1918 the Guntur Mission was oper-
> ated by the General Synod and the Rajahmundry Mission by the
> General Council. When the United Lutheran Church was organ-
> ized in 1918, these two Telugu missions were reunited under
> one board. The Augustana Synod did not enter the merger but
> retained a cooperative relationship in the India mission of
> the United Lutheran Church."[60]

Today the three major bodies mentioned above, the United, American

and Augustana Lutheran Churches, and all other Lutheran groups in

America  have foreign mission work in every part of the world.

But very little was done by most of the other bodies until the

turn of the century, and the greatest activity has been since the

close of the second World War.[61]

## Chronological Comparison of THE BEGINNINGS
## (Chapter II) of the Andhra Desa Missions

| | Guntur | Rajahmundry | Hermannsburg | Breklum |
|---|---|---|---|---|
| 1842 | Heyer arrives | | | |
| 1844 | Gunn (Gen.Syn.) begins work | | | |
| 1845 | | Valett opens field | | |
| 1846 | Heyer to U.S. | Groenning and Heise arrive | | |
| 1848 | Heyer returns | | | |
| 1849 | Palnad begun | Ellore Station opened | | |
| 1850 | | Work given to General Synod | | |
| 1851 | Death of Walter Gunn | | | |
| 1853 | First Lutheran Synod convenes | | | |
| 1857 | Heyer goes to U.S., only Groenning remains | | | |
| 1865 | Mylius, answering call for help, cannot cooperate | Mylius opens Sulurpeta Sta. | | |
| 1866 | | 3 more missionaries arrive | | |
| 1867 | | Nayudupeta and Gudur Stations | | |
| 1868 | | First Synod & Constitution | | |
| 1876 | | Nine stations, 15 catechists. | | |
| 1882 | | | | Pohl & Bothman in Rajahmundry |
| 1883 | | | | Settle in Salur |
| 1885 | | | | First school |
| 1889 | | | | Parvitapur Sta. |
| 1890 | | | | Salur Ch. dedic. |

# CHAPTER II

## THE BEGINNINGS

### (Breaking the Ground)

#### A. The Andhra Desa

The Andhra Desa, the Telugu territory of India, until October 1, 1953, was not thought of as a country or state but rather the area in which the Telugu language was spoken. On that date, however, the Andhra State was inaugurated as a distinct unit, formed from eleven districts of the Madras Presidency or State.[1] Originally the nine Telugu-speaking districts in the Hyderabad State, known as Telengana, did not join the Andhra State; and since there is no Lutheran work in Telengana, our consideration of the missionary work in the Andhra Desa will be limited to the Andhra State as formed in 1953.[2]

#### 1. The land

The eleven original Districts of the Andhra State stretched from a short distance north of Madras along the coast of the Bay of Bengal for some 590 miles, and extended inland more than half way across the peninsula of India at the widest section and only twenty miles at the narrowest. Extremely irregular in its borders, Andhra touched Orissa and Madhya Pradesh in the north and northwest, Hyderabad and Mysore in the west, and the present Madras State in the south. It covered an area of 67,000 square miles and

29

had a population according to the last census[3] of 21,282,000.
Seven Districts were located along the coastal area, fed by three
great rivers, and comprised one of the richest agricultural areas
in all of India. The other four Districts were found in the plat-
eau area of the Deccan, divided from the coast by the so-called
Eastern Ghats, and suffered from a lack of rain. Although rich in
mineral resources, the area was largely undeveloped and "no detailed geological survey has been attempted."[4] Nearly one-fifth
of the area was covered by forests and in them were found some of
the ancient hill tribes, such as the Koyis and Chenchus.

The majority of the people are agriculturists. Although most
of the tobacco grown in India comes from the Andhra State, ninety
percent of the cultivated area is used for food crops, such as
millet and rice. Rice is grown along the coastal area where there
is adequate rain or irrigation; while small grains and ground-nuts
are the major crops in the interior and the south where there are
as little as 20 inches of rain a year and water sources are primarily wells and tanks.[5]

Industrially the Andhra Desa remains to this day one of the
most backward in all of India. Although much cotton is grown,
there are only two textile mills. The largest industries come out
of agricultural activities -- rice, oil-milling and sugar. The
mineral development is very small. About the only other industry
is ship-building at Visakhapatnam, a very recent development.[6]

30

Outside of this last-named city, there are no natural harbors along the coast line.[7]

## 2. Its history and language

The word 'Andhra' is a very ancient one. The earliest rulers of the Telugu section of India of whom there is any definite knowledge were the Andhras, a Dravidian race, who sprang up from the area located between the Godavari and Kistna rivers and spread across the Deccan. They are mentioned in the Ramayana and Mahabharata as a primitive tribe living in the inaccessible forests of the south.[8] They were on the fringe of Asoka's empire, acknowledging his authority and strongly influenced by his Buddhist missionary efforts. Following his death and the decline of the Mauryan empire, the Andhras became the dominant power in the Deccan for nearly 450 years, from 225 B.C. to A.D. 225, with an eastern capital at Amaravati and a western capital at Pratishthana, better known as Paithan, which had a rich trade with Alexandria and the west.[9] Strangely enough, Telugu literature tells nothing of the glories of this period. It is understandable, in part, when one realizes that there was no Telugu literature at that time, but rather it is probable that "the literature of the day existed in Prakrit, one form of which is considered to be the immediate literary ancestor of Telugu. The Pallavas, who conquered the country, must have exterminated Buddhism and Buddhistic literature, of which not a vestige has survived."[10]

31

The Pallavas and early Chalukyas, who were the next conquer-
ors, brought the Jain faith and culture into the area, but this
disappeared in the face of the revival of Hinduism following the
reforms of Sankara.  The Eastern branch of the Chalukyas, located
between the Godavari and Kistna rivers in what was known as Vengi
Nadu, ruled for nearly six centuries before joining the great
Chola Empire, which covered an area as great as that of the Andhras of the second century.[11]  It was during the height of this
empire that the first extant Telugu literature appears, beginning
with Nanniah's translation of the Mahabharata in 1020 A.D.  It
would appear, however, from the highly developed state of this
early literature that there had been a long period of growth previously.  Songs and sonnets were carried down from generation to
generation in an indigenous Telugu free of Sanskrit; but the religious revival of the eleventh century called for abstract,
scientific and religious words not found in the indigenous language
and thus a literary Telugu had to be developed artificially with
the help of Sanskrit derivatives and corruptions.  Words from foreign languages, especially Hindustani, were added in later periods as the land was conquered by the Mohammedans, French and English.  Today there is still this distinction between the higher
literary dialect and the dialect used in common conversation; and
they form separate branches of study.[12]

Telugu is a very melodious language and is commonly called the 'Italian of the East.'[13] It is spoken in its purest form in the Rajahmundry area.

> "The letters of the Telugu alphabet and their combinations are very numerous, and at first sight make the language appear difficult. But in reality they make it far more easy to acquire correctly; for there is a distinct letter for each sound, and therefore every word is pronounced exactly as it is spelt."[14]

Many of the missionaries have found, to their sorrow, that the meaning of a word depends to a great extent on "the exact pronunciation of each individual letter, especially ... the length of a vowel, or the harsh or smooth pronunciation of a consonant."[15]

The Telugu script comes from the same source as all modern Indian scripts, the Brahmi Lipi, which came to be known in southern India as Dravida Brahmi. By the thirteenth century, it had become distinct from other southern scripts and assumed its present form.

> "The modern Telugu character may fairly claim to be the most beautiful and the most convenient of all the Indian characters. It has a great fondness for rounded forms, derived from the habit of writing with the stylus on palm leaves, on which straight lines and angles could hardly be made without splitting the leaf. Every consonant has its vowel attached, so that each character really represents a syllable. The characters are very clear, and capable, unlike those of Hindustani, of being easily printed. Even when written rapidly by hand, they are far more legible than is generally the case with the Indian languages."[16]

Outside of the recent development under the influence of Western culture, the high point of Telugu literature was reached during the time of the famous Vijayanagar empire, A.D. 1327-1565,

33

which held back the inroads of the Muslim and united all of South India below the Kistna-Tungabhadra rivers. Whereas previously most literary work was in the form of translations of the great religious Sanskrit epics, the Telugu kings of Vijayanagar patronized much work that was original and independent. "Those were stirring, spacious times, of great heroes and glorious battles, of love and valour, and of splendid victories and spreading dominion -- a period altogether cast after the heart of a poet."[17] Moreover, this was a period in which the Vaishnavism of Ramanuja held sway in contrast to the earlier influence of Sankara and Saivism.[18] It was also during this time that Vemana is said to have lived and written his Sataka, which is the most popular poetry of the common people. "He is the greatest moral teacher of the Andhras. For well-nigh five centuries his Sataka has been the textbook of morals for Telugu boys, and a better book cannot be asked for."[19] Many of his ideas fitted in so closely with Christian truth that the missionaries found his poetry useful in achieving rapport with the people.[20]

3. Early Christian efforts -- before 1842

Up to 1842 and the entrance of the Lutherans into the Andhra Desa, very little Christian work had been accomplished in this tremendous area so close to Madras and so accessible from the sea. Two Christian poets, although not likely "formal members of the Christian Church,"[21] left contributions in Telugu on the life of St. Thomas and the life of Christ during the 17th and 18th centuries.[22] The first effort at evangelization came from the French

Jesuits of Pondicherry, with the work of M. Manduit in the Chitoor

District. His first converts came from Punganur in 1701;[23] and

from there the work spread in a northwesterly direction to Ananta-

pur and eastward to the territory of the Rajah of Venkatagiri.

Within thirty years 16 stations were established and some thousands

of caste converts gathered. The Jesuit priests zealously preached

and visited the villages around each station, lived in the homes

of Brahmans and merchants as they traveled, and catered the favor

of rajahs.

Wars in this area[24] forced many of the converts to move north-

east to the Northern Circars, where they could live under the pro-

tection of the French.[25] They settled on lands given them in the

Nellore and Guntur Districts. But further disasters arose with the

withdrawal of French troops from the region after the English took

over the Northern Circars in 1765, and the suspension of the Jes-

uit Order in 1773. The Society of Foreign Missions of Paris tried

to fill the empty gap, but lack of missionaries led to the return

of many to Hinduism. Only four priests remained in 1802 for the

whole Telugu Mission.[26]

Bartholomew Ziegenbalg was evidently the first Protestant and

Lutheran missionary to visit the Andhra Desa.[27] On one of his

visits to Madras he went to Tirupati to take a look at one of the

great Hindu temples of South India and did some preaching there which nearly cost him his life when the Brahmans plotted against him.[28] But it was his successor, Benjamin Schultze, who started work among the Telugu people shortly after his coming to Madras in 1726.[29] Less than two months after beginning the Tamil school he found it necessary to open a Telugu school with a Brahman teacher. He began to study Telugu and in two months was translating the Catechism and the New Testament.[30] When we learn that he completed the Gospels by May 30, 1727, five months later, as well as other translations, it becomes apparent how superficial his work must have been and why it was of little value to those who came after him.[31] As to conversions, the early reports of Schultze do not distinguish between the Tamil and Telugu converts. In speaking of the death of his Telugu Brahman teacher on November 2, 1728, a little over a month after the first baptisms in Madras on September 26, he states that the teacher was "fully convinced of the truth of Christianity; ... and had he survived, would not only have rendered us further service, but would have embraced Christianity with his whole family."[32]

Schultze's successor, John Philip Fabricius, continued to work among the Telugu people in Madras. When the French occupied Fort St. George in 1746, the mission buildings were destroyed to build up the defences of the fort. "Being thus rendered homeless, Fabricius retired with the children of his boarding school to the neighboring Dutch Settlement of Pulicat, where he was hospitably received."[33] This retreat was repeated during those difficult war days; and Fabricius found an opportunity to visit the villages around Pulicat and lay the foundation for village parishes which have continued to this day.[34] No effort was made to extend the work among the Telugus by those who came after Fabricius; in fact, it would appear that this work was neglected altogether in this period of the decline of the old Danish Tranquebar Mission and before the rise of modern missions with the arrival of Carey at the close of the century.[35]

To the London Missionary Society was given the privilege of opening up the Andhra Desa to the influence of Christian missions.[36] Established as a Society in 1795, three of their missionaries arrived in India in February, 1804, and the decision as to where they would locate was left up to them. Originally intending to work in the Tamilnad (Tamil Country), they were led by friends in Madras to Vizagapatam. The Reverends George Cran and Augustus Des Granges were cordially received by the Collector and the English residents in July of 1805; and they immediately turned to the study of Telugu while at the same time holding services for the English population.[37] These missionaries, and Gordon and Pritchett, who followed them, were leaders in the translation of the Telugu scriptures and made a real contribution to the field of Telugu Christian literature. At the same time they developed good schools and preached regularly to the natives; yet the Mission had to wait thirty years for its first convert, Purushottam Chowdhuri.[38]

The same Society is given credit for opening the second Telugu Mission in what is known as the Ceded Districts of Cuddapah, Bellary, Anantapur and Kurnool, given over to the British by the Nizam of Hyderabad in 1800. From the newly-developed station in the Canarese-speaking part of Bellary[39] work was extended into the Telugu-speaking sections until a Mr. William Howell was sent in November, 1822, to establish a station in Cuddapah. Much more successful than Vizagapatam, this Mission had over 100 converts ten years later and experienced a mass movement among Malas in the 1850s.[40]

In spite of the fact that India had been opened up to British missionaries in 1813 following renewal of the charter of the East India Company and a large number did come under the auspices of English Societies, the Andhra Desa remained neglected until after the Charter of 1833, which opened India to extensive efforts on the part of Continental and American Churches as well as trade with all nations.[41] When Anthony N. Groves' Christian work in Baghdad came to a complete standstill, Captain[42] Arthur Cotton, military engineer, urged him to come to India and establish work there. His tour in 1833 aroused the European community to their spiritual needs wherever he went. In 1836 he returned from England with thirteen missionaries of the Plymouth Brethren. Two of these, Bowden and Beer, established a station at Narsapur in the delta of the Godavari river.  As laymen, they were expected by Groves to make their work self-supporting by engaging in their respective trades.[43]

Besides Groves, still other voices were raised[44] in calling Americans and Europeans to the great needs of the Telugu area. The Rev. Dr. Amos Sutton of the General Baptist Mission in Orissa spoke of the neglected Telugu people on his visit to America in 1835, and this had a profound effect upon American Baptists.[45] The Reverends Howell and Smith of the London Mission in Cuddapah appealed in 1837 through the Missionary Herald, organ of the American Board of Commissioners for Foreign Missions, for workers in the Andhra Desa.  They emphasized that there were only four ordained missionaries attempting to serve over ten million people.  Other than the organized work at Vizagapatam and Cuddapah,[46] the only other effort being made was the distribution of some 25 publications of the Madras Religious Tract Society,[47] with some 37,000 copies being distributed in 1836.[48]  Over three years later the Rev. M. Winslow of the American Board reported in the Missionary Herald from Bangalore that there were only five missionaries in the Telugu country and there was an immediate need of two or more.[49]  The English people were also being moved to action by a stirring appeal on the part of the Rev. William Campbell, whose book on the situation in British India appeared in 1839.[50]

39

As early as 1836, the Rev. Samuel S. Day of the American Baptists arrived in India to serve the Telugus. After several preliminary efforts at Chicacole, near Vizagapatam, and at Madras, he moved to Nellore on February 26, 1840. Progress was so slow that on three different occasions, in 1848, 1853, and again in 1862,[51] the work was nearly terminated; but the faith and determination of such men as Lyman Jewett, who was willing to go back alone without support of the Baptists if they were going to give up the work, led the mission to a new day of tremendous mass movements among the outcastes under the leadership of the Rev. John E. Clough.[52]

Just about the time the pioneer American Lutheran missionary, C. F. Heyer, was sailing from Boston, the Rev. Robert T. Noble of the Church Missionary Society began his work among the Telugus at Masulipatam, October 28, 1841. Impetus for this new mission had come from Mr. John Goldingham, Collector at Masulipatam, who had since 1836 urged first the Society for the Propagation of the Gospel and then the C. M. S. to send out missionaries to the Andhra Desa. Even when turned down by both of them, he and his friends collected money and

"formed themselves into what they called the 'Telugu Missionary Society.' An anonymous gentleman in Masulipatam offered a house, his own property, for the residence of a missionary. A schoolroom was built, some fifty or sixty boys were put under instruction. Under these circumstances the C. M. S. was again approached; here was the money and the buildings, could they not now send men? But C. M. S. found a further difficulty, they had on their rolls nobody who could be trusted with so responsible a work."[53]

Still undaunted, Goldingham searched out the men himself; friends in Brighton, England, found Noble and Henry W. Fox. At last the C.M.S. decided it would take charge of the work. By this time Goldingham was Collector in Guntur and urged Noble to make it his headquarters; but Fox and Noble decided on Masulipatam because of its greater size and importance, leaving Guntur open for the American Lutherans.[54] This mission is known for its famous school for high caste boys where some outstanding conversions of Brahmans occurred. This later developed into Noble College, an affiliate of the Madras University. As with other missions in the Andhra Desa, converts were few and far between in the early years.

B. The Call from the Far East Answered

1. Father Heyer -- the Guntur Mission

By 1842 all vestige of early Lutheran work in the Andhra Desa had been absorbed by the English Societies who had taken over the old Tranquebar Mission.[55] To the American Lutheran Church was left the responsibility of establishing the first permanent work there; and the pioneer selected to perform this task was already 49 years of age when he reached Guntur on July 31, 1842. The American Board had advised using a much younger man, but to the Lutheran Church in America the Rev. Christian Frederick Heyer was the only logical choice.

This becomes apparent as one looks at his earlier life -- a true pioneer in every sense of the word and a man eminently fitted and prepared to answer the Call for help from the Telugu land. Born in Helmstedt, Germany, on July 10, 1793, he came to America when a boy of fourteen to help his uncle who was a master-furrier in the city of Philadelphia. The reason for his being sent away from home at such an early age arose out of his facile ability to acquire the French language, which he used as an interpreter for the company of French soldiers quartered in Helmstedt. His parents evidently feared that he might be drafted; and America was the safest place from the grasping hand of Napoleon.[56]

Coming from a deeply-religious family, Christian Frederick was soon active in the life of Zion Lutheran Church in Philadelphia, where the Rev. J. H. C. Helmuth, D.D., was the senior pastor. "He joined the choir, a promising tenor. He became a member of a young men's German and Bible study group, named after the theologian, Mosheim. Thereby he eventually qualified as one of the early teachers in Zion's Sunday School."[57] Much against the desire of his uncle, for Heyer was proving to be a good furrier, the young man began to study theology under Dr. Helmuth in 1810. He then directed a parochial school for Zion (1813). And in 1815 he went back to Germany to study at the University of Goettingen.[58] Upon his return he was licensed to preach by the Pennsylvania Ministerium at its seventieth convention in York, Pennsylvania, in May, 1817, and

42

sent out to serve in its most northwestern parish in Crawford and
Erie counties.

Then began twenty-three years of active missionary work on the
frontiers of the expanding Lutheran Church.  Immediately he found
it necessary to learn English, for there were groups of Lutherans
who spoke nothing else on the frontier.[59]  He developed a 'Lutheran' answer to the many revivals which were drawing his people away
while serving in 1820 in the Cumberland valley, Maryland; and "having mastered the art of winning souls for the Lord, Heyer also won
the friendship and respect of many of his erstwhile opponents."[60]
After his ordination at Lancaster, Pennsylvania, in 1820, he was
appointed a traveling preacher through parts of Kentucky and Indiana.

> "He spent three months, from July to October, 1820, on this
> tour, covering a territory of twenty-five hundred miles, trav-
> elling at first on foot and then on horseback, preaching wher-
> ever he could gather a few people, administering the holy
> sacraments, and distributing German and English tracts."[61]

His experience and interest in the missionary efforts of the Church
naturally pointed him up as the logical person to be the home missionary of the "Central Missionary Society" when it was organized
in 1835.[62]  He was directed to "traverse the principal portions of
the entire Mississippi Valley and ascertain all German settlements,
spending a short time in each."[63]  Leaving December 30, 1835, from
Somerset, Pa., in six months he covered parts of Ohio, Indiana and
Illinois, and crossed the Mississippi river into Missouri as far

as the Iron Mountain, enduring all sorts of hardships, winter weather and receptions on the part of the people. Heyer found at least fifty areas ready and eager to have home missionaries; and he felt that most of them could be developed if the missionary were willing to help support himself with farming.[64]

After this tour Heyer was sent to Pittsburgh, where in the next few years he founded three congregations, one English- and two German-speaking, and undertook a money-raising tour in the East to collect a building-fund for one of them.[65] It was just a month after the dedication on April 5, 1840, of this new building for Trinity Lutheran Church that Heyer was called by the Foreign Missionary Society of the Evangelical German Churches in the United States to be its foreign missionary to India.

One other interesting facet of Heyer's activities before he became a foreign missionary was his selection in 1830 as the agent for the Sunday School Union of the Evangelical Lutheran Church in the United States.[66]

"Heyer, who had been the chairman of the committee which drafted the constitution of the society, entered on the duties of the newly created office with much enthusiasm. He was convinced that what the church needed at that time, above all other things, was the organization of a Sunday School in every Lutheran congregation.[67] In the course of eighteen months he visited about three hundred congregations, travelled over 3000 miles, advised and aided pastors in the establishment of Sunday Schools, and distributed and sold about 13,000 German Sunday school hymnals and tracts."[68]

W. A. Lambert, who had gathered Heyer's autobiographical material for publication, concludes the period of his life from 1817 -

44

"Of his ability as a pastor and church worker there would seem to be no doubt whatever; nor of his popularity. Wherever he went, and whatever work he undertook, he was always successful. Among the pastors no less than among the congregations he was honored and respected, perhaps the more so because of the two years he had spent in a German university. In 1828 we find him not only the Secretary of the West Penna. Synod, Agent for the American S. S. Union, but also a member of the committee to draft the Constitution for a S. S. Union of the Lutheran Church, delegate to the Maryland Synod, a director of the Seminary at Gettysburg, and on the editing committee for the Zeitschrift. ...

"It is interesting to note how Father Heyer was during these years prepared for foreign mission work. His natural disposition inclined him to a roving life. His failure to receive the call to the Lehigh County congregation and the appointment as travelling preacher encouraged the inclination within him. His generally rapid success in congregations, and frequent calls still further tended to free him or keep him free from local attachment of a permanent character. His zeal for the work of gathering men into the Church added its quota, in leading him to accept travelling appointments, taking him away from home for months at a time. His sympathies widened and his courage increased. The knowledge he had gained among American people he felt fitted him for work among the heathen. The death of his wife still further loosened the bands binding him to a home (in 1839). His experience in crossing what were practically uncivilized portions of America accustomed him to the habit of enduring all things, and freed him from that dependence on the comforts and luxuries of life which frequently prove a hindrance to the missionary. When a missionary to foreign lands was talked of seriously, no man could be found better suited for the work than Father Heyer. To his qualifications -- only his age was spoken of as a hindrance -- must be added the fact of his large acquaintance in the Church and the confidence of the Church in him. Few men would have undertaken the work as he did, few could have done so, and very few would have been asked to do so by the Church itself. In India, or any other field that might have been chosen, the work must have been pioneer work, and Father Heyer was preeminently the pioneer of the Church in those days."

45

When Heyer left Pittsburgh in May, 1840, he went to Baltimore to prepare himself for the missionary task by attending lectures at the University of Maryland, now known as Johns Hopkins, on the subjects of medicine and Sanskrit.[70]    Commissioned in St. Paul's Church, Philadelphia, on October 5, 1841, he sailed from Boston on the 15th in the company of several missionaries of the American Board.  On the long journey around the Cape of Good Hope the missionaries found ample opportunity to learn about the land to which they were going, study the Tamil language and have revealed to them good missionary methods; their tutor was the veteran Rev. Benjamin Meigs, who had served for thirty years in Ceylon and was one of the most successful American Board missionaries.[71]

Landing at Tuticorin, the southern tip of India, on March 23, 1842, Father Heyer bought a second-hand palanquin, "a kind of covered bed or stretcher which is borne on the shoulders of a half-dozen porters,"[72] and engaged bearers to take him up the East coast of India by stages.  On his way he visited many of the existing mission stations and studied some of the methods used.  He found the missionaries friendly and helpful.  Especially did he enjoy visiting those missions started by the Lutheran missionaries from Halle more than a century before but now manned primarily by English or Danish men.[73]  He noted such customs as that of asking questions during the sermon and of writing the main points of discussion on palm leaves.  In Palamcotta Heyer visited the seminary established by Rhenius[74] and learned how the native workers were trained, and saw the boarding schools for Christian boys and girls as well as the schools for Hindu children.  Father Heyer reports:[75]

> "The more promising boys from the village schools are taken into the Seminary at Palamcotta; from among the Seminary students a further selection is made of young men, who are formed into a Preparandi class, and instructed by the Missionaries, to be employed as catechists in the various districts.  The Missionaries spend much of their time in visiting the different villages connected with the Mission.  Two catechists are sometimes placed in charge of a large village, and at other times one catechist has to superintend several villages.  Once a month all the catechists belonging to a particular District, assemble where the Mis. resides, and give in their reports; they are examined, receive advice and instructions, and the work to which they are to attend during the month, is pointed out to them.  Saturday is commonly the day on which they assemble; on the following Sunday the Lord's Supper is administered, and on Wednesday they return to their respective stations."

Heyer was struck especially by one of the societies, called the 'Pilgrim Society', which under the inspiration of a sermon by Rhenius had been formed by the congregation on their own initiative to send messengers of peace into areas where the light of the gospel had not penetrated.  A catechist told Heyer that from the offerings gathered two men were sent out to make known the word of God, and distribute tracts and portions of the Scriptures.[76]

Upon his arrival in Madras on April 16, Father Heyer was advised to remain there for several months to study Telugu, get acquainted with the Telugu people living in Madras and at the same time look around for a satisfactory location for the proposed mission.  But his restless spirit again came to the fore when a month later, on May 19, he traveled north on the canal from Madras to Pulicat in an open boat under the scorching sun, protected in his palanquin. He was cordially received four days later by the Baptist men, Stephen van Husen and Samuel S. Day, when he reached Nellore. Because of the excessive heat and also because one of the missionaries was planning shortly to take a trip distributing tracts and testaments and preaching in the northern regions, Heyer decided to remain for a while. Again it gave him an opportunity to study the schools and preaching methods, and practice his Telugu.

Heading northward with van Husen, Heyer found Ongole a definite possibility as there were, though in a rather run-down condition, bungalows formerly occupied by some Government officials.[77] Continuing on, they went from village to village, reaching Guntur on July 31, 1842.

Father Heyer was received most enthusiastically by Mr. J. Henry Stokes, Esq., Collector of the Guntur District, who had been very eager to secure a resident missionary for Guntur. As a member of the Church of England he had addressed several appeals to the Church Missionary Society without success. Stokes urged Heyer to stay in Guntur. In fact, he wrote immediately to the C. M. S. missionaries at Masulipatam telling them about the new arrival and inquiring whether they were planning to occupy this area. Realizing it would be many years before they could advance that far, the

secretary of the Society in Madras agreed with Fox and Noble that
Stokes should do all he could to keep Heyer there.  Heyer himself,
speaking of his reception by Collector Stokes, says that he was[78]

> "an ardent friend of Missions and Missionaries, as well as a
> very exemplary Christian gentleman.  The inducements which
> Mr. Stokes held out, and the kind offers of assistance which
> he made, were far preferable to anything that I could expect
> at Ongole; -- hence I decided in favor of Guntur, and after
> prayerful consideration concluded to commence Mis. operations
> forthwith."

Actual mission work began with the first Sunday in August when
a service was held in a building provided by Mr. Stokes on his
compound for a school and meeting house.  The Rev. Mr. Porter of
the London Missionary Society, on his way from Vizagapatam to
Cuddapah, preached in Telugu.  After that Heyer conducted the services with the help of an interpreter.  Two Telugu schools were
started and in September the English-Telugu school which had been
conducted for some years under the patronage of the Collectors and
other English residents was formally transferred to his care.[79]
With so much of the groundwork already laid by these devoted
Christian officials, and with large contributions coming from them
to supplement the inadequate provisions from America, it is no
wonder that the work advanced quickly.  Within six weeks, Heyer
could report that "as far as I am acquainted with the history of
modern Missions, I know of no Society, that has attained such a
sphere of operation in so short a time, and with such small means
as ours."[80]

About seventy poor, maimed, blind and helpless beggars came
to him the first thing each morning to receive alms contributed
by his English friends, amounting to about $15 a month. He took
this opportunity to read the Scriptures to them in Telugu, teach
them hymns and gospel verses, the Ten Commandments and the Lord's
Prayer, always closing with prayer. Following this he held devotions for thirty or forty servants of the Stokes' household who
were required to attend. At eight in the morning, he opened the
English-Telugu school with prayer and a Bible class; there were 30
pupils. Following breakfast he studied Telugu for four hours with
his native munshi; and then he visited the two Telugu schools, one
on the compound of Stokes having 13 scholars and the other in the
center of the town serving 27 more. On Sunday the Telugu worship
service reached about 70 individuals, mostly school children; and
Heyer also served as pastor to the English residents, with about
30 of them attending an English service Sundays and a prayer meeting Wednesday evenings.[81] Heyer employed four teachers, none of
them Christians, and their salaries amounted to $20 a month. He
instituted weekly meetings to help them increase their teaching efficiency and also win them, if possible, to Christianity. In addition, he took an orphan boy named Kotilingam into his home with
the hope of training him to be a catechist.[82]

A month later there were six schools, all Telugu except the
original English one, attended by children of the low castes and

outcastes.[83]   In November, Father Heyer organized, with the support

of the wife of Judge Walker, the first Hindu girls' school with 15

pupils in attendance.  He also took five boys from the English-Tel-

ugu school and spent extra time with them in a sort of normal

school in order to have more efficient teachers.  December saw the

opening of a Sunday School to give the children added instruction

in the Christian faith.  And on January 4, 1843, a day that Heyer

felt should in many respects be considered the true beginning of

the "American Evangelical Lutheran Mission in Guntur," the first

schoolhouse built with $15 from America was completed and put to

use.[84]

After a year Father Heyer could report in a letter dated Oct-

ober 11, 1843, that three adults had been instructed and baptized;

and that these three had joined two Tamil Christians of Stokes'

household to receive the Lord's Supper.  He had held one wedding

and six funerals.  The seven schools served a total of 180 pupils,

22 of them girls.  Nearly 200 Telugu people were reached reg-

ularly through the preaching at the one o'clock service on Sunday

and to the poor each morning.  At the instigation of the Rev. Win-

slow[85] the A. B. C. F. M. sent a $10 contribution to provide a col-

porteur to visit the villages, read portions of scriptures to the

people and distribute tracts.  The Madras Auxiliary Bible Society

sent 500 pamphlets in Telugu, 300 in Tamil, with the gospels, Gen-

esis and the Psalms separately bound.  This was the beginning of substantial help from the Bible and Tract Societies. Heyer also mentioned that the Government had provided about two acres for an annual ground rent of about $1.25 and that he was now in the process of erecting a brick building for the Church and schools.

In this same letter Heyer emphasized how happy he was to learn that the two Lutheran Missionary Societies in America had adopted a plan of agreement that would soon provide him with a fellow laborer.[86] He also noted that a missionary sent out by the North German Missionary Society had arrived in Madras and that he had written to welcome him and offer him help in getting started. The Rev. Louis P. Menno Valett accepted this offer and arrived in Guntur in February, 1844, and remained with Heyer the rest of that year before moving on to open new work in Rajahmundry, to which reference shall be made at a later time.[87]

With Valett, Heyer made a significant three-week tour westward into the Palnad, ceded to the British in 1817. Driver, cart and extra horse being provided by Mr. Stokes, they started on March 8 and made their first visit at the famous Roman Catholic mission of Father Bonnand in Peringapuram.[88] Going on from there they visited many villages, distributing tracts and preaching wherever possible. At Pedugural Heyer found the people as hard as any he had met in India, refusing to listen to him or take any of the books. Part of the reason for his tour was to determine whether the native school at Timmeracotta supported by English residents in Guntur should be moved to Dachepalle with its more favorable location and fresh, running water from a brook. The houses in this area were built of marble stones which lay around plentifully on the ground. They conducted a Sunday service for Roman Catholics and others who would attend at Rentachintala, and found that they knew the gospel to some extent and considered worship of the Virgin Mary and the Saints to be wrong. They were served by a priest from Peringapuram.

Heyer gives a sample of his preaching on the streets of Macherla:[89]

> "We pointed out to the people that their village contained temples for Vishnu, Siva, Rahmaswamy, etc., but no temple for the only true and living God. Some of the Brahmin priests asserted, that they did not worship wood and stone, but God in the wood and stone. When the question was put: Do you believe, that the true God can hear and see? -- they answered: Yes, God is omniscient. I then asked one of the by-standers, if he could hear and see? He said yes. Well then, said I, if you were stuck into a large stone or block, would you be able to hear and see better, than you do now? This caused a great laughter. I immediately made the application, and wished to know, why they believed, that God could hear and see better in a stone, than if they would pray to him in spirit and in truth."

This trip was of significance as Heyer believed he and Valett were the first Protestant missionaries to preach in that region; and this area was soon to become the fastest growing part of the Mission. Heyer made such an impression on Malapati John of Polepalli that he came to Guntur to study and learn to read, returning again in 1847 to be baptized. During this time John worked dili-

53

gently among his relatives and people of the weaver caste, telling them about his Lord. "Such Mis. tours," Father Heyer reported, "should often be engaged in; but one missionary alone cannot do everything; if there were more laborers, we could better cultivate the field."[90]

The Rev. Walter Gunn, second missionary to Guntur and the first to represent the General Synod, arrived on June 18, 1844, after a long, circuitous and expensive voyage that lasted seven months. He and his wife had stayed for a short time in Burma, sat fearfully for seven days in Calcutta in the midst of an outbreak of cholera that killed 28,000 in two months, went from there to Madras which was far south of the Guntur mission, and then returned north to Masulipatam, always traveling in inconvenient and most uncomfortable sailing vessels. After such a harrowing experience they were pleasantly surprised with the excited reception of Father Heyer and the English residents in Guntur.[91] Gunn entered the work with enthusiasm , studying Telugu, teaching English to a class of Hindu boys, conducting a Bible study class for the English residents and occasionally preaching at the English services on Sunday; while his wife began to teach English and needle-work to Hindu girls. Gunn took part with Heyer and Valett in the consecration of the new brick mission-house on June 30; about 200 attended the service.[92]

Meanwhile there appeared on the scene three more missionaries who were from the Dresden (Leipzig) Society and were considering work among the Telugus. Heyer received them gladly and was willing to provide them with young natives from his school as interpreters and schoolmasters. He also was looking forward to the day in the near future when they could hold a 'Lutheran Synod' meeting. But a month later the Leipzig missionaries had decided to return to Tranquebar and open up work in the surrounding area.[93]

### 2. Valett -- the Rajahmundry Mission

Valett, having decided upon the location of the new Mission of the North German Society, felt that he had enough of a start in the Telugu language to move to Rajahmundry in January, 1845. Rajahmundry, the ancient capital of the Eastern Chalukyas and the center of Telugu culture and literature, was situated 115 miles from Guntur on the Godavari river. At this time the city was of interest because of the great irrigation dam about to be built near by at Dowlaishwaram under the direction of Captain Arthur Cotton.[94] Cotton encouraged Valett and promised support of any new mission work established in the area.

The Rev. Louis P. Menno Valett, born in 1813 in Glueckstadt, Germany, had offered himself to the North German Missionary Society of Hamburg (later Bremen) through the Stade Society, which had been the first to initiate the organization of the North German Society.[95] After his commissioning he had sailed from Hamburg May 26, 1843, and arrived in Madras October 2, and then came on to

Guntur early the next year to study Telugu under Heyer.[96]   In
Rajahmundry Valett began to preach right from the beginning in
both Telugu and English.  Daily devotions were conducted for the
native servants of resident English families; but unfortunately
their attendance was compulsory, as had been the case in Guntur,
and this was not a way to win converts in spite of the good intentions of the English officials.

Two schools were opened, one in English-Telugu and the other
purely Telugu.  He found derelict East India Company property
available and with the permission of the Government leased for a
99-year period what is now known as the Church Compound.  Valett
was in the process of building the first mission house when two
more missionaries arrived on July 22, 1846, to strengthen the work.[97]
Two months later the Rev. Walter Gunn came from Guntur to participate in the ordination of the new missionaries, the Rev. Charles
W. Groenning and the Rev. Ferdinand A. Heise.[98]

In spite of the promising outlook of three missionaries and
the support of the English residents, progress was very slow; Valett reported his first baptism on February 18, 1849, followed by
two others in January, 1850.  When Groenning and Heise were considered capable of taking over work on their own, a new station
was opened at Ellore where Groenning began to preach in May, 1849,
while Heise remained in Rajahmundry.  But matters were developing on the home front in Germany which changed the whole picture.

## 3. Reverses in Rajahmundry and Guntur

The disturbed political affairs and revolution in 1848 drastically reduced the income of the North German Society. Internal disunity and the closing of the Mission School led the Society to
give up one of its mission fields. Having had difficulty all
along in providing what they considered adequately-trained men
for the work in India,[99] the Society decided in May, 1850, to
give up its work there. The close-working relationship with the
American Lutherans in Guntur made them the natural choice for taking over the work. Ellore was formally transferred in August,
Rajahmundry by January 1, 1851, and this at no cost other than the
assumption of a debt of Rs. 1,000 in the School Fund.[100] As Valett had been in India more than seven years, he asked for a furlough and left Rajahmundry March 9, 1851; but when he was ready
to return, the Foreign Missionary Society felt it was unable to
support him with the sudden increase of the work in India. Therefore, he joined the London Missionary Society and served in Bellary and Chicacole until 1859.[101]

Turning our attention again to Father Heyer and the Guntur
Mission, progress was slow but steady after the arrival of Gunn.
A total of 18 adult and 6 child baptisms was reported at the end
of three years, of whom only four were permitted to commune.[102]
Four schools, three of them Telugu, with an enrollment of more
than 100 met in the Guntur mission-house; two other schools with
25 students were conducted in the vicinity of the city. The Girls'
School had 25 pupils, unusual for that day when there was still

57

so much opposition to the education of women.  Heyer's greatest

pride was the English school which had three grades, taught arith-

metic, geography, grammar and Biblical history, and served quite a

number of castes.[103]

What discouraged Heyer the most was the lack of support from

the Church in America.  Only two or three hundred dollars had come

each year in addition to his salary from the Society, plus small

amounts from individual churches, while the faithful English offic-

ials in Guntur had contributed a total of Rs. 2910 ($1164) up to

September 16, 1844.  He complained about this in most of his let-

ters, and emphasized that it hardly seemed proper for a Lutheran

Mission to be supported primarily by those of another Church.  Yet,

at the same time, it must be realized that the amount of money com-

ing from the churches and individuals to the Missionary Society of

the Synod of Pennsylvania was so small that nearly all of it was

used to support the work in India with little left over for any

Home Mission efforts.  Since the foreign mission was started with

the understanding that it would not hurt the work in America, there

was a good bit of criticism.  This came to a head when Heyer, be-

fore he had been granted permission to do so, left Guntur on Dec-

ember 22, 1845, and was back in America by August, 1846.[104]  He

left the work in the hands of Gunn, who had not yet mastered the

Telugu language.  Bachmann says in this connection:[105]

"Heyer's bolting for home may be accounted for on several

58

grounds. He had motherless children at home. He was home-
sick as well as innately restless. Above all he was discouraged with the aid which the church had hitherto supplied the
work in Guntur. He felt he could risk the inevitable crit-
icisms which a precipitous return would heap upon him, and
hoped in spite of it to stir up greater interest in missions
among those who still favored the station in India. He probably was sufficiently sure of himself to feel that, as a
missionary fresh from the field, his stories would do more
to inspire the church to renewed effort than could all his
letters from India, printed though they were in the church
papers."

Yet the Ministerium's Missionary Society evidently thought

his return was permanent, for they terminated his salary as soon

as he left Guntur and authorized the executive committee to turn

the Mission over to the Foreign Missionary Society of the General

Synod. Not permitted to make a campaign of missionary visitation

and education, he started a mission congregation in northwestern

Baltimore for the Home Missionary Society of the General Synod.

At the same time he completed his course in medicine and received

the degree of Doctor of Medicine at the age of fifty-four. Friends

were urging him to speak up and volunteer his services to India

once more; finally a letter of his appeared April 9, 1847, in The

Lutheran Observer, explaining his reasons for coming home when he

did and volunteering to take two or three young men with him to

India and help them in the study of Telugu.

The Missionary Society of the Pennsylvania Ministerium voted

at its annual meeting in June, 1847, to send Heyer back to India

(without the men) with the understanding that "he would not leave the mission field unless the society failed to pay his salary or ill-health compelled him to leave India."[106]  Following a four-month tour of the churches, he sailed on December 4, 1847, and arrived in Guntur May 15, 1848.  While in Madras he came across an independent congregation which had separated itself from the oldest native congregation in Madras, Vepery, with the intention of carrying on alone.  They were dissatisfied with the way the English missionaries were handling matters and wanted to return to the ways of the old German missionaries.  Feeling the need of a regular pastor, they expressed to Heyer the hope that he or one of the Tranquebar missionaries could serve them.  Heyer reports in this connection:[107]

> "As far as I can ascertain, this is the first attempt, made by native Christians in India, to carry on their operations independent of European agency.  I indulge the hope, that they will persevere in their undertaking, build a church, and form a native Lutheran Church in Madras.  If the missionaries at Tranquebar decline to attend to them, we ought to try and provide for them."

However, the Tranquebar Mission did send the Rev. C. F. Kremmer to them in 1848.[108]

The Rev. Walter Gunn had begun his work in Guntur with much consecration, but ill health forced him to do little more than maintain the status quo during Heyer's absence.  The mission house had been destroyed by a storm in October, 1846, and was rebuilt through the contribution of $350 (Rs. 1100) by Collector Stokes. A bungalow for the Gunns also was built, with funds from the For-

eign Missionary Society.  Although only two adults were baptized
in this period, they were significant: one of them was Malapati
John[109] who became the leader in a mass movement in the Palnad;
and the other was Stephen, a Mala and a former disciple of a
priest, who became the first Indian Christian teacher.  The first
native catechist, Nicodemus, was employed in March, 1847, but he
proved to be little more than a colporteur.  In December, 1847, and
January, 1848, Gunn felt strong enough to make a trip through the
Palnad in the company of Heise of Rajahmundry and Beer of Narsapur,[110] but he had a severe attack of malaria.  A long siege of
illness followed and he died in Guntur on July 5, 1851, the first
Lutheran missionary to give his life for the Telugu people.

4.  The Movement in the Palnad

In January, 1849, Heyer began another tour[111] into the Palnad
which produced such excellent results with twenty-two baptisms at
Polepalli on February 12th that Mr. Stokes persuaded him that he
should move to the area and open a new station.[112]  Heyer was offered a house and lot in Gurzala by Stokes; and at the same time
several other events occurred which led him to feel that this was
indeed a special call to duty.  He writes:[113]

> "A respectable native catechist connected with the American
> Mission in Madras, wrote to me stating that he felt an im-
> pression on his mind as though it were the Lord's will that
> he should go north and preach the Gospel among the Telugus,
> and wished to know whether we could employ him.  A pensioned
> dresser, (i.e., a kind of native doctor) a Christian man
> whose son wished to be employed as a Telugu teacher or read-
> er, also expressed himself willing to remove with his family
> whithersoever the catechist might be called to labor.  These

and other circumstances seemed plainly to indicate that the
time had come for commencing a new station, and that the Lord
designed to open a door of usefulness for us in the Palnad.
Therefore, notwithstanding the statements which were made
about the excessive heat during one part of the year, and
the unhealthiness of the climate during another part, I resolved in the fear of the Lord to commence the work."

Public worship was started Sunday, April 15, and the following
Sunday a congregation was organized with the adoption of a few
resolutions and the appointment of two elders and two deacons.[114]
Three schools were opened in short order at Gurzala, Polepalli
and Dachepalle with about 20 students in each.  Being without
trained teachers, the more intelligent converts were used; yet
Heyer realized he had to have trained men if there was to be any
real development and so he took five promising boys into his own
home and provided for their room and board at a cost of approximately Rs. 12.  One of these, Paulus, nephew of Malapati John, became one of the first pastors of the Church.

Forty-two persons were baptized at the end of eight months in
the Palnad in contrast to one-half that number in the first six
years in Guntur.  Fourteen communicants came forward to receive
the Lord's Supper when it was administered for the first time on
November 25, 1849.[115]  Heyer continued to live and work in the Palnad until February, 1853, baptizing a total of 243 persons in
eight villages.[116]

Reinforcements to the Mission field came in the persons of the
Rev. George J. Martz, a graduate of Gettysburg College and Semin-

ary, who stayed less than three years (1849-1852); the Rev. and Mrs. William J. Cutter, who also resigned after three years (1852-1855); and the Rev. and Mrs. William E. Snyder, who served from 1852 to 1859. Cutter and Snyder were graduates of Hartwick Seminary, New York. The widowed Mrs. Walter Gunn remained, at the request of the Executive Committee of the Foreign Missionary Society, to maintain charge of the Girls' School and thus became the first regularly called and salaried woman missionary. Now that the Rajahmundry field had been added to the Mission, and the work looked most encouraging, the five missionaries and fourteen Indian Christians met in Guntur to organize the first "Lutheran Synod in India" on January 31, 1853, the same year in which the Pennsylvania Ministerium returned to the ranks of the General Synod after an absence of thirty years. Heyer was elected the first president, Snyder the secretary. Changes in areas of work sent Groenning to the Palnad and Heyer to Guntur; Cutter had joined Heise in Rajahmundry early in 1852 while Snyder remained in Guntur. After the departure of Martz in 1852, the Ellore station was turned over to the C. M. S., so that the work now centered in Rajahmundry, Guntur (with very little work being done outside of the two towns themselves) and Gurzala in the Palnad.

Heyer found the progress had been very slow in Guntur during his absence with only fifteen adult communicants belonging to the congregation. There were 150 pupils in six schools with all eight teachers Christian, the only real improvement in the situation. Heyer had brought four boys with him from the Palnad; and, adding three more, he opened the first regular boarding school for boys in Guntur. Even less could be said for the progress in Rajahmundry where Heise could report only four adult baptisms up to April, 1851. Cutter revived the schools, so that by the end of 1852 five schools had 175 pupils. He had personal charge of the Anglo-vernacular school while Mrs. Cutter opened the first Girls' School in Rajahmundry.

The second annual meeting of the Synod in 1854 was significant in the proposal made by Heyer in his report "to make some step toward establishing an official correspondence with all Lutheran missionaries in India, which might eventually lead to the formation of a general synod."[117] In this Father Heyer was too much of a pioneer, for nothing came of this excellent proposal until more than fifty years later when the All India Lutheran Conference was organized in 1908. That he had other advanced ideas is revealed in a letter to Dr. Schmucker where he discussed the relation of the India church either as a Synod of the General Synod or as a corresponding Synod. He realized the difficulties involved, however, such as the distance, the traveling expenses of the delegates and location outside the bounds of the United States.

In this same letter he renewed his concern about the lack of support from America, especially since Mr. Stokes and other interested friends moved away from Guntur and the new officials did next to nothing to help the work. With adequate support Christian schools could be opened in four or five villages in the vicinity of Guntur where persons had applied for Christian instruction; and results similar to the Palnad might develop. He went on to say:[118]

> "It is a mistaken notion to think, that the Mission preaching is to do all the business; other instruction must be employed. To feed the lambs is of the greatest importance. From Missionary schools taught by heathen teachers and attended by heathen children, I have witnessed no good results, and therefore do not ask for money, to support schools of this kind."

Nor did Heyer want to go to the extreme of some missions who had taken boys and trained them for 12 or 15 years in European style, even sending some to Europe. The students trained for teachers and preachers should not be raised so far above the level of the people they were to work with. His plan was, rather, the one adopted in the Palnad:[119]

> "That we station a Christian school teacher in each village where two or three or more families have become or are will-to become Christians. After the children are able to read and write, we wish to select the most promising among them, and keep them one or two years in Guntoor, to establish them more fully in gospel principles; after having received this extra schooling, they go home to their parents and friends, to work with them for their living; a very few of the boys may be selected or employed as teachers."

Heyer also pleaded with the Ministerium of Pennsylvania to permit him to return to the United States and be replaced by

65

younger men, now that he was over sixty. But he was prevented by the sudden depletion of the staff. The Cutters and Snyder (his wife had died September, 1854) returned home because of health reasons; Heise took a much-needed furlough and stayed over to tour the congregations in America;[120] Heyer took charge of the Rajahmundry station at the close of 1854 while Groenning moved to Guntur and tried to continue work in the Palnad from there.[121] At this point (1856) the staff was smaller than at any time since 1844. But without waiting for the return of Heise or Snyder, who brought two new missionary families, Heyer showed once more his restlessness by turning Rajahmundry over to the care of a Captain George N. Taylor and leaving for America in April, 1857, with the entire work in the hands of one missionary, Groenning.[122]

For a time there appeared the definite possibility that four missionary recruits could be obtained from India itself when a group of Leipzig missionaries led by the Rev. C. C. E. Ochs resigned over a caste controversy and asked to be united with the American Lutherans;[123] but nothing came out of the development. Three of them went to Australia and Africa while Ochs started his own work in South Arcot which became the Mission of the Danish Missionary Society in 1864.

## 5. Mylius -- the Hermannsburg Mission

When, during the Civil War, there was no sign of new missionaries coming from America, Groenning, now located at Rajahmundry as the missionary of the Pennsylvania Ministerium Society, appealed to his brother-in-law, Nagel, a merchant in Hamburg, to come and help, saying: "You must come over and help us, else I will lay it upon your conscience that the mission here must cease to be a German and a Lutheran one."[124] Nagel was a very good friend of Louis Harms of Hermannsburg and turned the letter over to him. About the same time the Rev. August Mylius wrote to Harms from the Friederikenstift in Hanover, saying that he would like to return to India as a missionary of the Hermannsburg Society. He had been a missionary for the Leipzig Society in charge of Porayar near Tranquebar from 1847 to 1851 at which time he was forced to return to Germany because of a heat stroke.[125] Harms felt that this was more than coincidental; and he wrote to Groenning to say that he had a man.

During the course of correspondence between America and India, and Germany and India, several misunderstandings evidently arose. The Executive Committee in America understood from Groenning that Mylius was being sent to maintain the field for them, with his support coming from Hermannsburg for the time being;[126] but Mylius left for India on August 27, 1864 following his commissioning on St. Bartholomew's Day with specific instructions from Harms to occupy a new field for the Hermannsburg Society.[127] When Mylius arrived in Rajahmundry in March, 1865, it was clear to him that the General Synod had no intention or desire to give up the work or any part of it, although they were willing to have him stay if he joined the Synod. Mylius, on his part, was a strict confessional Lutheran and conscious of the furor developing in America over the laxity of the General Synod in this regard;[128] so he decided to take Groenning's kindly advice and look for a new area of work. He returned to Madras to consult the Rev. Mr. Kremmer of the Leipzig Mission.[129]

On a tour into the Telugu country during September, Mylius came to Nellore where he was graciously received by the Baptist missionary Jewett and invited to work there, as there was plenty of work for two missions. "Not wishing to work in an already occupied area, Mylius headed south where he found a rather extensive field in which no mission work was being done."[130] This was the territory between Arambakam (near the southern tip of Pulicat Lake) and Gudur, the southern part of the Nellore District, stretching for some ninety miles along the Bay of Bengal and inland about seventy-five miles. The town of Sulurpet especially attracted him. It was a center for merchants and traders although it had a population of only 1200, and boasted an English officer of peace, a police station and a post office. The friendly reception of a law official who had been trained in a famous mission school and the willingness of the people to listen to the word of God preached to them persuaded Mylius to stay.

He made his headquarters in the travelers' bungalow; and it was not long before Mylius had converted the caretaker whose name was Rangaja. This man was living illegally with a Roman Catholic woman. When he straightened out his married life, Mylius baptized him and his two children on February 11, 1866, the first fruits of the Hermannsburg Mission in India. Mylius named him Johannes; his wife was called Maria and the children Jesudasen and Gabriel. He was hired as the first catechist at ten rupees (Rs. 10) a month, and served in Sulurpet intermittently for ten years. Near the bungalow and close to the main road was a native house which Mylius was able to buy for about Rs. 100 and make his first permanent residence.

Traveling north eighteen miles to Nayudupeta, Mylius was given another kindly reception on the part of a Mr. Jackman, an Eurasian who served under the Rajah of Venkatagiri.[131] Whenever in Nayudupeta he stayed in Mr. Jackman's home; the latter aided in purchasing land both in Nayudupeta and Gudur and contributed toward material needed to construct houses on the land. He helped overcome the opposition on the part of Brahmans led by Swamutavaru, a Sannyasi, who tried to persuade the Rajah not to sell any land.[132]

In May, Mylius baptized the second family, a young policeman named Paul, his wife Maria and child Lydia. They had been under instruction by Johannes in Sulurpet, and made two visits in April to see Mylius in Nayudupeta. After the baptism they joined in communion -- Johannes' and Paul's families, the Brahman Telugu teacher and Mylius.[133]

Three new missionaries, Heinrich Brunotte, Jens Dahl and
Thomas Petersen, ordained May 25, 1866, in Hanover, arrived in
Madras in September and studied Telugu with Kremmer for three
months before going to Sulurpet at the close of the year. Dahl
supervised the building of the bungalow in Nayudupeta which was
dedicated August 4, 1867; the next month the bungalow in Gudur
was completed by Petersen. Mylius and Dahl settled in Nayudupeta, making that the center of the Mission; while Petersen went
to Gudur and Brunotte remained in Sulurpet. Four more missionaries arrived in the early part of 1868, bringing along the future
wives of two of the first group of missionaries, Brunotte and
Petersen. This interesting and unusual policy was continued;
with the advice of Mylius, Director Harms in Germany would select
the women from a list of volunteers and send them to the field a
year or more after the men had arrived.[134]

With astounding rapidity new fields were occupied and bungalows built. Help in purchasing properties came from the Collector
of the District, Bothwell, who came to Nellore in 1867, and proved
to be a very good friend of missionary efforts. Grants of land
were procured on Sriharikota Island opposite Pulicat; Durgara-
japatnam, twenty miles farther north and secured for a rest house
on the shore; and at Vakadu when it turned out that Durgaraja-
patnam was in too malarial an area. Brunotte went to Sriharikota,
but this work was never successful as it also was a very unhealthy

place. Moreover, the people were primarily forest Janadis, who proved very inaccessible and cut off from the services of the mission. They thought Brunotte was insane when he visited them in the forest, which no white man had done before.[135]

In the region Mylius had selected for the Mission, the largest towns were Venkatagiri and Kalahasti. Realizing it was important to set up stations there, Mylius was forced to move faster than he had anticipated by the news that the Baptists were planning to start work in the former, and the Dutch Reformed from the Arcot Mission in the latter. In 1868, Dahl accompanied Mylius to interview the Rajah of Venkatagiri, who held the largest Zemindari in the Madras Presidency. They approached him in typical oriental fashion with many gifts and were cordially received. In the course of the conversation the missionaries found he owned a Bible but did not know the difference between Christianity and Mohammedanism. They thus seized the opportunity to preach the Gospel and found him interested and most friendly. With this introduction and the help of Collector Bothwell it was not difficult to get some land. The Rajah even permitted Dahl to live in one of his houses until the mission house was built, provided him with meat and fruit and building materials, and was helpful in many ways. On one occasion he refused thirty rupees for wood that he provided Dahl. He commanded his people to help in every way and revealed to the missionaries in the course of conversation things which he had refused to tell the British government.

Dahl's greatest joy, however, was that he could speak often to the Rajah on religious questions and witness to the truth of Christianity. The Brahman who taught the Rajah's children was receptive and dared debate in favor of Christianity with all the scholars in the court. But he found it difficult to be baptized because of his wife's opposition. Dahl realized it was a great step to take from mere interest to conversion for high caste men such as these; yet what progress Dahl might have made in the Rajah's court was cut short by Dahl's dismissal in 1873 over the caste problem. Mylius found Dahl a true and eager missionary, but he tended toward the Leipzig position of leniency, permitting caste to exist in the mission and yet at the same time struggling against the spirit of caste with God's word rather than with the church discipline. He was accused also of spending too much time with the upper caste people to the neglect of the lower. This action turned the Rajah of Venkatagiri against the Lutheran Mission and made progress very difficult in his domain.[136]

The position of Mylius and Dahl regarding the use of upper caste converts is seen in the case of a wealthy Dasari or wandering priest who was sent back to his home and village to study from books rather than taken to the Mission center for further education. His parents were fearful that the missionaries would take

their son and ship him off to another country, as the Brahmans
claimed. Dahl saw the value of local Christian influence:[137]

> I wished that he would return home because I want to see that
> there are some Christians in the villages. Hence they are a
> light to the other village inhabitants if the Lord gives them
> the grace to be upright and to overcome the temptations of
> lying and deception which they will encounter in the vill-
> ages."

Far different was the reception Mylius and Dahl received at
Kalahasti, where the Rajah was under the complete control of the
many Brahmans who flooded his domain. The missionaries called it
a Brahman paradise for the Brahmans lived off the Rajah and the
rich temples, one of which is said to be where Siva had one of his
1008 revelations. The Rajah would not have anything to do with
these "ambassadors of a false god," as he called the two missionaries;[138] but the two Collectors of Nellore and Arcot urged the
Rajah to reconsider. It was not until August, 1872, that Thomas
Petersen began work there at a rented location one mile outside
the town, removed from the noise of the Siva festivals. In order
to get the lease, Mylius had to travel to the court and sit
patiently in the sun until the Rajah felt inclined to give it to
him. Work was very difficult in Kalahasti and there were only
eight baptisms up to 1876.

Rapur, at the northern end of the Mission field, was started
in 1873; this was another difficult field with only six baptisms
up to 1880. It was an unhealthy place for missionaries, Kiehne

losing two wives and two children in less than eighteen months.
It pointed up one of the great problems of this Mission field: the
great number of deaths or forced resignations because of health,
especially among the women and children. In one area ten missionaries served in the period of eleven years, with seven of them
succumbing to the heat and three forced to return home; during the
same period nine women and 32 children died, while five women had
to return to Germany.[139]

Efforts to open a station at Tirupati, one of the great holy
places of South India, where Ziegenbalg had nearly lost his life,[1]
proved to be difficult because of the opposition of the Brahmans;
but the Collector offered the Mission a valuable piece of property
and the greed of the Muslims for money overcame any fear they had
of the Hindu priests and provided laborers for construction work.
Work was started by Paul Petersen and Woerrlein in 1876. At the
end of this same year, after eleven years of concentrated effort
on the Hermannsburg Mission field and the occupation of nine stations, Mylius could report a total of 401 baptisms since the beginning, 98 of them in the past year. Most of the buildings were
of rather temporary construction, made of mud, but now three stone
churches and chapels were completed at Nayudupet (1874), Rapur and
Vakadu (both 1876); and money was available for two more at Gudur
and Kalahasti. Each station had its catechetical (baptismal
training) school; there were two boarding schools in the Mission,

one for boys in Nayudupet started in 1868, and the other for girls organized the following year in Gudur. In 1874, there were 15 catechists, of whom 12 were baptized by the mission. Two of these were Brahmans who had broken with their caste entirely and had been very useful because of their respected position and helpful contact with Hindu officials.

The first convention or Synod was held in 1868 at which time a constitution was drawn up that remained in force until 1892. This gave the Superintendent, Mylius, almost unlimited power over the missionaries and the native workers, and created a number of conflicts which led to resignations of some excellent missionaries. For one thing Mylius, rarely in good health, overrode his weakness with an iron will; hence he had little sympathy for sickly missionaries. For another, he opposed most vehemently any leniency toward caste. At the same time he was held in deepest respect by missionary and worker alike for his consecrated service, his brillant mind, his teaching ability and his strict adherence to Lutheran theology. They loved him as a father in spite of his sternness. Mylius also could be humble and ask for forgiveness if he realized he was in the wrong. His successor, Woerrlein, said of him:[141]

> "The brethren learned order under the guidance of Mylius and they now know how to keep order. It is through his conscientious faithfulness in the little things that he became the standard for all the missionaries; and is to this very day. That is because he lived wholly in the mission, and not for his own sake and honor."

75

## 6. Pohl and Bothmann -- the Breklum Mission

Among the first twelve students in the Mission Institute
opened by the Schleswig-Holstein Missionary Society[142] on April
10, 1877, was Hans H. Bothmann, born April 12, 1856, in Sarz-
buettel.  He was joined shortly by Ernst Georg G. Pohl, born December 25, 1860, in Fraustadt.  Their teacher and director of the
Society from March, 1879, on[143] was the son of the Rajahmundry
missionary, the Rev. Charles William Groenning.  William, Jr.,
also served in Rajahmundry from 1885 to 1889 as teacher in the
preacher's seminary following his directorship.  It is certain that
both father and son had much to do with influencing the Schleswig-
Holstein Missionary Society to open work in India.  A pupil of the
elder Groenning, the Rev. Hans C. Schmidt, also from Schleswig,
had been serving as the head of the Rajahmundry Mission since 1871
and correspondence between him and the Groennings brought out the
suggestion that the new Society should attempt to make Bastar
State their field of work.

Pohl and Bothmann were selected for the task, were ordained
on November 24, 1881, landed in Madras January 23, 1882, where
they were welcomed by the Leipzig missionary Handmann, visited
Petersen, who also was originally from Schleswig, at Tirupati, and
reached Rajahmundry February 13.  At this time the Rajah of Bastar
was most unfriendly to Christian missions; his State was one of
the most backward and isolated in all of India and there were
large numbers of Khonds and Kois, aboriginal tribes, living in the

forests that covered a large portion of the State. At the southern edge of Bastar, Colonel Cotton and his brother-in-law, Major-
General Felix Thackerey Haig, were in the midst of constructing
new irrigation works on the Godavari River, with their headquarters at Dummagudem. They also were active in helping the Church
Missionary Society reach the Kois and outcastes of the area, looking toward the day when an entrance could be made into Bastar.[144]
General Haig had written the Rajah concerning such a possibility.
When he heard that the Schleswig-Holstein missionaries were planning to go there, he advised them to go to Vizagapatam and work
their way inland to Bastar by establishing stations in Jeypore.

Schmidt, however, suggested taking the land route, from the
south border of Bastar, in order to reach the capital itself, Jagdalpur. Not realizing what was ahead of them, Pohl and Bothmann
agreed to this, since their Society wanted them to begin work in
Bastar. In the company of Schmidt, Artman of the Rajahmundry
mission and Heelis of the Godavery Delta mission at Narsapur,[145]
they started the voyage on March 15. They traveled 80 miles in
Schmidt's boat, the "Dove of Peace," up the Godavari and its trib-
utary, the Saveri, pushing the boat through shallow places. They
entered Bastar State through Manikidevikomta March 23, got porters
to carry their baggage and marched to Jagdalpur, 120 miles away,
in 18 days, having crossed three mountain ranges and nearly im-
penetrable forests. Travelers on the way told them that they

would indeed be welcomed and showered with gifts, but would end up being robbed.

They were received heartily and the Rajah gave promises of assistance; yet he kept putting off the decision to give them a piece of property. He invited them to participate in a hunt, during which Mr. Heelis became ill from sunstroke and almost died. As time went on the hostile attitude of the Rajah became apparent. The missionaries paid for food supplies and building materials only to find that the Rajah had given strict orders to the people not to help them. The Rajah told them he wanted a gift of Rs. 2,000; and when they could not and would not give it to him, he turned against them still further and saw that they were completely ostracized, with no contact with the people whatsoever. During this time they were living in a tent under a mango tree and several bad storms seriously damaged the tent. Several of the party came down with malarial fever. Realizing that they would have to leave, they made one more attempt on May 4th to purchase land, but without success. Then they found that they could not hire anyone to carry their baggage, for the original group of porters had been taken on a hunt by the Rajah.

Nearly a month had gone by when some friendly Rohillas, a robber caste, brought word that the whole party was to be massacre With their help the missionaries obtained some bandies (two-wheeled carts) which had come filled with rice and were returning empty to Kotapad in Jeypore State. The night before the plot was to have been perpetrated they fled seventy miles east to Koraput. Mr. Heelis had to be carried all the way slung in a cot. Fatigue coupled with fever left the group in utter collapse for some time. Bothmann and Pohl decided to stay in Koraput and begin their work there while the rest of the party descended to the plains on their return to Rajahmundry. The heat was unbearable and all except Schmidt came down with fever; at one point Heelis, Artman and two of the native servants were so prostrated that they lapsed into delirium. Somehow they reached Vizagapatam, found a steamer to Cocanada, seaport of Rajahmundry, and arrived home June 22 weak and emaciated. It took many months of nursing and care before Heelis was on his feet again. The Rev. Mr. Artman never did recover fully, as he continued to have fever attacks which took his life September 18, 1884.[146]

Koraput proved to be an unhealthy place for Bothmann, even though it was 3,000 feet above sea level; he was sick for four months, beginning August 1. Although the missionaries did not want to give up the work and retreat once more, a doctor advised them that they must return to the plains. A rich man offered them the use of his palanquin, and after a difficult journey they reached Vizianagram and were received graciously by the London Society missionaries. They arrived in Madras September 26 and Bothmann stayed in the hospital ten weeks and with missionary Handmann another five months.

Once again they returned to Rajahmundry and then on to Vizianagram where they studied Telugu. After an exploratory trip in July, 1883, they decided to locate at Salur which was on a new commercial road between Bastar, Jeypore and the coast. The Zamindar here proved to be a weak personality controlled by his mother and indifferent to Christian missions. He went through the formality of exchanging gifts with the missionaries and quite evidently was relieved when that obligation to the white men was completed. The site picked was across the river from Salur on a high and lofty spot along the main road. Building was started February, 1884, and completed before the rainy season set in. It was a very simple place with one room and a porch and soon proved to be too small when two more missionaries arrived in the Fall. The men studied on the porch, two of them noisily repeating Telugu phrases after their munshi or teacher at one end, and the other two busily occupied with the Oriya language at the other end, a sight that attracted large audiences from travelers on the road. In regard to opening the work in Salur the Rev. R. Tauscher states:[147]

"The Home Board of the S.H.E.L.M. only reluctantly gave its permission because they still thought of mission work in Bastar or in the Jeypore country. They saw the difficulty of having a mission field with two or even three languages. Telugu is spoken in and around Salur, Kuvi in the hilly range

between Salur and Jeypore proper, and Oriya in the Jeypore
country. The history of the mission work, however, has
proved the necessity of having Salur as a base for the work
in the Jeypore area. ... Everything necessary for the establishment of the mission stations in the West Jeypore field
had to be bought, packed and dispatched by the missionaries
in Salur, and very often the sick brethren of the Jeypore
stations had to take refuge there."

Bothmann began to build a more spacious bungalow large enough

for two families and this was completed and occupied May 23, 1885.

A rumor that the missionaries were going to sacrifice a child to

dedicate the new house emptied the school that had been started.

In June the original house burned down, evidently started delib-

erately, with a loss of nearly all the property and books of sev-

eral of the missionaries.

A happier occasion was the arrival of the brides of Pohl and

Bothmann and the double wedding in Waltair on September 14. And

on December 10, 1885, occurred the first baptisms -- four men,

three women, five children and three boys old enough to be con-

firmed in a short time. They had been prepared by a catechist

named David who had come from Nellore; he had worked for the Her-

mannsburg Mission but they had found him inadequately trained by

the Baptists in Nellore. He was not too capable but at least

could train the students in their catechism, having them say it

over and over again until memorized.

Most of these early converts soon relapsed over the caste

problem. Two of the boys refused to live with the Catechist David who was a Mala outcaste; and the others refused to take communion with the missionaries. They also wanted to marry their children to caste Hindus. No amount of admonishing or warning helped, so they were dismissed. Some of them returned at a later date. Opposition on the part of Brahmans and some moral lapses of the servants working for the missionaries added to the difficult task of establishing the work. The missionaries found that many were interested just as long as they expected to receive some money or rewards. On their preaching tours, people were more willing to listen in those places where Europeans had been before; elsewhere they ran away. They quickly learned that the people had no consciousness of sin and did not understand its meaning; they considered it a sin to cut down a tree or kill a mosquito, but they were blind to their entire sinful condition before God.

Realizing that little would be accomplished without native helpers stationed in the centers, they opened a school in 1885 with four classes. Soon twenty children were attending, including the daughter of the Tahsildar or local native judge. But trouble arose when the first outcaste boy attended. The attempt also was made to force the newly-baptized boys out of the school as they were considered to be casteless. Yet the school continued to grow in spite of opposition and rumors spread around that the missionaries were going to slaughter men. Each day was opened with prayer and the study of Biblical history. Because there was only

82

one room in this rented house, pandemonium reigned as the various classes studied arithmetic and reading aloud. On June 28, 1887, was the dedication of the new two-room schoolhouse which now had the approval and support of the government. Worship on Sunday was held in the larger of the two rooms. Sunday afternoons were devoted to catechetical training at which time the children learned and repeated the catechism and answered questions about the sermon of the morning. The missionaries found the children had small capacity for divine things and at the same time a good mind for misunderstandings. They were easily swayed by rumors spread and fostered by the Brahmans and other enemies of the Mission.

While William Groenning was still director of the Breklum Mission, a friend gave him 3,000 marks which Groenning decided should be used for a new church at Salur provided the Society would give another 1,500. Property in the center of town, at the entrance to a street of Brahman homes and just two blocks from the temple, was purchased for Rs. 60 from a Brahman. The other Brahmans were astonished to have such a thing happen, and fifty of them came to the missionaries and begged that the church should not be built so near their homes and temple, as it would be a disgrace and insult to them. Attempts at friendly persuasion changed to threats and rumors and finally court action; but the court and the District Collector, Turner, upheld the missionaries. Construction started September 23, 1886. The dedication was held February

83

15, 1890, of a building in good style to be used only for church purposes. The mission school and the house of the caretaker also were built on this property. The hostility of the Brahmans disappeared after a time, especially when they realized how the church improved the appearance of the area.

In 1889 a new field was opened up to the Breklum missionaries when the London Missionary Society offered Parvatipur[148] with a catechist and teacher. Although the congregation was not well organized and had been neglacted by the lack of regular missionary visits, there was a favorable piece of land on the main street of the old part of town that contained a catechist's house and a good well. The land had ample room for a chapel, school and a boarding house for orphan girls. Parvatipur appeared to be one of the most hopeful areas for development in the whole district. The Rev. Lucas P. M. Harless, born July 25, 1862, in Segeberg, who came to India in 1885, was stationed there and immediately began to preach daily in the bazaar, going two mornings in the villages and three evenings into the center of town. Many of the people appeared to be well acquainted with Christianity and received him cordially. Eight children and two adults were baptized by Pentecost, 1890. The first wedding of Indian Christians in the mission was held on April 29, 1890.

Although large mass movements have occurred in other sections of the Telugu country, the development in Salur and Parvatipur proved to be very slow and difficult. Part of it may be explained by the fact that the Schleswig-Holstein Mission had such outstanding success in Jeypore State and the Oriya language area that they naturally tended to emphasize the work there to the neglect of the Telugu mission.[149]

CHAPTER III

THE WAY PREPARED

(Sowing the Seed)

In the establishment of the work in the Andhra Desa, as it was developed in the previous chapter, certain features become apparent, both as to the way the missionaries were received when they arrived and the early policies that were established to face the situation. By bringing these factors together in this chapter a clearer view of the total groundwork of the missionary effort will become apparent.

A. The Reception of the Missionaries

1. <u>By the Government and civil leaders</u>

The early successes of the Lutheran Missions established in the Andhra Desa, meager as they were, can be traced to the preparation made beforehand and the substantial support afterward by the officials of the East India Company and the English residents in the centers where the work was begun.

This interest and cooperation of the English officials was a recent development. As the East India Company became the master power in India through military victories its attitude toward Christian Missions changed from that of tolerance and even friend-

liness in the time of Schwartz to open opposition. Missionaries
were refused entrance into its territories during the 1790s and
1800s because it was feared that they would arouse the anger of
the Indians with their proselyting, create discontent among the
people with their preaching and educational processes, and weaken
the authority of British rule.[1]  On the other hand, there were
chaplains of the East India Company, such as the famous Henry Mar-
tyn, who took a great interest in the promotion of missionary work a-
mong the natives and were able to do worthwhile work even while
the Government violently opposed missionaries definitely commissioned to such work.[2]

The turn of the century brought a keener consciousness among
the Christian Churches in England as to the obligation of the British Government to bring educational and religious and moral advance-
ment to the peoples under its rule.  Under the leadership of Wilberforce in the Parliament they tried but failed to change sufficiently the charter of 1793 of the East India Company to open the
land to missionaries, but by the time of the renewal of the charter
in 1813 the situation changed enough to permit the establishment
of the episcopacy and the opening of India to English missionaries.[3]

This was an important victory for the cause of Christianity.
It led to its acceptance as one of the religions of India; and in
time the government guaranteed the same protection to Christians

in the exercise of their faith as to those of other religions.
The East India Company became more conscious of its responsibility
toward the governed rather than of its profits.[4]  With greater
courage and consciousness of Christian ethics, it dealt with the
long-accepted public immoralities and cruelties that India had and
which were often closely tied to its religious ceremonies and
practices.  It found the Christian Missions strong allies in working out a program of education for the people, a task too great to
be done alone.[5]

Chaplains and devoted laymen turned more and more attention
to the needs of the native people around them.  They formed groups
which supported schools, gave funds for regular distribution to
the poor, and helped the newly-arriving missionaries establish
their work.[6]  With the great shortage of missionaries some of
these men organized congregations of English and native Christians
and conducted services, providing space in their homes or small
chapels and instructing converts until the missionaries from the
main centers could make their occasional visits to administer the
sacraments.[7]

Without the persistence of Mr. John Goldingham, Collector of
Masulipatam, the Church Missionary Society may not have begun work
in the Andhra Desa for years.[8]  When he moved to Guntur, he established a school and worked for the opening of Christian work
there.  Mr. J. Henry Stokes followed him in Guntur and was there

when Father Heyer reached that area on his tour of investigation. It was the fervor and interest of Stokes in establishing Christian missions that persuaded Heyer to make Guntur his headquarters.[9] This can be seen clearly in a letter Stokes wrote to friends in America who had showered him with gifts of appreciation after Father Heyer had told them how much he had done for the work. He said in part, after thanking them profusely:[10]

> "At the same time we cannot but find this touching remembrance deeply humiliating, reminding us of what we ought to have done in His service, whose blood-bought ones we profess to be, and encouraged by the kindness we have already so undeservedly experienced, beg of yourselves and the congregation of Zion's Church the further favor: (1) That you will set apart a special season to pray for us, that we may have grace to be faithful unto the end and not hinder the Lord's work by our deadness and inconsistency, and for the Guntur Mission and District; and (2) that you will try and send us more help. The fields are white already to harvest, adults wishing to listen to the Gospel, boys and girls anxious to be instructed, the children asking for bread and no man breaketh it unto them."

Even after Stokes left for England in 1856 he continued to show keen interest in the Guntur Mission, especially the Palnad field, relieved it of all financial indebtedness to him, and was frequently in correspondence with the Executive Committee of the Foreign Missionary Society when they sought his advice.[11]

In the same way Colonel Arthur T. Cotton, engineering genius who played such a large part in the building of the great irrigation systems of South India,[12] went out of his way to bring missionaries to the Godavari area with the assurance of moral and financial support from him and many of the engineers who worked with

him.  When he came to the area in 1844 to see what could be done
to retrieve the economic decay, his heart was deeply moved by the
plight of the people following the great famine of 1831-1833 and
the failure of the rains in the years 1836, 1837 and 1838 culminating in a destructive cyclone.  The population of the Godavari
district declined by one-third in a period of twenty years, from
738,308 in 1821-22 to 533,836 in the year 1840-41.[13]  When Missionary Valett traveled through the area looking for a new field
of work, Cotton did not find it difficult to persuade him to come
to Rajahmundry and become a pastor to the English residents as
well as work with their servants and the natives of the community.[14]  Bowden of the Godaveri Delta Mission[15] moved to Dowlaishwaram to evangelize the great labor camps brought there by the
Colonel to build the Anicut across the Godavari river.  Cotton's
interest in mission work is revealed by his son who states:[16]

> "He had the greatest love for Christian mission work; he
> loved the missionaries too.  He hardly asked or knew the
> section of the Church of Christ to which they belonged; they
> were God's servants; they were carrying the personal message
> of the gospel, with its present blessedness and its future
> joys, to those around who knew not the Gospel."

One of the ablest assistants to Colonel Sir Arthur Cotton was
Lieutenant, later Major-General, Felix Thackerey Haig, who proved
to be an even greater friend to Christian missions.[17]  Helping at
Rajahmundry in support of the Lutheran Mission, later on he moved
up the river to Dummagudem where he came in contact with the abor-

91

iginal hill tribe, the Kois, and took a special interest in them.
Urgent appeals from Haig and Cotton[18] finally led the Church Missionary Society to adopt this new field already well-started with
twenty-two members. Haig translated the Gospel of Luke and the
First Epistle of John into the Koi language. He returned from
England in 1881 to take charge of the field for eighteen months
during the furlough of the missionary.[19] To the end of his life
he remained keenly interested in missions throughout the world.[20]

Mention has been made previously of the important help given
the missionaries by the District Collectors,[21] especially in the
obtaining of properties and influencing native Rajahs. Assistant
Collector Henry Newill of Guntur not only contributed generously
for schools and gifts for the poor but also made use of his famil-
iarity with the Telugu language to translate a number of tracts
for the missionaries and prepare "a Telugu hymn book and an almanac for the year 1849. These he had published at his own expense
for use in the Mission."[22] The generosity of the English residents is indicated by the fact that in 1854 of the Rupees 1300
needed for the work in Rajahmundry, apart from the salaries of
missionaries, Rs. 1,000 was given by Colonel Cotton and his assistants. And this was not an unusual year.[23] It is certainly true
that several of the Lutheran missions would have been doomed to
failure right from the start without the keen interest and support
of English officials and civilians. When Heyer decided to leave

for America suddenly in 1857, he left Rajahmundry in the hands of a Captain C. Taylor for nine months until another missionary arrived;[24] and this same gentleman, together with Judge J. Henry Morris, was responsible for the schools and general oversight of the Rajahmundry area during the period following the Civil War when there was only one missionary for the whole General Synod Mission.[25]

Although government had gone a long way in changing its attitude toward missionaries since 1813, there were still areas of disharmony and some officials remained indifferent and even suspicious. The enthusiastic help from some English officials and residents at times proved to be a hindrance to the work of missions. This was true in the Guntur field where the missionaries had come to depend so much on the generous contributions of Henry Stokes and those who worked with him that they found themselves high and dry and the whole work in jeopardy after his departure and the arrival in Guntur of indifferent officials. This occurred at the time of the American Civil War and no additional funds were available from the American Churches. All the schools were closed for a time. This drastically retarded the children's progress and many returned to Hinduism.[26]

The English residents also expected their servants to attend the Telugu services conducted by the missionaries but few conversions resulted from such pressure. It was only when attendance became voluntary that greater progress was made with the servants, even though fewer came.[27] Moreover, this close working between government officials and missionaries left a distinct impression upon the people that the missions were run by the government or were sponsored by it, with the same type of leaders and the same large resources of money which seemed nearly inexhaustible.[28]

On the other hand, the missionaries found adequate reasons for claiming that the government was rather indifferent and perhaps too condescending toward Hinduism and Mohammedanism. Christians were rarely employed by the government for fear that the Hindus would raise strong objections.[29] There were many other restrictions.

"Converts to Christianity were legally subject to disinheritance; and native Christians, whether Protestants or the Roman Catholics who were very numerous in Southern India, suffered from civil disabilities and restrictions, while Hindu and Muhammadan religious usages, institutions and ceremonies were treated with profound official deference. Troops were turned out and salutes were fired when festivals occurred. The British Government administered Hindu and Muhammadan religious endowments and levied pilgrim taxes in order to pay for keeping temples in order, for supporting priests and for providing guards on particular occasions; it repaired sacred buildings and managed landed estates the net proceeds from which went to ministers of temples and mosques. As meantime only scanty sums were allotted to the service of the religion which the rulers of the country themselves professed, the contrast gave point to the charge that these rulers neither had nor cared for any religion."[30]

The missionaries often would go to the great Hindu festivals and set up booths from which they distributed tracts and preached to small groups that gathered. Again and again they were rebuffed by the people who pointed out that English officers and officials evidently approved of their religion for they attended in large numbers and raised no objections to the ceremonies.[31]   In this and many other matters both missionaries and Christian officials were concerned that the Government did not take a definite stand in favor of Christianity.  They pointed to India's past as evidence that the Ruler's definite position on religion did not cause disturbances and rebellions, but rather was expected.  To vacillate only brought disrespect and contempt and suspicion.[32]

The important place missionaries came to have in the eyes of the British Government and most of its officials may be summarized in this quotation from Sir Rivers Thompson, Lieutenant-Governor of Bengal:[33]

> "In my judgment Christian missionaries have done more real and lasting good to the people of India than all other agencies combined.  By their pure, unselfish lives, by their fearless, brave exposure of all wrong and injustice, by their self-sacrificing sympathy with distress and sorrow, by their living with the people and for the people, they have exercised a power and produced results that words cannot fully set forth; they have been the salt of the country and the true saviours of the Empire."

## 2. By the religious leaders

In the previous section we have been speaking primarily of the Government and civil leaders insofar as they were English. They were centered primarily in the large towns and cities.  But the Andhra Desa, as is true of all of India, is mostly rural and the leaders of the local governments Indians.  Their reception of the missionaries in most cases was quite different from the English.

We have noted already that the missionaries found a poor reception where the rajahs of zemindaris were controlled by the Brahman priests, as was the case at Kalahasti.[34] On the other hand the Brahmans were not able to overcome the influence of an Eurasian, Mr. Jackman, who worked for the Rajah of Venkatagiri and was friendly to Missionary Mylius at Nayudupet.[35] The difference between the two situations becomes clear when one learns that the former was deeply in debt and completely under the control of the Brahmans who flooded his estate and found it a veritable paradise. Poor farmers had to deliver half their harvest to the rajah who in turn gave much of it to the temples and the support of the priests. After returning from greeting Lord Napier when he became governor of Madras, this same rajah was required to give large sums of money to the Brahman priests and to dedicate offerings in the temples so as to be cleansed of the terrible desecration of touching an outcaste white man's hand.[36]

And this was not an unusual situation. In the rural areas away from the influence and stern hand of the English official, the Brahman controlled the life of the people as he had for centuries. Different from North India, there are no middle castes in the Telugu country. This is evidently explained by the fact that Brahmans came into the area in small numbers as teachers and military leaders. They taught Aryan culture and religion to the

Dravidians and classified the Dravidians as Sudras; and the people in turn accepted the term as honorable. Those who had been the servants and slaves of the Dravidians were called Pariahs or out-castes. In time it was natural for descendents of former rulers of the Telugu country such as the Rāzu caste to claim that they were Kshatriyas, second in importance to the Brahmans; and the trading castes such as the Komatis to claim they were Vaisyas. There were also some groups who said they were not Sudras at all and took to wearing the sacred thread and claimed equality with the Brahmans, but there is no real foundation for these claims. They were leaders in the area before the arrival of the Brahman priests and remained so after, but subordinate to the Brahmans.[37]

A study of the ranking Sudra castes, from higher to lower, makes it difficult to understand how some of them gained the position they did. In some cases it may have been because the caste occupation appears cleaner than others. It is more likely, how-ever, that the classification which developed was dependent upon the willingness of the caste to make use of the services of the Brahmans and admit their complete authority. Hibbert-Ware sug-gests the following determining factors:[38]

> "first, the extent to which they acknowledge the supremacy of the Brahmans and use them in a sacerdotal capacity; sec-ondly, their retention of customs not countenanced by the Brahmans, such as the eating of beef, and the remarriage of widows; and thirdly, their social position and their oc-cupation."

This is an indication of the complete control the Brahmans had over each village community.

Supposedly the priestly caste, the Brahmans branched out into other fields of endeavor because of their large numbers. The Neyogi (ambassador) Brahman is traditionally "the divinely appointed government servant, entrusted with the prerogative of advising the rajahs or hereditary princes, of managing the affairs of their states, and of governing the towns and managing the treasuries."[39] With the advent of British rule it was natural that they became the source of supply for most government positions. They were the educated ones and the logical choice for positions where intelligence and intellectual training were necessary. They won the leadership in all departments of intellectual and economic life.

The Vidiki (priest) Brahmans traditionally take care of

"the religious rites in the temple, ... perform all marriages and ... carry on the many religious rites in every town and family, ... ascertain the auspicious days for the planting of seed and the harvesting of grain, and ... attend to all the religious needs of a very religious people."[40]

Although they will not officiate at bloody sacrifices, they will at times stand by during these festivals as advisers and silent participants.[41] In every way possible the Brahmans try to make the people dependent upon them in their religious life. Combined with their wealth, economic power, control of much valuable land, and their social influence as the superior people by inheritance and education, this religious dominance and the demand for large offerings and gifts for festivals and the necessary services leaves the Brahmans in absolute power.

Together with the merchants they lend large sums of money to the rajahs and large land-owners, as well as small amounts to the rest, at exhorbitant rates of interest. In speaking of the 20,000 Brahmans in the Narasaravupet taluk (county) Dr. J. E. Graefe feels it would be safe to say[42]

> "that three-fourths of the remaining people in the county either have all their property mortgaged to them [money lenders] , or are so heavily in debt to them that it amounts to practically the same thing as mortgage. The prevailing rate of interest [about 1920] in this whole section of India is 12%, (that is one per cent each month) and very often this rate is so manipulated as to amount to double this percent. Moreover, seemingly with diabolical purpose, the religious customs of the people have been established by the Brahmins as to fit right in with this system of financial dominance, and so make positively sure their dominance over almost all the people."

Funerals and marriages are very expensive, from which the Brahmans receive large fees and presents. Families often go so far in debt on such occasions as to enslave the family and even relatives for life, and perhaps for several generations.[43]

The Brahmans and upper caste Sudras were naturally reluctant to allow any outside force or influence to enter village life so as to break down their power and control over the people. They opposed the missionaries violently at first and did all in their power to influence the leaders, whether rajahs or village headmen or tahsildars,[44] to create difficulties in their work.[45]

Although this opposition was fairly general on the part of
Brahmans and high caste Sudras, it was not true of all of them.
The attraction of a good mission school overcame the reluctance of
some who wished to see their sons gain high governmental posts.
Father Heyer had several Brahman boys right from the start until
it became apparent to their parents that he was including the
truths of Christianity along with the ABCs, and then their opposition became quite vociferous.[46] Sudras attended the schools
also; their opposition arose only after some of their children
asked for baptism. Children were withdrawn and the schools had to
be rebuilt gradually. But the survival of a school through such
an ordeal very often strengthened it in the long run and attracted
still more pupils.[47]

Since the Brahmans would not have anything to do with the
bloody sacrifices and many of the ceremonies connected with the
village gods, there were Sudra and Outcaste priests who performed
these functions. Their response to the missionary was often quite
different from the Brahmans. Some of the early converts were
Dasaris, wandering Vaishnava beggars and priests. Their independent life brought them into contact with the missionaries and
freed them at the same time from the control of the Brahmans. The
first native Christian teacher in Guntur, Stephen, was the disciple of a priest.[48] Many of the early catechists in the Hermannsburg Mission had been priests or gurus, with fairly good educa-

100

tions. Some of them were poets, and most of them well-trained speakers.[49]

Their response was due in part to the Ramanuja movement, known in the Telugu area as the Raja-Yoga movement, which swept through this part of India several centuries ago and apparently served as a bridge-over to the Gospel when it arrived. The Raja-yogis were sincere seekers after truth. Emphases were on a pure life, that God is a spirit, the expectation of an incarnation of divine life and that caste did not count before God. Many outcastes eagerly became disciples.

J. E. Clough, the great Telugu Baptist missionary,[50] tells how the forerunner of the Mass Movement in the Ongole area, Yerraguntla Periah, was spiritually prepared for Christianity by his discipleship to a woman Guru, Veerama, a caste woman who accepted all in her circle. His initiation

> "gave him a standing in the Madiga community which nothing else could have given him. ... As time passed he was asked to come here and there to teach. He had a Guru-staff in his hand, which he never discarded, not even after he became a Christian preacher. Where he stayed in a village and taught the people, they gave him to eat. It seems there was little in his teaching which he afterwards had to contradict as evil, when he went among the same people to tell them about Jesus. ... He had ceased to be a Raja Yoga Guru and had become a Christian preacher by a simple sequence of events. These believers who were waiting out there were his disciples. He wanted me [Clough] now to come as one of long experience in the Christian life and give sanction to all that had been done. Among the Gurus there is a hierarchy. He of deeper experience and higher initiation leads those of less. These oriental conceptions were all a part of Periah's mental equipment. His request now to me was practically that I should let this Christian movement go in the channels formed by Indian movements of spiritual significance."[51]

101

Such men, in their wandering search for truth, heard about
Christianity through relatives or other religious leaders. They
voluntarily searched out the missionary or heard him when he came
on a preaching tour to their area. Malapati John, the first convert of the Palnad, heard Heyer preach on his first tour in 1844.[52]
Realizing in the days following that this was what he had been
searching for, he made the long trip to Guntur, some seventy miles,
in order to hear more. He stayed for two weeks to receive Christian advice and instruction, and went back home with a Telugu book
in his hand. Heyer says:[53]

> "In order to give him sufficient time for trial and consider-
> ation, we advised him to return to his home, at that time
> without receiving the ordinance of Baptism. During my ab-
> sence [in America], this man came on a second visit to Gun-
> tur, and Bro. Gunn baptized him, on which occasion he adopt-
> ed the Christian name John, instead of his former heathen
> name. In December 1847 this region of country was visited
> by a German, an American and English Missionary. These
> brethren encouraged John to let his light shine among the
> people; they preached in Polipally, and the neighboring
> villages and gave books to such of the people as could read.
> It now appears, that the grace of God has produced a blessed
> change in the hearts and minds of some of these villages."

It is quite apparent from the early history of the Lutheran missions that without these religious leaders the success of the work
would have amounted to almost nothing. They were the key to opening the hearts of the common people in the villages.


3. By the common people

On the whole, the missionaries found the common people ready
to hear them preach. These people were accustomed to traveling

102

Gurus of their own faith and of the reform Raja-Yoga movement going from village to village. To listen to them was a break in the monotony of their dull, poverty-stricken lives. The missionaries had the added novelty of being white and were received with great curiosity and respect.[54] The tracts distributed were received eagerly by those who could read. News spread from village to village concerning the visit of these white Gurus and audiences were usually quite large.

These people also found it easy to agree with what the missionaries had to say. They had already heard much of this from the Raja-Yoga Gurus; and with their willing acceptance of all and any gods in the Hindu pantheon, they found no difficulty in accepting a new incarnation of this man Jesus. But as for actual conversion that was another matter altogether. The village community was bound too close together to make a break from it any easy matter. Where the Brahmans ruled with an iron hand, little or nothing was accomplished. Dr. Martin L. Dolbeer, Sr., states in a letter to the author:[55]

> "In the case of Agraharams, which are villages owned by Brahmins, (usually the gift of some former Rajah to some Brahmin courtier) we can see even today how the thing works. Many an Agraharam is still practically untouched by the Christian movement. Reason, naturally, being that the Brahmin landlord has been adamant against the very entrance into his little private domain of such a non-Hindu movement. Fortunately there are relatively few Agraharams in our area."

Where the Hindu land owners did not want the Christian movement to get a foothold in their village, economic and social

103

pressure made it almost impossible to effect any change in the hearts of the people. Occasionally, however, there would be an independent farmer who would stand as a bulwark of defense for any of the low caste or outcaste laborers on his farms who desired to embrace the new religion. The bonds of master and employee are at times stronger than religious prejudices; many of the panchama (fifth caste) families have worked for generations for the same ryot (farmer), formerly as agricultural slaves, but since the British abolished slavery more as serfs

> "still semi-attached to the land -- or rather, to the land-lord. When your grandfather worked for the grandfather of the present farmer, and your father for his son and now you for the grandson -- well, there is a kind of relationship that even caste differences cannot destroy. And usually the laborer is tied to the landlord by debt -- money borrowed for a wedding or to build a house."[56]

Some of the farmers felt enough concern for those who worked for them loyally and faithfully that they were willing to permit them some such diversion as this new religion if it would please and make them at all happy in their admittedly hard lot in life.

Heyer relates the cordial reception he received in 1852 when he came to a village of the zemindar estate of Bangaru Naiyakudu, "one of the few remaining Indian Chiefs, who are still permitted to manage the revenue affairs of their small principality." He goes on to say:[57]

> "We were much pleased with a Tassildar and other officials, who are employed by Naiyakudu in his cutcherry or county court. The tassildar treated us well, and set an example to the people with regard to receiving and examining our

books. This encouraged many of the villagers to assemble, so that the ground near the cutcherry presented quite an animated scene. There appears to be an impression among the people, that the time is not far distant, when great changes will take place among the Hindus, throughout India, in their long established customs and religions."

The missionaries of the Hermannsburg field in the south part of the Andhra Desa found that at times the people received them gladly and willingly, and yet at other times there was open opposition to the Gospel, and that it was hard at times to determine the reason.[58] It was true that in that area there were more Brahmans and large sections of land were owned by the great Hindu temples. But this was not always the determining factor. In the larger towns conversions came one by one,[59] and not in family groups, and these individuals were mostly those with rather loose ties to the community. Many were disgusted with the Hindu faith and were ready for something new. Still others had motives for showing great interest in the missionaries that became evident only at a much later date -- such as getting an education, or a financial position, or basking in the prestige of being connected with a white man's organization.[60]

In the Palnad area where Heyer had his initial success, there is not as great a gap between the Mala outcaste and the lower class Sudra; and Hindu landowners of large estates are practically non-existent. Small farmers could not exert the same pressure over laborers as the rich owner of many thousands of acres. There was greater independence and greater willingness to listen to and accept a new religion.[61]

This is also true to a less extent throughout the northern
part of the Andhra Desa. The farther away from Tamil Southern
India, there are fewer temples, although there are still many of
them, and fewer towns and surrounding farming districts completely
owned by the wealthy temples.[62] One valid theory for this is that
the Telugu area was a stronghold of Buddhism from 250 B.C. to A.D.
500.

> "Remains of Buddhist shrines and monastic centers dot the
> Telugu land. Amravati on the Kistna river (in our Guntur
> Mission Field) was one of the great educational centers of
> Buddhism. At Dharanikota, a few miles east, are remains of
> monasteries where at one time ten thousand monks and nuns
> lived. At Nagarjunakonda, fifty miles west along the same
> river, the Madras Bureau of Archeology during the 1920's dug
> up the ruins of another great Buddhist center, as great or
> greater than the two mentioned above. ... the missionaries
> who brought Buddhism to Burma, then to Siam, Java and beyond,
> set out, not from Northern India as hitherto taken for grant-
> ed, but from the Telugu coasts. ... the lines of commerce in
> those days between India and the lands to the East started
> from the mouths of the Godavery, Kistna, and Cauvery rivers,
> not from the northern coasts of what is now Bengal. And some
> of the earliest inscriptions of Buddhist culture in remote
> Siam and Java are written in an ancient form of Telugu
> script."[63]

These eight centuries of Buddhist rule broke the power of Brahmanism in this area from which it never fully recovered, although
there are few Buddhists there today. "Buddhism left a permanent
impress upon the life, character, and mentality of the Telugus
which is aiding our work today."[64] Whether the basis for it comes
from this or not, the Outcaste in the Telugu area has a bit of
self-respect, and some independence which is lacking in other

areas. Together with the preparation already made through the Raja-Yoga movement, this fact provided for the missionaries a cordial reception, on the whole, among the common people.

A typical reception of the missionaries while touring in the villages was described vividly by Ramme of the Hermansburg field.[65] He told how the people gathered around them as they entered the village. Going to a central point or in front of the school, if there was one, they began to talk to the people and offer books for sale. They usually refused the books; and in some cases the headman of the village suggested that they bring money instead of books on their next trip. The teacher and children of the school were avid listeners. At the back of the crowd were seen men with plows over their shoulders as they paused for a moment on their way to the fields. As one gazed over the audience some were writing or tracing on the ground, others chewed tobacco or betel nut while listening. On the whole Ramme found that they listened fairly well. Generally a Brahman would start to argue with the missionary, stating that Indians would be saved by their religion and Europeans by their own. Venkateswarudu is our Christ, he would say. But as the discussion continued, and especially if the catechist with the missionary was one of the brillant high caste educated men or former priests, the Brahman would very often admit that the Christian religion was the true one. After hearing some strong truths which the Brahman could not stand, he would

walk away and leave the audience quite impressed by this new religion of the white man.

## B. Early Policies Established

### 1. The primary purpose of missions

There was never any question among the Lutheran missionaries
as to the primary purpose of their work. This was the establishment and extension of the Church. Since the Church is present
where the Gospel is preached and the Sacraments rightly administered, the early missionaries concentrated on making these conditions possible. A meeting place was decided upon, regular services were started, and as soon as possible those in the community
who were already Christian -- English residents, their servants
and other natives, and the missionaries -- came together to participate in the Lord's Supper. Preaching became one of the primary
activities. At first it was done through an interpreter, but as
the missionary became proficient in the language he took over the
full task himself. This preaching was not limited by any means to
the place that had been selected for regular services, but the
missionary went into the bazaar, the streets and the surrounding
villages and spoke to crowds wherever he could gather them. Tracts
and portions of Scripture were regularly distributed.

Thus language study became a matter of prime importance right
from the beginning; and it was expected that every missionary con-

108

centrate on this when he first arrived. It is true that in many cases the early missionaries did not spend as much time as they should have to become highly proficient in the native tongue; it was hard to sit by idly , as it were, while forced to witness the great physical and spiritual needs about them. The busy schedule and the shortage of missionaries kept the men from spending adequate hours alone in study or with the munshi (language teacher). Father Heyer was accused of never learning Telugu well enough to do truly effective work,[66] yet he was able to translate Luther's Catechism into Telugu and later was chairman of the committee which revised it. Even after a twelve-year stay in America between his second and final trips to India, he still had enough command of the language to begin the "ambitious project of translating the new Church Book of the General Council into Telugu."[67] It is not likely that the common people would have listened to him, or Mr. Stokes and the other English officials supported him as they did, if he had spoken Telugu poorly.[68] The German missionaries emphasized language study strongly and placed the new men under the care of older missionaries for the first year or two.[69]

Catechetical training was another essential to fulfill the primary purpose of the Lutheran missions. By the end of the first year Heyer had instructed and baptized three adults.[70] Right from the start he spent a great deal of time in the schools established and with the beggars who gathered each morning, instructing them in the knowledge of the Bible, and teaching them hymns and Scripture passages. At the end of 1842, just five months after the work had been started, the pupils of all the schools were gathered for an examination, which indicates where the emphasis had been placed:[71]

> "The program rendered at this public examination greatly pleased the audience. After an opening prayer the children recited from memory, in English and in Telugu, Psalm 115, Luke 2:8-20, and John 4:21-26. Then a number of hymns which had been memorized, were sung in both languages. Catechetical exercises, conversation and an examination in geography were followed by a distribution of books and small coins."

It was evident that religious instruction was the most important subject in the schools. Daily classes were begun and ended with devotional and catechetical exercises. Bible history, grammar, geography and arithmetic were the main subjects in the English school in Guntur; and a real effort was made to help the children in the Telugu schools to learn at least to read, write and do simple mathematical problems.

In the Hermannsburg field, Mylius was very emphatic about the emphasis on preaching, not the schools. He could not go along with the Scottish missions and their primary emphasis on the schools as agents of evangelization. In 1871 he stated:[72]

> "We maintain the method of first sermons, then schools; first church, then school; first to gather parishes, then to arrange for the training of the Christian children, but to which schools the pagan child is also welcome. On the other hand, we can't do otherwise because our money is lacking. We are always distressed financially; if we would try this expensive school system, we would have nothing and could not continue. We preach to the pagans sometimes near the station,

going out early to be back before the heat; sometimes to a distance, riding by oxen wagon to any bungalow or Sattiram [rest bungalow] or shaded place under a tree. There we stay for some days, and visit the surrounding area. Our sermons are addressed to everyone without distinction -- Brahmans, Sudras and Pariahs. We teach the catechetical schools, we supply our parishes with Sunday and weekday worship services, according to the church order of Lueneberg; also we supply private pastoral counselling. We teach in our schools, we prepare our catechists, our native mission workers, and finally we translate our hymns and good books into Telugu."

Of interest, before leaving this section, is the following description of a typical worship service in the village, as told by Heyer in a letter written December 8, 1849:[73]

"At first we read one or more of the Psalms of David; I read the first verse, and the persons who can read and have books, the second verse, and so on, alternately to the end. After reading we sing from the small collection of telugu hymns, which a friend of our mission, H. Newill, Esq. has got printed at his own expense; we next unite in the confession and Lord's prayer, all kneeling; after this I read a portion of Scripture, and then we sing again to the praise of God. At the close of the singing, the congregation arises and all unite with the minister, in repeating the articles of the creed; next follows the sermon; prayer, singing and the benediction, close the exercises. At morning prayers I generally have all the people who are with me, to repeat the ten commandments, and thus by frequent repetition I endeavor to inculcate a knowledge of Christian truth upon the minds of all who are willing to hear and receive the Gospel."

2. The importance of education and native literature

From what has been said it would appear that education, as emphasized in the Lutheran missions, was of value only to provide the Gospel and catechetical training for the children. It was through the schools that the native children heard the Bible stories and learned to know Jesus. By learning how to read and write,

they were able to study the Bible themselves and the religious
tracts and books which were being printed in Telugu. This knowledge was of value in turn for the parents of the children, who
delighted to hear their children able to read what had been given
them. It was quite apparent that in this way the missionaries
hoped to reach the hearts and minds of children and parents, and
perhaps in the course of time lead them to conversion and dedication to Christ.

The children learned quickly by rote. Those in the Telugu
schools and the beggars daily cared for by Heyer were able to repeat the commandments, the Lord's prayer, several hymns and Scripture passages in a short time. The boys in the English school, in
addition to grammar, geography and history, "committed to memory a
Scripture catechism with proof passages."[74] How much of this they
understood is another question. That Heyer made a real effort to
get the older boys to think things through for themselves is indicated by the fact that at the school examination in September,
1848, in addition to questions being asked from the catechism on
the order of salvation, some students gave addresses and discour-
ses. The one creating the greatest interest was on the question:
"Is Caste, as it exists in India, a divine appointment, or is it
merely a human institution?"[75] Afterward an exhibit of things
most of the Indians had never seen, such as a powerful magnet, a
small air-pump, a microscope, a planetarium or solar system, and

a galvanic battery, created much interest and curious questioning.
Heyer often used these articles to open up a way to talk on religious subjects.

About a month later he commented, in a letter to America, when relating how quickly the children memorized and how well they recited the Catechism and Scripture passages: "But whilst the memory is thus exercised, the hearts of the children appear not to be influenced by the important truths which they are taught. Great, lamentably great is the moral degradation of parents and children."[76]

In the Hermannsburg mission the first schools were outgrowths of the instruction necessary to prepare people for baptism. A definite order of procedure was adopted: first came the building of a small mud hut to house the missionary and provide a place of worship;[77] then preaching was carried on far and near; when a few were willing to receive catechetical training, they came together regularly at the hut for instruction. The memorization was carried on by a liturgist or reader, as few could read or write, and the missionary interpreted the meaning. During this period of catechetical training, the people could not work. Many of them came from outlying villages and remained at the center during the instruction which lasted at least seven weeks -- three for memory work, four for the explanation. Six hours each day and three on Saturday were devoted to the training. Therefore the missionaries found it necessary, much as they disliked the practice, to help these people financially; but this help ended upon completion of the catechetical training.[78]

Mylius' first school was begun at Nayudupeta in 1868 for the training of native workers. Each missionary needed catechists and liturgists; the best-educated converts were taken to Nayudupeta and given a short period of instruction that usually did not last more than half a year. Historian Hartwig Harms points out that the mission was fortunate in that its first converts were men of some education. After their short period of preparation they continued their studies privately under Mylius' supervision.[79]

The second school was for girls, and was started in Gudur the next year to serve the children of catechists and missionaries' servants, and also some orphans and illegitimate waifs. Both these schools developed into boarding schools for training the Christian boys and girls of all the stations, as well as the catechists, native helpers and wives.[80] But as these grew and became inadequate, requests poured in from the centers where missionaries were located that permission be given by Superintendent Mylius to open elementary schools in connection with each congregation. The experiment was started at Sulurpeta January, 1877, with the teacher Jesudasen, oldest son of the very first convert of the Hermannsburg mission,[81] and one of the first Christian boys to complete his training at the Nayudupeta school. There were soon 18 pupils; and the school proved successful enough that Mylius gradually ex-

114

tended the system, as money was available, and as the need arose
for training Christian boys and girls in each particular center,
and as the teachers were found who were capable or had completed
the training course. Most of the early graduates of the Nayudupeta school were needed as catechists and liturgists rather than
as teachers, although many fulfilled both duties. All this was
consonant with the policy of church first, then schools.

One of the primary problems at first was the lack of Christian teachers. The Hermannsburg missionaries found Hindu teachers
so unsatisfactory that they felt it was better to do without a
school than employ them. The early schools in Guntur and Rajahmundry were conducted by Hindu teachers with the missionary taking
charge of the religious courses. Until the missionaries became
familiar with the language they were quite often deceived by these
teachers. Although the educational methods were superior to the
Telugu schools run by Brahmans and high caste Hindus, the schools
were generally ineffective as agents for conversion.[82] This was
all the more unfortunate in that some missionaries thought it necessary to give up preaching trips throughout the surrounding area
rather than neglect the schools; they went so far as to give up
preaching in the bazaars and streets in order to concentrate every
effort upon the schools.[83]

That there was often a great difference of opinion between
missionaries, and between missionaries and the Home Boards, on the

school problem is clearly indicated by the frequent references
made to it in correspondence to the Home Boards and Missionary
Societies.  The Guntur and Rajahmundry missionaries had taken
charge of English schools started and supported by English residents.  Although both Hindu teachers and pupils were interested in
these schools mostly as stepping stones to civil service,[84] yet as
long as the missionaries could have personal supervision and teach
the religious courses, they were considered agencies of evangelism,
since Hindu children could be reached and receive instruction in
Bible truths and facts.  They were reluctant, however, to take
charge of English schools at a distance from the centers, where
supervision would be lacking.  Some of these were taken over but
soon given up.

Heyer, on one occasion, attempted an experiment with Assistant
Collector Newill's support of just such a Telugu and English
school at Narasaravupet, about 28 miles from Guntur.  Two young
men trained in the Guntur Mission school were to teach.  He says
in this regard:[85]

"There will be some difference, however, between this and our
regular Mis. schools.  Religious instruction is the principal teaching in our schools; this keeps many of the Caste
boys from attending, who are closely joined to their idols.
But in this new school, which is to be kept at Mr. Newill's
expense, besides reading, writing, etc., some attention is
to be paid to grammar, geography, etc.  The teachers are
sometimes to read a portion of the Holy Scriptures, without
insisting on it, that the scholars themselves are to use the
Bible as one of their school books.  This school therefore
will occupy an intermediate place between the old heathen

and our Mis. schools. Time will show whether the people will make use of this opportunity to obtain useful knowledge or not."

In time Heyer changed his mind about the value of such schools. Several years later he defended the schools as they were being conducted in the Guntur Mission, especially in the Palnad, where right from the start he employed converts and Christian teachers, even if it meant sacrificing proficient education, in order to give the people enough learning so that they could read the Telugu tracts and scripture portions. He suggested that Guntur adopt the system used in the Danish Tranquebar Mission. The most promising children from the village schools would be trained for a year or two in Guntur. Fully established in gospel principles, they would then return to their homes where they would earn their own living. The best of these would be employed as teachers.[86] This type of education, Heyer felt, would have the most lasting effect in the beginning stages of the mission development. Such students, taught by Christian teachers, would influence the whole community in which they lived and in time might bring about a completely Christian community.[87]

In 1860 an interesting set of resolutions drawn up by the missionaries of the Guntur-Rajahmundry field for the Foreign Missionary Society in America emphasized that English schools[88]

"are to be considered as a secondary means of spreading the truth, wherein the higher castes, desiring to learn the English language, consent to listen to Bible teaching. An

117

English school, however, should not occupy more than two
hours a day of a missionary's time. The rest of the day
should be devoted to evangelistic effort."

Other resolutions pointed out that "Telugu schools are necessary

means of disseminating the good seed into the hearts of children

and parents;" and that "public preaching in the bazaars and vill-

ages affords the best opportunity of learning the difficulties and

hindrances which prevent the masses from accepting Christianity,

and of preparing the way for inquiry concerning the truth as it is

in Jesus."[89]

Although the Hermannsburg Mission had set for itself a strict

policy of running Telugu schools only for its Christian children

and the training of workers and teachers, it was unable to main-

tain that position one hundred percent. In Tirupati a government

English language school, attended mostly by Brahmans, had such a

poor reputation and inadequate control over the conduct of the

pupils that many parents came to missionary Paul Petersen and

begged him to take over the school. Mission schools had gained an

excellent reputation around Madras through the Scottish and Eng-

lish Missions. He started to give one hour of Biblical instruction

in the school with voluntary attendance, but the mission did not

feel it could afford to take complete charge of such an expensive

proposition. In 1880 Mylius changed his mind when he learned that

a neighboring mission[90] was willing to answer the request of the

people. At the same time Petersen learned from Pastor Clausen in

Dueppel that a mission society in North Schleswig had been established to support Tirupati and especially the school.

Reluctantly Mylius authorized the start of this English
school, laying down four conditions: (1) that the entire conduct
of the school be by the mission -- the employment and dismissal of
teachers, the schedule, the enrollment and dismissal of pupils,
the tuition and fees were to be determined entirely by the mission;
(2) that there was to be no caste distinction and all students were
to meet in the same rented building; (3) that the mission would be
obligated to run the school only so long as the North Schleswig
mission society and the people of Tirupati supported it; and (4)
that every day the school was to begin and close with prayer in
the name of Jesus Christ.[91]

Opposition to these conditions was tremendous at first, especially on the part of the Brahman priesthood of the great temple at
Tirupati and the teachers of the government school. Biblical education and the removal of caste kept all but four pupils away.
But this number quickly increased to seventy. Its influence continued to grow as the results of the annual examinations improved;
more and more Brahmans sent their sons to its classes. The government school closed down completely, and the government placed its
stamp of approval on the Mission school.

There was by no means unanimous approval among the missionaries concerning this school. The discussion came to a climax in

119

1882.  Some felt that the English school should be maintained as
of great value in spreading the Word of God to many of the higher
caste people (not accessible otherwise) who were destined to be
the future leaders in the area.  The opponents felt it was not
worth the high cost and the valuable man-power expended; the Brahmans could run their own schools and do it well with proper supervision.  Brahman boys were not interested in the religious subjects and would take them just to get the rest of the education.
In fact, there was the feeling that the Hindu parents were rather
amused at the missionary's efforts to instill Biblical education
and were confident that they could counteract anything he might
try to teach.  The opponents went on to point out that in some
cases intellectual teaching of Christian truths turned students
into enemies, rather than friends, of missions.

Woerrlein, in his history of the Hermannsburg Mission, felt
that a middle position should be taken in regard to providing
schools for non-Christian students.  Realizing that open conversion rarely occurred through such methods, the mission still
should provide such institutions if money and an adequate number
of Christian teachers were available in order to plant the seed of
the divine word in the hearts of many of the students.  Here it
would grow, usually unconsciously, and influence their whole outlook on life.  He felt it was most important that at least one-
third of the future leaders of India should receive their educa-

tion in a mission high school to counteract the anti-Christian materialistic view of the West that was promulgated in the "religious-less state schools."[92] Extremely important was the living witness of the divine power of the Gospel that capable and faithful teachers could give.

With the strong emphasis on Telugu schools, the problem of adequate literature in the native tongue greatly concerned the Lutheran missionaries. We have already noted how Heyer translated Luther's catechism into Telugu.[93] This was completed in 1851 and printed in Madras. Later he worked on translating the new Church Book of the General Council, which he had helped prepare for its first English publication in America in 1868.[94] The Telugu version was not completed and printed until 1881.[95] Assistant Collector Newill made a distinct contribution to the Guntur Mission in 1849 by his translation of a number of tracts and the preparation of a Telugu hymn book and an almanac.[96]

Tracts and portions of the scripture were available through the Madras Auxiliary Bible Society (1812) and the Religious Tract and Book Society of Madras (1818). Although Gordon and Pritchett of the London Missionary Society had completed translations of the Old and New Testaments by 1823,[97] the Madras Bible Society did not finish revision and the printing of the whole Telugu Bible until the 1850s.[98] Even then the Bible was in need of further revision; and from 1852 until 1907 expert missionary linguists and

121

revision committees worked almost steadily on the Telugu Bible. The Rev. Hans C. Schmidt of Rajahmundry was a member of the committee which began work in 1873 and continued to meet at intervals for twenty-five years.[99] Charles Groenning of Rajahmundry evidently worked on the Bible independently; for Woerrlein tells in his history that Mylius revised a translation of the Bible and catechism by Groenning.[100]

On the whole, however, the missionaries of the Rajahmundry and Guntur Missions, especially the Americans, did very little work in the field of translation and development of native literature in the early days. This is largely because the fields were understaffed and the missionaries greatly overworked. In the Hermannsburg field the situation was quite different. There the work was done in a concentrated manner in a small area with a fairly adequate number of missionaries. Moreover, Mylius not only was a specialist in languages himself, but he kept prodding the rest to spend time in private study, concentrating on one particular field of interest. Thus Kiehne, beside the study of Telugu, specialized in dogmatics; Th. Petersen did translations and aural transcriptions of Telugu melodies he heard, besides keeping up his Latin and Greek; Woerrlein, in addition to his interest in Martin Luther, studied the history, language, geography and general information about India; Wahl assisted Mylius in the work of translation and development of native literature for the schools and catechetical training; and Mylius, in addition, enjoyed the study of history and genealogy.[101]

Mylius did most of the literary work while he was superintendent of the mission, and also directed the publications. He headed the training school in Nayudupet for native workers and teachers. He prepared and translated a liturgy for the Telugu church. Under his leadership the Mission had a songbook with 128 hymns translated and edited in 1879, soon followed by a second edition with 172 hymns. In 1872 Mylius went to Madras to have the Hannoverian catechism of 1862 printed in Telugu. A little book on dogmatics, entitled The First Milk and similar to the one used by the Tamil Leipzig missionaries, was prepared for the catechetical students as a basic course for baptism and church membership.[102] Another theological work was the Augsburg Confession. More devotional was the translation of Johann Gerhard's Holy Meditations printed in 1880. As Mylius approached the last years of his life, he spent more and more time translating and gave up preaching and traveling. Before his death in 1887 he started a collection of his own gospel sermons but only completed a series according to the Church year from the First Sunday in Advent to Rogate Sunday. This was published in 1890 by Woerrlein who commented: "It is a pity that this collection is not finished; his sermons are so simple and childlike and full of faith that they will be an everlasting blessing for our Telugu church."[103] Mylius had a good knowledge of the Telugu language. His contributions to native literature were primarily translations from German, as was true of most of the German missionaries of this period, and those who came after him revised and improved what he had done. One educated Telugu made this remark about his translations: "It is the smooth way of speaking that we understand and love. It speaks to our hearts. In this way the Telugu Bible should be translated. Mylius is the right man for the translation."[104]

Leopold Wahl, who was considered to have the best command of languages, made his primary contribution with the translation of a prayer book, and a revision of Petersen's translation of Zahn's Biblical History. After Mylius' death, Hartwig Harms took over the seminary at Nayudupeta and also did most of the literary work with such contributions as a new translation of Luther's small catechism, a Biblical History of the Old and New Testament, ten or fifteen simplified and clear books on Kurz's Church History, and a book on World History. He prepared a Telugu song book in conjunction with Rayapa Joseph, a good poet and musician, who in turn translated several books of poems from Tamil.[105] A few natives, such as the catechist Ravuri Paul,[106] aided in the work of translation in the early days, but generally the Christians were unable to help the missionaries in this work because of inadequate education. They came primarily from the lower castes or outcastes. The Hermannsburg Mission also was faced with the shortage of money for

publications since most of the small amounts received from Germany
went toward construction of chapels, schoolhouses and missionary
bungalows.[107]

Pohl of the Schleswig-Holstein Mission also was active in the
field of translation. He worked with Hartwig Harms on Telugu historical literature,[108] and with Wilhelm Groenning of Rajahmundry
and Dr. John Hay of the London Missionary Society in the development of a new hymn book, aided by well-known linguists and Christian professors in Rajahmundry.[109] They found it difficult to
bring the original German rhythms in line with the Telugu poetry.
Pohl also translated the Passion History for use in Biblical story
telling in the villages.

### 3. The attitude toward caste and social customs

The attitude toward caste was similar to that of all Protestant missions except the Leipzig Lutherans, who had inherited the
lenient position of the old Tranquebar Mission in Tamil land.
Little is said about the problem among most of the Telugu Lutheran groups other than their opposition to it and continual struggle
against it. But the Hermannsburg Mission made it a matter of detailed discussion because of a conflict which developed with Leipzig missionaries. Close contact and friendship had been maintained with some of them, especially Kremmer in Madras.[110] August
Mylius had served the Leipzig Mission at Porayar near Tranquebar

and was quite familiar with the position of that Mission on caste; in fact, this had been one of the reasons for his resignation in 1851.[111] When he established the Hermannsburg Mission he realized that a dispute between the two neighboring missions was inevitable. His friendliness with Kremmer did not prevent criticism on the part of others in letters and communications to societies in Germany concerning Mylius' position on caste. Director Harms and Mylius found it necessary to explain their attitude in the Missionsblatt in 1872.[112]

The position of Bishop Wilson of the Church of England in Calcutta was cited: that Christians shall not be separated according to caste; that they shall not commune separately; that native catechists and helpers must be willing to entertain catechists in their houses, no matter what caste they are; that a native preacher is not allowed to leave the position to which he has been appointed just because there are only lower castes in the parish; that godparents should not specifically be picked from the same caste at the time of baptisms; that entire congregational assemblies cannot exclude lower castes; and that there shall be no difference in burying people in the church cemetery. Mylius comments that he would add two more: that catechists and mission helpers have to be willing to entertain anybody, not only those who visit them at the time of Christian celebrations; and that the parishioners have to be educated to eat with lower castes not only at communion but also in daily life. He pointed out two prime examples in the Hermannsburg Mission in the persons of the Brahman catechists Sivaramaya and Ramaya, the latter even having married a Pariah girl.[113]

Mylius believed he could have no part in a Mission which allowed caste to remain or allowed the missionaries to do as they wanted in regard to it. When Jens Dahl became a close friend of the Rajah of Venkatagiri,[114] he began to associate more and more with the high caste people in his area with some success. He came to the conclusion that he could accomplish more by adopting the rather lenient position of the Leipzig Mission. Although he was opposed to the caste system in itself, he believed it should be endured at the start and through the working of the spirit of God's Word in their hearts gradually change the attitude of the Christian converts, rather than by strict Church discipline. Quite a number of high caste men had told Dahl they would be baptized if he would be lenient in this respect. It was inevitable that tensions should arise and missionaries take sides on the matter. Woerrlein agreed with Dahl at first, but later on, by experience in Sriharikota and especially in Kalahasti, he became convinced that the caste system could not be tolerated.[115] Finally Mylius demanded that Director Harms recall Dahl for his refusal to use Church discipline against the practice of caste.

Harms agreed with Mylius and in 1873 gave Dahl the choice of going to Africa or America, since he was an excellent missionary and the conflict was only on the matter of caste in India. Harms considered the caste problem in the same category as polygamy or adultery. Can adultery be accepted in the Church while at the same time the Church is struggling against the spirit of it? The practice as well as the spirit of the caste system must be opposed; there can be no difference between the word of God and the spirit of God. And if the caste system has a place in the Mission, then it has a place in the Church and its worship. Serious problems would develop in the Lord's Supper, such as the decision as to who would go first, the matter of drinking out of the same chalice and other difficulties.[116]

At Mylius' request Director Harms added a supplement to the statutes of the Hermannsburg Mission: (a) No one is to be baptized without knowing the Church's principles on caste; (b) especially must the catechists and mission workers, supported by the Mission, agree with the missionaries and be willing to be hospitable and eat with every Christian if God so ordains the occasion; and (c) the weaker members of the parish shall be treated firmly yet with much patience and forbearance, but if at last they cannot bring themselves to eat with people of a lower caste at occasions brought about naturally then they are to be refused the Holy Communion.[117]

Over and over again difficulties were encountered in the schools started by the missionaries when children of lower castes were enrolled or there was danger of caste children being baptized; but the desire for education usually overcame any initial repugnance to having contact with the missionaries or those of other castes. Father Heyer tells of his experience in one village in the Palnad where the weavers refused to send their children to the newly-established school because the teacher was of a lower caste. He writes:[118]

"But since the people in the other villages, when they found that I would not and could not yield to their unreasonable prejudices, no longer manifest any dissatisfaction, it may be expected, that the Mutkoor applicants will also become reconciled and submit; otherwise the school must be discontinued."

The missionaries found the same difficulties when it came to receiving members into the Church. The first candidates for baptism of the Schleswig-Holstein Mission at Salur, fifteen of them in all, fell away almost as a body because of caste difficulties. Their catechist, David, was a Mala from Nellore who had served in the Hermannsburg Mission. Two of the young boys, Nathanael and Josua, refused to live with him as boarding pupils because of caste differences. Others refused to take communion with the missionaries. Some of them insisted that their children should marry only non-Christian caste people. In spite of all admonishment nothing could be done with the group so that they had to be dismissed. Some of them repented and asked for communion at a later date.[119]

It was evident that the Lutheran Missions considered caste as opposed to the very core of the Christian faith and not merely a social custom of the people. Mylius felt it was a great evil and that he would be disobedient to God and betray the Indian people if he were lenient in the matter. At the same time he realized that the problem was not easy to solve; to think that there was a Christian community in India that no longer had any inclination toward caste was nonsense.[120] The Lutheran Missions had converts primarily from the outcastes and thus the problem did not stand out as much as elsewhere.[121] Yet even among the outcastes themselves tensions occurred between the various groups, often to such an extent that discipline and excommunication were necessary.[12]

The Rev. F. J. McCready, an Eurasian by birth who had been sent to America by missionary Horace G. B. Artman to be prepared for the holy ministry, speaks of the situation in the Tallapudi district of the Rajahmundry Mission. Different from the other areas, this particular district had Christians coming primarily from the Madigas, the great leather-working caste of the Telugu area and corresponding to the Chakkilyans or Chucklers of the Tamil area. They were considered very low in the social scale, especially by the Malas or Pariahs, weavers by trade, who placed themselves just above the Madigas. This created much bitterness between them.[123] Mr. McCready explains: "When Christianity first enters a place, should those who first embrace it be of the Mala

130

caste, which is one of the lower castes, others still lower will join us; but should the first converts be Chucklers, the Malas keep aloof."[124]

Heyer recounts in one of his letters the trouble he had in the Palnad when he obtained a worker in the kitchen who was of even a lower caste than the Malas, probably a Madiga. He writes:[125]

> "Malahs are almost as tenacious of their ranks as the Brahmins are of theirs. ... This gave great offense in those villages especially, where a number of the people have professedly embraced Christianity. Our enemies and opposers made use of this circumstance, to persuade the new converts, that it is our intention to degrade them, and to mix or amalgamate them with people of a lower grade, than they themselves are by birth. You can scarcely imagine, how much trouble such a trifling circumstance occasions."

It was difficult to make the Christians see that they all must be brothers in Christ.

Although opposition to caste stood as a principle of mission policy, how far this was carried out in practice depended greatly on the missionary in charge and the individual situation. At times the wisest step seemed to be a gradual change, such as the case when Father Heyer opened a school in Gurzala with a Brahman teacher, changed a month later to a young man trained in Guntur who did not yet profess to be a Christian, and then finally brought in a native Christian from a low caste to take charge.[126] Mylius, on the other hand, for the sake of principle and as an example to the other congregations in the Mission, started the practice of holding congregational meals on special occasions in Nayudupet.

It did not matter to him if the Christians held on to their vocations which they had learned as members of a particular caste, but in all things brotherly love must reign supreme.[127] Other missionaries felt it was wiser and incidentally less costly for families to bring their own food and cooking utensils and set up their own living quarters in the church compound when large groups came in from the villages for festival occasions. Less difficulty was encountered when an upper caste man was used in the kitchen of the boarding school. And in many places wells were built for the special use of the outcaste Christians when they were refused the use of non-Christian caste or outcaste tank or water supply.[128]

Because caste and many social customs were tied closely to the religious life of the people, it was a difficult task to determine what should be opposed by the missionaries and what should be accepted. The general policy of the Hermannsburg Mission seems to have been to accept customs and conduct which did not violate the Scriptures. For example, it was customary to retain the 'tali bottu' or small piece of gold tied around the neck of the bride by the bridegroom during the wedding ceremony.[129] Father Heyer, on the other hand, reported that he did away with the tali and tom toms at the first wedding held at Macherla in the Palnad. When explained, the use of the wedding ring appealed to the people; according to Heyer, they felt that the tali custom had given the impression of a bride being sold to be a servant or slave.[130]

It was expected that the converts were to give up all idol worship and the ceremonies connected with village life in order to be baptized. This affected two areas of their life. In the home the god-pots and idol pictures and figures must be removed and when the village became Christian the village shrine destroyed. In inter-group relationships the services of the Malas and Madigas in the idol worship ceremonies must be dispensed with. Neither one of these was an easy step to take, although the former proved to be less difficult than the latter. The great fear and superstition of the people made it hard for them to touch or remove the god-pots or destroy the shrines for fear the gods would strike them down. Often the missionary or catechist found it necessary to take the first blow with crowbar or hammer to demonstrate the impotence of the idol or demon spirit.[131] The community idols or shrine usually were not removed until the entire group had indicated their intention to become Christian. Heyer tells us that when the Mission purchased a piece of property with a shrine on it and he permitted the people to remove the stones in order to build elsewhere, they good-naturedly offered the stones for use in the new temple, "for they themselves would probably attend and unite with us in worshipping the only true and living God."[132] The caste people rarely opposed the removal of Mala and Madiga shrines, for it was only the outcastes' customs which were affected.

133

It was a different matter altogether when it came to ending

their services at the Hindu festivals and worship ceremonies.  The

Madigas, since they handled animals in their profession as leather

workers, killed the animals for the sacrifices and played the

drums.  No other group could perform these functions without being

polluted.  They also led certain dances.  The Malas generally had

charge of the music and dances, led the processions and took part

in some of the most revolting parts of the buffalo sacrificial

ceremonies.[133]  Certain Madigas and Malas served as priests in

the performance of ceremonies for lesser village deities.  When

the outcastes became Christian and refused to perform such reli-

gious duties any longer, the anger and persecution of the upper

caste was extreme in many cases.  For they feared the consequen-

ces if the demons and evil spirits were no longer appeased by the

drum-beating and special ceremonies performed by these outcastes.

Since the payment for these services and the drums made by the

Madigas, as well as for the leather-work and woven cloth, came in

the form of food and clothing, the pressure put on these outcastes

could be great.  Hibbert-Ware states:[134]

> "The actual presents that they receive for their share in the
> shape of grain, cloth, and the flesh of the slaughtered an-
> imals, are to them, in their extreme poverty, of no small
> moment.  The loss of them makes a difference that is felt.
> But a further loss often follows.  The Sudras, angry at the
> defection of the Christians, sometimes, as far as possible,
> exclude them from employment, and make the struggle for a
> subsistence even harder than usual.

A partial solution of the problem is adopted by the Malas themselves. As a rule, in any particular village a member of a certain fixed family takes the chief part in the sacrifice. Such a man is called a 'Vetti,' and receives a more valuable perquisite than the rest. When the Malas of a village are baptised, the Vetti family commonly stands aloof and remains heathen. It is not allowed to them to do what they would gladly do -- that is, to set apart one member only to perform the sacrifices. The rule in our Mission is to baptise all of a family or none of it. But if the whole family stands out the Mission cannot interfere. It may be added that much trouble has arisen in the past from the baptism of Vetti families. The temptations are so great that members of these families almost always relapse into idolatry."

One of the hardest things for the missionaries to adjust to in India was the quite evident corrupt state of morals, especially among the lower castes. The early missionaries pointed out in communications to the Home Societies the complete lack of any real consciousness of sin as Christians understood it, nor any truly heart-felt grief and sorrow on account of sin.

"Lying, dishonesty, perjury, fornication, etc., are made light of, much more so than in Christian countries; consequently the mind becomes indifferent and hardened; but few are brought to see and feel the great evil and soul destroying nature of sin."[135]

It was felt that a strong stand must be taken in regard to the moral standards of the converts, and that strict disciplinary action must be enforced in the case of converts failing to live up to the proper standards.

The natives on their part found it hard to understand why the missionaries took such a strong stand on age-old customs such as polygamy and child marriages. When a man with more than one wife

135

desired baptism, the early missionaries required that only one
wife be kept and the others be sent away or sent back to their
parental homes.[136] At a later date Mrs. George Albrecht of the
Palnad tells of a situation which indicates a little leniency on
the part of the missionaries and yet a continued insistence that a
Christian can live only with one wife. She tells of an old pat-
riarch who was very sincere and brought many others to the Church.
He attended and gave regularly. Both his wives were old and he
treated them exactly alike. One had eleven children, the other
twelve. In bringing the matter up at a missionary conference, the
question asked was:[137]

> "Should we tell Abraham that baptism is essential to salva-
> tion and that it is better to seem to be unjust to one of the
> old ladies than to risk his soul's salvation; or shall we
> baptize him and his two wives; or shall we baptize the two
> women, and tell him, perhaps God would soon take one of them
> to heaven and then he could be baptized and be saved?"

A committee was appointed and a circular sent to neighboring missions asking about their policy in such matters. But the answers
were so varied that the conference suggested the Albrechts act as
they thought best. As a result the old man and his two wives were
baptized, and one wife was sent to live with her daughter.

The Lutheran missionaries were cautious about performing any
marriages except between baptized Christians. Church approval had
to be obtained. The Breklum Mission accepted marriages that had
been performed before baptism and usually blessed them at a later
date. Soon the custom grew to bless them on the same day as the

baptism. All marriage problems had to be settled before catechetical instruction for baptism was even started.[138] Approval
was all that was necessary in the Hermannsburg Mission if the marriage before baptism was a real one; otherwise, remarriage was
required.[139] Nor did the missionaries marry couples considered
too young, although this aroused some bitterness and many complaints. When such requests came to Father Heyer, he made every
effort to explain why he could not permit such marriages. He felt
that they should wait until they could answer the marriage questions intelligently themselves. Although he permitted marriage
between a couple where the bride was 14 and the groom 18, he turned down a request where the girl was only 6 and the boy 16.[140]

Toddy-drinking was a serious problem among the outcastes.
Both Brahmanism and Islam opposed the use of intoxicants, so it
was a question whether the Lutheran missionaries could be any less
strict in this matter even though the outcaste, living beyond the
bounds of the Brahmanic code, thought nothing improper about it.
The Roman Catholics condoned it among their converts while the
Baptists opposed it strongly and considered it a sin, dismissing
workers who drank. The Lutherans took a middle position: that
drinking or smoking is not a sin in itself, but that it is dangerous like thin ice. The people should be warned of the danger. And
it certainly would not be good for the teachers and catechists to
be seen in a toddy shop or at a festival where the use of the drink

137

of the palm tree was unlimited. If they fell down in this regard, the workers were fined; or if they still continued, they
were finally dismissed. Heyer in his sermons emphasized that ab-
stinence from toddy drinking "would henceforth be one of the marks
of the new life in Christ."[141]

From the records it would appear that more disciplinary action was necessary in the matter of adultery and sex offenses than
anything else. This could be understood by the fact that it was
customary for outcaste boys even before marriage to go to prosti-
tutes and to have a great deal of freedom afterward. One of the
big arguments for child marriages was to protect the chastity of
young girls.[142] The prevalence of this problem is indicated by the
difficulty the missionaries had with their teachers and catechists, who were expected to be setting an example to the others.[14]
In one flagrant case a teacher, deciding to run away to Mauritius,
stole five rupees from the catechist in Nayudupet, took the catechist's wife with him, persuaded the oldest of his pupils to go
with him and take the wife of the cook. The Mission had them
pursued and brought to court. The teacher was given a six months'
sentence and the pupil only two, since the latter did not succeed
in his efforts to take the wife of the cook. The home village of
the pupil was very angry at the missionary for not appealing the
sentence. But missionary Petersen felt that the shame of having
the pupil in jail for two months would be good for the Kalahasti

Christians, since such sin should not be hid but rather the importance of the wrong strongly emphasized.[144]

Discipline in a congregation for backsliding or other failure to come up to the standards expected of a Christian took the form in the Hermannsburg Mission of a person being required to sit in a special place in the church during worship services and not being permitted to take Communion. Such discipline disturbed the whole congregation for they did not want to be known as having such members. When this discipline was coupled with the customary village discipline, it could be very effective. The missionaries permitted the Christians to keep as many of their social controls as possible. For adultery such village discipline might consist of the individual and his family not being permitted to have his clothes washed by the village washerman, not entering the houses of any other persons, and having to pay a fine. Church records kept by the missionaries in the Guntur field indicate that fines were a common form of punishment used by the church, especially since money was a scarce item. Fines were exacted for backsliding, absence from church worship, attempting pagan marriages and eating carrion or meat of animals sacrificed at Hindu festivals.[145]

Because of the closely-knit social unity of a village, the missionaries found it advisable to make use of village discipline insofar as it was in keeping with Christian principles. The vill-

139

ages themselves preferred this to bringing in an outside force, such as the British government. If a majority in a palem, a section of the village belonging to one caste, were Christian, the control of serious sins could be most effective. The missionaries would give the elders or Church Council responsibility to observe the ethical conduct and life of the people. They saw more and knew better than the missionaries what the people were doing and could institute effective social pressure to correct irregularities.[146]

The Hermannsburg missionaries were extremely cautious about those desiring to return to the church after having fallen back into Hinduism. They were visited personally by the missionary to see if they were truly penitent and wanted forgiveness of sin, and to determine the motive for their return. Too often it was because they were badly in debt and believed the missionary would help them. Public church punishment followed penitence. If the persons behaved well during this probationary period, they were reaffiliated.[147]

It became apparent right from the start of the missionary effort in the Andhra Desa that the Gospel message and the presence of the missionaries would be a disruptive force in the social makeup of village life. When a group of people interested in learning more about Christianity asked for instruction and a Christian teacher, a chain of events began which could not be stopped. It was a Brahmanical maxim, as Heyer pointed out, "that the lower classes of the people shall not be permitted to learn to read."[148] Often the Kornam or head man of the village would try to prevent the teacher from beginning his work, driving him out of the village and threatening dire punishment if he returned. This drew the missionary into the picture; and he would inform the Tahsildar or judge of the district and register his complaint. Even though the judge might be a Brahman, fear of what the Collector, always an Englishman in those days, might say or do led him to warn the Kornam of the consequences of his action. As these people learned to read and write, and as they realized that they had a champion in the person of the missionary, their attitude toward life and toward those who had always dominated their lives changed drastically. As Fishman points out:[149]

> "To those who were never even approached by a respectable person except for exploitation, the unstinted, wholehearted friendship of one associated on terms of equality with the highest class in the land, the British officials, was a very precious possession. The emotional satisfaction of this experience was very great; for, although it brought little immediate increase in status, it appreciably enhanced status-feeling. This feeling of worth became a vehicle of progress."

These people took pride in their new status. Even though it meant persecution and privation, they found a certain joy in refusing to perform their expected functions in Hindu religious ceremonies, in making Sunday a day of worship rather than a day of work, and depriving themselves of meat sacrificed before idols.

141

Just being a Christian had its effect, so that they felt they could not do certain things. Gradually they gave up uncleanliness, drunkenness, carrion, filthy language, evil customs and vicious habits. This in turn profoundly affected others in the community.

Father Heyer tells of seven boys from a neighboring village who attended worship in Gurzala and were so influenced by what they heard that they did not want to go back home. For the villagers were about to sacrifice a sheep to the village goddess, Ammavaru, after which the meat would be eaten in the homes. They were afraid that they might be forced to eat such meat or that their parents would insist on them doing so even though they did not want to. The boys were told to return home, for no one could force them to eat such meat. And if the parents insisted, they could eat it and remember that sacrifice to idols could make the meat neither better nor worse. A report later revealed that the parents also had abstained. Heyer indicated that this incident shows the profound influence of the word of God even upon people still heathen.[150]

The extreme poverty of the people, the unhealthiness of their daily living habits, their lack of any consciousness of sin from the Christian viewpoint and their indifference to human pain and suffering were factors which disturbed the missionaries greatly and brought about greater or lesser efforts to relieve the situation.   In witnessing a hook-swinging ceremony, Mrs. Albrecht

reported:[151]

> "Many years ago when old Father Heyer, our first missionary,
> came here he found not a goat but a man swung up on that
> very same pole, with that very same hook thrust through his
> back and no rope supporting him.  Through Father Heyer's
> appeal to Government, man-swinging was prohibited, and ever
> since a goat has taken the place on the hook."

Heyer's knowledge of medicine helped him to bring much relief and

institute habits of cleanliness.  He showed concern about the

primitive weaving methods of the Malas who could not earn more

than six to nine cents a day, if they worked steadily.  He felt

that the situation could be improved by introducing a better hand

loom, warping mill and filling wheel.  But this would take money

and there was no possibility of the people themselves changing

from machinery costing only three dollars to some costing forty or

fifty.  Heyer also envisioned the establishment of Christian vill-

ages and asked friends in America to contribute funds for the land

and looms.  As an experiment he permitted four young families to

build on mission property at Polepalli with the provision that

they could remain there only through good behaviour and as long as

they belonged to the church.  But lack of funds and the large num-

ber of converts in many different villages prevented any further-

ance of such plans for the social betterment of the Christians.[152]

When fire destroyed 100 dwellings in Adugopala, including

those of all the families receiving instruction for baptism, Heyer

gave each family connected with the mission one rupee although

this would hardly replace the loss of the looms.  He also started
a subscription among the other congregations.  It did not amount
to much, but "it showed to the heathen around, that native Christians care for and assist each other in time of need."[153]

Another problem was the effort to save little girls in the
families.  Mrs. George Albrecht reports in her unpublished manuscript, In Tent and Bungalow, that it was still a problem as late
as 1906.  Although there was a law against throwing them to the
crocodiles, they now disposed of superfluous babies by feeding
them with thick indigestible buffalo milk, instead of the mother's
milk, and the little innocents died a "natural death."[154]

The Hermannsburg missionaries tried various schemes to bring
relief to the utter poverty of the converts.  When they came into
the centers for instruction for baptism, they were given money or
work to make up for their losses.  They were even given money to
come to the worship services on Sundays in order to compensate for
loss of a day's work for the Sudra farmers.  Efforts were made to
obtain land for the Christians, and loan societies were established
so that the Christians did not have to borrow at exhorbitant rates
of interest.  In one case a missionary lent money for a wedding
to prevent fornication or heavy debt.  The missionaries realized
the dangers involved in giving material aid: that it made people
lazy and too dependent on the missionary, a natural step from
their previous dependence on the Sudra farmers for whom they
worked, and it often proved a barrier between the Christian and

the missionary. On the other hand, it was felt to be worthwhile
if the Christians could gain some independence from the upper
caste landlords and moneylenders. They were less likely to backslide into idolatry, they were respected more by government officials because they were able to pay their rent on time, and the
missionary had more influence upon them.

Missionary Schepmann explained in the 1882 issue of _Missions-
blatt_ that money was rarely given as a gift. The people were
steeped in the idea already that the missionary had to do something for them since they were so poor. This moneylending could
be used to force the people to do something for the church and
school, since they now had money which could be spent wisely instead of wasted. Schepmann tried to get the people to pay for
half the cost of a chapel. He told them that he always had to
give money when they needed it; now they could do something for
the mission when it needed their help. He also tried to get them
into the habit of giving one-twentieth of their harvest to the
church and school. Often he lent money only on this condition.
In this way they were more willing to build a chapel than at
first. In time the people would be able to support their own
teacher.[155]

Missionaries have often been accused of not being interested
in, nor taking the time to study, the customs and religious habits
of the Indian people. Although this may have been true of some of

the later missionaries, it could certainly not be said of the
early men. Of course they were persuaded that there was salvation in none other than Christ, but this did not prevent them from
studying and appreciating that which was distinctively Indian.
Without too much thought they impressed western methods and techniques on the life of the Church, but there was a great deal of
adaptation. When something distinctively new was being introduced, it was perfectly natural for them to do it in the way they
were accustomed to doing in America and Europe. And, further, it
must be realized that the people themselves often preferred to
change to something distinctively different as part and parcel of
their complete break from caste and Hinduism. This is shown in
their preference up to recent years for western-style churches:
they did not want temple or mosque adaptations, as these were too
much a reminder of their former life of domination, fear and
misery.[156]

In the matter of adopting names at the time of baptism, the
Hermannsburg missionaries such as Hartwig Harms urged Indian names.
But the people liked European and Biblical names as something definitely Christian and distinctive. Too many of the native names
were connected with the Hindu religion or had evil connotations.
Parents were accustomed to giving bad names to their children to
keep the evil spirits from showing any interest in them and harm-
ing them.[157] The Schleswig-Holstein missionaries urged their

people to Christianize the native names rather than adopting European or Biblical ones.[158]

Woerrlein of the Hermannsburg Mission was told, shortly after his arrival in India, by an English official that it was not necessary to know the Hindu customs and fables in order to preach the Gospel, but Woerrlein learned differently on his very first preaching occasion. A shrewd Brahman told him: "You may know your Christian dogma, but not our Hindu religion. If you hope to speak to us at all, you have to be familiar with our teachings and customs; and then we'll listen and speak with you."[159] From that time on he made a life-time study of the history, language, geography, religions, customs and other general information about India. The director of the mission, Mylius, established in 1865 as one of the requirements for a missionary that "he must learn well the Hindu religion, scriptures, fairy-tales, and superstitions, so that he will not needlessly offend the Indians."[160] To further this study, discussions were held at the conference gatherings of the missionaries. Father Heyer at the first annual meeting of the Evangelical Lutheran Mission (Guntur and Rajahmundry) held January 30, 1853, discussed in an essay the origin of the aborigines of India. So we see that there was a great deal of interest on the part of the missionaries in the customs, religion and social problems of the Indian people.

Men such as Woerrlein could also see some value in the Hindu religious literature. In speaking of the Vedas he notes that in a few places Varuna is asked to forgive sins and that there is a faint reminiscence of God's pure revelation, which provides missionaries with the necessary point of contact to preach the Gospel to the Indian people. Concerning the great epics, the <u>Mahabharata</u> and <u>Ramayana</u>, he confesses that some passages are found recognizing the One God, but that these are rather obscure and insignificant when compared to the main body of the literature. On the whole there is little of real spiritual value as compared to the Bible.[161]

### 4. The relation of native worker to the missionary

The development of good native workers in the Lutheran Missions was a difficult problem and one that took many years to solve. In the Guntur and Rajahmundry fields the great shortage of missionaries made it impossible for any one missionary to devote most of his time to the training of workers. The Home Societies felt that most of the missionary's time should be spent in preaching the Gospel, and looked askance at any of the men who spent too much time in the schools.

The first workers were teachers in the schools and they were Hindus, primarily Brahmans, of little value as far as Christian education was concerned. All religious work had to be done by the missionaries; and their inadequate knowledge of the language and customs of the people proved a real barrier to conversion. The first Christian teacher in Guntur was Stephen and the first catechist employed by the Mission, Nicodemus, began his work in March, 1847. Nothing more is said of Nicodemus, so he evidently was not too satisfactory.[162] Colporteurs were used to distribute scripture portions and texts, receiving their support from the Bible and Tract Societies, but they could not be depended on for any real evangelistic preaching.

When Heyer moved to the Palnad in 1849, he determined to use only Christian teachers insofar as he possibly could. Although he had to sacrifice on the side of education, he found these men, working in their own villages, of real value because they were evangelists as well as teachers. They had a real influence in their community by virtue of their position of leadership and their close relationship to the people. Heyer had selected them originally because of their previous positions as leaders in their caste. And he gave them a great deal of responsibility which they took upon themselves proudly and with deep consecration. The tremendous growth in the Palnad field is an indication of the worth of these poorly educated but faithful teachers.[163]

The first catechist in the Palnad, Divasichamany, came from the American Mission in Madras.[164] There is no further indication as to how valuable he proved to be in the extension of the

149

work.  Heyer speaks more of the five boys he took into his own home
in Gurzala from three different villages to train for future usefulness.  Two of them, Jacob and Rettivardu, evidently were old
enough to assist the catechist and the colporteur Appiyah when
they visited the villages.  He emphasized in a letter to America
dated August 1, 1849, the great need for more native laborers, "for
by native instrumentality, the most of the work must be done."[165]
By January, 1851, Heyer was able to take twelve of the best students from the village schools and start a boarding school to prepare them for teaching.

It cannot be said that the teachers were completely satisfactory just because they were Christian.  Evidently there was
some falling down on their part, even as the Hermannsburg and
Breklum missionaries experienced, although Heyer does not say too
much about it.  He does tell of the removal of one older teacher
because he countenanced irregularities in his family.  In one of
his last letters from the Palnad Heyer mentioned that he deliber-
ately left out most of the persecutions and unpleasant things because it would not be happy reading nor pleasurable writing.[166]

That the teachers did not work exclusively in their own villages is brought out in a letter of May 3, 1852, where Heyer told
of commissioning nine of the teachers when school was closed to
act as colporteurs, going two or three together, to more than a
hundred villages distributing a thousand tracts and Scripture

portions. In some places the men were well received. In others, associations were already arising among the Malas formed to oppose the Gospel and defend their heathen practices. They had become alarmed by the large number of converts among their caste. Upper caste men, such as Kornams, village headmen and usually Brahmans, Komitees, the merchants, and Kamasalas, the goldsmiths, were happy to receive the reading material and absorbed it avidly. The teachers came back with many interesting experiences and reported that villages everywhere were requesting Christian schools.[167]

When Heyer moved back to Guntur in 1853, he started the first boarding school there, with four boys that he had brought from the Palnad as a core. Two years later three from the Guntur school went with him when he took charge of the Rajahmundry station. Groenning, and Unangst after him, continued the Guntur school.

It is not known to what extent the early Christian leaders took part in the administration of the Guntur and Rajahmundry missions. Fourteen of them participated in the organization of the first Lutheran Synod formed in Guntur January 31, 1853, under Heyer's leadership,[168] but none were elected to office. At the second annual meeting "three young native Christians were recommended for training as catechists and future pastors, namely: Chinsa Ramurdu of Rajahmundry, aged twenty-two; William Barnabas Passavant of the Palnad, aged sixteen; and Joseph of Guntur, aged fourteen."[169]

It was a long time before the missionaries found men well enough trained and experienced to be ordained. As most of the Christians were outcastes with very little education, their leaders could be used as teachers and evangelists in the village situation; but the missionaries felt they could not leave whole areas of work in charge of native men. Heyer commented in a letter dated May 9, 1851, that "our native converts from idolatry and heathenism, need constant guidance and superintendence."[170] And the same, to a great extent, was true of their leaders. Part of the difficulty in ordaining any of the native men, even when they had proved themselves by diligent and faithful work, was the high position in which the ministry is held in the Lutheran Church. As contrasted with the Telugu Baptist Missions[171] where poorly educated men were ordained in order to lead the great numbers of people received in mass movements, the Lutheran Church was most reluctant to ordain uneducated men. And this was true even when the Guntur and Rajahmundry missions were deprived of nearly all missionaries during and after the Civil War. No missionary recruits came between 1858 and 1870; and during the periods 1857-58 and 1866-70, only one man directed the whole work. (Six new men came between 1870 and 1874 to put new life into the effort.)

On October 5, 1873, Mr. R. E. Cully, the Anglo-Indian catechist who had proven his worth by taking complete charge of the Palnad since October 1862, and by directing the Guntur field for

152

one year in the absence of any missionary, was ordained as the first pastor and assigned to the Palnad. But a year later he became dissatisfied, resigned and moved to Rangoon.[172] At the time Cully was ordained, the missionaries also received authority from the Home Board to raise several of the catechists to the status of Evangelists after special instruction. Two of these men, Medikonduru Nathaniel and Bethala John, were licensed to administer the sacraments and placed over the western and eastern sections respectively of the Palnad. They were both ordained January 7, 1877, at the time the Stork Memorial Church was dedicated in Guntur. When misunderstandings arose between the two men and it was realized that the congregations suffered because of it, Pastor Nathaniel was transferred to the Narasaravupet-Vinukonda taluks. For almost fifteen years Pastor John was in sole charge of the Palnad and did an amazing piece of work. Cully had reported a Christian community of 600 when Father Heyer visited Gurzala on November 16, 1869; the baptized membership reached 4,903 in the year 1890.[173] In speaking of these newly-ordained native pastors, the 1877 report to America stated that "it is to this native agency that we must ultimately look for the redemption of India;"[174] and yet, strangely enough, not another pastor was ordained in the Guntur field for twenty-six years.

Because of the lack of native pastors and catechists, the Guntur field instituted what was known as the itinerant teacher to cover the tremendous area of the field. It was their duty to keep "constantly moving among the people, encouraging and instructing new converts, and persuading others to embrace the truth as it is in Jesus."[175] It was understood that in time these men would be promoted to higher positions and greater responsibilities. The 1877 report lists twenty-six of these plus twenty-nine village teachers, the two native pastors, three catechists, two Bible colporteurs and two tract colporteurs. A total of 3,045 Christians including children resided in 111 villages.

In the Rajahmundry field the first two catechists were Tota Joseph, one of the students Father Heyer brought with him when he was transferred in 1854,[176] and Nelaprolu Paulus, nephew of Malapati John, first convert from Hinduism in the Palnad and the first school teacher at Polepalli.[177] After a period of education, they were employed as colporteurs and then teachers. When Unangst was left as the only missionary in the whole Rajahmundry-Samalkot-Guntur-Palnad area in 1866, he made Joseph and Paulus catechists with complete responsibility for their districts. Joseph was located in Rajahmundry and directed work in the surrounding villages where there were 85 Christians in March of 1870 and three families of inquirers; while Paulus was located at Muramunda, in which area there were 76 baptized Christians and two families of inquirers.[178] So faithfully had these men performed their task and held the fields that Father Heyer, missionaries Becker, Schmidt and Poulsen, who came to Rajahmundry in 1870 and 1871, placed tremendous responsibilities in their hands while the new men learned the language and customs of the people. They acted as interpreters on long tours of the villages in the whole Godavari delta. The Synod of Pennsylvania authorized their ordination, and on December 25, 1878 they were ordained at the same time the new church at Rajahmundry was consecrated. Previously, the following agreement was drawn up for them to sign:[179]

"1. The end in view in every Mission must be the establishment of independent native churches with native pastors.

2. In the event of the ordination of Joseph and Paulus, the General Council promises to pay in future their salaries, namely, Rs. 20 per month and travelling expenses.

3. They are to reside in a central village and be the pastors of a number of surrounding villages, where they are to try to develop an independent ministry. A district is to be assigned them for special evangelistic work among the heathen. They are to accompany the missionaries on longer mission tours.

4. The foreign missionaries are to remain superintendents of these congregations; but they are to regard the native pastors as fellow-ministers who with them are members of the General Council of the Evangelical Lutheran Church in North America.

5. With regard to money received from foreign sources the foreign missionaries remain the only agents, but with regard to money collected in their own congregations, the native pastors have equal vote with the foreign missionaries.

6. As soon as a third missionary arrives, church government is to be vested in a Conference or Synod."

This Conference was organized February 3, 1879. Pastor Joseph was stationed at Jegurapad to care for the congregations

155

east of the Godavari river and Pastor Paulus at Velpur to care for
the west side.

"The wisdom of their ordination and appointment to special
parishes soon became evident. Unlike the foreign missionaries, they had no building operations to superintend, no boats
to build, no salaries to distribute, no work of any secular
kind whatever to do. Accustomed to the climate, thoroughly
familiar with the habits of thought and modes of life in
their own country, having a good command of the conversa-
tional vernacular, these sons of the soil, Telugus of the
Telugus, whom all foreign missionaries who had known them
-- Heyer, Groenning, Schmidt and Poulsen -- had recommended
for ordination, proved to be a power for good in the mission
that can scarcely be overestimated."[180]

Schmidt, as director of the Rajahmundry Mission, took the position

that these two native leaders were in complete charge of their

areas as 'pastores loci.' In speaking of Paulus at the time of

his death in 1897 he said:[181]

"Although it [Paulus' charge] remained part of my work and I
came twice a year to visit the Christian villages, examine
the schools and congregations, still I never performed ministerial acts or interfered with his work, except as supervisor. He always consulted me on important matters, and he
never did anything without my consent. He managed the work
remarkably well and showed as much sound judgment as if he
had grown up in congregational work at home. He paid all
the teachers and preachers, between fifty and sixty of them,
and looked after buildings and repairs. I always found that
he got more help and labor out of the Christians than a missionary could have done. But he was principally an evangelist
and understood how to bring the people into the Church.

He could not write English well enough to compose glorious reports, else the missionary journals would have printed
them and not forgotten to record that this native pastor in
little more than eighteen years baptized close to five thousand persons."

Other Christians who gained places of honor and responsibil-

ity among the Rajahmundry missionaries in the early period were

P. V. Ratnam, S. James and J. William, all ordained after years of service. The first was a Sudra converted in 1877. Already a teacher and a man of some education, he took charge of the Christian school in Rajahmundry when Paulus and Joseph took up their special pastorates. In 1882 he helped start the Caste Girls' School and was a very capable headmaster for twenty years until his ordination in 1902. He also served in this period as Catechist in Rajahmundry town. He "became an outstanding figure in Rajahmundry for many years."[182]

Srikotla James and Jeriprolu William were two of the three boys in Father Heyer's boarding school opened in 1870 when he returned to India for the third time at the age of seventy-six to save the Rajahmundry Mission for the Lutheran Church.[183] William's father was one of the early native converts brought by Groenning from Guntur to Rajahmundry; he became a warden in the Rajahmundry jail and a faithful lay leader in the local church. His mother, Ruth, was the first girl to be converted at the Guntur Girls' School in 1853; she became a teacher in that school and helped lead a number of other girls to Christianity, two of whom became the wives of Pastors Paulus and Joseph. Every member of this large Jeriprolu family has been in the employ of the Mission.

James and William entered the Government High School in 1872, meeting with a missionary each day for one hour of religious instruction. James, after having passed the matriculation examination at the Government College in 1880, assisted Ratnam in the school work in Rajahmundry. William became headmaster in 1882 of the Rajahmundry school after Ratnam started the Girls' Caste School. He also was elected Telugu Secretary of the Conference of missionaries and native agents held on December 26, 1881; and he held that post for a number of years. James followed him in that post for a period. At this same conference James was appointed Inspector of Schools for the Rajahmundry Mission following complaints that were made against some of the village teachers. "He was to visit each school at least twice a year and hold semi-annual examinations."[184] Later on James became headmaster of the Rajahmundry school when William was appointed a catechist outside of Rajahmundry. J. William was ordained in 1898 and James in 1900.

With the exception of a few outstanding men, such as those mentioned above, the early workers in this field received little more than an elementary education in the Mission school before being sent to the villages as teachers and leaders in the local congregations. Many turned out to be lazy and inefficient. McCready found it necessary to institute teachers' meetings on the first Monday of the month where he tried to increase their efficiency and systematize their work by setting up a schedule of duties, hours and lessons of instruction, and preaching appointments on Sunday and during the week. Missionary Dietrich wrote: "The children are few in number, irregular in attendance and carelessly

158

taught.  The teachers are indifferent. ... I am anxiously looking

forward to the time when we can obtain the men who are now being

trained by Rev. Groenning."  And Schmidt, along the same vein,

said:[185]

> "There are many who wish to enter mission employ, but alas,
> very few of them are fit for the work! They hardly satisfy
> the most meagre expectations as to Scriptural knowledge and
> gifts of teaching.  Our mission work constantly reminds us
> of Luther's saying, that we must plow with asses until we
> get horses."

A report of a conference held for these teachers in the sum-

mer of 1874 indicates that the missionaries continued instruction

whenever possible in Bible history, church history, the catechism,

and in learning to read publicly the Sacred Scriptures with run-

ning comments.  Luther's small catechism with an explanation, pre-

pared and published by the Hermannsburg Mission, was introduced

for use by the worker at this time.[186]

Before turning away from the work in Rajahmundry, mention

should be made of the experiment by Missionary Artman, who sent

Frederick J. McCready,[187] an Anglo-Indian by birth from a prom-

inent Rajahmundry family, to America to prepare for the ministry

at the Lutheran Theological Seminary in Philadelphia.  He was

graduated in 1884, ordained June 10th of the same year at Reading,

Pa., and commissioned as a regular missionary.  Artman felt that

this would be a good method of obtaining missionaries in an inex-

pensive way.  Although the missionaries had already resolved that

young men from India should not be on an equal level with the

American missionaries,[188] the Home Board determined that the Rev. Mr. McCready should have a starting salary of $1,000. This was in contrast to the policy of the missionaries who resolved to start themselves at $600 and increase to a maximum of $1200 by the twentieth year of service. This action of the Board created some friction which increased still further in later years. In the meantime, McCready worked on an equal basis with the other missionaries in all matters, taking active part in administration and policy-making. It is interesting to note that immediately following McCready's ordination, the Home Board changed its mind about training native Indians in America for the ministry. It refused to return to India another Anglo-Indian, the Rev. William G. Hudson, who was graduated from the Philadelphia Seminary in 1885 and remained in America serving parishes in Ohio and Pennsylvania; and it would not grant permission for the two sons of Pastor Paulus to come to America. The Board also adopted as the more expedient one the salary scale established by the missionaries.[189]

Wischan tells us that the other missionaries also were opposed to Artman's effort to train native Christians in America, especially to become missionaries on an equal basis with themselves. He points out that McCready, because he was an Anglo-Indian and married to one, the granddaughter of Captain Taylor,[190] did not have any social standing in the eyes of Europeans and was less acceptable to caste Hindus than the missionaries. His greatest

160

success as a missionary was with the Madigas, the very lowest caste.[191]

In the Hermannsburg Mission Mylius, with previous experience in the Leipzig Mission, knew the importance of native helpers. He brought two with him from Madras when he began his work in Sulurpet; they proved unsatisfactory. Those who came from Nellore proved to be too strongly grounded in Baptist ideas to satisfy the strict Lutherans of the Hermannsburg Mission. So Mylius determined very early to take the best of the new converts and give them a short, concentrated period of training to be catechists. Fortunately, most of these already had a fair education; and they had previous religious experience as Dasari priests and traveling Gurus. Some of them were poets. Among them were the best preachers and speakers that the Mission had in its whole history. With a half-year's initial preparation and supervised home study thereafter under Mylius' direction, these early catechists were fairly effective for the opening of mission work in a new area.[192]

Mylius was by no means entirely satisfied with these men. He was a strict disciplinarian and kept close control over missionaries and workers. Because many of these catechists had been wandering priests, they tended toward habits of laziness and too much independence. They were often accused of being pig-headed and unreliable for not being able to adjust themselves to the disciplined ways of the German missionary.

161

Hartwig Harms in his Chronik des Seminars für Gehilfen in
Nayudupeta gives short and blunt biographical sketches of these
early workers.  He speaks of Ravuri Paul,[193] the second man baptized in the mission, as very helpful in teaching the missionaries the Telugu language and helping in the work of translation,
but he became unreliable and disorderly when his good wife died.
He was discharged, later rehired, but his second wife caused him
more trouble.  Tupili Philip, who served from 1871-94, proved to
be an excellent catechist who knew how to economize and keep out
of debt; but he was very obstinate at times.  His brother, Tupili
Massilamonie (1872-96), not so good a catechist, was also not quite
so pig-headed.  Another pair of brothers from a very fine family
proved to be good workers and problems at the same time.  Sunduri
Andreas (1868-78) was exceptionally intelligent and energetic, a
well-converted and -convinced Christian, but he came into such
conflict with Wahl that he incited a young teacher, Joseph, to
join him in trying to beat the missionary with sticks.  He had to
be discharged.  His brother Johann (1870-86) was never an effective catechist but was an excellent poet.  He was familiar with
Indian beliefs and superstitions and could have served well in
this respect.  But he caused the missionaries so much trouble by
his unreliability that no one wanted to use him.  He was finally
retired and pensioned.  Tupili Thotaya (1869-76) was one of the
very best; he had been a beggar priest but was able to read and

162

write. He was converted by Andreas and studied under Dahl at Venkatagiri. He was the only helper missionary Kiehne was ever satisfied with; unfortunately he died of tuberculosis during his best years.

Harms spoke very highly of several who were still serving at the time he wrote most of his Chronik.[194] Palle Raguel, converted by Sunduri Andreas, was a heathen priest who sang and prayed at Hindu sacrifices. He had an excellent education; in fact, Harms says he was almost too intelligent and therefore difficult at times. He was a good economizer, never in debt, but a little too interested in furthering his own welfare. He had never been disciplined in any way by the missionaries. Neat, orderly and serious, he worked from 1872 on, especially in Gudur, Rapur, Venkatagiri and Nayudupeta. Sorrows caused mainly by his children aged him. Because of asthma and old-age weakness, he taught school in his later years.

Saverus Lazerus, who had been a vaccinator for the government, gave up a good job and became a catechist in 1883 at a very low salary. He worked diligently and faithfully and was so enthusiastic about Christianity that people gladly listened to him. Two brothers, Avilele Gottfried and Avilele Gad, were some of the first converts of Petersen in Tirupati. The former was quite conscious of his shortcomings and was willing to be employed on a part-time basis in lonely spots. He was a good and honest worker. Gadu was one of the finest preachers to the Hindu that the Mission ever

had.  He had been a Hindu priest and was very intelligent.  He
served from 1878, much of the time with Harms, who loved to hear
his excellent preaching.  He had a tendency to be too light-
hearted and superficial which got him into trouble with young
women.  And on one occasion out of fear for Sudras who were
threatening to persecute him, he swore wrongly, then would not ask
for forgiveness and had to be disciplined.  For a time he was
given a teaching position in a small school.

One of the best known of the early men was Rayapa Joseph, the
first boy educated in the seminary in Nayudupeta, who began his
service in 1872.  His parents were originally Tamil but resided
in Ongole.  He was exceptionally intelligent, had a logical mind,
was an excellent poet and musician, and learned languages very
easily.  He began his work as a teacher and became involved in the
incident previously mentioned[195] when he and Andreas attempted to
attack missionary Wahl.  Because he was not to blame and was still
very young, Mylius received him back into the church.  He developed into an excellent Bible teacher in the high school at Tirupati.  As a poet he did a great deal for the Telugu Lutheran
Church.  He also translated a number of books, especially from
Tamil into Telugu.  He had a side line and developed quite a reputation as a mechanic.  His big problem was his inability to keep
out of debt.  Also somewhat obstinate and proud, he found it difficult to give in when he was wrong.

164

Three men who began their service in 1882 as teachers were called back to the seminary ten years later to be in the first Catechist Class, 1892-94, in preparation for the ministry. The whole course of educational development was a long and slow one; and the Hermannsburg missionaries, in typical Lutheran fashion, were extremely cautious about ordaining inadequately trained men. Five years was the expected period of preparation in the teacher's seminary to qualify a man for the village schools. If, after at least six years of teaching, the missionaries felt that certain men had done a good job, they were called back for a two-year course in the catechist's seminary. Bible content, singing, catechism and church history were the main subjects. After passing the required examination they were employed as catechists for many years, teaching **catechetical** students, helping the missionary in the preaching and evangelism, and representing him in the worship services. The best of the catechists were then brought back for further preparation for ordination. In this way these three men, Nellaballe Isaak, Dasi Punitudu and U. B. Palle Daniel, were not ordained until December 14, 1904. It was felt that the Telugu people were too backward and the congregations not firmly enough established to be handled by native pastors.[196] Mylius told Hartwig Harms on one occasion: "From our present helpers, we will not be able to bring any so far as to ordain him. They are too depend-

ent, and too weak in character."[197]  Harms was happy to prove him
wrong by this ordination in 1904.

We see that the Hermannsburg missionaries insisted on maintaining high standards for their workers.  Because of this, they
were keenly disappointed again and again.  Mylius found it necessary on several occasions to remind the men that catechists were
very necessary for the present state of the work and therefore
ought to be treated with special care, giving them the honors belonging to their specific ministry, spending as much time as possible in their further training, and at all times showing patience
and understanding.  In many ways they were still children, just
recently come out of Hinduism and still very much involved in customs considered evil by the European Christian and from which the
Indians found it difficult to escape.  An essentially true catechist, he pointed out, is a real treasure, but a rotten or mal-
icious one is poison to the mission.  Mylius considered catechists
a necessary evil until the day when there would be adequately
trained men coming from the teacher's and preacher's seminaries.
Catechists would then wither away.  But now while the European
missionary must struggle with the people, language and customs,
he needs such a helper as an intermediary -- half secular, half
spiritual.  The day would come when the work of evangelism and administration of the church would be handled completely by efficient, independent teachers and pastors.[198]

166

Mylius found it necessary to restrain the missionaries by keeping the control of employment, amount of salaries and dismissal of native catechists and school teachers in his own hands as superintendent of the Mission. Otherwise, every missionary would have too much freedom in this regard and perhaps dismiss too hurriedly or without adequate forethought of the consequences, and thus create confusion and insecurity, both for the Mission and the native workers.[199]

On the whole, the missionaries took too much responsibility upon themselves. The catechists were completely dependent upon them for decisions and working orders and salary. Schaefer points out:[200]

> "The Christians themselves had little to do in the church or with the church. Even in the matters of personal evangelism they were not too well trained, because here too the missionary saw to everything personally. When some heathen expressed interest in Christianity, the people immediately were to tell their missionary, and then he took over completely. The general attitude of the missionaries can be best expressed by summarizing what Rev. Scriba wrote in 1887 when he complained that there were some missionaries who wanted to turn over more of the functions, duties and support of the work to the Indians. He strongly disagreed with them, saying that the Indians were too poor, uneducated and weak in faith to take on the responsibility. Therefore, he felt that the missionary should continue to handle and run everything."

The Schleswig-Holstein Mission, starting later than most of the missions in the Telugu area and realizing by their experience the great need of native workers, asked the Gossner and Hermannsburg Missions for catechists. They complied gladly; and these

167

evangelists usually stayed for several years, some never going back to their former homes. The first Telugu catechist was David from Nellore, converted by the London Missionary Society and a member of the Mala caste. His brother was employed by the Hermannsburg Mission; David himself did not have the proper training and was dismissed shortly after he began working for them. He was in great financial distress as a result, so that the request of the Breklum Mission was fortunate. Although he was admittedly not very capable, he had a great deal of patience and could train the students in the catechism. He had them go over and over it, learning by rote. Mention has been made previously of the difficulty the missionaries had with two of the first boys baptized who refused to live with David because of his lower caste standing.[201]

The second catechist also came from the Hermannsburg field. Chimaya Joseph had worked for the Church Missionary Society and the London Missionary Society before coming to teach in Tirupati under Petersen. He also served in Kodur as a catechist under Woerrlein. He was born in the Cuddapah district. In Salur he helped the catechist David in the school established in 1885. The school had both a Christian and a Hindu teacher; but the Christian teacher, Joseph Samuel, had to be dismissed for sex offenses. A colporteur, Ebenezer, distributed for the Bible Society and worked with the others in preaching and training catechumens.

When the Parvatipur station was handed over to the Breklum Mission by the London Missionary Society, a catechist, Appadu Philip, and a Christian teacher, Titus, were offered and accepted. The latter was also considered in the category of catechist as he did much work outside school hours. Philip proved to be faithful and well-loved. Nearly sixty years of age, he had been baptized in Vizagapatam when forty. Formerly he had been a merchant and superintendent of a factory. He went to England on three occasions to accompany mission children and sick wives. When he became a Christian, the people in his congregation liked him so much that they requested that he become a catechist, which he did in 1881. He accepted his position with the Breklum Mission on condition that he could return to the L. M. S. any time he wished if he found objections to Lutheran teachings or serving in a Lutheran church. He was sent to Salur for a period of instruction and was amazed at the simplicity of the Gospel message preached. He affiliated with the mission October 20, 1889.[202]

In 1885 the eleven-year-old son of a policeman was deserted by his widowed mother, and the Mission took him to start what became an orphanage supported by interested individuals in Germany. He learned quickly, proved to be very obedient and was baptized with the name Martin. Another boy, Josua, of a still higher caste, was confirmed with Martin in 1888. Missionary Pohl took these two to Rajahmundry in July, 1889, to be educated at the Anglo-vernacu-

lar school by Wilhelm Groenning, his former teacher in Germany.
On arrival in Rajahmundry he learned that Groenning had died very
suddenly July 7th. His presence in the city brought a request
from Schmidt that Pohl remain and take Groenning's place and carry
out his educational policies. The Breklum Society gave Pohl a
one-year leave of absence, so that he was himself able to train
the boys he had brought from Salur to become catechists. It was
not until after Pohl's long-delayed return in 1897 that the
Schleswig-Holstein Mission established a school of its own in Parvitapur for the training of teachers and evangelists.[203]

The work in the Breklum field proved extremely difficult. A
number of times catechists just disappeared while out on a preaching tour. Much responsibility had to be placed on leading laymen
to handle the evangelistic work and maintain discipline. This was
possible because of the very careful catechetical training which
these missionaries maintained. Based somewhat on old German in-
structional systems, the training came in stages. There was a
period of pre-catechetical training which could last for years if
the person was unable to fulfill necessary requirements, such as
giving up of idols, caste and polygamy. Transgression of Christian ethics required a stop in the educational process; the elders
in the congregations helped the missionaries observe the actions
of the applicants.

170

Then came neophyte education for those who applied for baptism or affiliation. This could last for two or more years and never less than one. At the end of this period was a concentrated session under the missionary lasting three or four weeks. Previous training was done primarily by the catechists. In this whole time the individual under training would learn to know the catechism, gain a profound knowledge of the Bible, especially its historical parts, cover the life of Jesus and the parables, and learn hymns. The missionary concentrated primarily on inward conversion, since the Breklum Mission felt that without baptism there was no conversion; and without conversion, there was no baptism. Special consideration in this training process was given old and sickly people. At the end of the training period and just previous to baptism, a final examination was held in public before the congregation, lasting one or more days, covering all areas of the Christian faith which had been taught. There was usually still further instruction between baptism and the first communion.[204]

Elders in the congregations were established when the problem of settling disputes and other matters prevented the catechists from spending much time on preaching tours.

> "These men tried to settle the disputes among the Christians or between them and the Hindus. They became very valuable helpers not only to the workers but also to the Christians and the enquirers. Even the Hindus respected them. Their position became rather similar to that of the village headman."[205]

## 5. Station-centered congregations

The establishment of any new Mission must begin at a central point and spread out from there into the villages. In order to form any type of congregation at all for worship, it is natural for the converts to come to that central point for worship, study and inspiration.

The tendency of the Lutheran Churches in the Andhra Desa, however, was to hold on too long to concentrating the life of the church around the station where the missionary lived. Lack of native catechists, evangelists and pastors may have accounted for part of this. The German missionaries were strongly influenced by the system in Europe whereby people from the surrounding countryside came into town to worship in the large parish church. It must be realized as well that the majority of converts were from the outcastes, who had merely transferred their complete dependence and loyalty from the Sudra farmers, who practically owned them, to the missionary. The missionary was the father and his converts the little children who gathered around him for guidance, protection and help -- both spiritual and physical.

This tendency was fostered by every move made by the missionary to free the outcaste convert from the shackles placed on him by the caste people who had controlled his life for so long. In India, for example, there were many holidays but they came on religious festival occasions. Sunday was normally a work day. If

172

the missionary expected his people not to labor on Sunday, then he often found it necessary to supplement the income of the poverty-stricken outcaste in order to make up for the loss of one work day.[206] Serious, too, was the loss of the gifts and privileges which had been the right of generations of Malas and Madigas when they gave up their customary duties at festival occasions. Other work must be provided or gifts doled out by the missionaries. Or if the persecution became too intense in the village community, what simpler situation was there than to have the converts move into the station center and work for the mission?

Both the Guntur and Rajahmundry stations existed for a long time as centers to which all the converts in the surrounding area came for worship. The lack of native Christian workers and the heavy schedule of schools kept the missionaries tied down so that they could not conduct services regularly in outlying villages. When Father Heyer arrived in Rajahmundry twenty-five years after that work had been started by Valett, he called all the Christians in the territory together for the Lord's Supper on Christmas day, 1869. By Easter, however, he began diffusing the work by administering the Lord's Supper also at Muramunda, oldest outlying station and the headquarters of Catechist Paulus.[207]

Quite different was the situation in the Palnad where from the beginning the congregations were village-centered and Heyer went from village to village with his workers to perform the functions of a minister at baptisms, weddings and the Lord's Supper. Occasionally the people gathered for a Christian festival in the center, Gurzala. The local Christian teachers carried on public worship in the schoolhouses on Sundays and looked forward to the periodical visits of the missionary or catechist to bring inspiration and encouragement.[208]

When we turn to the Hermannsburg Mission, Plitt characterizes Harms' view of missions as emphasizing the establishment of a congregation, with missionaries constituting the nucleus, which will develop and grow into a self-supporting church, spreading to others both by word and deed. The idea was for the missionaries to form a Christian family as an oasis in the desert of Hinduism, not only preaching but working to support themselves, and setting a living example to those about them. Thus they were not so much a center from which missionaries would go out into the various villages and form congregations, but rather a center where several missionaries drew people to them and formed a central congregation. Although this idea was successful in Africa, it could not be worked out very satisfactorily in the Indian atmosphere. Adaptations had to be made.[209]

The missionaries did not work to support themselves, but they did establish themselves as the center of a congregation to which all the surrounding Christians were drawn. All the converts in the villages automatically were made members of the congregation

in the mission center and owed their allegiance to it.  Statistical reports up to the first World War listed the members of the
Hermannsburg Mission by these congregational centers.[210]  While
the congregations were small and most of the people lived nearby
in the neighboring palems, the system was fairly effective.  The
missionary kept the congregation together by personal contact.  He
could check when anyone was not at the worship service on Sunday.

But as the members became scattered in more distant villages,
and the missionary became involved in the local school and other
projects, many of the people were not visited more than three or
four times a year by the missionary.  Within ten years it became
apparent that the Christians farthest away were not regular in attendance and could not be properly supervised.  It was determined
to hold services in the more distant places at least once a month
by the missionary or catechist.[211]  In 1878 the members of the
Nayudupeta congregation were scattered in 12 villages.  It took
some two to four hours to walk to the center.  Two services were
held each Sunday and one on Wednesday, plus morning chapel services, but all of these were in the center.[212]  By 1894 Nayudupeta
was divided into several sub-congregations.  Two Sundays the
people were expected to come to the center for worship; the other
Sundays seminary students directed worship services in the particular villages where chapels were built: outstations Ekollu,
Pannur, Kundam and Vojeli.  By 1896 there were 750 Christians in

26 villages. The response to having worship services out of the center every other Sunday was marked with joy and eagerness. Vojeli became almost entirely Christian in 1893.[213]

Another completely Christian village or palem was Mitta near Kalahasti. Because most of the Christians of the Kalahasti congregation lived there, regular worship services were arranged and a little chapel was built in 1880.[214] Woerrlein reported that after thirty years there were ten main stations which had six churches and three chapels where there was worship every Sunday; and in addition, there were several outstations with very simple chapels built for regular worship.[215]

The people in Venkatagiri were so scattered that it almost destroyed the effectiveness of the work altogether, especially when no missionary resided there in 1892; for the workers turned out to be most unreliable without the direct supervision of the missionary.[216] Missionary Schepmann found that there were real problems when it came to baptizing people who were some distance from the center. He wrote in a letter:[217]

> "[One family] wanted at first to learn in their village, which is three hours from here. If they learn in their houses, it is an advantage, because they are not supported by the mission; and they remain in their proper environment. But one doesn't get to know them and one cannot teach them as well in the village. Philip [the catechist] should stay with them every week for three days, and I will visit them sometimes. We both have been there once. When I was there, the house was crowded the whole day with people listening; but afterwards they came to Nayudupet and learned here for three weeks. ... I think it would be better if we could have them learn several hours a day and work the rest of the day;

and so learn for three months. But how can that be done here
in India? If they want to be employed by the heathen, they
have to work the entire day and don't get very much money.
If we want to employ them, as I would like to, there are many
hindrances and the work would not be practical financially.
The people are very ambitious to learn, not only in the six
hours, but among themselves afterwards."

Schepmann found it worked very well to have them come to the miss-

ion center for a concentrated course of three weeks, six hours a

day and three hours on Saturday. They learned eagerly and answer-

ed the questions very well on the day of baptism. Moreover, other

people were strongly influenced by this family in their village;

they were much more valuable than the missionaries or catechists,

who the people felt did their work because they were paid for it.

An experience such as this plus the testimony to surrounding Hin-

dus of a village nearly completely Christian, such as Mitta or

Vojeli, would seem to be enough to persuade the Hermannsburg miss-

ionaries of the value of local, active and worshiping congrega-

tions; but such was not the case. The Breklum Mission tended to-

ward the same position in its early years.

# Chronological Comparison of THE DIFFICULT YEARS
## (CHAPTER IV) of the Andhra Desa Missions

| | Guntur | Rajahmundry | Hermannsburg | Breklum |
|---|---|---|---|---|
| 1865 | Departure of Groenning | | | |
| 1866 | Death of Long, Unangst alone | | | |
| 1867 | Formation of General Council | | | |
| 1869 | For. Missions Board estab. | Heyer saves Rajah. Mission | | |
| 1870 | | Schmidt takes charge | | |
| 1871 | No missionary | Poulsen comes, Heyer retires | | |
| 1872 | Unangst back with Harpster | Attempt to convert Hill tribe | | |
| 1873 | Cully ordained | Death of Heyer | | |
| 1874 | Uhl reopens Eng. school as High school | Schmidt begins Industrial & Land program | | |
| 1877 | New church, 2 Indians ordain. | | | |
| | Famine and relief Work in all Andhra Desa | | | |
| 1878 | | New church, 2 Indians ordain. | 4 Sta. vacant, heavy missionary losses | |
| 1879 | | Conf. organiz. | 5 new miss. | |
| 1880 | 5,432 Chr. in 100 congreg. | 334 Chr. in 20 congreg. | 592 Christians in 9 congreg. | |
| 1887 | | | Mylius' death | |
| 1891 | | | Dir. Harms' visit, Woerrlein new supt. | Mission understaffed, Pohl in Rajahmundry |
| 1892 | | | New Constitution, Council | |
| 1897 | | | | Pohl returns, opens Cat. Sem. |
| 1900 | | | | Bothman moves to East Jeypore |
| 1906 | | | | Leper Home begun |
| 1914 | | | | 934 Christians, 45 Inquirers |

CHAPTER IV

THE DIFFICULT YEARS

(Awaiting the Harvest)

Each one of the Lutheran Missions established in the Andhra Desa experienced periods when the work almost was overwhelmed by the difficulties which arose. Some of these difficulties came from the situations which developed in America and Europe. Others arose out of the conditions the Missions had to meet and overcome in India itself. These problems seemed to reach their climax during what might be considered the middle period of our historical survey, between 1860 and 1914.

A. The Effect of the American and European
Situations on the Lutheran Missions

### 1. The Guntur-Rajahmundry fields

We have already noted the effect the Home situation had on the development of the Missions as they began their work.[1] The decade previous to the Civil War appeared most hopeful in the Guntur and Rajahmundry fields when the Ministerium of Pennsylvania returned to the General Synod in 1853 after thirty years;[2] and a number of reinforcements were sent out by the fast growing Synod[3] to strengthen the work in India. Sickness and death in India and the Civil War in America changed the picture completely.[4]

179

The Rev. William Snyder had brought two new families with him on his return to India late in 1858, the Rev. and Mrs. Adam Long and the Rev. and Mrs. Erias Unangst. Groenning took a much-needed furlough after twelve years. With Heyer's departure in 1857, Heise became the missionary supported by the Ministerium of Pennsylvania. Long opened a new mission station east of Rajahmundry at Samalkot, headquarters for the 28th regiment of English soldiers. Snyder took charge of Guntur and Unangst worked with him, covering the Palnad from Guntur. Income from America was gratifying[5] and the work was developing smoothly when Snyder was stricken suddenly with cholera and died March 5, 1859. The Civil War cut off much financial help from America and sidetracked the growing missionary interest of the churches. Heise was forced to resign and return to Germany because of ill health in March, 1862.

It was at this juncture that Groenning, realizing that reinforcements would not be coming from America for years, made an effort to obtain help from Germany and thus brought Mylius to India. We have already seen how misunderstandings and suspicions, both on his part and the General Synod, turned him away from the Rajahmundry field to begin new work for the Hermannsburg Missionary Society.[6]

The suspicions which Mylius and the Hermannsburg Missionary Society had concerning the laxness in Lutheran doctrine of the

General Synod also were held by many Lutheran groups, both inside and outside the Synod. A struggle had been developing between what was known as "American" Lutheranism and conservative Lutheranism. The Synod or Ministerium of Pennsylvania had entered the General Synod in 1853 with the understanding that it was simply[7]

> " an association of Evangelical Lutheran Synods, entertaining the same views of the fundamental doctrines of the gospel, as these are expressed in the confessional writings of our Evangelical Lutheran Church, and especially in the Unaltered Augsburg Confession, and that we advert to the fact that the General Synod is denied the right by its Constitution of making any innovations or alterations of this faith."

Two years later, however, there appeared anonymously a publication entitled The American Recension of the Augsburg Confession, known more popularly as The Definite Synodical Platform. It was an open secret that this had been prepared by three of the leaders in the General Synod, The Rev. Drs. S. S. Schmucker, S. Sprecher and B. Kurtz. Schmucker considered it to be, in his words:[8]

> "a faithful and definite exhibition of the import of the generic doctrinal pledge of the General Synod. The pledge includes, in connection with absolute assent to the Word of God, as the only infallible rule of faith and practice, the belief 'that the fundamental doctrines of Scripture are taught in a manner substantially correct in the doctrinal articles of the Augsburg Confessions;' and the Platform is an unaltered copy of these articles of that confession, only omitting those parts which we know by long acquaintance with American Lutherans to be generally regarded by them not only as non-fundamental, but erroneous."

The proponents of this "American Lutheranism" were not in the majority by any means, but the leaders held strong positions in the General Synod and their voices were loud. Wentz points out that they were alarmed at the growing confessional reaction which was permeating the Lutheran Church. They believed it would hurt its spirituality and aggressiveness: and so they determined to oppose it vigorously.

> "To that end they proposed a modification of **historic** Lutheranism, its confessions and its practices, so as to infuse into it the vigor of Presbyterianism and the warmth of Methodism. In short, they sought to adapt Lutheranism to American soil by divesting it of its distinctive traits and making it conform to the average American type of religion."[9]

The differences between the two parties in the General Synod came to a head at the convention in 1859 when the Melanchthon Synod, formed two years before by certain 'liberal' churches in Maryland with a Declaration of Faith almost identical to the articles of the Evangelical Alliance,[10] sought entrance into the General Synod. After much protest, the Synod was admitted with the understanding that it would remove from its Declaration any implied charges against the Augsburg Confession. The next year a large number of Scandinavian churches left the Synod of Northern Illinois to form the Augustana Synod.[11]

The Civil War brought about a further separation when five southern Synods left the General Synod in 1863 to form the General Synod of the Evangelical Lutheran Church in the Confederate States of America. It is likely they would have returned to the General Synod after the War if it had remained united.[12]

When in 1864 the Franckean Synod, formed in 1837 in definite

opposition to parts of the Augsburg Confession and with its own

Declaration of faith,[13] asked for admission to the General Synod

on the same basis as the Melanchthon Synod, the conservative party

found it had a real problem on its hands if it did not stand firm-

ly in opposition to such admissions.  The majority voted to ac-

cept the Franckean Synod on the word of its delegates that they

understood acceptance of the Constitution of the General Synod also

meant that they had accepted its confession of faith; and that at

its next convention it would adopt the Augsburg Confession as its

doctrinal basis.  The conservatives contended that it made the

confessional position of the general body extremely insecure to

permit a group to enter before it had formally accepted the Augs-

burg Confession.  It violated the terms of the constitution which

permitted the admittance only of Lutheran synods that had accepted

the fundamental doctrines of the Bible as taught by the Lutheran

Church, in the Augsburg Confession.  The Ministerium of Pennsyl-

vania withdrew its delegates with the claim that the terms of its

affiliation in 1853 to the General Synod had been broken.[14]

In spite of the fact that the General Synod adopted in this

same convention at York in 1864 a firm conservative statement of

doctrinal standard,[15] the rift could not be repaired.  A definite

break came at the 1866 convention at Fort Wayne, Indiana; and at

the same place the next year the General Council came into exist-

ence. The losses of the General Synod between 1860 and 1870 were
tremendous. Two-thirds of the Lutherans in America belonged to
the General Synod in 1860; a decade later only one-fourth.[16] Not
until 1918 could the damage be repaired and the Synods brought
back together.

This tragic disunity, plus the Civil War, brought about a
period of disinterest in the work of foreign missions which was
almost fatal. The men that the General Synod were sure they
could get, when they turned down Mylius, did not come forward.
The lack of funds created real problems for the missionaries who
were on the field. Salaries arrived so late that they had to
borrow at exhorbitant rates of interest. At one time they owed
$3,000. With the loss of income both from America and from local
English officials, all the schools were closed for a time. This
was especially true in Guntur after Stokes' departure for England
in 1856. Judge J. H. Morris and Captain C. Taylor kept things
going in Rajahmundry by giving as much as Rs. 60 a month. The
mission lost its rights to run the only government English schools
in certain localities through lack of funds and found it impossible to compete with the ones which were set up by the government.
Instead, the missionaries were forced to hire cheap teachers with
limited qualifications.[17] Exchange of moneys was against the Foreign Missionary Society; it was pointed out in 1864 that a mission
budget of $6,000 in India would really cost $10,000. And the

gifts coming in did not make up for the difference, much less allow for any expansion of the work.[18]

Fortunately, Groenning on his own initiative made a special
effort to get local support for the mission.  In 1862 he was able
to pay toward a colporteur, teachers, boarding children and day
scholars, in addition to Rs. 200 for Mr. Cully in the Palnad, out
of a total of Rs. 677 received.  The next year Rs. 1436 provided
for the expansion of the work.[19]

Still further trouble hit the mission when Groenning, his
wife and their two younger sons were seriously ill during the hot
season of 1865.  One of the children died and physicians ordered
the family to return to Germany.  The Executive Committee in America was willing to grant him a furlough but was unable to forward
the money needed to travel.  Friends in India and Denmark, who
had helped for two and a half years to support Mr. Cully as a
teacher and catechist in the Palnad, came through in his need and
he was able to leave September, 1865.  Long, who had been working
at Samalkot, took his place in Rajahmundry.  He had hardly entered into the work when he died March 5, 1866, a victim of smallpox
contracted from a little boy whom he nursed.  Of his three children, also ill at the same time, two died and were buried with him
in the mission cemetery.

"One missionary was left, Unangst, at Guntur.  He continued
his residence there and undertook to supervise the whole
Mission.  Cully was the catechist for the Palnad.  Joseph and

Paulus were appointed catechists for the Rajahmundry work,
Joseph residing at Rajahmundry and Paulus at Muramunda.
Judge Morris and Captain Taylor agreed to look after the
school work in Rajahmundry."[20]

News in America of the death of Long brought resolutions from the

Foreign Missionary Society inviting the entire Lutheran Church to

unite in "the great and blessed work of Foreign Missions" and this

in spite of the divisions occurring; and that the "Executive Com-

mittee be authorized to seek out and employ an efficient Financial

Secretary, whose whole time shall be given to the financial depart-

ment of the Mission work, and the management of the Mission Jour-

nal, if such a publication be established."[21]

The breakup of the General Synod brought loss of income to the

Society when the synods associated with the General Council with-

drew their support; and the groups remaining in the General Synod

lost interest or turned their attention to the new mission in Af-

rica, started as an independent project but later placed under

the control of the Society. After a concerted appeal, a few appli-

cations to become missionaries were made but they had to be turned

down for various reasons.

So the Corresponding Secretary contacted Groenning in Ger-

many, but he declined. However, he did agree to take two young

men into his home to prepare them in Telugu and give them an ac-

quaintance with customs and religions of India. He was to re-

ceive financial assistance. Later, however, when it became ap-

186

parent that "every Synod, in which the Germanic influence largely predominated" had joined the General Council, the Committee
found it necessary to inform Groenning "of its unwillingness for
the present, to employ these men, and the uncertainty that hung
over their employment in the future." Rather than leave everything in an unsettled state, the Executive Committee suggested
offering the Rajahmundry or Samalkot Mission to the Synod of Pennsylvania. "Thus these stations would be saved, and our foreign
mission work carried on more effectively."[22]

A letter from the Rev. Mr. Unangst dated Guntur, December 5,
1868, helps us to understand the terrible effects the situation
in America was having on the mission:[23]

"To the Evangelical Lutheran Churches in the United States.
  Dear Friends: I regret very much that we are obliged to
inform you, that we and our Mission are in want and distress.
The last letter from our corresponding secretary gives a
rather gloomy picture of the condition of the foreign mission enterprise in our Church, so that we have little or no
hope of a reinforcement of missionaries at present. Our
treasurer's last letter is dated May 4, 1868. By this letter we got only $1,000 for us and our Mission. Since that
time we have received nothing, and yet we have had to live
and meet all the pecuniary demands of the Mission. Ten
teachers and a catechist in the Guntur district, Mr. Cully
and eight teachers in the Palnad district, a catechist, a
colporteur and five teachers in Rajahmundry and Samulkot,
had all to be paid their salaries. Incidental expenses and
our own living had also to be met. In order to do all this
we have been obliged to borrow upward of $1000 (Rs. 2000)
from native merchants. The interest on this amount is $15
a month. ... I do not know what you would do under similar
circumstances. Perhaps you would resign, attach the mission property, clear your debts, secure your own lawful share
and retire. If not, then do you wish us to go on and manage the Mission and conduct its various operations by means

of borrowed capital? We can hardly believe that you have such a wish, nor can we think that your hearts are so callous as to be insensible to the loud appeals of humanity and the cause of Christ. We, therefore, appeal to you for relief. Some new missionaries are wanted in our Mission, with several thousand dollars, or else you must give up the work to those who would be willing and ready to furnish both missionaries and money for this field. Our good work here is increasing on our hands, and we feel powerless to take hold of it and carry it on vigorously. Only recently news came from five villages where there are new inquirers. All we can do is to invite the people to come to Guntur. How can we incur additional expense for travelling and go to see these and other places in our mission field, unless you promptly relieve us and pay the Mission's debt which, by the time you see and read this appeal, will have increased to $1500. ..."

Statistics for 1867, at the end of 25 years, were not very impressive for they revealed how slow the work had been; but they did bear out Unangst's contention that much could be done with adequate missionaries and financial support. A total of 1099 members had been received since 1842 and the present membership was 633. The candidates for baptism were an impressive total of nearly 375.[24]

Realizing that the work was too much for one man to supervise and that the Plymouth Brethren were enticing teachers and members away in the Rajahmundry-Samalkot districts without a resident missionary,[25] Unangst consulted with English residents and missionaries of the Church Missionary Society as to the possibility of transferring the work to the C. M. S. With no immediate response from the Ministerium, the Executive Committee had the same thought and suggested such a move even before receiving a

188

letter from Unangst in regard to his suggestion. Authority was

given by the Synod to act as it saw fit. When the Church Mission-

ary Society at Madras was informed that the Foreign Mission

Board[26] had resolved to make the transfer, they authorized the

Rev. Mr. Alexander to take charge and start paying the workers as

of May 1, 1869.

> "While negotiations were pending between The Foreign Mission-
> ary Society of the General Synod and The Church Missionary
> Society of England..., Dr. Heyer was living temporarily at
> Helmstedt, Germany, whither he had gone with a granddaughter
> to direct her education. When he heard of the proposed
> transaction, he hastened, in April, 1869, to Apenrade, to
> confer with Groenning and, if possible, to prevent the trans-
> fer. Apart from the keen personal interest which these
> pioneers took in the Rajahmundry Mission, they were unwilling
> that the condition should be violated on which The North
> German Missionary Society had transferred it, in 1850, to
> The Foreign Missionary Society, namely, that it should re-
> main a Lutheran Mission."[27]

When Heyer found two young men, Hans Christian Schmidt and

Christian Friedrich J. Becker, studying under Groenning in prepar-

ation for service in India, he took it upon himself to take them

with him to America and offer their services to the Ministerium

of Pennsylvania with the hope that the Synod would be willing to

take over responsibility of the Rajahmundry Mission. Only Schmidt

could go immediately. They arrived in America in time for the

annual meeting of the Ministerium at Reading, Pa., May 23, 1869.

Heyer made an impassioned and dramatic plea which stirred the

audience profoundly. After having introduced Schmidt, he brought

his speech to a close by holding up his suitcase , and declaring

189

that he too "was ready to go at a moment's notice, if the synod wished it, even though he was seventy-seven years old and it would be his third journey to India, in order that he might direct his younger brethren in the reorganization of the mission work."[28]

The Foreign Mission Board of the General Synod was contacted immediately, the transfer of the Mission to the C. M. S. was stopped, and the field was formally accepted by the Executive Committee of the Ministerium on August 27, 1869. Four days later Heyer was on his way to India. In November the General Council approved the action of the Ministerium and accepted the custody and control of the Rajahmundry Mission. The executive committee of the Ministerium was elected to be its committee on foreign missions. An appeal went out for funds.

Arriving in Rajahmundry December 1, 1869, Father Heyer found the Mission in a weak state, but with some encouraging signs. There were about 135 Christians, a total of 73 children in the mission schools and 49 in attendance at the first administration of the Lord's Supper on Christmas Day. Becker arrived in February, 1870, but died after a brief illness on May 8, 1870. Heyer applied himself diligently and made some extended tours throughout the area with the two catechists, Paulus and Joseph. The schools were reorganized. He started to translate the new General Council Church book into Telugu.[29] When Schmidt arrived on August 4,

Heyer introduced him to the work by visiting the principal out-stations and giving him a clear insight into the work which would soon be placed in his hands. The boundless energy of Heyer showed in his end-of-the-year report which told of 102 baptisms during the year and the establishment of five new schools. On Christmas Day, 1870, seventy individuals communed in Rajahmundry; and over 200 gathered to celebrate Christmas at an elaborate dinner of rice and curry served at the expense of Judge Morris. Captain Taylor presented gifts of clothing, books and fruit.[30]

Following the arrival January 22, 1871, of the Rev. Iver K. Poulsen from Denmark to assist Schmidt and Poulsen's ordination January 26, Heyer felt he had completed his task and left for America on the 30th. The last year of his life he served as chaplain and house-father at the Lutheran Theological Seminary at Philadelphia, dying on November 7, 1873, at the age of eighty years, three months and twenty days. This amazing man with the boundless energy has often been accused of doing very superficial work and baptizing too many to be considered a great missionary. It is true that his restlessness kept him on the move too much for concentrated work; but as was true of Heyer throughout his life, whether in America or in India, he was principally a pioneer who laid foundations for others to build on. Whatever he set himself to do, he did quickly and effectively, not sparing himself at all. He saw the tremendous work which needed to be done and did all he could of it.  His fault lay in that "he could lay more foundations

than the Church was ready to build upon ... it seems there were

few to take up the work when he had to lay it down."[31]  In speak-

ing of Heyer, Schmidt stated:[32]

> "He was a peculiar man, but he was a good missionary, and
> his memory will remain blessed.  He was a pioneer, and show-
> ed to many the way to Jesus, even if he was neither writer
> of books and keeper of accounts.  The mission bureaucracy of
> our days, with its infinite exactness and rules for mission
> work, has hardly converted as many heathens."

With the revival of the work and the coming of missionary re-

cruits to the Rajahmundry field under the auspices of the General

Council, a new day for the mission was expected.  But the two in-

experienced men did little more than hold the field until more

men arrived eight years later in 1879.  There was much illness be-

tween 1875 and 1878.  The Church at home still failed to furnish

sufficient funds to take advantage of opportunities as they arose.

One interesting development was the effort by Schmidt to

reach the hill-tribes of Kois and Reddis north and northwest of

Rajahmundry.  The people fled in fear to the jungle when he first

approached the villages, for they had never seen a white man; but

when the native workers were able to assure them of their peaceful

intentions, Schmidt found that they received the Gospel eagerly.

They said to him, "We live like wild beasts, separated from men.

No one has cared for us or taught us the truth; but now we will no

longer pray to stones, but to the Living God."  Others said, "We

are too ignorant to be able to believe in Jesus."[33]  The Christ-

192

ians in Rajahmundry heard the results of this difficult journey into the hills with great interest, and four teachers offered their
services.  But it was not easy country to live in; all contracted
jungle fever, one died, another lost his reason and the others refused to stay.  Another attempt was made in 1874 when three other
teachers went to the hill country.  Two returned within a month,
the third a month later, all sick with hill fever.  Schmidt then
made an effort to bring boys from the hills and train them for
use among their own people; but the parents objected strenuously
to having their sons sent so far away, as if to another world.

In 1876, the Rev. C. W. Groenning made a special visit to the
United States for the express purpose of urging the General Council to support its work in India more liberally.  He had been receiving reports from Schmidt and Poulsen that only about $500 more
than the missionaries' salaries was being sent to carry on the
work.  For some years the expenses were greater than the receipts
and the missionaries went into debt.  Rather than pay exhorbitant
amounts of interest to local moneylenders, Schmidt tried to make
up the difference by selling photographs, and repairing watches,
sewing machines and other mechanical devices.  As a result of
Groenning's visit, $2,000 was sent out in 1877 instead of the us-
ual $500.  A special committee for Foreign Missions was appointed
to relieve the over-worked Executive Committee of the Ministerium, which was so involved in home missions and educational inter-

ests; and a real effort was made to spread the news of the work to the congregations through church publications. In January, 1878, a new paper, Der Missionsbote, was started under the editorship of the Rev. F. Wischan and by the end of the year had 8,000 subscriptions.

In the Guntur field, illness of his wife and physical exhaustion on his part made it necessary for the Rev. Erias Unangst, who had stood alone in the Guntur field for nine years and had been in India for thirteen, to leave for America in March, 1871. For a year the field had no missionary and sole responsibility was in the hands of Mr. R. E. Cully who had been serving as superintendent of schools and Evangelist in the Palnad since 1862.[34] Unangst came home with encouraging news and urged immediate reinforcement of the work with at least three missionary families. Whole communities were showing interest in the Gospel, he reported, with more than 400 members added to the Church in the past year and more than a thousand candidates receiving instruction toward baptism. Four new outstations had been added. The schools were flourishing. Three men were being prepared as pastors to take over parts of the work.[35]

The change on May 20, 1869, from a Foreign Missionary Society to a Board of Foreign Missions directly responsible to the General Synod began to have noticeable results in increased interest and contributions. Unangst' short furlough of nine months in

America was filled with visits to congregations, Synods and Seminaries. The Rev. J. H. Harpster was ordained December 20, 1871, and returned with Unangst to India in January. The Rev. L. L. Uhl left for India December 7, 1872, and four other students showed their interest by becoming missionary candidates. Deeply impressed by Uhl's farewell meeting in Harrisburg, A. D. Rowe, a student at Gettysburg Seminary, determined to go to India even though there were no funds available.

> "He conceived the idea of raising the needed funds through the children of the church. The plan met with approval. The 'Children's Foreign Missionary Society' was formed and from that time his support was assured. He organized within the space of a year, 315 societies, having 21,000 members, and collected almost $6,000 for the cause." [36]

He arrived in India in December, 1874.

Receipts from the congregations of the General Synod increased from $5,890.31 in the 1868-69 biennium to $13,640.70 in 1870-71 and $28,014.13 in 1872-73.[37] The panic of 1873 stopped progress for a few years, but did not decrease the giving. This financial support meant increased activity in India where the first pastor was ordained October 5, 1873, the Rev. R. E. Cully, and two more ordained January 7, 1877, at the time a new church was dedicated in Guntur. Funds for this church were raised through a special appeal. Although not completely successful, the Rev. Dr. and Mrs. Stork completed the fund and the church became known as Stork Memorial.

The Anglo-vernacular school started by Heyer in 1842 had been closed in 1863 because of financial difficulties and the loss of support from English residents. Missionary Uhl reorganized the school and reopened it in 1874. He acted as principal, assisted by Christian teachers. Outcaste and caste sat side by side, although the caste students left the school in great indignation for the first few days. The Board showed some concern when the promised help from the government was slow in coming and decided that the English department of the school should be closed and Uhl sent to the Palnad where he would be more useful. The General Synod approved this action; but the missionaries protested very strongly, claiming that the future success of the Mission depended largely on this high school as organized. When the government aid of $18.75 per month started coming, the Board permitted the continuance of the English department of the school. There were 127 students the year after it was opened.

The first Sunday School in the Guntur field was organized in 1875 and set the pace for Christian work in four directions:[38]

"It increased the benevolent spirit of the Christians; it helped in a notably larger way to support the church; it began collections of contributions for the Madras Bible Society and for the Madras Tract and Book Society; it started the support of a native worker in non-Christian hamlets and villages."

The size of the Church began to increase perceptibly year by year. Membership increased from 1452 in 1870 to 4712 in 1879, a total of 1227 being baptized in 1878 alone.[39] Harpster baptized 1300

adults and children during his four years of residence at Dachepalle, Palnad, between 1872 and 1876. Efforts were made to reach
the higher castes, not only through the high school, but also by
the establishment in 1879 of a Bible, Tract and Book Depot in a
main street of Guntur. A reading and lecture room was fixed up
in connection with it and regular meetings -- which were well attended -- were conducted for educated people.

## 2. The Hermannsburg field

The effect of the situation in Europe on the Hermannsburg
Mission was quite different from that of America on the Rajahmundry and Guntur Missions. In the case of Hermannsburg, the problems arose out of the missionary policies of the Harms brothers.
Louis Harms' intention was to send missionaries to foreign lands
who not only would preach but also support themselves. He did not
attempt to select highly-educated men for the work, but rather accepted volunteers from his parish, many of them farmers, who had
the zeal and enthusiasm for devoted service. Since university-
trained men were most difficult to obtain for mission work, and
partially educated men were neither profound nor of much value,
Harms felt it would be better to take young people and educate
them thoroughly in the Scriptures, the confessions of the Church
and those subjects which served the understanding of the Scriptures. The only foreign language necessary, felt Theodore Harms,
Louis' brother and successor in 1865, was English, as a missionary could not get along without it in India.

Although Louis Harms could carry through his policies in
Africa and establish colonies of missionaries who supported themselves to a large extent and formed the nucleus of a congregation, these ideas did not succeed in India.  However, he and
Theodore Harms did insist, through the leadership of the Mission
superintendent Mylius, that the missionaries live in the utmost
simplicity and economy.  Mud houses were built at first, similar
to native houses.  The missionaries ate the native food, sometimes dressed like them, and in every way possible tried to keep
the cost of living down to a minimum.  This was detrimental to
the health and welfare of the missionaries and cut down their efficiency.  Living under such conditions and not permitted to take
rest periods away from the heat and fever, because of the cost,
the missionaries had a heavy toll of sickness and death.[40]  It was
not until 1891 that an attempt was made to correct this situation.
An appeal went out to the Hermannsburg Society for funds to provide missionary rest homes in the mountains and to rebuild better
houses in the plains, the houses to have thick stone walls, tile
roofs, high ceilings, second floors, verandas, and screens or mosquito netting for the beds.[41]  In order to obtain a better diet,
the missionaries were urged to plant their own gardens and irri-
gate them from wells provided them.  Hartwig Harms speaks in his
Autobiography of the exhilarating experience of his first vaca-
tion in the mountains; he was privileged to be one of the first to

go. This family had lost two children previously, but they had little real sickness after that.[42] From this time on, tents were provided for the missionary tours which, with mosquito netting for the cots, helped immensely in preventing fever, sore eyes and other common village diseases.

Much of this was an expense which could have been prevented by the output of some extra funds in the early years of the Mission. As it was, missionary homes had to be built twice. And the loss of work and manpower through sickness and death never could be fully estimated.

Another problem which caused untold headaches and tragedy was the complete authority given the superintendent of the Mission, August Mylius. From one point of view, because of their lack of university education, it was felt necessary that Mylius must have complete supervision over the missionaries to see that they continued their studies, did not make any unwise decisions in their work and did not go foolishly beyond the financial means of the mission in any new project. The constitution drawn up in 1868 at the first convention was based on the Church Order authorized by Director Harms. It provided that the superintendent guide the whole mission, especially the maintenance of the Church Order insofar as the conditions of the land and people did not make changes necessary.

199

The superintendent kept in touch with each missionary and station through annual synods, annual reports of the missionaries, annual visitations of each station, bimonthly conferences of all the missionaries, regular exchange of letters and extraordinary visits to the stations if special conditions arose, or if Mylius decided to do it. He represented the mission in all outside contacts and in all personal and legal negotiations with English and Hindu officials. He decided where new stations were to be established, distributed the missionaries among them, and decided when they could take vacations. Any leave of absence for more than eight days or over a Sunday had to be reported and permission granted. He could suspend missionaries if they failed to fulfill their ministry, although final dismissal could be made only by Director Harms. He checked the employment, salaries, and dismissal of native catechists and school teachers. He kept very close supervision over the education and catechetical training of students. He was responsible for all mission property. No missionary was permitted to print anything without the knowledge and permission of the superintendent.[43]

Schaefer points out that such absolute power had its good points in maintaining the unity of the mission and preventing the usual tendency of missionaries to become independent and dictatorial over their own domain. "It was good in that it assured unity of action and policy and an administrative set-up which provided

prompt action. It fell down, on the other hand, in that it concentrated too much power in one man."[44] This was especially true
when Mylius permitted his personal feelings to enter into his
dealings with the men. Just in the short period of a little more
than a year occurred the following events.

Leopold Wahl, who was a teacher in the Nayudupeta school because of his grasp of Telugu, was never very well and could not do
much touring of the villages. Mylius felt that anyone who was
consecrated to the cause would be willing to preach and visit.
Moreover, when Wahl asked to be married, Mylius would not ask the
Home Board to send out a woman for him, as was the custom in the
Mission.[45] Hot words followed and Mylius transferred Wahl to Venkatagiri and took over the school himself. Later, without Mylius'
permission, Wahl married a girl who had been a maid for children
of Leipzig missionaries. Mylius felt that this was a dishonor to
the office of the ministry. Later on, when the entire family was
sick with malaria and the two children dying, Mylius permitted
them to go to Madras. This did not improve matters. Because his
relatives had moved to America, Wahl requested permission to go
there instead of Germany. This Director Harms refused to do.
Some English missionaries found them very sick in a dirty tenement
in Madras and immediately started a collection to help the Wahls
get to America. The German missionaries were very upset by this
bad publicity. Too late Mylius realized the disgrace he had

brought the Mission and had an equivalent amount of money given to the English friends who had helped Wahl. With it was established a fund to care for any future happenings of like nature.

Moritz Otto served at Sriharikota where he got swollen legs which some diagnosed as elephantiasis, common in that area. He was moved to Vakadu but was still expected to tour Sriharikota, which he feared to do. He had already refused to move to Tirupati on a previous occasion because of its unhealthy location. Mylius had little sympathy for him and discord continued between the two men until Otto, having lost a wife and child, lost courage and left for America in 1878.[46] In the same year missionary Kiehne returned to Germany with a near breakdown after the loss of two wives and two children in the short period of eighteen months; and Boettcher died in June, 1879, after a long illness which was not properly cared for. Hartwig Harms states in his history that both Wahl and Boettcher were great men and that their health should have been taken care of. They could have served the mission for many more years.[47]

Another incident was the discord between Mylius and Heinrich Brunotte. One of the first missionaries, coming in 1866 with Dahl and Th. Petersen, he had worked hard and faithfully in spite of tragedy. He had lost a wife and two children. When Director Harms appointed Th. Petersen to be assistant provost under Mylius, to assist him in his later years, Brunotte took the action

as a personal affront. The rest of the missionaries had felt
with Brunotte that he was the logical choice, as Petersen was often sick and was not a person who could carry authority. But
they had not been consulted. Mylius may have felt that Petersen
would be better to work with, as Brunotte was of a somewhat taci-
turn and stubborn nature.

Brunotte refused to acknowledge the authority of Petersen.
In fact, he fasted in his home for three days in protest and would
not let Petersen in when he came to make peace with him. In an
effort to solve the problem, a number of missionaries wrote to
Mylius. But he would not listen to their suggestions. Brunotte
found it impossible to work under Petersen and left to enter the
Leipzig Mission in August of 1878. Woerrlein considered him an
efficient missionary, respected by the Hindus, loved by his congregation, and admired by his co-workers. He believed that if
Mylius had had a Council of missionaries working with him to advise and recommend that the many troubles which hit the Mission
in just little more than a year would not have happened.[48]
Hartwig Harms spoke of this period as a tragic year, a time of
crisis, much of which was caused by the too-personal atmosphere
of the all-powerful director. As a result the missionaries urged
that Director Harms give Mylius an advisory Council to assist him,
to be chosen by Mylius. This kept the control in his hands, but
permitted some of the missionaries to help him reach his decisions.[49]

These losses in 1878 and 1879 left the Mission depleted,
with four of the nine stations vacant. Five men hurriedly were
sent out at the close of 1879. Because of the trouble Director
Theodore Harms was having in Germany with the Landeskirche,[50]
these men had not been ordained. Mylius also was concerned that
the new financial difficulties in Germany, with the loss of offerings from the State Church in Hanover, would not provide
enough money to care for such a large number of recruits. Woerrlein assured him that the Lord would provide if the men came.
At a conference and mission festival in Nayudupeta, June 23-24,
1880, the five men were examined by Mylius and Petersen, and ordained. Although the ordination was not recognized by the state
church, it held good for all foreign missions and in all the German free churches.[51]

### 3. The Breklum field

In the Schleswig-Holstein Mission, the disturbing factor for
real progress in the Telugu area, as has been mentioned before,[52]
was the fact that the directors were primarily interested in making an entrance into the forbidden Bastar State through these
stations. Language complications made it impossible to provide
very many missionaries for the Telugu area when the work was ad-
vancing so quickly in the Oriya language area of Jeypore. From
1899, 15 years after the work began, when there were 687 Christians in both language areas, progress is shown by the statistics
five years later of 5285 Christians. Five years after that there

were 10, 239; and on April 1, 1914 there were 16,550, and 7,471
catechetical or preparatory students in addition.  Of this last
figure, however, only 934 baptized and 45 catechetical students
could be claimed by the Telugu area of Salur and Parvatipur.[53]
If the Telugu area had produced some early results, it is likely
that greater effort would have been made there.  The mass movement in Jeypore, when it came, taxed the powers of the Schleswig-
Holstein Mission and all available missionaries.  The Mission cannot be judged for following the direction which produced the
greatest results.

It is amazing, in the face of events, that the work was maintained at all in the two stations of Salur and Parvatipur.  Pohl
and Bothmann, the founders of the mission, were used elsewhere at
times.  We have mentioned that Pohl stayed in Rajahmundry with
the permission of the Breklum Society to take the place of Wilhelm
Groenning, when he died suddenly in 1889,[54] and took charge of the
educational program.  This was to be for one year, but he remained
until August, 1897, and even then the Rajahmundry Mission was very
reluctant to give him up.  With his previous experience at Salur,
he had proved to be a very effective missionary and a stabilizing
force for the new men.  "In its report to the General Council in
1897 the Board bore him the following testimony:

> 'His seven years of labor before he came to our Mission gave
> him an experience that made him a valuable and efficient
> missionary, and his fidelity to his calling and his Lord

secured for his labors a blessing from God that none could fail to recognize.'"55

It was not until after Pohl's return that the Schleswig-Holstein Mission could find a man to take charge of a long-planned seminary for catechists. And it was more than twenty years before one of the older, experienced catechists was ordained as the first pastor.

Bothmann, on his part, was called away from Parvatipur station to begin new work in 1900 in the eastern part of Jeypore. Since much Telugu was spoken in this area around Gunupur, it was not until 1907 that Bothmann decided that his age and his inability to master Oriya made it a wiser step for some other man to take up the work there and for him to return to Parvatipur. He had worked faithfully at Gunupur and was helped immensely by an evangelist, Ch. Jesudas, the son of a non-Brahman priest of the Site-Rama temple there. Jesudas had assisted his father in the temple for several years.

> "A Christian bhajan which he heard made him desirous to learn more about Christianity. ... He walked and begged his way ... to the South, and reached Rajahmundry. Here he met Dr. H. C. Schmidt, who, after proper instruction, baptized him. In 1903 he returned to Gunupur with his wife and became an evangelist. He knew Telugu and Oriya, and later on acquired also Savara, into which language he translated the Ten Commandments, the Apostles' Creed and the Lord's Prayer. For many years he served the mission faithfully."56

Some of the effort of the Telugu missionaries also was side-tracked to work among the Kuvi Khonds, hill people who lived between the Telugu and Oriya areas.

> "[Rev. P. Schulze] started work among the Kuvi Khonds. He
> learned their language, translated Bible stories and the
> Gospel of St. Luke into Kuvi written in Telugu characters
> and did much for the uplift of this backward tribe. Pniel
> became a Khond station on the 4000 feet high hill range
> near Salur. In 1911 the first church was dedicated for the
> service of the Khonds. There were about 500 Christians
> from among this tribe. Even a small seminary was started
> to train some of them for work among their fellow-tribes-
> men."[57]

Sambari was founded as a station for work among these people.

The Rev. J. Staecker was in charge, assisted by his wife, who was

the daughter of Dr. H. C. Schmidt of Rajahmundry. In the later

years of his life, Schmidt helped them also.

Before the first World War eight missionaries, three of them

single women, had worked in the Salur-Parvatipur area over a per-

iod of thirty years. Less than a thousand persons had become

Christian. Tragedy struck here and in the Hermannsburg field with

the beginning of the War. At first it was thought that the mis-

sionaries would be permitted to continue working in their stations

with certain restrictions as to travel. Those of army age were

imprisoned and the police gave close supervision over the others.

The missionaries assured the Governor of Madras that the natives

would remain loyal to India and were instructed as to their duty

to king and government. The government continued to support the

schools, realizing their importance. The governor permitted the

German missions to form a committee to collect money from America,

since funds had been cut off from Germany.

Unfortunately, however, the press began attacking the missionaries and also the Governor and the chief secretary of the government for their interest and helpfulness toward the German mission work.[58] Although the missionaries had promised to do nothing against England and the allies in order to continue in the work, public opinion finally forced the government to intern them. Haccius reports that at first Nikolaus Wittmann was permitted to stay in Kodur and Johann Maneke at Puttur.[59] Winfried Wickert was released from prison after a short time to direct the high school with the condition that he would not leave Tirupati. However, they all had to leave finally and were sent back to Germany, the last leaving by March, 1916.[60]

Only Carl Scriba, son of one of the earliest missionaries in the Hermannsburg Mission and born in India, could stay as he was considered a British citizen. He had been working in Gudur and taking charge of all the Hermannsburg field; but he was required to move to Kodur and work only in the area which had been supported by the Ohio Synod. The Hermannsburg field was taken over by the government and responsibility given to a committee consisting of representatives from various surrounding missions. Its main concern was supervision of the school work. Because the Hermannsburg missionaries had always done most of the work of preaching and leading the worship, it can be seen that the work was seriously affected by the War and the removal of the missionaries.

B. Social Pressure and the Opposition of Hindu Religious Leaders

1. The Common People

The progress of the missionary work was made difficult, not only by problems in the Church in America and Europe, but also by the tremendous social pressure which could be exerted by the relatives of those who were considering baptism, or by the leaders in the village community. We have mentioned already some of these problems in connection with the missionary's attitude toward caste and social customs.[61]

As the missionary toured the villages and was often gladly received and willingly heard, his enthusiasm would rise to great heights with the feeling that he was accomplishing something. It became quite apparent that many of the people actually feared and hated their idols and gods and goddesses and would have wished to give them up. But they did not dare for fear of the ridicule and censure of relatives and neighbors. Charms and religious symbols handed down from parents were worn with almost holy reverence. To remove them would bring the curse of their parents and relatives upon them.[62]

Over and over again the missionaries would be assured by one of the villagers privately that "there were one hundred men in the town, whom he knew, who were like Nicodemus, afraid of their friends, afraid of being put out of caste, but who were Christ's at heart."[63]

For the majority of the village people, religion was bound up with their daily life. If everything was going well, material progress satisfactory and the family was blessed with sons, then it was quite apparent that the gods approved. If times were hard, and things were going against them, then it was just as apparent that the gods were angered and must be appeased by special gifts, sacrifices and the customary ceremonials. The Brahman priests fostered this attitude.

Mrs. Albrecht reported one experience where the priests aroused the people (non-Christian) to action by telling them "that the goddess Mutyalamma was angry because since the missionaries came, they had neglected her temple; if her anger were appeased, she would send rain."[64] So a feast was declared in which everyone had to take part or contribute. The village officials assured Albrecht they would have nothing to do with it, and that it was the farmers who wanted the feast. Albrecht made some efforts to explain the situation to the people, that the lack of rain was not because of the anger of a goddess; but the farmers created a disturbance and threatened the crowds so that they finally dispersed. A sudden shower on what appeared to be an almost cloudless day stopped any further preparations at that time. Some days later, however, Albrecht met a procession with the foremost carts filled

210

with the village officials and their families. At the sight of him and conscious of his preaching against idol worship, the procession broke up in confusion. But the feast went on, and for three months Albrecht did no preaching in the village. Much conversation was going on, however, during this time, for it had not rained since. Finally the village accountant, a Brahman, came to the missionary bungalow and admitted they had made a mistake. This did not mean, of course, that he would become a Christian; "it simply shows that these people are ashamed to be seen taking part in that in which they have in reality lost faith. Three of those who took part in this feast have truly repented, and two of them have already been baptized."[65] When the monsoon finally did come it was so long after the feast that no one connected the two.

Here was a case where the continual preaching of the missionary was beginning to have its effect, but this was not true in the majority of the tiny villages. In fact, since each village was a complete unit in itself, the struggle had to go on in every community. For every one of the thousands of village congregations now situated in the Andhra Desa there was some courageous pioneer who fought the battle for religious freedom some forty to ninety years ago.[66]

For the outcaste desirous of becoming a Christian, the battle was very often just as difficult as for the caste man. The landowners and upper castes were rarely willing to have their privil-

eged status in the community changed in any respect. This was especially true in regard to the outcastes who were virtually hereditary serfs without rights and privileges, obedient to every wish
of the landowners for whom they worked. Moreover, as has been
mentioned previously, their essential place in the religious ceremonies and their hereditary responsibilities to the village community made it necessary, as far as the leaders were concerned, that
the outcastes remain as they had always been.[67] It is a mistaken
idea to assume that the outcaste had nothing to lose by becoming
a Christian. Although he had little in worldly goods, he could be
ostracized by the community, refused an opportunity to work, and
denied the use of water and washing privileges. His own caste
would react very harshly against any sign of independence from
group loyalty, as they understood it, on the part of one of their
members. For a man and his family in the beginning of the Christian movement to dare to separate from his group and accept and
openly declare a new faith meant the severest of persecution.

In many ways, it is amazing that more of the early converts
did not backslide. Phillips points out:[68]

> "The Christian pariah has to submit to more cruel hardships
> and greater indignities than ever before. When he is in
> trouble he cannot get his heathen employer or the village
> trader to allow him the concessions allowed to everyone else.
> If he applies for a loan of seed he receives the mocking
> answer, 'You have left the religion of your forefathers and
> fallen into the Christian way. Go to your Padres (the mis-
> sionaries); you have no right to come to us.' Many a poor
> pariah is beaten, many a false prosecution is filed in

court, many an ancient mortgage is pitilessly foreclosed ...
many a poor outcaste suffers for his new-found Lord in ways
which sound vulgar and unromantic but which are terribly
hard to bear."

And it must be pointed out that very often it was the simple fact
that the missionary was in the background, giving his encouragement, ready to step in if the persecution came to the point of
violence, that made it possible for the outcaste people to stand
up against the pressure.[69]

In this period the missionary was always willing and ready to
fight for the rights of the Christian converts. A white man was
a person of some consequence, who could do things on the basis of
his own personal authority that are quite impossible now. Men
such as Albrecht in the Palnad developed quite a reputation in
this respect. They did not hesitate to use corporal punishment
on some landowner or village official who had dealt unjustly with
a Christian. And they were feared by the village officials should
the missionaries decide to report what had been going on to the
English District Collector. Dr. Ernst Neudoerffer is remembered
yet in the Rajahmundry field around Bhimavaram for the way he defended the Christian communities from the very proud and stubborn
Kshatriyas who were the landowners in that area. A few such in-
cidents in an area sufficed to drive home the fact that the despised outcastes had definite rights in the eyes of the law, and that
the missionary was ready to stand up to the limit for these
rights.[70] Such backing by the missionary helped relieve the more

flagrant methods of persecution, but did not stop much of the petty persecution. This the Christian had to endure himself.[71]

This social pressure of the village community could have been overcome by moving the people into the mission centers under the wing and protection of the missionary, or by establishing new Christian villages on land provided by the Mission. Several experiments were made in this regard,[72] but lack of finances prevented any elaborate developments. Fortunately for the Lutheran Missions, the new converts remained, for the most part, in their own villages, fought their own battles and laid the groundwork for the great movement toward Christianity which has occurred since 1900.[73]

It did not take the missionaries long to learn how mixed were the motives which led people to come to them for Baptism. It was difficult to preach the Gospel to starving people who were mainly concerned about hunger. There was the strongest temptation to feed them, to give them that little extra to tide them over periods of famine and disease. How often the missionary heard a statement like this: "If Jesus Christ can give us a little more rice, we will call Him a good Swami, and worship Him."[74]

Others were perfectly willing to accept Christ as one of their gods, but not the only one, for they felt that something might be lacking if they left out the worship of one of the gods, just as the effect is spoiled if one ingredient is left out of their usual "chew" consisting of betel nut, betel leaves, tobacco and lime.[75]

And, of course, there was the continual problem of natives who were willing to become Christian if they would be employed by the Mission as teachers or catechists.[76]

## 2. The Failure to reach the upper castes

Richter has pointed out that the effort of most of the early missionaries in India was directed toward the middle and higher castes with the understanding that their conversion would more quickly lead to the conversion of the lower castes.[77] The outcastes were not rejected when they came, but the emphasis was placed on reaching the upper castes through village preaching, schools and private discussions. The Lutheran missionaries tended toward this same attitude, especially in the centers of Guntur and Rajahmundry. Mylius had to discipline some of his missionaries in the Hermannsburg area for concentrating too much time and effort on the higher castes.

Heyer's early successes with the lower castes in the Palnad pointed out, however, the great possibilities for work among them and saved the Lutheran Missions from many years of wasted effort. The mass movements which began to occur after the great famine of 1876-79[78] added to this impetus, so that the Missions in the Andhra Desa became known primarily as Mala or Madiga religions. This presented a serious problem to the missionaries.  Such people,

they felt, would be a disgrace to Christianity,[79]

> "if it could not uplift them in every way, spiritually,
> morally, intellectually, socially and economically, and that
> despite all the obstacles which the higher castes would nat-
> urally place in the upward path of their quondam slaves; des-
> pite all the hindrances resulting from the depravity of past
> ages, their weak moral character, the beggarliness and
> brutishness of the new converts; despite too all the dangers
> which the elevation of lower classes of a people always en-
> tail, for the individual as for the community."

Moreover, not only were there the dangers of lowered moral,

spiritual and intellectual standards, but also the refusal of the

upper castes to have anything at all to do with the Christian

Church reached serious proportions.  To a great extent the initial

successes with some of the upper castes were rarely repeated when

the outcastes dominated the churches.  This does not mean that the

missionaries gave up their efforts to reach them.  Again and again

reports and letters from the missionaries point out the deep con-

cern that they were unable to accomplish much with the higher

castes.  The new missionaries criticized the older men for not do-

ing more.  We find Schmidt of the Rajahmundry Mission defending

himself by noting that he had started the work among the high

caste people in Rajahmundry, and that long before women mission-

aries arrived he, together with Poulsen, Carlson, Artman, Diet-

rich, Groenning and their wives, worked steadily among these

people through personal intercourse and public English addresses.

He realized that not enough was being done, but this was because of the burden of work thrown on too few missionaries. The lack of native pastors forced missionaries to take charge of congregational work. The lack of adequately trained teachers and headmasters drew valuable missionaries away from evangelistic work to take charge of Christian boarding schools.[80]

Along the same line Mrs. Albrecht states that her husband did a great deal of work among the Sudra classes; but he found it most difficult to visit 80 villages over 1041 square miles, direct the building program going on in Rentachintala, maintain close contact with the new converts who tended to fall back into Hinduism very quickly without continual encouragement, and at the same time spend much time with the upper castes.[81] However, there was much interest among them and they could not be forgotten. In describing a worship service, she relates:[82]

> "On one side the caste people hold back their skirts with an 'I am holier than thou' attitude, while the depressed classes hold back their garments with a deprecatory air out of respect or fear. After the Christians and inquirers from the lower classes have gone, the caste people come and sit around the tent for hours. 'A very good religion,' they say, 'very good -- for you; ours is a good one for us. Our forefathers' religion is the one we must keep; how they believed and did so must we believe and do.'"

Albrecht found the Sudras go just so far and no further. He decided it was because the missionaries are considered outcastes because of their association with the lower castes and their food being cooked by them. He determined to use Sudra cooks and servants. "A higher caste can fall to a lower, but a lower caste can

217

never by any means rise to a higher. We are going to attempt the impossible, and try to get admittance into the lower aristocracy of India."[83] And what a time they had trying to train Sudra cooks! The Albrechts had to get used to. eating the same thing day after day until the cook finally mastered the menu and could try something else. Innumerable times cooks had to be changed because of the threats of the caste people to debar from the village well anyone who worked for those who had eaten outcaste food.

Failure to follow up street preaching with close personal work was due primarily to the fact that the native catechists and evangelists, being from the lower castes, were not fitted to deal successfully with the high caste people who were interested. It is no wonder the Lutheran Missions made every effort to obtain some upper caste workers and gave a great deal of recognition to such converts. Mention has been made of P. Venkata Ratnam,[84] who was baptized by the Rev. Iver Poulsen in 1877.

> "His conversion aroused the enmity of his relatives, caste
> people, to such an extent that they sought by every possible
> means to get him away from the missionaries. They followed
> the house-boat in which Poulsen took him from Peravaram to
> Rajahmundry, and met it at the landing-place, accompanied by
> a crowd of two hundred persons, intent on getting Ratnam away.
> Schmidt secured an escort of police who conducted Ratnam in
> safety to the mission house. There he was confronted by his
> relatives, but he told them that he had become a Christian
> because he believed in Christ as the Saviour, and exhorted
> them to become Christians. They pleaded with him, mocked,
> scolded and threatened him, but all to no avail."[85]

In the Hermannsburg Field Woerrlein speaks very highly of Devadattam, baptized by Hartwig Harms about 1893. He went through

quite a period of persecution, even being carried off and held
prisoner by his Brahman associates. Finally the police and the
District Collector had to enter into the matter to settle it. He
was trained to be a catechist, married the daughter of the catechist Totaya,[86] and worked successfully among the Sudras and
Brahmans. He was at home in the social customs and formalities
"upon which the educated Hindu lays so much stress, and therefore
receives the respectful attention of the cultured classes. At the
same time he has the gift of accomodating himself to the limited
comprehension of the lower classes, when he brings them the message
of redemption."[87]

Another young Brahman, who became a teacher in the girls'
school at Gudur, went through much difficulty to become a Christian. He had to leave home and stay with the missionary for protection; the relatives, temple priests and holy beggars came in
large groups and stood outside the missionary home and wept and
cried out. The father said he himself would have a terrible
birth in the next life if such a thing should happen to his son;
finally he informed his son that he must go into the desert as a
penitent since he must have committed many sins in his previous
birth to have such a karma.[88] The young man tried to point out
to his father and those with him that although he loved them, he
must take this step for his Lord. Because of his example, his
aunt started learning the small catechism secretly.[89]

The schools established by the Lutheran Missions were one of the most effective agents for reaching the caste people. Not only did the schools have to fight the battle of caste,[90] but the storm would rage again when the regular Bible teaching led some of the caste students to be baptized. Puttur, an outstation of Tirupati in the Hermannsburg Field, became an independent station in 1901. It was declared the Jubilee station of the Hermannsburg Church (1849-1899). A Government school, upon the request of the Hindus, was taken over by missionary Wittman and developed into a Higher Elementary School under the leadership of a Christian headmaster. In a few months the attendance jumped from 30 to 100, and by the end of the year there were 170 students. This quick growth stopped suddenly at 200 and dropped drastically when two of the higher caste pupils became interested in Christianity and asked for baptism. They attended the services in Tirupati, 22 miles away. When the father of one boy discovered what was happening, he took his son to a distant city and arranged his marriage. In the meantime the father of the other boy died, and relatives withdrew him from the school. As the boy still desired to continue his schooling, missionary Wittman paid his tuition. This caused much criticism, children were taken out of the school, and the parents accused Wittman of hurting their religion and drawing children away from domestic worship. This, of course, he was

happy to admit.  The government examination of the school was
very successful and calmed the rebellious parents.[91]

The missionaries found that the upper castes would go to almost any extreme to prevent one of their people from becoming
Christian and thus degrading both family and caste.  Where the
Brahman influence was strong, all sorts of threats and rumors
were used to keep caste people from sending their children to the
schools.  They would try to frighten the people by saying the
missionaries would marry the children to low caste people;[92] or
that they would betray them and take them to another country.[93]

Mrs. Albrecht told the experience of a young Brahman who
came to them and asked to be instructed in Christianity.  This was
just before his final year in a Hindu college.

"All during the hot season he sat every morning with the English Bible, asking me questions and listening to the things
I told him.  One day he announced, 'I have decided to take
Christ as my Saviour and to trust Him for everything no
matter what happens to me.'  He decided to leave the Hindu
college and to join the Christian institution.  As he could
not expect any help from Brahman sources for his final year
in college, we arranged to pay for his support to the close
of the year, when he expected to pass his matriculation examination.  The money was deposited with a Christian professor in the college to be paid out according to need.  Not
one cent of the money was ever touched.  Within one week the
following lines were received: 'Dear Madame, Having been instructed in the doctrines of our sacred Hindu religion, I
have decided to remain an orthodox Hindu.'  He failed in his
examination and is now wandering around ... a slobbering
idiot."[94]

On another occasion a Sudra widow was persuaded by her husband
before he died to study Christianity.  The little son was sent to

one of the mission schools.  Then one day their house was locked

up tight, and no one in the neighborhood seemed to know anything

about the situation.  Finally the Bible woman learned that "two

hundred members of their caste had joined together, each giving a

rupee, and had hurriedly married the little boy to a baby girl in

an influential heathen family.  Medicine had been poured into the

ears of the poor widow, whilst she slept and she would never again

hear a sound."[95]

Drach pointed out that in those early years "Albrecht in Pal-

nad country received more of these caste people than all the rest

of the missionaries combined."[96]  And Mrs. Albrecht mentioned

that the Sudras were coming in ever greater numbers, but were hav-

ing a very difficult time.  Their cattle were poisoned, or all

sorts of accusations were brought against them, falsely made up;

they were excluded from the wells, their water pots smashed; they

were socially ostracised, abused in public and called by low

caste names.  "In a recent case the police sergeant told the

people that they would have no trouble if they gave up Christian-

ity; if they persisted, their troubles would increase."[97]

The tendency for the Lutheran Missions to avoid schools

which were not primarily for the training of Christian pupils to

become teachers and evangelists, removed many opportunities to

reach the upper caste students.  Haccius points out in the case

of Vakadu, a difficult field of work because of the predominance

222

of Sudras, that progress was retarded by not opening a school before the Government stepped in and opened one of its own.[98]

In Rajahmundry, the Mission school which had been developing under the headmasterships of Ratnam and William[99] was raised to a high school by the Rev. H. G. Artman in 1883. But his sudden death at the age of 27 on September 18, 1884, cut short the ambitious program of education which he had laid out.[100] At the same time, the Home Board, faced with serious financial difficulties and disapproving any educational emphasis other than preparation for evangelistic and pastoral work, voted to close the high school. This was done in 1886 despite the desire of all the missionaries, except one, to retain it. The development of a strong Government high school removed an important avenue of approach to the high caste people in the very center of the Rajahmundry field and the center of Telugu culture. "The closing of the High School was for many years deeply regretted by the leaders of our Christian Community in Rajahmundry."[101] This action seemed doubly strange in that the Board continued to maintain a school at Peddapur, raised to high school in 1900, which had only Hindu students, while the Rajahmundry school had been training most of the workers for the Church.

Missionary Dietrich, in a letter from Rajahmundry, dated October 19, 1883, stated that it is hard to convert Brahmans, not in convincing them, but in implanting "the idea that they should become equal to other men for whom they have no more feeling than for a beast, yea even less."[102] The distaste for those people in castes below them was so ingrained that it proved to be one of the most serious barriers to any true understanding of the Christian message.

Although the task was difficult, the missionaries did not fail entirely to reach the upper castes. The next chapter will bring out how they were reached through the women's work and hospitals. And although the influence of the missionary was small in this group of people, it was found to be increasing. More and more of them came with requests on the theory that the missionary was a white man and therefore likely to have great influence with the Government. They would turn to the missionary to settle fights and disputes. If their purposes were not very worthy, yet it gave the missionary an opportunity to contact the upper castes, through tact and patience to plant the Word of God at the right moment, and with continued friendship to help bring the Gospel to bear on their lives.[103] A few missionaries found opportunities to further the missionary cause among the high castes through public service. Wilhelm Groenning was elected to the municipal board of Rajahmundry, and was a member of the Local Fund Board.[104]

## C. The Problems of Conversion

### 1. Rehabilitation, moral and spiritual growth

The Lutheran missionaries were deeply concerned about the moral and spiritual development of their Christian people. Although there may have been a tendency on the part of a few to baptize too quickly, with the result that the converts went back into Hinduism under social pressure or adverse circumstances, the majority were very cautious about adequate preparation for Church membership.

Also a few of the missionaries had little patience with the converts when they continued many of their Hindu religious customs or committed serious immoral acts. Most of them understood the tremendous difference between the degraded and despised lives which the outcastes had been living and the moral standards which they, as missionaries, had learned to expect of a convinced Christian.

Missionary Rohwer of the Hermannsburg field pointed out that the outcastes have had no justice under the rajahs or the British Government, in spite of any laws which may have been put into effect. He stated:[105]

"But if the people have no rights, they have little scruple about wrong doing; for why should they be called to account for their acts if they have no claims and no recognized rights? If a Mala is dishonest, if he lies and steals or lives in shame, it is regarded as natural, and public opinion does not condemn him unless he carries it to excess. His wrongdoing is condemned with the remark: 'Why, he is a Mala.'"

He admitted that progress was very slow and far from satisfactory. The low caste people lacked will power and character. They were too weak to carry out good intentions. However, there were many who were upright and staunch, especially among the native helpers, deacons and catechists, and they helped lead the weaker ones.

There was a much closer relationship between the missionary and convert in the Hermannsburg field than in the Guntur or Rajahmundry areas. For example, the Hermannsburg missionaries insisted that each Christian come to them previous to the Confessional and Holy Communion Services to announce their intention to confess and commune. The missionaries would take that opportunity to emphasize spiritual growth, review the five chief parts of the catechism, ask questions about their understanding of confession and the Lord' Supper, and instruct those who were ignorant.[106]

It was emphasized that the methods of the Hermannsburg Mission were preaching, ministering of the sacraments, worship service, education and counselling. And that the education was primarily to teach the native people how to live as Christians, the improvement of their moral and religious life. Thus the total effort of this Mission was toward the spiritual development of its converts. When the Christians fell back into former ways, much time was spent in rehabilitating them. Haccius wrote of the outstation Vojeli connected with Nayudupeta , which had become entirely Christian under the devoted work of catechist Jacob. After his death in 1894 many of the Christians were pressured by neighboring palems to take part in Hindu sacrifices despite the efforts of the new catechist Aharon and one of the members of the Church Council, V. Nalaya. Missionary Maneke visited them, and spoke at length with the men of the village. They could not deny their sin. After a long time the larger part were brought back into the Church while the rest were publicly required to leave the Church.[107]

In the Sulurpeta area many of the Christians fell away during the famine conditions of 1892 and missionary Kothe tried to bring them back without complete success. With much patience the work continued until the missionaries could report that the congregations were found to be fairly faithful to word and sacrament, giving their penny or three each Sunday. Occasionally difficulties arose because the Sudras demanded that the Christians work on Sunday. By 1901 only a few were excommunicated each year. They were taught the responsibility to care for their own poor and widowed. Much of the work was done by Church Councils. Leading laymen among them were Adam in Sulur and Padam Adaja in Sulurpeta, who directed the congregational development with patience, love and proper discipline.[108]

In the Gudur area difficulties arose by the failures of some of the catechists and teachers. One of the worst blows was the falling away of Isaak, who held the confidence of many of the congregations and had been chosen head of some of them. He committed adultery, leaving his family to live with a prostitute. Excommunication followed. A teacher also committed a serious sexual sin, a real problem to the Christian people, but later he repented. However, it was stated that among the baptized there were quite a number who remained true to the word and sacraments, and revealed by their lives that the Spirit of God had started His work in them.[109]

Turning to the Venkatagiri field, Haccius noted that when one Christian participated in idol worship and then later asked to be readmitted to the congregation, he was required to take the place of the sinner in the church for two months, and then publicly asked for forgiveness.[110] In many cases it was found necessary to prolong the period of preparation before baptism.

In Rapur, a little parish of only 14 adults and 15 children in 1890, a crisis arose when some of the members attended a Hindu festival and others reported them. The whole parish was brought together, the problem presented, and the unfaithful asked for forgiveness and repented. Two weeks later they asked for communion as an evidence of their peace and solution of the problem. In January, 1905, Pastor Isaak[111] was given charge of Rapur, the first time a main station was given to a native pastor. Isaak reported that he developed spiritual insight among the members through much visitation. After the Sunday services, he would visit those 'lazy' Christians who had not come to church and point out to them that they had despised the divine Word and warn them not to miss again without reason. If the Christians were ill, he visited them frequently, talked with them about their salvation, prayed at their bedsides, and offered communion when they asked for it. He spent much time with those who had fallen back into Hinduism, talked with them sincerely about their sins, and asked them to be led to penitence by the love of Christ. Frequently he would check on the work people were doing, finding out if they were active or lazy in their employment, and urging them to get rid of some of their debts.[112]

When many of the Christians in Puttur moved away to find employment, missionary Maneke traced them down and took care of them in the surrounding villages. Quite a number had moved away as far as Madras. As economic difficulties forced more and more Hermannsburg Christians to migrate to Madras, the Lutheran missionaries found it necessary to open a new station there in 1909. The Leipzig missionaries had work there, but only among the Tamil-speaking people, and an agreement was reached with them.[113]

Kodur proved to be an especially difficult field because of moral lapses on the part of Christians. In 1903 trouble at Gallapalle necessitated the excommunication of seven members. One of them repented and was given employment by Councilman Abraham. In Kodur itself, a theft among the Christians, and others committing

229

perjury and having to be put in jail, prevented any growth in the
Church for a number of years. There were only two baptisms in
1910, seven in 1911. But the improvement in the spiritual atmosphere in those two years is indicated by the fact that while 76
communed in 1910, more than 200 communed the next year. Progress
also was made in church offerings. Bible study was conducted on
Wednesday evenings by missionary Wittman in the church for the
Christians, but it was attended by Hindus also. A number admitted that they would like to join the church if only some others
from the village and caste would make the move.[114]

The somewhat meager reports from the Breklum Mission reveal
that the missionaries were deeply concerned with the spiritual
development of the Christians. Tauscher tells us:[115]

> "Many an obstacle will be overcome if the true witness of
> the individual Christian as well as of the congregation is
> accompanied by a sanctified and disciplined life. ... The
> temptation of relapsing into former habits such as heathen
> worship, especially in times of distress and Hindu festi-
> vals, polygamy and adultery, conduct that is branded as
> typically outcaste by the caste Hindu, as well as the tempta-
> tion of leading a superficial Christian life has always
> been present. ... Besides pastoral and congregational admoni-
> tions, the sitting in a separate place during divine service,
> temporary exclusion from Holy Communion, excommunication
> and finally, the striking out of one's name from the regis-
> ter of Christians are some of the means employed. In spite
> of strong opposition from many quarters even the fine has
> still a place as a means of discipline."

Missionary Pohl reported that in addition to emphasis on attending of the worship service and listening closely to the sermon,
home devotions were fostered. The Christians were to go home and

pray for that which they had heard in the sermons and periods of instruction. And the missionaries helped them in this regard by visiting the homes as often as possible. The educational emphasis at all times was to increase and deepen spiritual life. With a revivalistic emphasis, a clear conversion experience was expected and individuals were taught to examine their lives daily. Private confession was voluntary, but the people seemed to find it of much value and it was often practiced. The old pietistic ideal of developing a church in a church was fostered in the Breklum Mission.[116]

In the more rapidly-growing Guntur and Rajahmundry Missions the problem of close supervision over the spiritual development of individual Christians was a continual source of discussion. The Rev. Lemon L. Uhl, who came to Guntur in 1873 and devoted 50 years of service in one of the most outstanding missionary careers among the Lutheran missionaries,[117] pointed out that more and more effort was made to reach the people in the village congregations. Under the supervision of missionaries, catechists and evangelists kept in constant touch with the Christians. As the staff of missionaries increased, new stations were established where the missionaries could more easily cover the village congregations and keep in touch with the native workers. Uhl himself helped establish the new stations of Tenali, Repalle and Chirala, and began the difficult work at Tarlupad.

Two primary goals for the village congregations were: "first, personal Christian character and, secondly, the organization of Christians in congregations."[118] Better results were achieved when whole families were baptized rather than individuals. The missionaries tended to hold off baptism, even for years, until every individual in a family reached the point of decision. It was found, for example, that women were under the severest temptations and pressures when their husbands were opposed to Christianity. Secret baptisms were condemned; instead, women were urged to work on their husbands and children.[119]

This slow, careful approach on a family basis helped to keep family and village solidarity and not to disrupt community life, so basic to the Indian people. The group was more willing to give up Hindu religious customs voluntarily when the decision was made by common agreement, whereas it would have fought desperately to prevent any individual from the group taking the same step. At first the appeal was made to outcastes to give up eating carrion flesh and stop drunkenness. Catechists would report to the missionaries that certain villages showed definite improvement because they were earnest and sincere in their endeavor to "act as Christians in observing the Sabbath and abstaining from eating carrion, and attending to prayer meetings."[120]

Once this initial criterion became standard practice for the Christian congregation, then the missionary and catechist could

take further steps in the spiritual development of the congregation through the common effort of all the people and by the leading example of the church elders.  Congregational discipline was
often necessary, as Fiedler has pointed out:[121]

> "The positive, always the positive encouragement they must
> have.  Do good and choose the right and thus live true to
> our belief in the pure sinless Christ.  But there are oc-
> casions when the plain word of the law must be spoken: 'thou
> shalt and thou shalt not.'  For to some the only language
> understood is the language of absolute authority.  I know
> that missionaries who have been unable to shame Christians
> out of it have actually fined them for partaking of feasts
> of carrion flesh.  Summary but decisive, it stopped them."

It soon became evident to the non-Christian in the community, in
spite of the many who failed to fulfill even the simplest Christian requirements, that there was a definite difference, a distinct
line of cleavage, between the outcaste Hindu and the outcaste
Christian.  They learned that Christians "are not allowed to live
the same life of sin that they live without being brought to confession and repentance."[122]

The boarding school was one of the best agents for developing the moral and spiritual life of the church.  Here the future
teachers and catechists could be supervised closely in their
growth, mental, physical, moral and spiritual; and much of value
could be instilled.

> "[Orderliness, cleanliness,] mutual love, kindness, thought-
> fulness, consideration for the little ones, the weak and the
> sick, truthfulness, industry, honesty and obedience were en-
> joined.  Transgressions demanded daily rebuke and discipline.
> The dormitory life became a sphere for the practical applica-

tion of the religious instruction received in the schoolroom."[123]

Mrs. Albrecht gave an illustration of the results of such train-

ing when, at the time of famine, the boarding boys came in a body

requesting[124]

> "us not to give them their weekly allowance of meat -- they
> are given meat on Wednesdays and Saturdays -- but to allow
> them to use the money to give meals to the hungry. Also
> from their daily allowance of grain they took out a handful
> for each boy and put it into a pot to save for the poor.
> When the boarding girls and women converts heard of this,
> they wanted to do the same. Could we do less? We had also
> little desire for food, and we fasted."

It must not be surmised from what has been said that the

moral and spiritual growth of the Christians was ever very satis-

factory to the missionaries. The majority had come a long way

from what they had been and far beyond the expectations of their

Hindu and English civilian neighbors:[125]

> "A Tahsildar, or native official in charge of a region with
> a population of about one hundred thousand people, told ...
> that the Mala hamlet of the village of Bodagunta used to
> have a very unsavoury reputation, but that a perceptible
> change had taken place, which was commonly attributed to the
> efforts of the Christian teacher and the Christian Bible-
> women."

But there were still many who became Christians and maintained a

semblance of Christian life for ulterior motives, especially

those who desired to find work in the Lutheran Missions. Because

of this, the native workers brought as much sorrow and heartache

to the missionary as did any group within the Church. Mrs. Al-

brecht commented:[126]

"Some of the teachers are such poor weak Christians themselves that I wonder sometimes whether they can do much
good. ... I am hoping and praying, that as these poor teachers in their ignorance and weakness try to teach his commandments, the Master Himself will be present and make up where
they lack."

Along the same vein, Missionary Dietrich while at Dowlaishwaram
touched on a sore spot when he reported:[127]

"The Hindus seem never so happy than when they are engaged
in a wedding, in a law-suit or in making debts. The Christian converts seem unable to shake off this characteristic.
It is pitiable to note that nearly two-thirds of our mission
agents are in debt. I have taken special notice of this
evil during the last six months and am fully persuaded that
it has had a baneful influence on our mission work. Agents
contract debts and then allow the exorbitant interest to ac-
cumulate, until it becomes impossible for them to liquidate
them. The consequence is that they shirk their debts, liti-
gation follows, and in the end they disgrace the Christian
name."

It was not unusual for Christians and native workers discharged from one Mission to make the rounds and cause many different churches years of trouble. Missionary J. E. Davis of the Telugu Canadian Baptist Mission recounted the confession of old
Aaron, who first heard the gospel through the Lutheran missionaries, was baptized by them and taught in a village school. He was
a good singer and played the violin well. He had never experienced a real change of heart, but had come to the conclusion that
idolatry was wrong and accepted Christianity just as a person
might put on a new suit of clothes. He continued to drink and
commit flagrant sins until the Hindu people themselves became disgusted and burned down the schoolhouse. When this happened, the

235

missionaries learned about him for the first time and immediately
discharged him.  Later on he worked for the Godavari Delta Mission,
believed he was truly converted, but ended up in the same trouble.
The Canadian Baptist missionaries Timpany and McLaurin went
through the same experience with him.  In his old age he came to
Davis asking for forgiveness and desiring to be taken back into
the Church.  Davis concluded his remarks by saying:[128]

> "One of the native men told me that it was a common saying
> among them that though a white man might confess his sins,
> a black man never would.  But he said they had all learned
> that the Holy Spirit could make a black man confess just as
> easily as He could a white man."

## 2. Movement toward village-centered churches

In this period all the Lutheran Missions in the Andhra Desa
made advances toward congregational development in the villages.
We had noted previously that, outside of the Palnad area, congregations were station-centered and members were expected to come to
the church located in the towns where the missionaries lived.[129]

Greatest development in this regard occurred in the Guntur
field.  The increased missionary staff and the ordination of
three native pastors in the 1870s[130] permitted a great deal of
village touring.  Uhl on his first tour lasting 42 days traveled
542 miles, stopped in 96 villages, held 63 services, and visited
729 families consisting of 2,232 Christians.[131]  Results of this
work can be shown in the increase from 14 congregations and less

than a thousand members in 1870 in the Palnad-Guntur field[132]

to a total of 100 village congregations in 1880 with a membership

of 5,423.[133]  Pioneer workers in this great expansion in addition

to the three native pastors, Cully, Nathaniel and John,[134] were

Chikkala William, Murari Samuel, Govatoti Luke and Penumala Abra-

ham.  Samuel worked diligently among Mala and Madiga alike, with-

out distinction, going from village to village as an evangelist.

He and Luke "were the chief human factors in establishing the

Church in Eastern Guntur District."[135]  Luke rose to the position

of sub-pastor; he

> "lived among the people he served, showing them by example
> as well as by word what Christian living means.  He too dis-
> regarded caste and is said to have been instrumental in es-
> tablishing a number of congregations among the large group
> of outcastes among whom he did not happen to be born."[136]

These pioneers are remembered not only for their faithful service,

but also because from their families came some of the finest pas-

tors and workers in the Guntur Mission.  All five of William's

sons became workers.  Samuel's daughter had two sons who became

leading pastors and Seminary professors.  Samuel's sons were pil-

lars of the Guntur Mission, David becoming the fifth pastor and

"unequalled in his day as a preacher both to Christians and non-

Christians, a man to whom all listened not only on account of his

eloquence but because they realized that his inner life corres-

ponded with what he preached."[137]

* * *

In 1871 when Heyer left India for the last time,[138] the Rajahmundry Mission had a total of 13 congregations with 241 Christians. Five of the congregations had been started in the previous year, showing Heyer's desire to spread the work out from the center. Although the progress was not as apparent in the 1870s as was true of Guntur, it must be remembered that Heyer found the work in Rajahmundry in a feeble condition and it was necessary to reorganize the work almost to the point of starting over again.[139] Only 30 of the 241 Christians in 1871 were in Rajahmundry town. In speaking of such meager results after 25 years of the missionaries concentrating primarily in the center, Dolbeer comments:[140]

> "Rajahmundry Town and the surrounding area has always proven a hard and comparatively unfruitful field. Perhaps in the early days too much time and effort of missionaries were spent on the town to the neglect of the villages where the real harvest awaited."

Moreover, the Mission was much under-staffed. The two catechists Paulus and Joseph did tremendous work in spreading the Gospel message throughout the Delta region, but the rest of the workers were inadequately trained to achieve any immediate results.[141] The outstanding among them were Lanka Jeremiah, a colporteur and itinerant preacher, Mallepula William, noted for his evangelistic preaching, Battini John, a builder both of congregations and houses of worship, and Merugu Alfred, who had come to the Mission during the brief period the Church Missionary Society was responsible for the work[142] and served as an Evangelist and teacher.

Statistics for 1879 reveal that there were 86 Christians in Rajahmundry town and 248 in the district in a total of about 20 congregations.[143] The native staff consisted of 15, of whom two were recently-ordained pastors, Paulus and Joseph.[144] That a new day was ahead for the Mission is revealed by the fact that there were 124 baptisms in 1880 and 170 in 1881. The extension of the work into the villages of the Godavari Delta began to have its effect.

* * *

In 1879 the Hermannsburg field had a total of nine stations, all but one of which had been organized within the first eight years of the Mission's existence.[145] The total baptisms up to that time had been 871 of whom 582 were still living and members of the Church.[146] Over one-half of the baptisms had occurred in the last three years. However, the work developed very slowly during the 1880s, with baptisms ranging from 41 to 86 a year, and only one new station was opened, Kodur, in 1883. Most of the baptisms during these early years were on an individual basis with few families baptized all at the same time. Motives for conversion also were suspect, although very often a true conversion occurred later in the lives of such individuals. Woerrlein cites the case of a young girl who was baptized in order to marry a catechist. At first she found Christianity a nuisance and was quite a hindrance to her husband in his work; but in time she proved to be a true and faithful Christian.[147]

By 1884 Mylius could report a staff of 28 native workers, a large staff when we consider the total number of Christians that had been baptized up to that time, 1,101. This was, of course, a feature of all the Missions -- a large staff in comparison to the number of Christians. Concerning the Christians, Mylius reported: "Our Christians belong with the exception of one Sudra family in Tirupati to the Pariahs. In former times we had some who just wandered around; but now praise be to God, either we kicked them out or they ran away by themselves."[148]

With the death of Mylius in 1887, the work put under the responsibility of the Missionary Council instead of one man, a reorganization of much of the field and a new constitution in 1892, the Hermannsburg Mission made notable advances so that 306 baptisms could be reported for the year 1891, 576 in 1892 and 296 in 1893. Again in a three-year period occurred nearly one-half of the total baptisms since the establishment of the Mission.[149]

In 1891 the outstanding event was the visitation of Director Egmont Harms from the Hermannsburg Missionary Society in Germany. He made a complete survey of the situation, held many conferences with the missionaries, and placed the superintendentship of the Mission in the hands of the Rev. Johann Woerrlein. The new con-

stitution was built on the principle that all the men were interested in the total work of the Mission and should have a part in
the decisions made through regular conventions.  Th. Petersen was
elected president of the Mission Council.  Other members of this
Council, which worked closely with Woerrlein and handled all matters between conventions, were Carl Scriba and Hartwig Harms.[150]

Decisions made at the final conference of all the missionaries with Director Harms on January 5 to 15, 1892, helped further
the spread of the work into the villages and the establishment of
more local congregations.  Catechumens were to be instructed by
the catechists in their own villages or as close to their homes as
possible.  Only on the final eight days before reception into the
church were they to come into the center to be instructed by the
missionary and given the final examination.  Preaching to the non-
christians and congregational work were to be closely connected.
As the catechists cared for the congregations, the Hindu population of the community also was to be visited and invited to take
part in the worship services.  Elders were to be elected for each
congregation to lead and direct the physical affairs, be responsible for collecting the apportionment of contributions that each
congregation would be expected to give, care for the poor and the
widowed, and take charge of disciplinary action when necessary.
A suggested constitution for a local congregation was drawn up.

The rank of the native worker was raised and his training improved.[151]

By 1897 there were nine main stations, Kodur having been established in 1883 but Sriharikota no longer considered as one, and eighteen outstations plus four regular preaching places. Thirteen missionaries, twenty-one catechists, forty teachers and twenty-two volunteer workers (probably the elders) made up the total staff of 96. The total baptisms since the beginning were 3,081, of whom 1,740 were living. A few of these had moved to other areas; of the rest 875 were adults and 846 were children.[152]

At the time the missionaries were forced to leave India because of the first World War, statistics revealed that there were twelve men missionaries, three single women missionaries, two native pastors, thirty catechists and deacons, 136 teachers, eighteen Bible women and women teachers, and 32 Church Councilors or Elders. This gave a total native staff of 218 serving 3,116 members. Of the members, 2,007 were adults and 1,109 were children. About 7,000 had been baptized since the beginning of the Mission.[153] No information is available as to whether services were held each Sunday in every outstation. It is apparent that there were not enough pastors and catechists, but since Hermannsburg rarely used teachers in the elementary schools that were not trained in the teacher's seminary, it is likely that many of the teachers also were trained to conduct the worship service. A

242

one-year laymen's class was held in the seminary in 1895 to overcome the shortage of teachers and 'prayers' in the local congregations after the large number of baptisms in 1891-1892.[154] Haccius reported also that in addition to every center having its
own large church, many of the outstations had chapels or school
houses which could be used for worship. The worship services
held were complete in all details. Besides preaching and instruction for the children, the singing of hymns and the use of
the liturgy were cherished. He stated also that with great sincerity pastoral counseling was carried on by the missionaries
and native pastors to further the welfare of congregational
life.[155]

D. The Tragedies of Famine, Starvation and Disease

A terrible famine occurred between 1876 and 1879 which affected the Andhra Desa as severely as any part of India. There
had been no rain since 1874. The Government opened up vast relief projects for those who could work and relief camps for the
helpless ones. In August, 1877, nearly one million people were
active on relief work in the Madras Presidency with another million receiving gratuitous relief. Hundreds of thousands died and
their bodies had to be burned to prevent cholera.

The missionaries practically stopped all their evangelistic
work to give the Government their assistance in the distribution

of relief and direction of work camps.  J. E. Clough of the Baptist Mission performed a great task for the area around Ongole when he took the responsibility of constructing three miles of the Buckingham Canal, which had been started as a famine work and was to unite Madras with Bezwada and the Kistna Delta.  His teachers and catechists helped him direct the work and see that everyone was fairly treated.  He gave employment to thousands of natives.[156]

The Rev. Adam Rowe undertook operations in the Guntur area in cooperation with the Famine Relief Committee of Madras.[157] Through such work, it was possible to come face to face with a great number of people in scores of villages, gain their confidence and good will through the relief given, and receive a respectful hearing of the Gospel message where many refused to listen before.

Woerrlein told of visiting villages and distributing gifts to the needy, and assisting the Government in the work camps where sometimes it was possible to preach before thousands.  One of the big problems which arose was the tendency toward graft and black-marketing among Indian officials who were in charge of the distribution of relief funds.  Brahmans in Kalahasti dominated the relief committee and saw that most of the funds went to needy Brahmans.  Missionary Schepmann objected, but he was only on the committee in an advisory capacity, without vote.  Woerrlein in Tirupati reported the situation to the government and the situation was corrected. But the anger of the Brahmans was turned upon Schepmann and they tried to poison him. The result of the trouble was that Schepmann was given greater authority and directed an impartial distribution of gifts to all who were in need, high caste, low caste and Christian.[158]

Not only did the missionaries cooperate on the Relief Committees, but they did all they could with funds from the churches in Europe and America, as well as from their own meager salaries, to help the suffering people around them. Schepmann tried to help the Christians in their economic conditions by lending them money to buy seed and to pay rents. A number of the Christians in the Hermannsburg field were employed in the building of the new station at Tirupati and various village chapels. The church at Tirupati was completed in three months and, together with the missionary homes, was dedicated October 10, 1877. A new church was dedicated at Kalahasti June 26, 1878.

Many of those who assisted in the building program at Tirupati came from the village of Mitta where the remarkable courage of Rangama, the first person baptized, opened the way to the majority of the community becoming Christian. When the famine came, the Hindus left the town and the Christians remained. A few managed to save some cattle. Missionary Woerrlein visited them frequently and helped them with little gifts. When the rains came again, although they were nearly starved, they were able to start right in with the planting of seed, rebuilding of their homes, and the establishing of community life. The Hindus returned to find the Christians living in neat and orderly homes, the stalls and streets full of cattle, the gardens blossoming and the rice ready for harvest. The joy and assurance of these newly-converted Christians amazed them; and the God of the Christians was praised because he helped the people maintain themselves during the time of distress. The Hindus with their sacrifices of roosters and other animals only made the distress worse and speeded the death of many. As a result of this experience, the whole community became Christian. Schepmann built a little chapel in 1880 and arranged for a regular worship service each Wednesday afternoon.[159]

Reports in the Missionsblatt of the Hermannsburg Society gave a tragic picture of the famine. The lack of water almost stopped the building program, because bricks could not be baked. Where there were relief projects sponsored by the Government, the missionaries found that men had to give one day's pay a week to their supervisor if they expected to keep their jobs. This was done secretly and the British officials could not stop it, even when it went as far as the supervisor taking most of the pay. Nor was it possible to have the Christians free from the work on Sunday as long as the majority in any one group were Hindu. Twenty men usually worked under one superintendent.

Prices rose so drastically that rice cost four times what it had. The cost for one meal equaled the average salary for one day, and the worker had to share that one meal a day with his whole family. The missionaries were disturbed to see the merchants building better houses while the poor farmers were mostly without cattle and corn. A large part of the Christians lived on leaves and grass seed. Those who had a little land, through mission help and friends in Germany, were given seed to till their plot of ground. In the Kalahasti zemindari alone the Mission in 1878 distributed 17,000 rupees to 2,500 people for seed. In order to keep them from spending the money immediately on food, four men were assigned to go around through the villages to keep a check on the people.

The dread cholera came in 1876 and stopped much of the work on the canals and roads. There was not enough rain in 1877, so that what seed was planted withered away. Missionary Kiehne reported that half of the village of Rapur burned, hitting the wealthiest homes the hardest. The starving people participated freely in stealing whatever they could, doing so primarily in order to be put in jail where food was available. The jails became so full that the punishment for thievery had to be changed to whippings. When the rain fell in October, 1877, seed again was sown and appeared to be developing well when locusts suddenly appeared and consumed everything.[160]

Typhoid fever and cholera raged in the little village of Rapur so that ten to fifteen died each day at the height of the epidemic. One-half the Christians and 150 of the 1200 inhabitants died; the Collector reported 700 deaths in the District. It was at this time that Missionary Kiehne suffered such tragic losses in his own family.[161] Such setbacks stopped all baptisms in Rapur for several years.[162]

Missionary Brunotte attempted to isolate the cases of cholera in Gudur where one-fourth of the congregation died; but the Hindu people would have none of it, saying that,[163]

> "as their forefathers drove the spirits from the village by much wailing, noise and festival-making, so they would get rid of the dread disease. This only served to spread the cholera so that finally the stench of the dead and the burning of their bodies made living at the station almost impossible."

The Hermannsburg Mission experienced with the rest of the churches in the famine area an upsurge of interest on the part of the people. Baptisms in three years equaled the previous twelve. One of the outstanding conversions was that of the catechist, Avilele Gad,[164] who was a Hindu priest. He had come in contact with the Gospel message and was deeply disturbed by it. But his final decision came when his mother was stricken with cholera. Full of fear, Gadu read the little catechism of Martin Luther twice during the night. This removed his fear, except that he wanted to be baptized before he died. He vowed to God that he would accept Him if his mother recovered.  At the end of the fifth

day, she improved.  After a period of instruction he was baptized

and became a very effective preacher to the non-Christian.  During

the famine period, he helped Woerrlein and Petersen distribute

the relief money.  He knew all the villages and the leaders in

them.  Within a few years he had drawn a small group of 34 Christ-

ians around him in his own village and served as their elder.[165]

More will be said in the next chapter concerning the effect

the famine had on the growth of the churches in the Andhra Desa

after 1880.  It is of interest to quote Richter who points out

that a fivefold increase in the Telugu Territory occurred between

1871 and 1881, from 15,393 Christians to a total of 77,041 for all

the Missions.[166]  He states:[167]

> "To an extent never known before, the Hindus came to perceive
> that the missionaries meant well by them, and still more,
> that connection with the Christian community in such seasons
> of distress was the best protection, and afforded the safest
> prospect of help for those of the lower castes or of no
> caste at all.  It thus came about that when the famine
> ceased -- as a matter of principle none had been baptized
> during its actual duration -- vast numbers of the people
> went over to Christianity."

E. Cooperation Among the Lutheran Missions

Our story of the Beginnings of the Lutheran Missions in the

Andhra Desa in Chapter II brought out that there was a close con-

nection between each of them and a certain amount of cooperation.

In the period covered by this Chapter, it continued to be so.

It was pointed out that the General Council came to the aid of the General Synod at the time there was danger of losing the Rajahmundry field. In the time of crisis Heyer called upon a former missionary, the Rev. Charles Groenning, to provide two Danish missionaries to assist him in reviving Rajahmundry.[168] When Becker died suddenly, another missionary came from Denmark, the Rev. Iver K. Poulsen.[169]

The cosmopolitan atmosphere of the Rajahmundry field was increased with the arrival in 1879 of the Rev. August B. Carlson, who had been born in Sweden, and represented the Augustana Synod, a member of the General Council when it was organized in 1867.[170] He was the first missionary to represent the Augustana Synod on any foreign mission field; he had been led to the service through the inspiration of meeting the Rev. Charles Groenning when Groenning visited America in 1876.[171] Unfortunately Carlson did not live long enough to accomplish much. He made an extensive tour throughout the Delta region by houseboat in January - February, 1881, baptizing 29 persons. But he returned to Rajahmundry suffering from fever. From this time on he was oppressed by severe headaches which were aggravated by the sun. He moved to Samalkot in May with the hope that the climate there would be less harmful to him. But his eagerness to preach in the many surrounding villages led him to take too many chances. He suffered a sunstroke in September, had to be taken to Madras and died there March 29, 1882, at the age of 36.  It was a severe blow to the Rajahmundry Mission as he was to take charge of the educational work.[172]  He was instrumental in converting F. J. McCready and persuading him to become a missionary of the General Council.[173]

Another tragedy, the death of the Rev. Horace G. B. Artman,[174] who had been sent to India to develop the educational work of the Rajahmundry Mission following Carlson's death, brought the Rev. Wilhelm Groenning in 1885 to Rajahmundry for the same purpose.  He had been the Inspector of the Breklum Society for a number of years.  His coming not only points out the continuing interest of his father in the Rajahmundry Mission, but also the close relationship maintained with the Breklum Society. This was continued when the Rev. Ernst G. Pohl spent eight years in Rajahmundry, from 1889 to 1897, directing the educational institutions Wilhelm Groenning had started.[175]  The Rev. Franklin S. Dietrich, who had come to India in 1883, and was proving to be a most energetic missionary, died from a sunstroke June 11, 1889.[176]  The tragic loss of four men in seven years (Carlson, 1882, Artman, 1884, and Dietrich and Groenning, 1889) and the resignation of Poulsen in 1888 left the Rajahmundry field almost depleted.  Only Dr. and Mrs. Schmidt, and the Rev. and Mrs. McCready were left.  It is no wonder that Pohl was urged to stay in Rajahmundry where he gave such worthwhile service in a time of need.[177]

The Hermannsburg Mission, organized by Mylius because he
and Harms were not willing to work with the General Synod, continued to have some suspicion of the Guntur Mission and did not
have much association with it.  Contact with the Breklum and
Rajahmundry Missions was primarily in the field of literature.[178]
But a new day of closer cooperation and association was ahead.

Chronological Comparison of THE UPSURGE

(CHAPTER V) of the Andhra Desa Missions

(1881 - 1900)

| | Guntur | Rajahmundry | Hermannsburg |
|---|---|---|---|
| 1881 | First single woman miss., K. Boggs | Conf. has 3 miss., 2 pastors, 15 work. | |
| 1883 | | High school begun | |
| 1885 | Schnure disrupts Mission; College & dispensary opened | Wm. Groenning comes to direct schools. Rampa Fund started. | |
| 1889 | | Heavy losses, only Schmidt & McCready. Pohl loaned by Brek. | |
| 1890 | Uhl reorganizes Repalle & Bapatla. 5 missionaries | Dr. Edman arrives, urges medical work. First 2 wom. miss. | |
| 1891 | | Board of For. Miss. estab. 21 teachers grad. Rajah. Semin. | |
| 1892 | Narasaravupet St. Girls' Train. Sch. | Valett dies in Germany | Full-time man in Cat. & Teachers' Seminary |
| 1893 | Golden Jubilee; Watts College Bldg. | 3 new missionaries | |
| 1894 | Bible Train. School | | 1st Cat. Class grad. |
| 1895 | Rentachintala new headquarters Palnad | Golden Jub. Celeb. Central Girls' Sch. | |
| | First joint Conference of the Andhra Desa Lutherans | | |
| | Pastor John dies | Bhimawaram Church | |
| 1896 | | | Poppe, first layman, opens Industrial sch. |
| 1897 | Missionaries assist government in Famine Relief Projects | | |
| | Hospital opened; Christians receive Govt. land | Pastor Paulus dies | Warber begins Agric. and Land program |
| 1899 | Nurses' Tr. School | Pastor Joseph dies, William ordained. | 1740 Christ. in 9 congr., 18 outstat., 83 Indian workers. |
| 1900 | 18, 664 Christ. in 426 cong., 418 workers, 27 miss. | 6,199 Christ. in 210 cong., 142 Indian workers. Peddapur High School | |

Chronological Comparison of THE UPSURGE
(CHAPTER V) of the Andhra Desa Missions (1900 - 1920)

| | Guntur | Rajahmundry | Hermannsburg |
|---|---|---|---|
| 1901 | | | Puttur Station opened. First woman miss. |
| 1902 | Sattenapalle Stat. | Harpster reorganizes Mission. Dispensary opened. | |
| 1903 | Ordain 4th and only living Pastor. | Schmidt retires | Tirupati church built |
| 1904 | Chirala Station, Rentachintala Ch. Orphanage started. | | 1st 3 Indian pastors ord. Sulurpeta Ch. Workers' Annual Conf. |
| 1905 | Publication of The Gospel Witness | | Leper Asylum, Kodur |
| 1906 | Guntur Synod org. | | |
| 1907 | St. Matthew's Ch. | | Puttur Church dedic. |
| 1908 | | Luthergiri Semin. | Widows' home estab. |
| | All-India Lutheran Conference held in Guntur | | |
| 1909 | | Miss. Council reestablished | Renigunta,Madras St. First Women's Conf. |
| 1910 | 40,198 Christ.in 526 congregations | 16,953 Christ., 347 Indian work. | |
| 1911 | Girls' High School, School for Blind. | Hospital completed, Samalkot Church. | |
| 1912 | Taluk High Schools authorized. | | 2 Deaconesses arrive |
| 1913 | | Bhimawaram Stat. | Joint Synod of Ohio buys two Stations. |
| 1915 | | Industrial work, full-time Wom.Miss. | 3,116 Christians, 218 Indian workers |
| 1916 | Cooperate with NMS in Rewa Mission | Bhimawaram H.S. | German Miss. interned (Breklum, also) |
| 1917 | Diamond Jubilee, Care for Breklum | Bible Train. Sch. | Mission given to Synod of Ohio. Scriba miss. |
| 1920 | 63,370 Christians 1,941 Ind. workers | 28,600 Christians, 1,362 Ind.workers. Diamond Jubilee. | Ohio Syn. Missionaries arrive, Conf. organiz. |
| | United Lutheran Church Mission formed. | | |

# CHAPTER V

## THE UPSURGE

### (Reaping the Harvest)

This final period of our History is a time of surging movements, rapid development of congregations and institutions,
changing policies in the approach of missionary to the native,
and increasing struggles between the old and the new, the East
and the West. The action is so swift that it is not possible to
give more than a rapid survey of growth of Lutheranism in the Andhra Desa. This can be done best by considering the development
under the headings which have been selected for this chapter
rather than a chronological recitation of facts.

### A. The Developing Church

In the process of change from Mission to Church, a natural
aspect of the devolution is the struggle for control and authority between missionary and the native Christian community. No
matter how willing the missionary may be to turn the work over to
the native leaders, he is held back by the uncertainty as to
whether they are truly prepared to assume the responsibility. On
the other hand, the native leaders never feel that the devolution
is being carried on rapidly enough. The missionaries find themselves in sharp disagreement with each other over the steps to
take, and the speed with which they should be taken.

In this period the struggle in the Lutheran Missions seemed to be primarily between the missionaries themselves and between the missionaries and the Home Boards. With the completely inadequate educational system used so far, and realizing that the Christian leaders were coming out of the outcaste society accustomed to humble obedience, it was not surprising that the tensions between missionary and native workers did not pose a serious problem until the close of our period of survey.

## 1. The Guntur Mission

The Lutheran Synod which had been organized with such high hopes in 1853 in Guntur by the missionaries from Rajahmundry, Guntur and the Palnad, did not continue to meet after 1858.[1] This was understandable, for the missionary staff was scattered from Samalkot, organized by Missionary Long in 1859, to Guntur; and the stringent financial conditions caused by the Civil War in America precluded any travel. It was not until October, 1872, after the return of Unangst with a new missionary recruit in the person of the Rev. John H. Harpster that some effort was made to establish a regular Conference of missionaries.[2] The decisions made were referred to the Foreign Mission Board of the General Synod for approval. One of the first was permission to ordain Mr. R. E. Cully and prepare several of the catechists to be Evangelists in anticipation of their ordination in several years.[3]

Evidently a certain amount of freedom of action was permitted the Missionary Conference, although it was expected to report all decisions to the Board. Difficulty of communicating back and forth quickly enough to deal with every situation was a large factor. The Board, for example, did not approve the establishment of the Anglo-vernacular school in 1874 under the direction of the Rev. L. L. Uhl, who had arrived March, 1873.[4] And the General Synod backed up the Board in its proposition to abolish the English department of the school. A very strong protest by the Missionary Conference led the Board to permit the continuation of the school as organized with the proviso that this arrangement was not necessarily permanent.[5]

The Rev. and Mrs. Charles Schnure arrived in Guntur in February, 1881, accompanied by Miss Kate Boggs, the first missionary to come under the sponsorship of the Women's Missionary Society established in the General Synod two years previously. Miss Kate Boggs had to return to America in two years because of ill health, but she was replaced in 1883 by Miss Anna S. Kugler, M.D., and Miss Fannie Dryden. Accompanying them were the Rev. and Mrs. L. B. Wolf. Two years later the Rev. William P. Schwartz arrived.[6]

Such reinforcement of the missionary staff was most encouraging. It helped to offset the tragic death of Missionary Rowe on September 16, 1882. He was one of the most energetic missionaries Guntur had seen and great things had been expected of him.

257

He had been active in the famine relief work, and as the Children's Missionary created keen interest in the Sunday Schools of American Lutheran churches through his lectures and books.[7]

Rowe had been assigned in 1876 to the southern division of the Guntur District while Dr. Unangst had charge of the northern. Missionary Schnure took Rowe's field after his death. Less conservative than the other missionaries and able to get down to the level of the people, he drew large crowds as he toured throughout the region. But he came in conflict with the Missionary Conference on the matter of policy and was not willing to go along with the decisions made. He had definite theories as to the approach which must be made to reach the non-Christian population, probably close to the thinking of modern-day missionaries, but the rest of the Conference was unable to accept them. They felt he was too easily influenced and led by some of his native workers. As a result, serious dissension arose, charges and counter-charges were made, rumors were spread, and the work was seriously hampered until the Home Board found it necessary to recall Schnure in 1885.

However he had a large following in the Bapatla and Repalle taluks (districts), especially among the native workers. He determined to establish an independent mission which drew most of the congregations in that area into its fold.[8] He was sure that he would receive support from sympathetic individuals in America. When that support did not come, the misled workers and the congregations began from 1888 on to return to the Guntur Mission.[9]

The bitterness and ill-will created by this incident prevented any progress for several years in those two taluks.  There
were almost no baptisms while the western and central parts of
the field showed steady growth through the diligent supervision
of Missionary Unangst aided by Pastors John and Nathaniel.  The
membership of the Guntur Mission increased from 5,423 in 223 villages in 1880 to 13,566 in 371 villages in 1890 and 18,664 in 529
villages in 1900.  The work was decentralized by establishing two
new missionary headquarters.  Two bungalows and a small church
were constructed in Narasaravupet in 1892 and 1893.  Miss Susan
Kistler, who had come to India in 1888, and the Rev. and Mrs.
Noah E. Yeiser, who had come in 1892, were the first to live
there.  When Dr. Harpster was in the Palnad between 1872 and
1875, he had lived in a small house in Dachepalle, which was used
by Pastor John from 1875 to 1890.  Dr. George W. Albrecht, who
came to India in 1892, moved the headquarters of the Palnad to
Rentachintala in 1895 and completed the construction of the bungalow two years later.

Much construction was going on in Guntur also.  Swavely reports:[10]

> "In Guntur the Watts Memorial College building was erected
> at a cost of $33,000; the hospital plant was constructed and
> cost fully as much; the girls' boarding school dormitory
> was built; Heyer Memorial was constructed in the Groenning
> compound.  In 1890 the property of the Mission was worth
> $15,000; in 1900 it was worth at least $100,000."

It was given to Dr. Uhl to resurrect the work in the Bapatla and Repalle taluks after the Schnure defection.  He became a familiar figure in the whole area as he covered village after village on his famous horse, Nizam.

> "From 1890-1902 he toured everywhere, and in every season, ignoring all kinds of weather.  Like St. Paul, he endured labours which would have killed any lesser man.  The great Christian community in East Guntur Synod today stands on firm foundation because of Dr. Uhl's great work."[11]

Uhl tells us in his autobiography that the many congregations which were restored for the Mission were reestablished on broader lines.  He emphasized evangelism, giving, better houses of worship and schools.  As time went on more and more of the building was done by the congregations themselves, some of them contributing from 350 to 1000 rupees toward the cost of a church.  The average giving of a communicant member was raised from 36 cents a year in 1894 to 42 cents in 1898.[12]

Another indication of the growth of the work is the fact that only five missionaries were on the field in 1890 while by 1900 a strong staff of twenty-seven had arrived to develop the work in ever-widening aspects through education, women's work, medicine, and more thorough evangelism.

With the death of the two native pastors, the Rev. Bethala John in June, 1895, and the Rev. Medikonduru Nathaniel, April, 1900, the Mission Conference was faced with the seriousness of the lack of native leadership.  The Rev. John Aberly, who came to India in 1890, was primarily a teacher. He started by teaching Bible in the college and hostels in Guntur. By 1894 a Bible Training School for workers was established. Dr. Aberly was given charge of this together with the Central Boarding School. For thirty years he trained hundreds of workers for the Guntur Mission. Under his supervision outstanding workers were prepared for ordination. Peravalli Abraham was ordained in 1903, only the fourth ordination in 61 years of the Mission's history! Murari David was the next, ordained in 1905. Two more men became pastors in 1913, and still two others in 1916. The staff of native workers increased from 375 in 1890 to 418 in 1900 and 723 in 1910.

A big event in the life of the Guntur Mission was its jubilee celebration in 1893. Postponed a year because of the threat of famine, a Jubilee Tour was made which covered 192 villages in 59 days. All the missionaries and workers participated in this event. The sum of 15,000 rupees was received through offerings and subscriptions and used for the construction of Heyer Memorial Hall in the Groenning compound in 1897, a building for the Bible Training School. "The tour was especially successful in binding the whole church together in a consciousness of unity in one fellowship throughout the whole of the area."[13]

During this time the Missionary Conference functioned as the governing body of the Mission. Increasing numbers of missionaries reduced the danger of dissensions serious enough to retard the work, as occurred in the early 1880s. A big step forward came in 1906 when the Guntur Synod was officially organized on October 29. The Rev. L. B. Wolf, president of the Conference, issued the call to nine ordained missionaries, two Indian pastors, and eleven lay delegates to meet in the Stork Memorial Church in Guntur. Dr. Uhl preached the opening sermon on the subject, "The organization and government of the groups of congregations for the work of the Church."[14] The officers elected were Dr. Uhl, president, the Rev. P. Abraham, vice-president, the Rev. E. C. Harris, who had come to India in 1899, secretary, and Dr. Aberly, treasurer. The objects of the Synod as adopted were:[15]

> "To promote the work of Christ in India, by establishing self-supporting and self-governing Evangelical Lutheran Congregations; by constituting charges among the individual congregations; by licensing and ordaining suitable candidates for its ministry and exercising discipline over its members; by hearing appeals from all Church Councils and special Conferences; and by distributing or supplying all funds contributed by the congregations or entrusted to it by the Mission Conference or otherwise."

From the beginning the Synod was concerned with the development of the Church and its organizations, its work and congregational life. Some of the standing committees established were: Examination of Candidates, Workers, State of the Church, and Ways and Means. Other committees added as the work of the Synod developed were: Synod Publication, Workers' Conference, Nomination, Budget and Home Missions.

Right from the start a Church paper was edited and published, entitled Mission News.  Later on the title was changed to Telugu Lutheran in 1916 and Andhra Lutheran in 1919.  Dr. Uhl was
the first editor.

The Synod took up the problem of Lutheran Christians moving
to areas outside of the Mission.  This led to diaspora work in
1915 in Hubli, near Bombay, where Christians had gone to work in
the Railway colony.

It entered into cooperation with the Lutheran National Missionary Society in 1916, sending contributions toward the effort
that was being made to enter Rewa, a native state in central India.  This was a big step forward for the Indian church to carry
the Gospel message with its own men and money to other parts of
India where the doors had been closed so far to missionary work.[16]

Moreover, the Guntur Synod opened up its own mission work in
1918 by selecting a field to develop at Tripurantakam in the Kurnool District.  Church workers especially contributed toward this
effort.[17]

The Field Councils were developed under the direction of the
Synod to relieve the missionary in each area of a great deal of
responsibility.  Dr. J. R. Fink points out that the missionaries
had so much power in their own fields that it was almost like a
dictatorship.[18]  More democratic principles were achieved and
native leaders developed by the formation of these Field Coun-

cils, which correspond in many ways to the Synod. An example is
that formed in the Palnad in 1918-19 by the Rev. J. Roy Strock,
who came to India in 1908. The officers are elected. They are
responsible for the preparation of the budget for that particular
field, the expenditure of funds received from local and Synod
sources, the spread of evangelistic work and the development of
elementary schools. Strock states in a letter, dated June 4,
1919:[19]

> "We have a small body of five, with four other co-opted mem-
> bers, which each month considers such matters as transfers
> of workers, appointment and dismissal of workers, opening or
> closing of work (schools, e.g.), Church discipline, & etc.
> This cabinet, as it were, is very valuable, as its advice is
> generally excellent. It has legislative functions as well
> as advisory ones, and also serves as a sort of court of ap-
> peal in matters affecting both church-members and workers.
> Every month a large number of matters come up for disposal,
> . . ."

Strock also described the organization of his field. His
main responsibility covered 110 surrounding villages, 80 of which
had congregations. Catechists were in charge of the village congregations, some of them having as many as four or five to take
care of. There were about 60 villages that had schools. Some of
these had male teachers, but the majority were cared for by the
wives of the catechists, or by catechists who had charge of just
one or two congregations. The field was divided into six areas,
each one under the direction of a supervisor, who inspected the
congregations and schools and reported to Mrs. Strock concerning

the schools and Dr. Strock concerning the congregations. Each

supervisor had from 17 to 20 villages and from 7 to 12 schools.

He concluded the description:[20]

> "Although we may not visit a congregation or school more
> than once or twice in a year, we are constantly doing our
> best for each through the Supervisor. The success of our
> work depends to a very great extent upon the intelligence,
> tact, faithfulness and honesty of the supervisors. In ad-
> dition to the supervisors, catechists and teachers, we have
> about a half-dozen evangelists who work among the higher
> castes, especially among the non-Christians."

The period from 1900 to 1920 in the Guntur Mission was marked

by rapid growth in every respect. Baptized membership rose from

18,964 in 1900 to 40,198 in 1910 and 63,370 in 1920. The move-

ment of caste people into the church was increasingly apparent.

Between 400 and 500 were baptized between 1900 and 1910 and by

1920 more than 3,800 of the total baptized membership were from

Sudra castes. Of the 10,177 Christians on the roll in the Palnad

field, one-fourth came from Sudra groups.[21] The number of vil-

lage congregations rose from 426 in 1900 to 526 in 1910.[22] The

native staff increased from 418 in 1900 to 1,941 in 1920. This

meant that there were 33 Christians in the mission for every

worker. When we notice that there were 36 Christians for each

worker in 1890, it is apparent that the educational process of

the Mission had kept pace with the rapid growth. Not only that,

but also the quality of the training of the workers was improved

and the schools were localized. Rentachintala had led the way in

establishing a Boarding School, the first outside of Guntur, in

1895. Others followed after 1912, when the Synod made the decision to open such schools in each taluk. New ones were opened
at Narasaravupet, Sattenapalle, Chirala, Tenali and Tarlupad.
In time these became Higher Elementary Schools. The task that
these schools set out to fulfill is indicated by the fact that
Dr. Uhl reported in 1901 that the best qualified workers that he
could get for the Repalle taluk were men of no more than third
grade education.[23]

In this period of twenty years thirteen men missionaries,
five medical missionaries and ten zenana missionaries came to the
Guntur Mission. Four new centers of work were opened. Sattenapalle was selected as the first in 1902. The bungalow was completed the next year and the Rev. and Mrs. Victor McCauley, who
had come in 1898 and 1900 respectively, were the first missionaries to work there. To care for the work south of Guntur, the Kin-
singer Memorial Bungalow was built in Chirala on land secured by
Dr. Uhl. The Rev. and Mrs. E. C. Harris moved there in 1904.
Very rapidly the work developed so that in the 15 years after 1901
the number of Christians increased from 1,836 to 7,179. Uhl's re-
claiming of this area finally showed fruit.[24] By 1912 a hospital
was built, and in 1918 St. Mark's Church was dedicated.

The Tenali-Repalle taluks were separated from Bapatla (Chirala the headquarters) in 1911 and a bungalow was built in Tenali

266

and occupied by the Rev. and Mrs. S. C. Burger, who came to India in 1898.

The missionary in Narasaravupet faced an almost impossible task in serving the vast area assigned to him, covering parts or all of Markapur, Cumbum, Ongole, Kanigiri, Darsi, Podili, Narasar-avupet and Vinukonda taluks. In 1898 Christians lived in 236 villages covering 5,000 square miles in area. In 1910 the Synod divided the field into three parts: Narasaravupet, Vinukonda, Ongole and Darsi taluks under the missionary located at Nara-saravupet; Markapur, Cumbum and a small portion of Podili in a new charge with the missionary to be located at Tarlupad; and Kanigiri and the rest of Podili taluks under an Indian pastor with a missionary supervisor. The Rev. and Mrs. E. J. H. Mueller, who had come originally to Rajahmundry in 1896,[25] took charge of the Markapur-Cumbum field, and occupied the Tarlupad bungalow in 1912.

Mention will be made later of other important buildings con-structed during this period in the sections concerning women's work, medical work, education and institutions of mercy.[26] Addi-tional missionary homes were being built in Guntur also, to take care of the enlarging staff in the various institutions.

A new Church building for St. Matthew's congregation, Guntur, was completed and dedicated October 8, 1907. Known as Stork Mem-

orial Church previously, it is the largest building in both the
Guntur and Rajahmundry Missions and cost only Rs. 40,000.

An amazing amount of building went on in Rentachintala --
two missionary homes, a hospital and the building that is considered to be the finest Church in the Andhra Evangelical Lutheran
Church today.[27]  Built entirely of Palnad marble, it was dedicated on December 17, 1904.  Twenty-two missionaries were present,
delegations came from nearly every village in the taluk, and a
great procession through the streets impressed the native population.  Mrs. Albrecht described the church:[28]

> "The floor is of red stone -- slabs from three to nine feet
> long.  The beautiful stained glass windows are from Quedlin-
> burg, a town in the Harz mountains and are copies of paint-
> ings by Hofman and Plockhorst -- Christ in the temple, the
> Wise Men, the Good Shepherd, Christ in Gethsemane and the
> Crucifixion.  The baptismal font is of polished light red
> marble and the pulpit is the same with inlaid slabs of
> beautifully veined green marble which reminds me in a very
> faint degree of the wonderful green marble in the Church of
> St. Paul without the gates in Rome.  $1,000 of the cost was
> paid by our Foreign Board, and the balance of perhaps $8,000
> was from other sources.  The most of the work was done by
> the people themselves.  They quarried the stone; in places
> where bullocks could not go they hitched themselves en masse
> to the carts and hauled the great stones; they learned to
> trim and polish stone and to build walls.  Some who used to
> be glad to get work at 6 cents a day have since been called
> to do mason work and earn 1 Rupee (33 1/3 cents) or even
> more."

The Diamond Jubilee was celebrated even more elaborately than
the Golden with a great tour of the village congregations and ending with a week's celebration in Guntur which closed July 31, 1917,
seventy-five years to the day after Father Heyer arrived in Guntur.

Highlight of the final day was the ordination of eleven Indian pastors, two more than had been ordained in the whole history of the Mission.[29]

## 2. The Rajahmundry Mission

We have mentioned already the formation of the Rajahmundry Conference on February 3, 1879. In accordance with the agreement signed with the two newly-ordained pastors, Joseph and Paulus, this occurred upon the arrival of the third missionary, the Rev. Augustus Carlson.[30] Schmidt was the first president, Poulsen, secretary-treasurer. Among the decisions the Conference made was to have Carlson conduct regular English services in the new St. Paul's Church for the benefit of English-speaking families. They sent an appeal to the Foreign Missions Committee to permit the opening of a mission school of a higher grade so that the eleven boarding boys did not have to attend the Government schools of the town. Also emphasized was the need of missionary teachers.

Correspondence between the Committee in America and the Conference points out that the Committee expected its decisions to be carried out implicitly.[31] With Carlson of the Augustana Synod in India, the Committee was expanded to include representation from that Synod in 1879. For the first time an American-born and educated missionary came to the Rajahmundry field in 1880, the Rev. Horace G. B. Artman.

The next convention of the Conference, December, 1881, included fifteen of the twenty-three native workers in addition to the Indian pastors and missionaries. Efforts were made to improve the school system, encourage regular contributions on the part of each worker, organize Sunday Schools in every village, and establish a Christian 'satram' or rest house in Rajahmundry from funds to be gathered from the native Christians.[32]

A year later the Conference learned that funds were coming in for the satram, but not a single pice (about one-half a cent) had been contributed by the native workers. Offerings taken each Sunday in St. Paul's Church, however, showed that something could be done in the way of self-support with continued emphasis and education. At this Conference seven new teachers, graduates of the excellent school which Artman had been developing for a year and a half, were given employment and admitted to the Conference as members. Three of them had been students in the school for only six months.[33]

Following this Conference, the missionaries met as a Ministerium and decided, among other things, to revise the Telugu version of Luther's Catechism. Assisting them were the native pastors, together with S. James and J. William[34] and a Telugu pundit, Subbarayadu.

Forty delegates, among them two laymen, attended the Conference held January 3-5, 1884. Poulsen was elected chairman. Schmidt was taking his first furlough at this time after thirteen years. Questions considered for discussion were the baptism of a person who had more than one wife, the problem of government grants and annual inspections of the schools, the caste situation, and self-support. They voted not to accept the government grant-in-aid system for the village schools. Each worker in the mission was expected to give four pice in contributions for every rupee of salary. The Ministerium designated the northern part of the Rajahmundry field as the fever district with the understanding that teachers would receive a higher salary when stationed there. Other salary schedules were set. "The missionaries requested the Foreign Missions Committee of the General Council to formulate rules and regulations for the better government of the Mission."[35]

In the absence of Schmidt, Artman was in every respect the director pro tem. of the Mission. He threw himself into the work and within a few months organized a high school for boys on January 1, 1884, with seven teachers and fifty students, ten of whom were Christian. Thirty-four of the boarding boys and girls in Rajahmundry were supported by patrons in America. A Mohammedan boys' school was opened January 10 and a Mohammedan girls' school July 1. Artman attempted to run the last two without cost to the mission. We have noted already how suddenly this ambitious program of Artman's came to an end.[36]

The Rev. Wilhelm Groenning was called from Germany to take Artman's place directing the schools. With the arrival of the Rev. F. S. Dietrich in 1883 and the completion of the education of the Rev. F. J. McCready in America and his return October, 1884,[37] the Mission had an adequate staff to expand its work outside of Rajahmundry. McCready was assigned to open up a new field to the north, on the west side of the Godavari River. The missionary bungalow at Tallapudi was completed in 1887 and the cornerstone laid for St. Peter's Church November 16, 1888.

Missionary Poulsen was assigned to revive the work at Samalkot in 1882.[38] He began a boarding school in 1884, but lack of interest in education on the part of the native people led to its closure.

Missionary Dietrich was given the responsibility of the Dowlaishwaram area. A small chapel called St. Mark's had been dedicated by Artman in 1884. Property now was bought for a missionary bungalow. The school which Heyer had started had long since been abandoned, but a retired engineer, Mr. Theodore Van Stavern had established and maintained several schools at his own expense. He offered to cooperate with the mission and turn the schools over to the mission after his death. A separate girls' school was started early in 1886. It was while Dietrich was working on the new bungalow in the hot sun that he was struck down by fever and died the next day.[39]

We have noted how the Home Committee would not go along with the wish of the Mission Conference to maintain the high school.[40] Instead they authorized the Rev. Wm. Groenning to study the whole educational program of the mission and recommend a definite plan for the future. Faced also with the lack of support from the churches in America, Groenning finally decided that the educational work must be limited at first to the training of elementary teachers, preachers and catechists. He took the Rajahmundry Mission school with its three departments[41] and added higher grades with instruction in theology. This might be considered the beginning of the institution that later became known as Luthergiri Theological College and Bible training School. The Mohammedan schools were closed.

The financial condition of the Foreign Missions Committee was so serious between 1886 and 1890 that salaries were not paid promptly and the work in general slowed up drastically. Schmidt reported:[42]

> "For the first three months of the year I was able to pay only a few mission agents. Rev. N. Paulus and others lost much time by coming to Rajahmundry and waiting for money. P. V. Ratnam, the headmaster of the Caste Girls' School, thought it best to resign and seek government employment."

The first Mission Conference held after the new Rules and Regulations went into effect occurred January 4-6, 1887.[43] There were present five missionaries, two native pastors, and 60 native workers and lay delegates. Discussion revolved around the training of boys and girls for future workers, using only the most promising students from the village schools; the difficulty of using Dawson's Telugu hymn-book because its language was not intelligible and simple enough; the evils of drunkenness and how to control it among the Christians; and the development of the Rampa Fund from the workers' regular contributions. The Rampa Fund was to be used for two purposes: first the salary of a catechist or evangelist in the district to the north (thus the name Rampa), and secondly for teachers' widows and poor Christians. No district could claim for this latter purpose more than one-half the amount contributed by it to the Fund.

The Rules and Regulations transferred the administration of the Mission on the field into the hands of the foreign missionaries meeting semi-annually as a Mission Council. Drach-Kuder explained that:[44]

"To this Council was delegated the duty of considering and recommending to the Home Committee, with whom the final decision rested, whatever measures were necessary for the proper administration and development of the mission work, the erection of buildings, the appointment of native agents, the schools and whatever pertained to the care and control of the Mission. At each meeting of the Council each missionary was required to submit a written semi-annual report of all official acts and expenditures, and an estimate of expenses for the coming six months, to be approved by the vote of the Council and sent as an official communication to the Committee in America for its sanction or amendment.

The Rules and Regulations also provided for an Annual Conference of foreign missionaries, native agents and delegates of native congregations, which was to receive the written reports of the pastors, catechists and evangelists, and oral

274

reports of the teachers, and consider such matters as pertained to their work."

Essentially there was little change from the previous arrangement

of Conference and Ministerium, other than the organization being

more clearly defined and the areas of work delineated.

At the Conference held in January , 1888, an interesting

item of business was the resolution made to express the Mission's

gratitude to Sir Arthur Cotton for his continued interest, espec-

ially through the support of the colporteur Talluri Joseph.  The

Conference recommended weekly prayer meetings to be held in the

homes of Christians.

Missionary Poulsen was elected president of the Mission Coun-

cil which met immediately after the Conference.  But in April, he

resigned from the Mission and returned to the United States.  He

had served the General Council sixteen years, six of them in the

very difficult and almost fruitless field at Samalkot.  In short

order the missionary staff was cut still further by the deaths of

Dietrich and Groenning in 1889.[45]  The latter had been serving as

Chairman of the Rajahmundry Municipality in the absence of the

regular chairman.  In that official capacity he was directing the

work of scavengers, who were disposing of refuse from the city,

when he contracted cholera and died within twenty-four hours.[46]

In spite of the loss of missionaries, the Church itself was

beginning to grow through the diligent work of the catechists,

teachers and Pastors Joseph and Paulus. Where there were only
about twenty congregations with 334 Christians in 1879, by 1890
the work had spread into 100 villages and drawn into the Christian community 2,433 people. The staff of 15 in 1879 had increased to 62. Ten years later there were 142 workers serving 6,199
Christians in 210 congregations.[47]

Pastor Paulus had charge of a tremendous area: the three
large taluks of Tanuku, Narsapur and Bhimawaram. The story of
his work there is one series of persecutions after another against
him and his workers. His life was threatened many times, his home
burned down on one occasion, and a group of fanatical Hindus called "Rama Dandu" made serious efforts to destroy the Christian
work in the Delta.[48] When Paulus was given his parish in 1879
following his ordination, there were six villages with 96 Christians. By 1890 more than half the Christians in the Rajahmundry
Mission were under his care, a total of 1,580 in 55 villages. At
the time of his death, May 25, 1897, he left as his legacy to the
Lutheran Church a strong and growing Christian community of 2,580
Christians in 65 villages.[49]

Pastor Joseph had a much more difficult field in the East
Godavari area. But he worked it faithfully, as shown by the fact
that he baptized 57 persons in 1883 alone. Toward the last his
health failed and for years he was almost blind. He died March
26, 1899, having preached the Sunday before.

The effectiveness of the Seminary as organized by Groenning was seen in the reception on March 4, 1891, of twenty-one men into the service of the church following their graduation. The growing church could use them all and they helped to overcome the loss of the missionaries. Additional missionary staff was not long in coming, however. Mention has been made previously of the Rev. Ernst G. Pohl coming from the Breklum Mission to take Groenning's place in the school system.[50] Strong recruitment came from America: the Rev. Emmanuel Edman, M.D., in 1890; the Rev. C. F. Kuder in 1891; the Reverends P. A. Baenisch, Rudolph F. Arps and Hans E. Isaacson in 1893; the Rev. J. H. Mueller in 1896; the Rev. Peter Holler in 1897; and the Reverends Ernst Neudoerffer and Gomer Matthews in 1900. The women missionaries will be mentioned later. Dr. Edman and Missionary Isaacson were representatives of the Augustana Synod. Dr. Edman did some medical work and urged the establishment of a mission hospital. Although funds were being raised as early as 1894, medical work was not started until 1901 and the Rajahmundry Hospital was not opened until 1911.

In 1895 the Rajahmundry Mission celebrated its Jubilee with much fanfare, opening it with the dedication of the new church at Dowlaishwaram. Many neighboring missions took part in the three-day Thanksgiving held in November; and Dr. Schmidt presented the mission with a gift of thirty acres just north of Rajahmundry,

the land where now the Luthergiri Theological College and Bible
Training School is located. Other activities at the close of the
century were the completion of St. Peter's Church at Tallapudi,
the construction of Transfiguration Church, Bhimawaram, 1894-1895,
the opening of the Tadepalligudem station in 1896 with the construction of a bungalow and chapel, and the start of work in the
inner agency at Addetigala through the gift of a site for a
school.[51] Of interest also is the fact that S. Abraham, the evangelist supported by the Rampa Fund, was having some initial
success in the Rampa district. He brought quite a number of inquirers to Rajahmundry in 1892 to be examined. Schmidt baptized
twenty-four of them, three from the village of Rampa and the rest
from the Yellavaram Division.[52]

The Foreign Missions Committee was changed officially to the
Board of Foreign Missions of the General Council in 1891. A "Missionary Superintendent" was chosen to work full time in visiting
synods, conferences, missionary societies, congregations and individuals in the interest of foreign mission work. The Rules and
Regulations of the Mission were revised in 1895 while Dr. Schmidt
was on furlough in the United States. The Mission Council, now
composed of all missionaries, women as well as men, was to have
charge of mission work, constitute the governing body and serve
as the executive committee of the Board on the mission field.

The control of the Board would be maintained through official correspondence concerning all decisions made.

To all appearances this put a great deal of power in the hands of the Mission Council. The new plan may have worked if some of the missionaries had not written private letters to members of the Board, some of which were read and made the basis of decisions. The dissension which resulted came to a climax in what is known as the 'J. William Case,' which was as follows:

It is apparent from all the materials on file in the Philadelphia Seminary archives that Mr. Jeriprolu William[53] was the innocent victim used as a target to defeat Dr. Schmidt. Dr. Schmidt had been given the directorship of the Rajahmundry Mission by Father Heyer before his departure in 1871. He was the Senior Missionary.[54] With the exception of McCready, who was a native Eurasian from Rajahmundry, the others had come to the Mission twenty years or more after Schmidt. Moreover, there was a very interesting mixture of nationalities and backgrounds among the missionaries: Schmidt from Denmark, Isaacson and Edman from Sweden, Arps, Mueller and Pohl from Germany, McCready from East India, Matthews from England, Neudoerffer from Canada and Kuder from the United States. Matthews and Neudoerffer arrived after the trouble started, but they became deeply involved in it.

> "Beautiful as the mingling of these diverse nationalities
> was in theory, in practice it could not work. There has
> to be a certain community of national and local interests

to cultivate unity and harmony among persons closely associated."[55]

These two factors created much of the tension among the missionaries. Dr. Schmidt felt that his position on the Mission
Council was based purely on longer experience and acquaintance
with the early days of the Mission. It is likely he angered the
new missionaries when they disagreed with him by pointing out
that the judgment of a young and inexperienced man can hardly
carry the same weight as that of the older men. Mueller, for example, was very critical of the lack of organization and order
and spiritual care in the Christian schools in the Tadepalligudem
field. Schmidt's answer to this was:[56]

> "Rev. E. H. Mueller is no doubt a man of ability. But he
> made the same mistake as many young missionaries make, that
> they condemn everything what others have done before they
> show their ability to do it better."

At the time of the Jubilee celebration, plans were carried
out with the Board's approval to build the Seminary building on
the property given by Schmidt.[57] Kuder, Schmidt and Pohl were
on the building committee; but Schmidt was on furlough in Germany
and America. So the other men went ahead, and were ready to lay
the foundations by the time Schmidt returned. Drach-Kuder states:[58]

> "[Schmidt] objected to the arrangements which had been made
> and to the plans, some difficulty arose with regard to the
> transfer of the site to the Mission, the Board's treasury
> became somewhat embarrassed because of a lack of funds and
> the whole undertaking was indefinitely postponed."

It was not until thirteen years later in 1908 that the Seminary
building was completed.

Schmidt also was the appointed Treasurer for the Mission.  He
felt responsible to the Board alone in the distribution of the
funds he received.  McCready led an effort over a period of years
to shift the control and administration of the Telugu Mission from
the Board to the Mission Council, especially in deciding where the
funds were to be distributed.  Schmidt recognized in this,natural
differences of view on the matter of administration, differences
which were apparent throughout mission work in India; the struggle
between the Home Board and the Indian Church for control and
authority.[59]  Schmidt emphasized that the money was all spent on
the Mission, and the majority of it on the native assistants and
the schools.  It was true that the native assistants had no vote
in the management of the funds from America, but neither did the
missionaries have the final say.  They could only recommend, while
the Board sanctioned every expenditure.  Schmidt noted the following development:[60]

> "The Missionaries in Council have of late gone further than
> permitted by the Rules and that they intended to go still
> further is clear when they claimed that the decision of
> Council was final.  This would hardly have happened if Mr.
> McCready had not been in our Mission. ...
>
> May be that I saw more danger than even the Board.  But
> long before this it is clearly understood that the real
> question is about final authority in our Mission, whether
> this shall rest with the Board or with the Missionary Coun-
> cil where the youngest Missionary probably will have the

deciding vote whenever there is difference of opinion among the older Missionaries."

Missionary Kuder was easily led by McCready in this struggle, because he as an American was interested in developing more and more democratic processes in the workings of the Mission.

This opposition to the control of the Home Board centered in Schmidt as he was their official representative financially and could control the activities of the Mission by the distribution of funds, rather than by any decision made by the Mission Council. Schmidt, on his part, accustomed to the European system of Church government and the strong control over mission work held by the Home Board and its appointed Director on the field, was determined that the Board should have the final say in all matters.[61]

Much suspicion was cast on his position as Treasurer when it became apparent that he was handling large sums of money in real estate transactions. Rumors spread that Dr. Schmidt was mishandling the funds of the Mission in speculations, and these spread to America. When Schmidt was in America in 1895, he explained to the Board that a Mr. John G. Haas of Lancaster, Pa., and a former parishioner of his while he was pastor for one year at Carlisle, had put in his hands a sum of $8,000 to develop self-support among the native churches.[62] The gift was to be confidential and Dr. Schmidt was not placed under any obligation to render an account of the disposition of the funds. The Rev. Dr. Henry E. Jacobs,

president of the Board from November, 1901, stated in this connection:[63]

> "A great mistake undoubtedly was made by both Mr. Haas and
> Dr. Schmidt in surrounding the gift with such secrecy.  It
> is true the members of the Board had at last been admitted
> into the secret; but not the other missionaries.  Dr.
> Schmidt had also the unfortunate habit of defying opinion
> that was arrayed against him, and throwing darkness around
> his course when he could readily have explained all to the
> satisfaction of his opponents."

Ever since the first two native pastors were ordained in
1878, Schmidt had been urging the Mission to obtain others to be
placed in charge of self-supporting churches.  Schmidt spoke of
this while in America and felt that the ministers in America were
favorable to the idea.  But the missionaries were much opposed and
McCready wrote a long article stating that no need existed for
such a proposal or plan.  He emphasized that Pastors Paulus and
Joseph functioned more as missionaries and were not in special
pastoral charge of congregations organized with a view to self-
support and self-management.

Heyer had planned, even before he left in 1871, to have S.
James and J. William ordained to the ministry when they completed
their education.  Nothing was done for nearly thirty years.  When
Pastor Paulus died and Joseph was blind and feeble, the situation
became desperate.  There were differences of opinion among the
missionaries concerning which men were best qualified for ordination.  McCready wanted P. V. Ratnam, but Kuder did not consider

him a fit candidate.  Ratnam finally lost patience and left to
work with the Church Missionary Society.  James had the best education but did not manage his home affairs too well.  Pohl recommended at a meeting of ordained missionaries October, 1897, that
William be licensed to perform marriages rather than ordain him
at once.  Three voted for this motion and three against it.  But
in letters to the Board each missionary gave his personal opinion
on the matter.  From these, the Board received the impression
that the majority of the missionaries wanted William ordained.
Some of them were sidetracked from the intent of the motion to
discuss in the letters whether a person who is not ordained
should be permitted to perform marriages.[64]

Understanding the will of the majority to be in favor of ordination, the Board applied to the President of the Ministerium
of Pennsylvania and received the authorization for the officers
of the Mission Council, Kuder and McCready, to ordain Mr. William.
The officers of the Mission Council replied that the matter of
ordination had not been discussed.  However, the Council did meet
in April, 1898, and after much discussion voted three to two
against it.  As Schmidt was absent, his vote was recorded as a
matter of courtesy in favor of it, thus again making the vote
three to three.  If the Board so ordered, the Council declared itself ready to ordain William.

The officers were surprised to receive an answer that Schmidt
and Isaacson were to go ahead with the ordination, which was done

on January 8, 1899.  Pohl and Holler assisted.  Kuder, McCready,

Mueller and Arps resigned because of the Board's nullification of

the authority of the Mission Council.  Arps later withdrew his

resignation.  The Board again surprised the three men by accept-

ing their resignations and also suspending the Mission Council in

India.  Jacobs wrote in this connection:[65]

> "Rev. C. F. Kuder, coming home about New Year 1899, sur-
> prised me by announcing that he and Messrs. McCready and
> Mueller had resigned.  The aim was to bring the Board to
> terms, and to force the dismissal or resignation of Dr.
> Schmidt.  I expressed my disapproval of the course adopted,
> convinced as I was from all the evidence at hand that they
> had just grounds for complaint. ... The general judgment of
> the Church was that the Board had acted unwisely in forcing
> the ordination.  The deference paid to the Senior missionary
> to the disregard of the rest was unAmerican, and was still
> less relished because he was not an American.  But the resig-
> nation of Kuder, McCready and Mueller was not justified.
> There was no reason why the mission should be further troub-
> led by the withdrawal of its missionaries.  The cause was too
> important to be subjected to such additional suffering.
> Their resignation did not hasten the crisis. ... A general
> who will lay down his commission, while a battle is raging,
> even though there be justice in his quarrel with an admin-
> istration, ought never to expect to be with an army again."

The drastic step of suspending the Mission Council was fol-

lowed by the sending of the Rev. F. W. Weiskotten to investigate

the situation.  He arrived in October, 1900, stayed thirty-six

days, and then returned only to die at sea.  During his visit in

India, Inspector Weiskotten helped in the ordination of Srikotla

James.[66]  Accompanying Weiskotten to India were four new mission-

ary recruits -- two men and two single women.

285

Weiskotten's death left the Board without the information it needed, for he had said very little in his letters. There had been a revision of the Rules and Regulations, however, while he was in India. Also the decision was made to transfer to the Trustees of the General Council all properties of the Mission. They had been in the name of individual missionaries, previously. This created quite a problem, as far as Schmidt was concerned, which was not settled for several years.

The controversy continued. When Arps and Miss Schade came to America on furlough, they reported on the continuing difficulties, and the 1901 convention of the General Council spent much time discussing what to do. Finally, it was voted to ask Dr. Schmidt to report to America. Moreover, the Board was authorized to find a man who would go to India and spend a number of years there reorganizing the work and ending the controversy. Schmidt took this recall as an arbitrary and unjust dismissal and called for a trial in India before an impartial judge, so that he could present his side of the case. He refused to come to the United States.

The Rev. J. H. Harpster of the Guntur Mission was obtained to direct the work of reconstruction.[67] This was a most difficult task and he was reluctant to accept. But his previous knowledge of work in the Telugu country and acquaintance with the successful organizational program developed in the Guntur Mission

were of great value.  He arrived in India at the close of 1902
with two men and two women missionaries.  The new Rules agreed
upon at the time of Weiskotten's death were put into effect upon
Harpster's arrival.  They called for the transfer of the responsibility for decision from the Mission Council to an Executive
Committee composed of the chairman who was appointed by the Board
and one representative for every seven ordained missionaries and
one for every seven women missionaries.

Within a year Harpster was able to settle property arrangements with Dr. Schmidt.  Schmidt handed over everything with the
understanding that he and his wife would receive an annual pension
of $300 during one or the other's life.  He moved from Rajahmundry
in March, 1903, to retire at Kotagiri in the Nilgiri Hills, where
he had built two houses.  He died there March 6, 1911.  In spite
of the many difficulties which had developed to discolor the last
years of Schmidt's service in the Rajahmundry Mission, the Mission
Council adopted a statement of appreciation that pointed up the
brilliance of his work.  It was he rather than Father Heyer who
was the savior of the mission and carried it through its most
difficult years:[68]

> "He was a wise buyer, a cheap builder, a shrewd manager;
> and much of the excellent property now owned by the Mission
> is the fruit of his foresight.  As a fellow-missionary he
> was genial and easy to get along with.  His long experience
> with new missionaries, all of whom for a period of thirty
> years he was here to welcome, made him patient and sympa-
> thetic with them.  He was quick to recognize merit and re-

joiced in it for the sake of the Mission. His judgment was safe and his tenacity of purpose great. Connected for so many years with the Mission, there is scarcely a phase of its work today that does not, to a greater or less extent, bear his impress."

Although Rajahmundry Mission's problems were far from solved, definite progress was made in all branches of the work as is evidenced by the statistics available and the large number of buildings constructed. Nine men missionaries arrived in the 1900s, ten more the next decade. A strong force of women, both zenana and medical, spread the work into ever-widening circles. Whereas only four had arrived before 1900, eight came in the 1900s and ten between 1910 and 1920. The Church continued a steady growth from 6,159 Christians in 1900 to 16,953 in 1910 and 28,600 in 1920. The total number of native workers increased from 142 in 1900 to 347 in 1910 and 1,362 (including lace women) at the time of the merger in 1919.[69]

A new bungalow was completed in Dowlaishwaram in 1904, another in Bhimawaram when that station was opened in 1913, and the Augustana Church building at Samalkot was dedicated January 15, 1911. Funds for it came from the college and seminary of the Augustana Church at Rock Island, Illinois. On the same day, the sixth native Christian pastor, Pantagani Paradesi, was ordained. The Rev. Pamidipani V. Ratnam had been ordained March 2, 1902, and he became the Bible teacher for the Peddapur High School when it was turned over to the Mission in 1903.[70] Pastor Paradesi was called to serve St. Paul's Church in Rajahmundry which, under his outstanding leadership, soon developed into the first self-supporting congregation of the Rajahmundry Mission. Self-government was instigated through the use of a panchayat or council consisting of the missionary in charge of Rajahmundry, the pastor of the congregation and five members of the congregation.[71]

Since 1872 the Mission had been making attempts to reach the Koyas and Reddis of the agency tracts north of Rajahmundry.[72] This began to bear fruit after Mr. Andrew Petersen, a government employee in the forest department, voluntarily gave up his position to serve the spiritual needs of the hill tribes. He started an independent mission at first, called the Godavari Hill Mission, at Kannapuram. The Rev. A. F. A. Neudoerffer, who came to India in 1912, enlisted Mr. Petersen in the work of the Church and he served faithfully in that difficult area until his death in 1930.

Another difficult area was the Korukonda field, on the east side of the Godavari river opposite Polavaram. Missionaries residing in Rajahmundry attempted to supervise this area. Only 269 baptisms were performed between 1901 and 1910, 657 in the next decade. But the groundwork was being laid in this period for later growth through the patient work of such men as Battini John (1885-1910), Manubattula Prakasam (1879-1920) and Peetala Abraham (1894-1931).

"Dr. Harpster opened Diaspora Work in Rangoon in 1906 after a personal visit to that city. Vungara Sriramulu was sent as the first catechist, but returned in six months. Rev. Kuder paid a second visit to Rangoon in May 1911, and A. Anandappan was sent there later in the same year; he soon gathered together a congregation of some hundreds of Telugu Lutherans."[73]

Although the Board's establishment of an Executive Committee to run the Mission had been necessary to restore order under Harpster's supervision, it was apparent that this system could not last indefinitely. Protests and petitions from individual missionaries to the President of the General Council in America brought about the decision to send a special Commission to India to study the situation and bring back recommendations for future organization and planning. The men selected were Professor C. W. Foss of Augustana College, Rock Island, Illinois, and the Rev. C. Theodore Benze, pastor of St. Stephen's Church, Erie, Pa. and President of the Pittsburgh Synod. Under the new Rules and Regulations adopted in 1909 as a result of their visit to India, the Mission returned to a government similar to that which was in effect before 1900: a Mission Council consisting of all missionaries in charge of work as the governing body, and a Ministerium of the ordained missionaries in charge of district evangelistic work.[74]

The Rajahmundry Mission closed this period of its history with the celebration of its Diamond Jubilee from January 11 to 13, 1920. And similar to the Guntur celebration in 1917,[75] the high point was the ordination of the first class of six graduates from Luthergiri Seminary, equal to the number of ordinations throughout its whole history.[76]

### 3. The Hermannsburg Mission

We have spoken already about the great changes made in the Hermannsburg Mission following the death of Mylius in 1887. Democratic procedures were established in 1892 with the majority of decisions being placed in the hands of the Missionary Conference rather than the Superintendent. Assisting the Superintendent during the interim between conventions was an elected Mission Council consisting of three members.[77]

The missionaries voted at that time to put a full-time man in the Teacher's and Catechist's Seminary in Nayudupeta. This required new property which Th. Petersen bought from his own funds and offered to the Mission. Construction was started on a home for Missionary Krueger. At that time was started the first Catechist Class, from 1892 to 1894, in which three of the men enrolled later became pastors. By 1902 the work at the Seminary had developed to the point that a special class was started to train men for ordination. For the Hermannsburg Mission, the training of men was a long process, starting with preparation to be a teacher in the village school. After a long period of service, the best of the men came back to receive several years of training in purely religious subjects.  Further years of service qualified the best catechists to take the training which led to ordination.[78]

Such training for future pastors was not a regular thing, however, after 1902.  We find that various types of training classes were instituted.  A large class of catechists was given Bible Training from 1905 to 1906.  This was followed by a class for Church Elders from 1908 to 1910.  Between 1909 and 1915 three groups of teachers were trained specifically for school work.[79] This Normal Training School had been developed by Hartwig Harms, who took Krueger's place in 1902, and it was deeply regretted that it had to be closed down in 1914 with the removal of the German missionaries at the start of the first World War.[80]

In 1897 changes were necessary in Tirupati because of the unhealthy location of the missionary buildings on the east side. The boarding school and the main station were transferred to new buildings constructed on the west side of the town.  The high school was kept on the east side, however, and additional construction done in 1899.  A new Church was completed and dedicated November 11, 1903.  It was a very nice building, 60 feet by 30 feet, with a 70-foot steeple.  The chancel was impressive.  Unfortunately the best quality wood was not used in the building which necessitated occasional repairs.[81]

A sister Church to that in Tirupati was constructed by Hartwig Harms in Sulurpeta.  Built in 1904, it was designed in such a

292

way that it could be enlarged at a future date. It was a long church, with the side walls constructed with thin columns and the area of wall between them mostly Gothic windows. These could be removed at a later date and a side nave added on each side. The Church in Nayudupeta had to be reconstructed in this period. A Chapel was built at Mopur in the Venkatagiri field in 1897.

Adventists had started work in Renigunta but were never very successful. In 1909 they sold the chapel with its land to the Hermannsburg Mission for 800 marks.[82] By doing this, the Mission was able to maintain the position it had held since the beginning of its work in this area, to have a field without competition from any other Protestant group.[83]

The only new main station opened from 1883 until the German missionaries had to leave in 1914 was Puttur,[84] a substation of Tirupati. As early as 1884 a site had been chosen and a small bungalow built for a catechist. When the Mission took over the government school and distances prevented close supervision of the work from Tirupati, it was decided to place a missionary there. Part of the reason for this move was because the Hermanns- burg Mission learned that the Methodists from the southeast of that area (Chingleput District) were planning to take over Puttur and its substations if the Hermannsburg Mission did not develop it more thoroughly.[85]

Because of the unsatisfactory vegetation on the old site, a new one was selected and building started. Krueger was the first missionary to settle there. A shed was used for a church at first, but then services were held in the school. The congregation developed slowly. Scriba, son of one of the first missionaries, followed Krueger. In the first year he visited the entire district twice and the southern part three times. He was able to work with the Sudras also. When rich relatives of his wife offered to help pay for a church, Scriba chose an excellent location situated high on a knoll and began the construction. It was dedicated by Woerrlein October 9, 1907.

In 1909 because of the large number of Christians moving to Madras, Asirvadam was sent there as a catechist to serve them and to establish a congregation for Telugu-speaking Christians.[86] This was considered a substation to Sulurpeta, but within a year it was transferred to the responsibility of Puttur. Missionary Johann Maneke, who had come to India in 1898 with young Scriba, followed Scriba in Puttur and worked diligently in Puttur and Madras. He also revived the work at Sriharikota by placing the catechist Christian there, rebuilding the chapel and school, and visiting the area regularly. The congregation developed mostly from people who had moved to Sriharikota from other places.

Workers' Annual Conferences were established in December, 1904. This was quite a change from the old system in which the superintendent would visit each of the main stations, call in the teachers and catechists, and examine them in subjects of doctrine and have them write a sermon.  The Lutheran Publication Society established in Guntur by the Telugu Lutheran Missions[87] began the publication of a paper in 1904 entitled <u>Kraistava Bodhakudu</u> ("Christian Teacher"), which furnished both news and material on which workers' examinations could be held.  When the workers met in their Annual Conferences in Nayudupeta, they were examined on the topics printed in that magazine.  The Conference began with the Lord's Supper and continued for three days, with suitable addresses covering a large variety of subjects.[88]

Director Egmont Harms made a second visit to India in December, 1909 and January, 1910.  Problems had arisen in regard to the school system, social situation, the education and employment of native pastors, and self-support of the congregations.  He found the missionaries interested in their task, faithful and earnest. He was not so pleased about the native workers.  He felt many of them were unreliable; others, such as Pastors Punitudu and Isaak, were excellent.  Hartwig Harms comments in this connection that the native workers proved Director Harms wrong.  While the Director favored the system in the African Hermannsburg Mission, where education was not emphasized as much as experience, Hartwig Harms found real character-building in the educational process. The African leaders did not prove to be worthy even in peacetime, while the natives in India, trained and educated, stood up under the most trying situations.[89]

At this conference, the constitution was once more revised and brought into agreement with the new African constitution, with a few differences resulting naturally from the varying situations. The entire foreign work now had a unified church constitution and closer relations between the two missions were established.[90]

B. Evangelism and the Mass Movement among the Outcastes

1. The strengths and weaknesses of the Movement

The Telugu territory was one of the major areas in which the mass movement among outcastes occurred following the great famine in 1876-1879. Because of the tragic need of the people, the missionaries spent most of their time assisting the government in the distribution of the "Mansion House Relief." We have already noted how the people were drawn to the Christian Church as a result of this famine.[91]

The majority of the missionaries saw the dangers inherent in receiving people into the Church when they have been moved by the love and concern and aid brought to them in the time of hunger and disease. They were fearful that many would return to Hinduism after the period of need was over. Still others, accustomed to the American emphasis on individualism and personal conversion, found it difficult to accept such a mass movement where whole families and villages desired to enter the Christian Church at the same time.

The problem of preparing adequately such large numbers of people for baptism loomed large in the minds of the missionaries. Their native staff was entirely inadequate; the missionaries were too involved in supervisory tasks to spend the time needed for such instruction; and it would be well-nigh impossible to follow up the instruction with the proper pastoral care and discipline.

But the pressure on the missionaries to go ahead with the baptism of thousands desiring it increased to the point that it could no longer be held back.[92] Seventeen hundred persons were baptized in the Guntur Mission during the two years following the famine, but when the famine relief came to an end, about 600 backsliders were reported. A great deal of caution had been taken to prepare the newly-baptized before they received Holy Communion. The waiting period was used in the continued study of the Bible under catechists and teachers and the learning of Luther's Catechism.

The survey made under the direction of the Rev. Dr. J. Waskom Pickett throughout the Mass Movement areas in the Andhra Desa reveals that many of the fears of the missionaries concerning this great movement were unfounded. Rather than the people coming into the Church for purely selfish reasons and then in

297

turn showing much self-centeredness in ignoring others of their
castes still non-Christian, interview after interview revealed
that many of the people were drawn to the Church because of its
selfless devotion in relieving the suffering of all people.
While the Brahmans in positions of authority cared for their own
primarily, the missionaries remained as impartial as possible.[93]

The Mass Movements revealed that Father Heyer was correct
in developing village congregations in the Palnad and bringing
the people into the Church by family groups. Although there
seemed to be a definite danger that the spiritual level of the
group would be lower, the reverse was usually the case. When a
whole group became Christian, it was easier to give up their idol
worship, to oppose the pressure of the upper castes, to refuse to
participate in the festivals, and to encourage each other in that
which became the basic standards for being a Christian.[94] The
unity of village life was usually maintained in the Mass Movement
areas without the disruption which occurs so often when outside
forces enter an area that has been the same for thousands of
years. Of course, there were adjustments and many of them, since
the standards expected of the Christians were far different than
those of the Mala and Madiga outcaste; and the upper castes had
to become accustomed to the changing attitudes of these former
serfs who had deserved less respect than their cattle. To see

such changes in the life of the despised castes brought respect and approval in the long run.[95]

Pickett emphasizes the importance of this group life strongly when he says:[96]

> "We are persuaded that the quality of faith and experience is very much better in the areas where group or mass movements have taken place than in areas where converts have been won by independent, individual decision. In Andhra Desa we interviewed hundreds of converts of more than forty castes. In a high proportion of such interviews we heard convincing testimonies of personal and family experience of the grace of Jesus Christ. A typical testimony was given by an aged Erukala woman. 'I did not want to be a Christian until my sons and all the rest of our community urged it. They had more sense than I did and I agreed to follow them. Now I am glad, for my sins have been washed away. Every day I talk to Jesus, my Saviour, and He gives me joy.'"

The congregations which developed in the Mass Movement areas maintained village simplicity and did not tend to take on western ideas. When whole communities became Christian, the leaders previous to the change very often were the leaders in the congregation. Thus the panchayat maintained its discipline, and the congregation remained "thoroughly Indian in social patterns and customs."[97]

Perhaps the greatest concern of the missionaries when the large movements began among the outcastes was that the door would be closed entirely to the upper castes. At first this was true. In the Telugu area, the Baptists became known as the Madiga religion, the Lutherans the Mala religion. And there were many years when seemingly impossible barriers were built up between the

Christian community and the non-Christian neighbor. By 1920, however, these were breaking down and the example of the Christians
was drawing those in upper castes toward the Church. "So far
from proving an obstacle to the conversion of the higher classes,
mass movements of the depressed classes have actually increased
the number of such converts."[98]

This was especially true in the Palnad area where Heyer had
his initial successes. Mrs. George Albrecht cites many cases
where the Sudras were coming in ever greater numbers.[99] By 1920
one-fourth of the Christians in the Palnad belonged to Sudra
groups.[100]

### 2. The Mission meeting the life situation of the convert

In this period we find the missionaries realizing more and
more the importance of keeping the Christian within his own environment. Fortunately, for the Lutheran Church in the Andhra
Desa, there was never too much of the tendency to take Christians out of their villages and bring them into the station centers under the protection of the missionary.

Catechists and teachers were trained in ever greater numbers,
so that the people could be reached in their villages, worship
services held regularly, and life carried on as a Christian within the community where the individual had always lived. The
training of the teachers and catechists was primarily in the ver-

nacular. The village schools not only taught the ABCs, but they also introduced the children to simple rules of cleanliness, to growing gardens of vegetables and flowers, and to ways of improving their home life. These schools spread everywhere. In 1920 when the Guntur and Rajahmundry Missions merged, there were congregations in 1200 villages; and there were 900 elementary schools in which 1300 teachers were used to care for 28,000 pupils.[101]

It was freely admitted that there was much to be desired in many of the village schools. Mrs. Albrecht commented that in some schools in the Palnad there were improvements from year to year which could definitely be noticed; in other villages, however, even after there had been a school for many years, often only three or four or even twenty out of a congregation of 140 or 150 could read. Parents so often saw no value in an education much less considering it to be an advantage for their children. They were faced with immediate wants which forced them to take the boys of 8 or 10 years of age and have them add to the family income by earning their pennies. Mr. Albrecht planned to emphasize family worship, which meant that more and more fathers would be expected to be able to read the Bible.

The government inspection and the fact that aid would not be received unless the schools came up to certain standards in regard to the school house, facilities and furniture, and a qualified teacher, were considered to be beneficial in forcing improvement.

Among the government's requirements was the teaching of nature study, drawing and gardening.[102]

The strong emphasis of the Lutheran Church on catechetical training helped in nurturing family and congregational life. The Breklum missionaries reported that catechetical education was accompanied with education in Christian customs and prayer. Home devotions were cherished, and the missionaries assisted the families in this through regular visits in the homes.[103] The Breklum missionaries were not interested in large numbers so much as forming a strong and faithful native congregation. The Gospel was geared to the daily life of the people; every effort was made to raise the level of family life through practical instructions. To improve the social and physical situation of the women in the homes was part of the task of the missionary and his workers.[104]

The tendency for the boys and girls who went away to boarding schools in the mission centers not to return to their villages was met by the establishment of more higher elementary schools closer to their villages. The life in those schools was maintained on the simplest level; children returned home frequently at the time of vacations; and the courses developed were such as to be most useful in the village situation.[105] Very often the boys and girls had gardens to care for, regular tasks to perform in the school community, and house parents to give them the feel-

ing of family life.[106]  The girls were prepared for motherhood
and to be the center of Christian homes.[107]

## 3.  Efforts at self-support

With most of the Christians coming from the depressed classes and the Andhra Desa suffering from periodic famines, it is not
difficult to understand why progress toward self-support was extremely slow.  The early missionaries were so moved by the tragic
plight of the people that most of them distributed gifts regularly to the poor and helpless.  They tended to be lenient with the
converts and not insist on regular offerings; in fact, the Hermannsburg missionaries felt impelled to help the Christians when
they left work to attend worship services on Sunday.  The same
was true of the period of catechetical training.[108]  At the time
Director Egmont Harms visited Nayudupeta in 1892 he found more
than 100 catechumens in the compound receiving instructions.  Entire families were there, sleeping in the church, the school and
the porches of the missionary bungalows.  Harms realized some
were probably there to receive material help.  Others had planned
to come long before this but could not leave their employment.
Now that famine and lack of rain had put most people out of work,
they took this opportunity to receive instruction and, incidentally, receive enough food to keep them going for a while.[109]

303

Harms at that visit instituted a Savings and Loan Association, with the initial capital investment of 3,000 marks. He also recommended that as much land be secured as possible for the people. Although he did not feel the day of large industrial schools had arrived in the Mission, he urged the missionaries to search for other ways to teach the native Christians new crafts to take the place of the employment many of them lost when they became Christians.

He promised the congregation at Tirupati that he would raise funds in Germany for the purpose of buying land for the Christians. But he expected them to show diligence and faithfulness by repairing their chapel.[110] Missionary Maneke reported that he bought land for his people and at the same time trained them to support the poor and the widowed in the congregation.[111] While some missionaries felt that the outcaste, not being accustomed to ideas of independence and self-support, had lost all sense of initiative, thrift, industry and honesty, others felt that the Christian should be faced with the responsibility of contributing something just as he had given before his conversion. In times of festival and disease, most Hindus gave heavily to their gods. They must be trained to do so in the Church as well and not expect hand-outs from the missionary whenever needed. Part of the problem, of course, was that the native worker or pastor preferred his regular support from the Mission rather than the people.

This gave him greater freedom of action, for the people could not demand services of him when they did not pay for them. And he felt much more secure in the service of the Mission.[112]

Missionary Warber, who had come to India in 1894, was the first to make a real attempt at a large agricultural undertaking to help the Christians help themselves. About two miles from Kodur there was a river with an old dam and channel leading to rice fields. This had fallen into disrepair and the fields were not being used. Warber approached the government; and the land was given to him on condition that he repair the dam and channel and pay the taxes. Although the other missionaries favored the project since they were in the midst of one of India's worst famines,[113] they insisted he must take the entire risk on his own shoulders. It was a big project, but when done he had so much land that he could take care of all the Christians in the area and also lease some land to Brahmans and Sudras, for which he gained the respect of many. Money was lent to the Christians for oxen and wagons, which money they were to pay back gradually. Schaefer told of a similar experience by Harms at Kurigonda.[114]

> "When the farmers had saved enough to buy their own land they were to either buy the plot they had been working or move off and get some other piece of ground, permitting the mission to help some other poor Indian. The whole idea was good but it failed because it did not take the Indian personality into account. The Indians were only too glad to move onto the land, but they were not willing to do anything more. Since the mission was supplying seed, it did not matter to them whether they had a good crop or not, just so

305

long as there was enough there to keep them fed. Since the
mission was supplying equipment it did not matter what care
they took of it as they felt they could always get more.
Even for their food they became dependent upon the mission
and finally, when the mission said 'No' and refused to give
them anything for a while, they turned against the mission,
feeling hurt, and called in the heathen to the point even of
trying to obtain the land by going to court where they tried
to insist that they had bought the land through the crops
they turned over to the mission."

At the time of Egmont Harms' second inspection tour to India

at the close of 1909, the decision was made to give up the Savings

and Loan Association as it had not proved successful. Attention

was directed to establishing farm schools. Three of them were

started to teach the people better methods of farming without hav-

ing to use tools beyond their means. At the same time was offer-

ed elementary education for those who could not read and write,

together with religious instruction through classes and daily de-

votions. The most successful of the schools was at Nayudupeta.

Although they were not spectacular in any way, they were a means

of training people who had lost their jobs by becoming Christian,

and thereby giving them a means of livelihood. The Mission had

learned, by previous experience, that this preliminary education

was necessary if the outcaste was to hold onto the land he bought

through Mission assistance. And the schools, through the use of

good techniques and no labor costs, more than paid for the cost

of establishing and running them by the value of the crops raised

on the school farms.[115]

Hermann Poppe, the first layman to come to the Hermannsburg field, arrived in 1896. Hartwig Harms assisted him in organizing an industrial school in Nayudupeta. Most of the missionaries opposed the idea until they found what good dependable workers were supplied for the construction of Mission buildings. Various crafts were taught the boys during the day -- cabinet making, carpentering, bricklaying and the blacksmith trade. Weaving was added later. At night they received additional instruction over and above the elementary education which they had when they entered. The course took four years and was aimed at creating an effective 'skilled labor' class in the native congregations. Johannes Burmester was the industrial missionary from 1904 on and, under his direction, the school gained a wide reputation in the field of furniture-making. In 1909 he had more than 40 persons working, 13 already journeymen and past the apprentice stage. At first the school supplied only the needs of the Mission; but later it branched out and sold articles. The government helped the school through an annual grant. The greatest blessing, of course, was the improvement of the economic condition of many of the Christians. Moreover, they made excellent church members, contributing well and taking an active part as lay leaders. When Commissioner Benze stopped in Nayudupeta on his way to Rajahmundry,[116] he visited the industrial school and considered it to be superior to the one he saw in Madura. He commented:[117]

"It is wise to have a layman and not a preacher for such
work. This man produces fine furniture and can compete in
the open market with the firms of Madras. Thus he teaches
a good trade to such as would otherwise learn nothing and
puts into their hands the means of earning a good livelihood. It is the working out of a good missionary problem."

As early as 1879 the Mission Conference in the Guntur field
was taking steps toward self-support when, with the Board's approval, they "required the native congregations to contribute at
least a part of the salary of their teachers. ... It is hoped
that in this way the native Christians may be gradually trained
to entire self-support."[118] Stork Memorial Church in Guntur,
with some assistance from the missionaries, was supporting at this
same time a missionary teacher in the field and hoped to assume
the support of a village pastor in addition.

The missionaries, during the two great famines of 1897 and
1900, did a tremendous work in relieving starvation and giving
employment. The latter famine was the more severe in the Guntur
area. There was no rain for a year. One-half of the hill tribes
were said to have died; 95% of the cattle perished. The Lutheran
mission carried on relief for 100,000 people. A sum of 4,700
English pounds was sent from Lutherans in America to help in this
area.[119] Harpster directed the central famine camp. Uhl, in the
three southern Taluks where he was serving at the time, employed
4,613 people who earned at total of Rs. 10,212 on various construction projects paid for by the government and the Mission.[120]

It was at this time also that the missionaries helped many
of the Christians to obtain lands and home sites. Unangst secured lands for church members in Sattenapalle and Bapatla taluks.
High tide of the policy was from 1894 to 1899. Much land was re-
claimed from almost primeval waste and put up for sale at public
auction. Albrecht in the Palnad and Uhl in Tenali, Repalle and
Bapatla were leaders in purchasing this land for Christians. Uhl
declared: "Hundreds of acres passed through my hands and most of
them were paid for by the recipients within fifteen years."[121]
He was able to help about 1,000 people.

Schmidt in Rajahmundry helped in famine relief. People
wanted to offer children in exchange for a little food. Instead
he accepted jewelry and lands without interest in return for food.
The income from these lands he used in the work at the time funds
were so slow in coming from the United States.[122]

Even before this he started what later became a highly-devel-
oped industrial program in the Rajahmundry field. When in 1873
the bungalow Valett had constructed at the time of his marriage
needed rebuilding,[123] Schmidt employed Christian workers, even
some from the surrounding villages, and taught them how to do the
work. He realized it cost him more, and he spent a great deal of
time explaining how to make the various necessary items, but he
had the satisfaction of knowing that they profited by it and had
an opportunity, in addition, to attend the daily prayer service.

Three years later he employed boarding school boys and native
Christians in the construction of a houseboat to sail the network
of canals in the Delta. The cost of it, $600, came from the sel-
ling of photographs and disposing of some property which he had
bought at Dowlaishwaram. The "Dove of Peace" became a familiar
sight as it was used by many of the missionaries as they traveled
to the villages.

When the Executive Committee in America appealed for funds
to build the Rajahmundry Church, St. Paul's, this projected construction permitted Schmidt to expand his industrial school to include carpenter- and blacksmith-shops, a brick yard, a saw-pit and
a lumber-yard. In commenting about this Dolbeer stated:[124]

> "He was very proud of this project and devoted a great deal
> of time and energy to it. Creditable results can be seen
> even as late as today growing out of our Dr. Schmidt's labours,
> in that at Rajahmundry and Dowlaishwaram, more than any where
> else in our church, there may be found Christian families
> with a tradition of carpenter work, building contracting, a
> knowledge of mechanics, etc., handed down from grandfathers
> who were trained by Dr. Schmidt."

The Home Board never was convinced of the value of this industrial
school and refused to support it after 1896.

Very shortly after Schmidt had come to Rajahmundry in 1870,
he realized that he must do something to make it possible for the
Indian churches to be self-supporting and not depend on financial
aid from America. There were periods when he was receiving nothing
except what he earned with his own hands. And so he conceived

the idea of imitating the system whereby the Indian temples were endowed with lands, from which revenue priests received their income. He began by securing some land at Velpur and permitting Christians to use it with the understanding that they would pay for their portion in three or four years. He loaned money to them without interest.

His theory was to buy up land while it was cheap, construct a small church on it, and have it understood that every member of the congregation give a certain number of days each year to caring for the land. He pointed out the advantages of such an arrangement to be:[125]

> "1. That independent native churches would be established.
> 2. That the increase of the minister's salary would depend on the help of the congregation, and that he, therefore, would have to care for them as well as they for him. The qualifications of the minister would, in course of time, also depend on the pay they raise for him. 3. That a more brotherly feeling would exist between the missionary and his native ministers in spite of difference in pay, as each would draw his pay from his own country and remain a son of his own soil, and the one would no longer be the servant of the other."

Schmidt collected money to buy lands from the time of the 1876-1878 famine, investing funds of his own, and finally receiving a large amount, $8,000, from a former parishioner in America. We have already pointed out the trouble which ensued because of the secrecy with which he handled this fund.[126] Commissioner Benze investigated these lands, especially those bought by the Haas fund, when he was in India in 1908-1909, and found that some were well

taken care of by the Christians while others were sadly neglected.  At one place where the people were making no effort to improve their position, Dr. Harpster told Benze: "There is no way
to drive them from the place except to set fire to the roofs of
their hovels.  This is one of the sweet Christian things connected with such land schemes."[127]

It must be admitted that the scheme did not accomplish its
planned purpose.  The outcastes were not able to assume farming
responsibility, would not do any work without the accustomed supervision, could not maintain themselves (often because the land
was poor), and soon returned to their former coolie jobs.  Moreover, much discontent was created in the congregations since all
of them could not be provided land.  The whole history of the
land development in the Rajahmundry field caused much grief to
Dr. Schmidt and was a major factor in his being recalled from
service.[128]

A few congregations, however, which were favorably located
have prospered.  In a letter to the author, Dr. Dolbeer wrote:[129]

"Some of our good congregations in Bhimavaram taluk today
live on lands secured by Schmidt and given to their grand-
parents.  I visited such a village this last month, Dina-
samarru, about seven miles south of Bhimavaram.  A congregation of 900 people, every family owns at least some land,
from two or three acres, up to 40 acres among the most fortunate.  Quite an independent group, quite able to support
their own Christian work.  Across the drainage canal are two
similar villages.  In those early days these were merely
waste lands, marginal lands along the sea-coast, but Schmidt
secured them for our people and by dint of hard work they
have become fairly productive."

312

Commissioner Benze gathered the following facts regarding self-support in the Rajahmundry field when he visited there:[130]

"1st -- Our schoolhouses and most prayerhouses are built from native money, and in the case of the schoolhouses the grant must be added.

2nd -- The Rampa and Widows' Funds are raised by the natives.

3rd -- They raise the Congregational Funds for current expenses.

4th -- Propositions are being made for a Poor Fund: More ought to be done and could be done in the Bhimavaram Talug."

## C. The Zenana Work

One of the outstanding features of this final period of our survey is the entrance of single women missionaries into the foreign mission work of the Lutheran Church. The wives of the missionaries through the years had been active in the running of girls' schools, and in contact with the women in the zenanas, those areas in the homes of the upper castes where the women are secluded from the view of all men other than their husbands and near male relatives. In the beginning of the Guntur Mission, Father Heyer organized four months after his arrival a Hindu girls' school with the support of Judge Walker's wife.[131] Mrs. Walter Gunn started teaching English and needlework to Hindu girls shortly after her arrival.[132] After her husband's death she remained in India for two years to run the Girls' School.

"Through the aid of Mrs. Pardhasarathy, a native Christian lady, educated in the Free Church Mission School, Madras, who has done much to develop woman's work among her non-

Christian sisters of Guntur, Mrs. Uhl, in the year 1878, began a systematic visitation, and through Mrs. Pardhasarathy gave regular instruction in a few homes of some of the leading native gentlemen. This was a small beginning, but was the seed-corn of the Zenana work ... ."[133]

With other neighboring missions using or considering the use of women missionaries, it was natural for the Foreign Mission Board to suggest to the Synod the possibility of using women missionaries in Guntur. This occurred in 1871.[134] Again at the 1877 convention of the Synod the matter was re-entered with the suggestion by the Board that missionary societies for women be considered. Two years later the report of the Board indicates that both on the congregational and Synodical level women's societies were being organized and that the general organization would be in effect shortly. However, it was felt that the time was not ripe for sending single women missionaries and the suggestion was made to the Women's Societies that they take over the support of the Girls' Schools in the Guntur field, involving an annual expenditure of about $400.[135]

The first Zenana missionary to arrive in Guntur was Miss Kate Boggs, who came with the Rev. and Mrs. Schnure on February 15, 1881. She was compelled by ill health to return to America very shortly.[136] In 1883 came two more, Miss Anna S. Kugler, M.D., and Miss Fannie Dryden. Although Miss Kugler was a physician, the Board did not approve of medical work at that time and would not give an appropriation for such. Miss Dryden and Miss

314

Kugler started work by assisting Mrs. Unangst and P. Lucy, a Sudra convert, in the visiting of caste women's homes.

Two Hindu Girls' Schools were opened in 1883 in Guntur and Mangalagiri, which are flourishing to this day. They also took over the responsibility of the Girls' Boarding School from Mrs. Unangst and Mrs. Schnure. In February, 1892, a Training School for Mistresses was opened with an enrollment of eight. This was for girls who had finished the fifth standard. The next year Miss Minnie Moses became headmistress and continued to work in the Training School until 1929.[137] Miss Sadtler, later Mrs. George Albrecht, was the first manager of the school. The Girls' School became a secondary school in 1907, a high school in 1911. Dr. Sylvanus Stall, an American educator, gave most of the money for the present high school building completed in 1912. It is known as Stall High School.

Work among the Muslim women of Guntur has been carried on since 1884 when a school for Mohammedan Girls was opened. Miss Jeanne Rollier was the first single woman to learn Urdu, working among the Muslim women beginning in 1903. Miss Jessie Thomas was assigned to that work in 1908. This was most difficult work, but Miss Thomas had six girls who knew Urdu working with her as teachers and Zenana workers.

A refuge for convert women who had come for protection under the care of the missionaries in Guntur was established in 1914.

315

It became a place of instruction for those needing training in the Christian Faith and in the course of time naturally developed into a training school for Bible Women. Education was very elementary. The first class of fourteen finished in 1915. In 1920 there were 31 students. Only three remained in the Converts' Home.

By 1920 there had come to Guntur a total of 26 single women missionaries to serve in the Hospitals and the Women's Work. At the end of our period of discussion the work began to spread from Guntur to the other centers.[138]

* * *

Mrs. William J. Cutter opened the first Girls' School in Rajahmundry in 1852. How long it continued is not known. In 1882, Mrs. Schmidt started a little school on Riverdale compound for caste girls. Mr. P. V. Ratnam was the headmaster.

In the meantime, Christian girls had been attending the Central Boys' School and three of them were placed in the homes of native Christians as boarders in August, 1880. A year later, a separate boarding house was established for 13 girls under the care of Matron N. Deborah, a Christian widow. Mrs. Artman was the spirit behind the boarding school.

The first zenana work began when the district munsiff, Narasimham, permitted Mrs. Schmidt and Mrs. Artman to enter his home for the purpose of instructing his wife and daughter. Five others were present at the first meeting. This was continued two afternoons a week.

Before his death, Artman appealed to the Foreign Missions Committee to send out a single woman missionary to continue the work started among the women and girls in Rajahmundry. Mrs. Artman remained for a time after her husband's death as the first salaried woman missionary. At the close of 1890 two single women arrived, Miss Agnes Schade and Miss Katherine Sadtler. They took charge of the Mohammedan Girls' School that had been started by Artman, and also the Caste Girls' School.

In 1895 they also took charge of the Girls' Boarding School which had been conducted in conjunction with the Rajahmundry Boys' School. A building was rented and the school opened with 19 boarders and 25 day pupils. This was the beginning of the institution which became the Schade Girls' School. It started with six classes. Two more were added in 1898. By 1904 a teachers' training section was opened.

As more women missionaries arrived, the work was expanded. New Hindu Girls' Schools were established in different parts of Rajahmundry and its outskirts. Miss Charlotte Swenson, who arrived in 1895, directed the work of the Bible Women. She reported in 1906 that 270 homes were visited weekly and 1200 women and children were under instruction.

Commissioner Benze found that the girls in Miss Schade's
school knew the Bible very well. All the teachers were Christian. Even the Hindu Girls' Schools had mostly Christian teachers and were good missionary agents. A Rajahmundry Missionary
Society had been organized by Miss Schade among the Christian
women and missionaries. When Benze attended one of their meetings, he commented: "The program was furnished by the girls of
the school. It was of a very high order and filled us with ad-
miration for these women and girls."[139]

As early as 1878 Mrs. Schmidt had sent lace from Rajahmundry to Philadelphia, and thus was initiated an industry with a
long history. In 1908 Mrs. Harpster reported that 240 women were
engaged in making lace. This not only gave work to poor widows
and others in need, but through the work many were given spiritual guidance and religious training. The program was self-supporting; in fact, Rs. 1,000 was contributed in 1907 from this
program to build a Hindu Girls' School. Sites were purchased in
1912 and 1913 for other schools from profits of the industry.
Miss Charlotte Hollerbach became the first full-time missionary
responsible for the lace industry, arriving in 1915. In 1919 in
Samalkot, in connection with the lace industry being carried on
there, a Dorcas Home was started for helpless or crippled women
and girls. This was later placed under Miss Hollerbach's care
in Rajahmundry.

At the close of this period, in addition to the Central Girls' School in Rajahmundry conducted by Miss Schade, boarding schools were established in Samalkot and Bhimawaram -- in 1918-1919.[140] Twenty-two single women came to the Rajahmundry field before 1920 to serve in Zenana and medical work.

* * *

In the Hermannsburg field, a Girls' School was established in Gudur by Petersen in 1869, with a boarding school connected with it. After his death, the school was transferred to Kodur where Mrs. Woerrlein, who had an excellent knowledge of Telugu, developed the School and widened its activities. When Woerrlein became Mission Director, he made Gudur his headquarters in 1892, and the Girls' School was transferred once more back to that center.

At first this school was mostly for orphans and unwanted girls. The children were trained in cleanliness, orderliness and industry as well as the regular school subjects. Home making and fancy work, with special emphasis on lace making, were taught the older girls. The profit from the sale of lace, which was sold in Germany and America, helped to support the school. Many of these girls became the wives of native workers and set excellent examples of Christian homes in the villages.

When Woerrlein was in Germany in 1901 he strongly urged sending Zenana missionaries in an article entitled: "Is the Zenana Missionary necessary in India?" As a result, various women's associations were formed. Woerrlein's daughter, Magdalene, returned with her parents to become the first Zenana worker, on July 23, 1901. At the end of the first year, Mrs. Woerrlein and her daughter were busy visiting Hindu and Muslim homes, and also looking after the Christian mothers in Gudur. They were ably assisted by Rachel, the widow of a catechist, who had been teaching in the Girls' Boarding School.

Miss Adele Schickinz arrived in 1904 to take over the work from Mrs. Woerrlein and her daughter; the daughter returned to Germany to marry a pastor. As the work expanded, a native teacher was employed for the fancy lace work. A school was built and completed in 1906; and Miss Martha Woerrlein came the next year to take charge of the lace school. This relieved Miss Schickinz for full-time Zenana work. A new Zenana station was opened in Tirupati in 1908. Miss Schickinz moved there when she was replaced in Gudur by Miss Martha Drewes. The first baptism in Tirupati through Zenana work was the wife of the police inspector, on July 17, 1910. In the next year 24 were baptized at Gudur.

Miss Schickinz married Missionary Lindner in 1912, but continued in the work as her husband was located at Tirupati. The same year two deaconesses came out to India to enter the work, Elsie Kastens and Anna-Marie Meyberg. The work expanded in the next few years to Puttur, where Maneke's wife supervised the work of two Bible women and two women teachers, one in the Middle school and one in the Elementary school. Sister Elsie opened new work in Venkatagiri in 1914. She visited the Rajah's wife, but found her indifferent and illiterate. Three more Zenana women were ready to come from Germany when the War broke out. When the missionaries were removed, the work was left in the hands of the Bible women under the supervision of Mrs. Carl Scriba. The Girls' School and Lace School were moved to Kodur when the Scribas were required by the government to locate there.

A Widows' Home had been opened by Mrs. Scriba in Kalahasti in 1908, but this was closed during the War. Another interesting feature of the women's work was the first women's conference, held in Gudur under Mrs. Woerrlein's direction, March 31, 1909. Subjects for discussion were the place of women in the homes (Christian or Hindu), the visitation of the sick, the teaching of the uneducated and the improvement of home living. Local women's samajes (societies) were recommended, with one of the activities to be sewing so that clothing could be prepared for poor children. Latest figures before the War for the Zenana work in the Hermannsburg field were that 80 homes were being contacted weekly with the activities centering around handwork, Bible stories and hymn singing. Some were instructed in reading. Also, the workers visited many Christian women in their homes regularly.[141]

## D. The Expanding Horizon

### 1. In Education

The Lutheran Missions during this final period of our history have generally accepted the grant-in-aid program of the British government and thus have been able to expand their work to a great extent. The suspicions of the Rajahmundry and Hermannsburg Missions concerning government control that might go along with the grants evaporated.

There was an increasing concern that the village schools serve not only as schools preparing children for church membership, but also that the children receive enough education through the school system as to be considered literate. Too many of the children, because of the lack of interest on the part of the parents, or because they were needed to supplement the family income, never finished the few elementary grades that were offered in the village schools. Missionaries knew that much of the weakness of the village schools came from the lack of training and initiative of the teachers. A concentrated effort was made in this period to improve the quality of the village teachers as well as increase their numbers.

Even at that, the trained teachers were still in a minority in 1920, and of those who were supposedly trained, many had not gone beyond the primary (Fifth Standard) grades with normal training added.

A big step forward in the Rajahmundry and Guntur Missions was the establishment of Boarding Schools in the taluks. These were most helpful in providing more localized opportunity for village people to advance beyond elementary village education. It not only provided more and better-trained teachers and workers for the Missions, but it also led the way to a more educated laity. Such schools were started in Sattenapalle, Narasaravupet, Chirala, Tenali, Tarlupad, Bhimawaram, Peddapur, and Parvitapur.

Several of these schools advanced until they became High Schools. The school in Peddapur, started by Dr. Edman in 1891 as a primary school, developed into a Lower Secondary School with the Fourth Form added in 1899 under the direction of the Rev. Hans Isaacson. By April, 1900, recognition as a High School was obtained from the government. During this period it was managed privately by the missionaries. In 1903 the institution was turned over to the Rajahmundry Mission which took it on condition that a Christian would be added to the staff as a Bible teacher. At that time there were eighteen teachers, all Hindu, and 475 pupils, mostly Brahman by caste. The Rev. P. V. Ratnam was appointed to the position of Bible teacher following his ordination.[142] This was the only Mission High School on the Rajahmundry field until 1916. Its building was constructed in 1911 from proceeds of the sale of the Haas lands in Bhimawaram taluk.

The Rev. Ernst Neudoerffer established a school and hostel
in Bhimawaram in 1912. This fast growing area[143] soon necessitated introducing the Secondary section by 1914 and raising it to the
High School level by 1916. A well-planned building was completed
in 1918.

The oldest of Rajahmundry's mission institutions, the Central
Boys' School, which had had such an up-and-down career,[144] moved
to its new location north of Rajahmundry at Luthergiri in 1908.
This school had often been called the 'Seminary', although only
of lower secondary level, because of its thorough emphasis on
Christian teaching. It prepared the early leaders for Mission
service. When it was moved, Dr. Neudoerffer changed the school,
with the consent of the government, to a Normal Training School of
two grades, lower and higher. A Middle School was added to it in
1915.

Builder of this new school at Luthergiri was the Rev. F. J.
McCready, who had resigned in 1899, but who remained in Rajahmundry,
his home town, and was active as a building contractor.[145] The
school was organized to provide teachers and village catechists.
An important change took place, however, from 1915-1917. The Middle School and the Normal Training School, together with the Model
Primary School connected with them, were moved back into the center of Rajahmundry. Luthergiri was then developed distinctively
as a Bible Training School. Junior Bible Classes giving one or

two years of religious training were added about a year later. After seventy years of history, the Rajahmundry Mission finally
took steps to provide an adequate institution for the training of
pastors. In 1917 six men were admitted to a three-year course,
and they were ordained January 1, 1920, at the Jubilee celebration.[146]

Guntur established its Bible Training School in 1894 when
the Central Boarding School in the Groenning compound was placed
in the charge of the Rev. John Aberly. He directed this work for
nearly thirty years and trained hundreds of workers for the Guntur Mission. A building was constructed in 1897 using the Rs.
15,000 offering received in the Jubilee tour.[147]  It is known as
Heyer Memorial Hall.

The most outstanding institution of the Guntur-Rajahmundry
Missions was the High School which had been organized by Dr. Uhl
in 1874.[148]  The Rev. Luther B. Wolf came to India in 1883 and became principal two years later when Dr. Uhl went home on furlough.
He raised the school immediately to a Second Grade College affiliated with Madras University. It was named American Evangelical
Lutheran Mission College. Uhl raised money in America for the
college and a new building was completed by 1893, called the Arthur G. Watts Memorial building.[149]

From its small beginning, 19 students in the first Arts
Class of 1890, none of them Christian, it grew gradually to serve

an important function in the life of the Andhra Lutheran Church.
The first Christian student entered in 1895. In 1903 there were
64 students in all. At that time the Government Inspector reported that "the College bids fair to be the best in the Northern
Circars."[150] Seventy percent of the students passed the University examinations.

The Rev. J. Roy Strock, a science graduate, became the
Principal in 1913. The college classes held 211 students in 1914,
two of them women. Dr. Strock carried on negotiations with the
Rev. W. C. Penn, Principal of Noble College, Masulipatam, with
the suggestion that the Andhra Desa would be strengthened by having a Union College in a location such as Bezwada. But Mr. Penn
was rather reluctant to take the step, arguing that the fact that
Noble College was a 'first-grade' college ought to lead other
Missions to cooperate with it, and thus convert it into a United
Missions College rather than to establish a new institution. But
the Guntur Mission considered Masulipatam to be too far from the
center of its field ,and also felt a new institution would be
wiser than rebuilding one of the present ones. Guntur College
held off any building program or the raising of the institution
to a first-grade college until some decision could be made.[151]

Dr. Strock, as Principal of the Mission College, was also
in charge of the Guntur High School, the Middle School and four
branches of the Elementary School, located in various parts of

the city.  In 1920 there were 160 students in the two classes of the College, 279 in the three classes of the High School, 397 in the three classes of the Middle School.  All these used the main College buildings.  The four branches of the elementary school had a total of 405 students in the first five classes.  This made a grand total of 1,241 in the Institution.  There were 71 teachers.  One-sixth of the student body was Christian, most of them having come from the village schools.  The establishment of the taluk boarding schools was expected to bring many more students to the College.  The total cost to the Mission over the fees and grants-in-aid was $10,000 a year for the 1,241 students.[152]

By the time of the first World War the Hermannsburg Mission had developed, in addition to its village schools, one high school at Tirupati; three Middle Schools at Chandragiri, Puttur and Nayudupeta; four girls' schools at Tirupati, Gudur, Sulurpet and Puttur.  Of the girls' schools, those at Sulurpet and Tirupati were closed during the War.  The High School gained an outstanding record after 1907, especially during the time of the Rev. Winfried Wickert, 1910-1915.  Unfortunately, the War ended the fast-developing program in the field of Education which the Hermannsburg Mission.had undertaken after 1900.  Statistics for 1915 reveal that there were 136 men teachers and 18 Bible women or women teachers in all the schools, teaching a total of 2,862 students. Of these, 781 were Christian.  This last figure in itself indi-

327

cates the great change that had taken place in the Hermannsburg
educational system.  They had originally determined to serve only
the Christian children.[153]

## 2. In Medicine

Although early missionaries of the Lutheran Church in the
Andhra Desa had taken some training in medicine and practiced it
on the field,[154] it was not considered that doctors were an important part of the missionary program.  Later, as it became clearer
what a great service doctors could perform, the sending of medical missionaries was put off because of the financial situation
of the Foreign Mission effort.  As with the development of high
schools and colleges, so hospitals had to wait before the primary
task of spreading the Word of God through preaching and evangelism.

It took a woman pioneer to show the Lutheran Church how effective an agent the doctor can be in promoting the Gospel and
reaching especially the higher castes.  Miss Anna S. Kugler, M.D.,
came to India not as a doctor, but as a single woman missionary
whose duty was to carry on zenana work and assist in the Girls'
Schools.  Her medical knowledge might be useful, but it was not to
be her primary concern.  The Board would not make any appropriation
for medical service.

When she arrived in Guntur in 1883, the second Zenana missionary, and saw for herself the tremendous need for medical care among

the people, she began dispensary work in a quiet way in the midst of her other duties.  She treated some 600 patients the first year.  The rest of the missionaries were in favor of her entering the work full time.  In 1885 she was granted permission to rent a house in the Muslim quarter of the town; but the fees for the medicine were to cover the cost of the dispensary.  She was assisted by two women who served as Bible women and helpers.  Mrs. John Nichols, whose husband had just arrived to be a missionary in the Guntur field, helped when needed as a nurse.

By February, 1892, the enthusiastic response of the missionaries and natives, as well as the interest of the Women's Missionary Societies in America, opened the way to draw up plans and estimates for a hospital and dispensary.  Dr. Uhl carried on the campaign while in America and raised $9,000 to start the building program.  The missionaries themselves had given the first $300.  The dispensary was completed in 1893, the hospital by June, 1897.  It was not until 1895 that Dr. Kugler was released by the Board from her other zenana duties so as to enter full-time into the hospital work.  Interest was so great that the native people collected $1,100 for a wall around the 17½ acres of property.

The first missionary nurse was Miss Katherine Fahs, R.N., who opened the Training School for Nurses in 1899.  The first class was graduated in 1901, consisting primarily of Anglo-Indian women because of the stigma against the nursing profession.

A year after the completion of the hospital, Dr. Kugler
set down certain principles for Mission hospital activity: use the
best and latest scientific findings; avoid extravagance, but not
so as to sacrifice the work of the hospital; carry on not only
stated and regular religious teachings, but also reveal those
teachings by the actions of the doctors and nurses in their daily
ministrations; encourage the payment of fees so as to arrive at
self-support.  Dr. Kugler was persuaded that the hospital would
attract patients if it was run well and efficiently.  She concluded by saying that the hospital "will afford opportunity for
Christian work that will make it one of the most powerful evangelistic agencies of the present-day effort of foreign missions."[155]

The first twenty-five years the hospital served 25,531 in-
patients, 186,296 dispensary patients, 9,677 office or private
patients.  Of the in-patients, one-fourth were Christians, 19%
Brahmans, 34% Sudras, and the rest from the other castes and outcastes.  If the return visits and the many relatives were included
in the totals, close to a million people came in touch in some way
with the hospital.  Dr. Kugler never made an apology for telling
about Christ, even though the majority had to go to the Mangalagiri temple twelve miles away to be purified after their visit or
stay in the hospital.

A beautiful little chapel was built next to the hospital
and regular Sunday services and daily prayer services were held

there.  Sunday School for women and children was offered on Sunday afternoons.  Bible classes were held regularly for the employees; and several Bible women were constantly employed at the hospital to visit all the patients and tell Bible stories in the wards.  One of the best of these Bible women was Philip Sarah, a widow and sister of the Rev. Murari David.[156]  Her two sons were pastors, the Reverends Philip Leisenring and Philip Paul.

> "The importance of Christian medical work is illustrated by an experience of Dr. Kugler.  A neighboring Rajah, various members of whose family had been cured in the hospital, expressed his gratitude not only by a large gift, but also by the making of a metrical translation of the gospels into Telugu."[157]

In 1903 the first dispensary was opened at Chirala; in 1909 another was established at Tenali.  Dr. Mary Baer, who came to India in 1895, was put in charge of the work in that area.  The Chirala Hospital was completed in 1912.  Dr. Alfred Pfitsch, the first man doctor, took charge of the newly-opened Rentachintala hospital in May, 1918.

In the Rajahmundry Mission, Dr. Lydia Woerner arrived in 1899 to establish medical work.  Having opened a dispensary on March 26, 1902 in a rented house, she reported a total of 2,026 patients, 432 visits to homes and 84 surgical operations at the end of the first year.  A temporary hospital was opened two years later.

> "As early as 1895 the sum of 280 pennies, an offering made by the children of the surgical ward in the Lankenau Hospi-

tal [Philadelphia], had been presented to the Church to be
used in providing medical help and hospital care for the
children of lands where hospitals were as yet unknown. It
was this touching gift which was made the starting-point in
the plan for the erection of a mission-hospital at Rajahmundry. Very soon all the women's societies and ladies'
aids of the Lutheran General Council were interested in the
proposed hospital, and funds began to come in in necessary
quantities."[158]

A site was purchased in 1902, the cornerstone laid in 1910 and

the main building completed in 1911. The contractor was a

Christian, M. Ramanayya. The first missionary nurse was Miss Hed-

wig Wahlberg, who came in 1902. A Training School for Nurses,

conducted in Telugu, was started in 1918 under the direction of

Miss Anna Rohre and Miss Hilma Levine, who came to India in 1915.

The Hermannsburg Field was financially unable to enter the

medical missionary work although the individual missionaries

learned enough about medicine to distribute it when able to help

minor ills. This helped to create a friendly attitude on the

part of the native population.[159]

Director Egmont Harms discussed the role of the medical mis-

sionary at the time of his visit to India in 1892, but he stated

that it was impossible to do anything at that time because of the

expense.[160]

## 3. In Institutions of Mercy

The Rev. Nikolaus Wittman, who had come to the Hermannsburg

Mission in 1896, became interested in the plight of the lepers

in the region of Kodur.   In 1905 he started an asylum for them.
He was able to obtain a tax-free site from the government and
built five buildings on it, each to house four people.   An old
shed was rebuilt for a place of worship.   One of the catechists
named Visvasudu, who had contracted leprosy, was employed to
care for the spiritual welfare of the asylum.

Wittman received permission to go to England and receive
some training in leprosy care at the Livingstone House in London.   Friends of the Mission in America and Germany became interested in the project and aided it financially.   The Mission to
Lepers also contributed.

Although it was impossible to force the people to worship
on Sundays, Wittman found them sensitive and open to the Gospel
message.   In time some were baptized.   The catechist baptized
two in 1907, followed by three more baptized by Missionary Warber, who was serving in Kodur while Wittman was in England.

The people were given an opportunity to work on grape ar-
bors and thus keep their minds off their troubles.   During Wittman's absence Warber constructed a little chapel in gothic style
with a steeple and bell.

Wittman not only served the Asylum with his additional
knowledge of medicine, but he also set up a clinic and treated
about 3,000 individuals in the course of the first year.   Unob-
trusively he could also preach the gospel.   Of the first twenty

333

residents in Krupapalle, the name selected for this 'home of
mercy,' seventeen became Christians, fourteen of them while they
were still in the home.  Later the Home was expanded to care for
thirty persons and an operating room was built.[161]

About the same time, the Schleswig-Holstein Mission estab-
lished a Leper Asylum at Salur with financial assistance from
America and the Mission to Lepers.  The property was donated.
Opened in 1906, it was called the 'Philadelphia' Leper Home.
"The grounds are spacious, well landscaped, and large gardens
are under cultivation.  This work is done by inmates of the
Home, who also do all kinds of hand work needed in the upkeep of
the Asylum."[162]

Institutions of Mercy conducted by the Guntur and Rajahmundry Missions by 1920 were: the Dorcas Home for widows, deserted
wives, crippled women and children, young girls needing protection, and children, started in Samalkot and later moved to Rajahmundry and made a part of the Industrial Home;[163] the Orphanage
in Guntur, constructed in 1904 to take care of orphans from Pan-
dita Ramabai's home in Poona after the tragic famine of 1900; and
the School for the Blind, established in Rentachintala in 1911.
The Industrial Work in Guntur grew out of the Orphanage.  Efforts
were made to teach the orphan boys how to be cooks, carpenters,
tailors, weavers, motor-drivers as well as school teachers.  Never done on a large scale, the Orphanage was closed in 1926 but

the two main training institutions, the Carpenter Shop and the Printing Press, continued.[164]

Mrs. George Albrecht opened the School for the Blind in Rentachintala. The Braille system was adapted to Telugu, and in 1915 the school was recognized by the government and started to receive aid. Children came from all over the Telugu area. A full curriculum in six standards according to government requirements was provided; and in the industrial section crafts taught, such as rope-making, tape-making, mats, cloth and basket-weaving.[165]

### E. Cooperation and Union of the Lutheran Missions

### 1. Joint Conferences of the Telugu Lutheran Missions

In the late 1880s the Rev. Ernst Pohl of the Breklum Mission began to urge a conference of all Lutherans in the Telugu area. Some of the Hermannsburg missionaries opposed the idea; but when it was understood that no doctrinal matter would be touched upon, they gave their consent.[166] Maneke and Woerrlein were selected to attend the First Joint Conference, held at Guntur from January 17 to 20, 1895. Among the topics discussed were: education, Hindu preaching, divorce, Christian charity, and the cooperation of Lutheran Telugu Missions. All went away from the Conference inspired to do a better job in their own work. The exchange of experiences helped the missionaries to see

335

some of the deficiencies in their mission methods. They agreed to meet every two years.[167]

The second conference was held in Rajahmundry; and the third in Gudur in 1902, March 19-21. Among the subjects discussed were: family life among Christians, preservation and development of native workers after their education, the transfer of workers from one mission to another, problems involved in translating the Telugu Bible, the training of catechumens both before and after baptism, women's work and its difficulties, and the lack of Telugu Christian literature.

Out of this last item of discussion developed a literature committee consisting of two missionaries from each Mission. It was agreed that the old translations of the Bible were unsatisfactory and the new translation being done was also in need of some definite improvements. Suggestions for changes were made. The conference felt that if the Translation Committee would not consider their requests, the Lutherans should plan on making their own translation. There was a great lack of good books for the higher schools, theological books on dogmatics, church and world history books, and also general books of interest, such as folk tales. Each Mission had its own translation of Luther's catechism and this was a waste of money and time.

The Guntur Mission had been putting out a publication for its workers entitled _Mission News_. The Literature Committee enlarged

this and developed it into the <u>Kraistava Bodhakudu</u>[168] which proved to be of real value in the continued training of the native
workers. Harms was acting secretary of the Literature Committee
and had an influential part in the development of this magazine.
He explained that the first part contained material helpful for
use in the regular Sunday School lessons; the second was on
Church History, the third part Biblical History, the fourth part
explanation of the Catechism, and the fifth part stories for en-
tertainment. The subjects were used in the examinations for the
workers at the Annual Conferences of Workers. It was decided
that the workers should be placed in four classifications, according to their development in this program, and that they had
until their fiftieth year to pass the annual examinations and
reach the final classification. The idea, Harms admitted, came
from the American missionaries who were acquainted with the correspondence school system.[169]

In 1902 Hartwig Harms started the publication on his own initiative of a paper called <u>Missionary Correspondence</u>, partly in
German, partly in English, which was sent to all Lutheran missionaries in India. It dealt with all those things of especial
interest to the Indian missionaries. These Telugu Conferences
and the activity of the Telugu Literature Committee led to a
general conference in 1905 in which were representatives of the
Leipzig, Hermannsburg, Swedish, Guntur and Rajahmundry Missions.

It was decided to form an All India Lutheran Literature Society
and Dr. L. B. Wolf was requested to edit a monthly church periodical in English. Taking his ideas from Harm's Missionary Correspondence, Wolf began to publish, in September, 1905, The Gospel Witness, which has been in publication ever since. It is
now the official organ of the Federation of Evangelical Lutheran
Churches in India.

The first All India Lutheran Conference was held at Guntur,
January 2 to 9, 1908. There were 63 delegates present from nine
missions, including the Basel Mission.[170] Subjects discussed
were: the development of the Lutheran Church in self-government
and self-support, evangelism among outcastes, catechetical training, Christian literature, women's work, medical work, higher education, industrial work, Pensions and Widows Fund, Christian
marriage, the training of teachers, catechists and pastors, and
the attitude of the missionary in the struggle between the government and the Indian people. On this last subject, it was
felt the Lutheran missionaries should avoid everything that the
Indian people might find insulting, such as the typical domineer-
ing attitude of the European. They should be as a Hindu to the
Hindus, so that the people would feel that the missionaries loved them and wanted the best for them. Bothmann of Breklum expressed the opinion of the Conference when he said: "We missionaries must be the unifying element between government and people."[171]

In planning for the next Conference many spoke strongly about keeping this only for Lutherans. This meant that the Basel missionaries were eliminated, as that Mission was composed of both Lutheran and Reformed missionaries. The thought of closer unity had developed to the point that by the next Conference held in Rajahmundry in January, 1912, the word 'Federation' was used a great deal.

> "Proposals were made to establish a United Theological Seminary at Madras. Work among Lutherans scattered in South Africa, Rangoon, Penang and Assam was to be systematized and directed by the A.I.L. Conference. The Conference was constituted as a permanent body. The All India Lutheran Literature Society was merged with the A.I.L. Conference, and The Gospel Witness was made the organ of the Conference."[172]

Practically all Lutheran bodies in India were represented at the third All India Lutheran Conference at Guntur, October 4 to 7, 1921. Whereas the first Conference was entirely under the conduct of foreign missionaries, this one had equal representation of Indians and missionaries. Close cooperation of the Lutheran Missions during the War years to save the German Missions helped to make this Conference one filled with real unity of spirit. It was felt that an official organization was needed to represent all the Lutherans of India in facing any future emergency such as that. "The proposed constitution for a United Lutheran Church in India was referred to the constituent Missions and Churches."[173]

339

The Lutheran National Missionary Society was organized in 1916 to carry on mission work in India from contributions by the Indian Christians. Representatives to the organizing body included Mr. V. Ch. John of Guntur, the Rev. D. Punitudu of Nayudupeta, and the Rev. P. Paradesi of Rajahmundry. The first effort was to enter the native state of Rewa, situated between the Central and United Provinces.[174] The first missionary was Samuel Gnanabaranam of the Tamil Evangelical Lutheran Church.[175]

### 2. The Joint Evangelical Lutheran Synod of Ohio and the Hermannsburg Mission

For many years the Joint Evangelical Lutheran Synod of Ohio had shown interest in the mission work of Hermannsburg. Individual churches and pastors had been sending contributions before 1899, which averaged 10,000 to 20,000 marks. This increased in the next decade to 35,810, and in 1910 the giving reached a high of 50,317 marks.[176] Closer cooperation on an official basis was held back for a number of years because of the suspicion the Ohio pastors had about the agreement made in 1891 between the Hermannsburg Church and the Hannoverian Landeskirche.

By 1906 the stage was set for closer coordination of mission effort when communications between the two made it clear to the Ohio Synod that:[177]

"The declaration of Hermannsburg is clear and unequivocal to the effect that it is an Evangelical Lutheran Mission,

established upon the Holy Scriptures, entire and un-
abridged, and upon the original and unaltered confession of
the Ev. Lutheran Church, and that it intends to abide on
this foundation whatever friends and supporters may be lost
on account of this conservative position."

The Rev. Karl Roebbelen had come to America in 1904 to participate in the Annual Convention of the Ohio Synod and suggested
that the Synod might want to take over several of the Hermannsburg Mission Stations as their own in order to develop increased
interest among the churches.  However, in attempting to work out
the details it became apparent that Hermannsburg was not willing
to release these stations completely, but wanted the progress toward independence from Hermannsburg to be made gradually.[178]

There was a strong move in the Ohio Synod to start work in
South America or Mexico in order for it to have its own and definite field of operations.  The Joint Synod Convention in 1910
defeated a recommendation:[179]

"That the Synod enter into immediate negotiations with the
Hermannsburg (Germany) mission institution, looking to the
transfer to our Synod (upon payment of a price to be agreed
upon) of two or three of said institution's mission stations in India."

At this same convention a Board of Foreign Missions was established with authority to find a field of missionary endeavor.
Professor Edward Pfeiffer of Columbus, Ohio, was elected the
president.

It is evident that Hermannsburg did not want to lose the financial support of the Joint Synod of Ohio and yet did not want to

341

hand over complete control of any of its work. But when it was faced definitely with the proposition that the Synod would turn elsewhere and open up new work, thereby dropping all support to Hermannsburg, the missionaries in India made the proposal through Director Egmont Harms to transfer the two stations Kodur and Puttur to the Joint Synod.[180]

An impartial committee of Gaebler and Schomerus of the Leipzig Tamil Mission and Kuder and Neudoerffer of the Rajahmundry Mission evaluated the property in November, 1912, and arrived at the figure of Rupees 52,984 and 4 annas. This amounted to $16,733, part of which was paid immediately and the rest used to support the work in the Hermannsburg field during the War years when nothing could be sent from Germany.

Missionaries Maneke and Wittman plus the native helpers in those fields remained to continue the work until the Ohio Synod could replace them with their own missionaries. The Rev. Charles Pflueger, secretary of the Board of Foreign Missions, offered himself as the first missionary and he went to Hermannsburg to get acquainted with mission methods and practice, do some language study, and to help unify the work by familiarizing himself with Hermannsburg's system of organization and parish discipline. From Hermannsburg he was to go on to India, but the War prevented this. Returning to America, he made another attempt to reach India together with the Rev. W. Schmidt, but when they reached Ceylon they were required to return to America because of their German descent.

### 3. The War Years

After the German missionaries were required to evacuate,[181] the only missionary left in the Hermannsburg Mission was the Rev. Carl Scriba, who was born in India and thus considered to be a British subject. He lived in Kalahasti and attempted to direct the work of the whole Mission from there. He was appointed acting secretary for both the Hermannsburg and Ohio Synod fields. However, the administration and conduct of the Hermannsburg Mission was taken from him very shortly by the government and he was required to move to Kodur and the Ohio Synod Mission field. His wife transferred the Girls' School from Gudur in order to keep it in existence.

The administration of the Hermannsburg stations was assumed by the government through a Board of Trustees of Alien Mission Property. The field was divided into five districts and the responsibility for the schools given to missionaries of some of the neighboring Missions: Sulurpet and Nayudupeta to V. McCauley of the Guntur Mission; Gudur and Vakadu to Miss Tencate of the American Baptist Mission; Venkatagiri and Rapur to G. P. Gibbons of the Wesleyan Mission; Kalahasti to Turnbull of the Australian Presbyterian Mission; and Tirupati to Muyskens of the Dutch Reformed Mission. In his report for 1919 Scriba wrote concerning this committee:[182]

> "The missionaries gave as much time as they could to supervision, along with the work they had to do in their own missions. This supervision was confined mostly to school work, and all the mission workers, except seven, and two pastors, were given school work. Village preaching stopped, and only services conducted for the Christians of the mission.
>
> In October, 1918, your secretary [Burger] was given leave of his work in Guntur Mission and took up his residence in Tirupati. The other members of the committee declared that it would be best for him to take còmplete charge of supervision, and each transferred his work to him. The committee, however, still hold themselves responsible for the work and give to the secretary help and advice when required and necessary."

The Hermannsburg Mission realized it could not care for the field properly and that it would not be administered very well by a committee from various missions; so it transferred its entire India Mission to the Synod of Ohio on February 28, 1916.

The Rev. Theodore Fricke emphasized that the absence of missionaries on the field, even though the committee of five kept things going, was very hard on the Mission. He said:[183]

> "Great losses were sustained both in property and membership. Most of the buildings fell into disrepair and some into ruin. The report for the year 1917 recorded a loss of 314 souls. During five years, 1913-1918, losses in membership were 848 souls. The membership dropped from 3,116 in 1913 to 2,268 in 1918."

The Rev. S. C. Burger, who had come to India in 1898, maintained the work as best he could until the arrival in May, 1920, of the Ohio Synod missionaries, The Rev. A. W. Wilch, the Rev.

344

and Mrs. Elmer S. Nicholson, and Miss Laura Nicholson. They

were followed two months later by the Rev. Dr. C. V. Sheatsley

"who, as commissioner of the Board of Foreign Missions, was auth-

orized to organize the work and bring back to the board a report

on existing conditions. On July 24, 1920, the India Conference

was organized, ..."[184]

Other missionaries from the Guntur and Rajahmundry Missions

who assisted in the Hermannsburg Mission for short periods of

time were the Rev. Victor McCauley, H. R. Spangler, Henry Traf-

ford (industrial work) and Karl Wolters. The final recommenda-

tion Sheatsley gave his Home Board following his return from In-

dia was:[185]

> "That the United Lutheran Church Foreign Board as well as
> the missionaries, especially the Rev. S. C. Burger, be giv-
> en a hearty vote of thanks for the interest and assistance
> they have given us during the trying times of the war and
> subsequently."

The Schleswig-Holstein Mission had a similar experience dur-

ing the first World War. At first the missionaries were per-

mitted to stay; but then they were removed, interned and later

repatriated. The Mission was still in its beginnings in many

respects, for the first Hindu had become Christian just 28 years

before. The missionaries had not found a single person ready or

qualified to become a pastor. Thus, in a more desperate situa-

tion than the Hermannsburg field, there was no one to baptize and

administer the Holy Communion. It appeared that the people were at the mercy of their enemies.

"[However,] the Special Assistant Agent of Koraput promised
his assistance in case the police or anybody else would
create trouble for the Christians and their workers. This
meant at least peace and rest regarding the various forms
of persecution the Christians had been suffering when the
missionaries were among them. Every worker will gladly
testify that they did not get into trouble during the difficult times."[186]

The General Council assured the Breklum Mission that they
would supervise the field as best they could. Money for the
Mission was sent to India through the Foreign Mission Board in
America. The Rev. Ernst Neudoerffer and the Rev. T. A. Holmer,
who came to India in 1912, were appointed to care for the Breklum Mission field, but Holmer never was able to take charge, and
Neudoerffer was unable to move to the area. He made periodical
visits.

While Hermannsburg had had adequate funds from the Ohio Synod, the Breklum Mission found the situation so difficult that
all the assistant teachers had to be dismissed, the boarding
homes closed and the schools handed over to the government. In
1917 the General Council assumed the financial responsibility as
well.

To ease the situation and give the people adequate care,
the Rev. Neudoerffer selected two of the old, experienced catechists and ordained them on March 18, 1920. Pastor Theophilus
took care of the Telugu field especially. In 1921 the Rev. W. F.

Adolphsen (arrived in India 1919) and Miss L. A. Miller (1913) took up residence in Parvitapur. Others went to Kotapad and Jeypore in the Oriya section of the Breklum field. They did a great deal to revive the work, repair buildings, and start catechists' and pastors' classes.

> "When in 1926, the German mission societies were permitted to return to India, the U.L.C.M. offered the Telugu and Oriya field to the S.H.E.L.M. According to the agreement of 1917 Breklum would have had to repay the amount of all the expenditures made. This was nearly one million rupees. Yet nothing was asked. Generously the whole debt was cancelled. Besides this a certain sum was sanctioned to facilitate the new beginning."[187]

## 4. The United Lutheran Church Mission

With the merger of the General Synod, the General Council and the United Synod of the South to form the United Lutheran Church in America on November 15, 1918, it was the natural step for the Guntur and Rajahmundry Missions to unite once more. Conferences were held between the missionaries throughout 1919 and a constitution and rules were drawn up for the United Lutheran Church Mission. Just fifty years after they had been separated by the tragedy of the Civil War and the break up of the General Synod,[188] they came together again by adopting the new constitution at Rajahmundry October 20, 1920. The Rev. Ernst Neudoerffer was selected as the first President of the Mission Council. Shortly after this, the Rajahmundry Mission Conference dissolved itself, and the Rajahmundry Synod came into existence in 1921. At the time of the organization, the Synod consisted of 8 ordained missionaries, 8 Indian pastors and 8 lay delegates. Its organization and function were similar to the Guntur Synod.[189] Together they formed the United Lutheran Church Mission in the Telugu country.

# CHAPTER VI

## THE CONCLUSION

### A.  A Backward Look

As we gaze back over the first eighty years of the History of
Lutheranism in the Andhra Desa, from 1842 to 1920, it becomes apparent that, in many respects, this period is just a beginning,
and the story of the Lutheran missionary much more than the story
of a Church.  The missionary is in the center of the picture, and
the happenings in Europe and America affect the work and progress
of the Lutheran Missions even more than the historical and political development in India itself.  There is almost an isolation
from the rest of India and occurrences there, which is quite different from the situation after 1920.

The Lutheran Church, both in Europe and America, was slow to
respond to the rising tide of the modern missionary movement,
which began with William Carey.  In Germany, the official church
was largely opposed or indifferent to the missionary call, and the
societies which formed were inspired by individual pastors and
laymen.  To this day the work of foreign missions has been conducted through societies rather than by church bodies.  This has
resulted in greater lay participation, but at the same time funds
raised for mission work through the societies probably has been

less than would have occurred under the official supervision of the Lutheran Churches in Germany.

In America, the Lutheran Synods generally followed the pattern of the mother churches in Germany, but later on formed Boards of Foreign Missions under the control and supervision of the church officials. Missionary societies were maintained, but in time these consisted entirely of women who supported women missionaries which the Boards were unwilling or financially unable to support. These women have maintained a keen interest in the work of foreign missions, but laymen and many pastors lacked the information and, consequently, became largely indifferent to the missionary movement. In many ways the missionary movement has been hurt by this delegation of foreign missions on the congregational level to women's missionary societies.

An auspicious beginning was made in the Andhra Desa through the work of the first Lutheran missionary, Father Christian Frederick Heyer. His experience on the American frontier, his enthusiasm and clear understanding of the methods of missions offset his age and tendency to leave the work when only just started. His was the pioneer spirit that cleared the way through the wilderness, but left the task of more concentrated cultivation to those who came after him. Unfortunately, those who followed failed to carry on what he had begun, often because of circumstances beyond their control. Sickness and death were big factors, keeping the mission-

ary force to an ineffective minimum.  Discord among the Lutheran
Synods in America and the problem of following the thousands of
Lutherans settling on the rapidly-expanding frontiers of western
America prevented the churches from giving the financial assist-
ance and interest needed to further the work started by Heyer.

The early missionaries received a great deal of support from
English officials who were sincere Christians and interested in
furthering the Christian faith among the Indian people.  Schools
financed by the officials were handed over to the missionaries
with continuing support.  But this situation changed with the
change of officials; the combination of the loss of this support
together with the restriction of financial aid and personnel reinforcements from America at the time of the Civil War brought the
Lutheran Missions in Guntur and Rajahmundry to a standstill.
Twenty-five years after the founding of the Mission, there was
only one missionary and 633 Christians.  The Rajahmundry field almost was turned over to the Church Missionary Society.  Father
Heyer, at the age of 77, returned to India to hold the field until
reinforcements could arrive.

The lack of missionaries and support from America was also
the main cause for a change in policy that retarded the work for
many years.  Father Heyer had found that Christianity advanced
most quickly as the congregations were established in the local
villages and were fitted into the community life of the people.

Whole families were baptized at one time; they, in turn, contacted relatives in neighboring villages, so that the news spread from family to family, from village to village. The early leaders were taken from the leaders in the community. Although their education was meager, yet their enthusiasm and desire to spread the Gospel message, plus their influential position, far outweighed this lack.

Without missionaries or the necessary financial support, however, the work became concentrated in a few main centers. The Christian people were expected to come to these centers for worship and instruction; many had to travel great distances to do so. Others could not afford to leave their work without financial support from the missionaries during the period of catechetical instruction. This opened up opportunities for improper motivations for becoming Christians. Moreover, conversion and baptism was very often on an individualistic basis instead of by family units. This was especially true in the Hermannsburg Mission under the direction of the German missionaries. From the start they modeled the churches after the parishes in rural Germany. People came in from miles around to worship in the center on Sundays.

Another danger was the fact that many of the Christians and Indian workers, once they had become acclimated to the life in the Christian centers, and the protection, prestige and security which came out of living in the community of white men, did not wish to return to their villages. In some cases the loss of employment

352

when the people became Christian, the social persecution and os-
tracism, led the missionaries too easily to permit the Christians
to move to the centers and find employment through the Mission.
They persuaded themselves that a Christian could not do otherwise
than help those in need and suffering, not realizing that, in most
cases, if the Christians had remained in their native villages and
endured the preliminary stages of persecution, the people would
have accepted them in their new status and quietly admired them
for their stand. It must be remembered, too, that the native village was a complete and self-sufficient unit in itself, each person having his task to perform, menial as it might be, in the life
of the community. Drawing the Christians away from their normal
environment disrupted village community life and brought in destructive forces that the Hindu leaders learned in time were more
dangerous than the outcastes becoming Christian. These factors
gradually were understood by later missionaries.

The shortage of missionaries in the Guntur-Rajahmundry fields
would not have been so critical if native workers and pastors had
been trained and given responsibility for areas of work. At first
Hindu teachers were used in the schools, while the missionaries
taught the religious courses. But the missionaries learned to
their sorrow that these teachers deceived them because of their
unfamiliarity with the native language and customs. These schools
were ineffective channels of conversion and Christian training

until Christian teachers were available. But these were not easy to obtain. Most of the Christians came from the completely illiterate outcastes. Years of training were necessary to achieve the standards the missionaries required.

Father Heyer in his work in the Palnad was not so particular about standards; he found it more effective to take the early leaders in the villages and train them with just the necessary basic knowledge to instruct the pupils in reading and writing. This was necessarily a temporary measure, but one that proved effective when missionaries were unavailable. These men were trained well enough to preach and lead the worship services in the local villages, to prepare new converts in the knowledge of the Bible and the catechism, and to maintain the life of the village congregations. It must be remembered, however, that these teacher-evangelists were dealing only with outcaste people and were not faced with the task of teaching the children of the high caste Hindus, as was the case in Guntur and Rajahmundry. High standards in the main centers were necessary to compete with Hindu schools and to receive approval of the government.

It is true also that the missionaries might have felt greater urgency in the training of pastors and native leadership if they had known what a critical shortage of missionaries would occur. They preferred to keep the reins of leadership in their own hands; and when the time came that there were no missionaries available, it was already too late to rectify the situation.

The Hermannsburg Mission was more fortunate in its early leaders, most of whom were fairly-well educated and needed only a short period of religious instruction. Nor did they have the critical shortage of missionaries, and their work was in a more concentrated area. Yet they had difficulty obtaining the leaders they desired because of the very high moral and educational standards they required of the workers. And they were unwilling to place the responsibility of any congregations in the hands of Indian Christians. The missionaries maintained close supervision, working almost as dictators in their fields, and considered themselves as the only ones capable of serving as pastors. Those who were finally ordained forty years after the founding of the Mission had served for years as teachers and catechists, with occasional periods of concentrated training in between, before they were considered ready to serve. This Mission would have had greater success if it had not insisted on such high standards for its Indian Christian leaders in the early years, but rather had raised the standards gradually as the congregations themselves developed and the people became more conscious of the meaning of the Christian life. It was not to be expected that those just out of Hinduism and the binding customs of the caste system would be able to maintain the high standards expected of the Christian leader in Europe or America, where Christianity has been for centuries.

Yet, strangely enough, it was the amazing change in the
lives of the Outcastes, now become Christian, that led the upper
castes to be drawn to the Christian faith. Although the early
missionaries had spent much of their time preaching in the bazaars, teaching in the schools and carrying on endless discussions
with the upper caste Hindus, the results had been very discourag-
ing. Very few were converted. But the Outcastes came in greater
and greater numbers, especially after the two great famines. So
much so that the Christian Missions in the Andhra Desa became
known as Mala or Madiga religions. The missionaries began to feel
that no others would come; but as the village communities witnessed the change in many of the Outcastes, considered lower than dogs
and forced to live in hovels outside the village boundaries, into
clean, well-mannered, diligent, honest, intelligent and happy human
beings, more and more of the higher Castes became interested in and
studied this new Religion. It was accomplishing that which Hinduism had never done.

Other factors drawing the attention of the upper castes were
the impartial charity of the Christians during time of famine, the
help which the doctors and hospitals were able to give the sick
and their families, the institutions of mercy being established
and the positive efforts to better the social conditions and the
educational climate of the Indian people.

During the period under consideration, the Lutheran Missions
in the Andhra Desa had developed very slowly and their successes

had been few and far between.  Yet the period since 1920, when they developed rapidly, especially the Guntur-Rajahmundry fields, to become some of the most successful areas of Christian work in all of India, indicates that foundations were well laid.  We can be critical of the system which neglected higher education for so many years, and the Home Boards which would not provide the finances and the full-time personnel nor develop an over-all strategy for a thorough educational system; but we must admit they used what little they had to further the primary purposes for which the Missions were organized: to preach the Gospel and care for the spiritual needs of the converts.

We can claim that the famines drew people to the Church for economic reasons.  Yet events showed that those who fell away afterward were few compared with the ones who remained for spiritual reasons.  The missionaries knew the dangers and held off the incoming tide during probation periods of instruction and moral discipline.  For the majority in these mass movements, their economic welfare was little improved by becoming Christian.  They remained in the village environment, continued to be considered outcastes, and moreover had to endure the persecutions which normally followed the first conversions in any area.

The Lutheran Missions were slow in developing adequate literature in Telugu; many of the missionaries never learned the language and customs well enough to be effective; they maintained too dictatorial a position over the Indian workers; and they were reluctant to cooperate with other Christian Missions in the Andhra Desa. It took many years for them to cooperate with each other, and only then in limited areas. Yet, in spite of these defects, there were enough missionaries with a keen interest in the Telugu language, customs and literature; with a willingness to place more and more responsibility in the hands of the Indian workers; and with a clear-enough understanding of the larger aspects of the Christian task in India to overcome these defects and build the foundations for a strong Lutheran Church in the Andhra Desa.

If we compare the Missions with each other, we come to the apparent conclusion that greatest progress was made where the missionaries were not so dictatorial in their administration and were willing to place much of the responsibility in the hands of the Indian pastors, catechists and teachers. Thus, the Guntur Mission advanced far more quickly than the others. The German Missions, in spite of their more concentrated and more thorough work, lagged far behind because of their insistence on missionaries carrying on the pastoral duties. We must not forget, however, that the climate for growth was more favorable in the beginning in the Guntur field. The German Missions also were held back by the tragic policy of not providing adequate housing and vacations for the missionaries, causing sickness and deaths far out of proportion to the other Missions. Internment of the German missionaries at the time of the

first World War almost sounded the death-knell to their work.  The
Indian leaders had remained too dependent upon them for leadership
and financial assistance.  Fortunate indeed was the willingness of
these Missions to cooperate with others in maintaining the work,
finally allowing the American Lutheran churches to take over the
fields and advance them more quickly than would have been possible
with the limited resources and personnel of the German Missionary
Societies since that time.

B.  A Forward Look

The entrance of the Joint Evangelical Lutheran Synod of Ohio
into the Andhra Desa and the union of the Rajahmundry and Guntur
Missions to form the United Lutheran Church Mission bring our
History to a close.  The pioneering stage is completed; the groundwork is laid.

From 1920 to the present, the history of the Church in this
area takes on a completely different aspect.  It is a history in
itself.  From 1842 to 1920 the emphasis has been at all time on
the Mission and its work.  The missionary has played the predominant part; the decisions have been in his hands; and the Home
Boards have thought of their foreign mission work primarily in
the light of what their missionaries were doing.

The years since 1920 center around the growth of the Church.
The missionary more and more takes a back seat.  His duty is to

359

work himself out of a job. This becomes apparent when we find that although the Church grew by leaps and bounds, the missionary staff decreased. It is the Church which makes the decisions. The missionary serves now as one of the pastors or in the role of a specialist until he is no longer needed. He comes to work in India, not because he is sent by the Foreign Mission Board of the Lutheran Church in America, but because the Lutheran Church in India has need of his ability and dedication in a special task.

Another significant reason for the closing of our History at the date 1920 is that the political atmosphere in which the Church had developed throughout nearly 80 years came to an end with the movement for Indian Independence which began with the Non-Cooperative Movement in 1921. Up to this point, other than the helpfulness or lack of helpfulness of British officials, and the willingness of the government to aid the school program of the Missions, the development of the Missions has not been greatly affected by the decisions of the government. With the growing restlessness of the Independence movement and the national consciousness of students and leaders increasingly apparent, the Lutheran Church found itself faced with many adjustments that it did not have to make before. No longer could the government be ignored. The stirring events leading up to the transfer of power from the British to the Indian people on August 15, 1947, have had great influence on the story of the Church in the Andhra Desa.

We spoke of the Mass Movements which occurred in the Andhra Desa following the great famines of the 1870s and 1900s. But this growth was as nothing compared to the rapid development since 1920. The United Lutheran Church Mission has averaged about 9,000 baptisms a year. Its total membership in 1950 was 239,887 as compared to 91,764 in 1920. This is an increase of 162.5% in just thirty years. Even more outstanding is the development of its native leadership. Only 24 pastors were expected to lead a Church of over 90,000. In 1950 there were 130. This is far from adequate, but it indicates the trend. Another interesting development is the fact that, although there were no more schools in 1950 than in 1920 because of the stricter regulations enforced by the government, yet the pupils in them and the staff of teachers more than doubled. This indicates a vastly improved and more effective school system, better able to serve and educate the people.[1]

The development toward self-support which hardly had its beginnings before 1920 goes forth in tremendous strides afterward. The congregational offerings of the United Lutheran Church Mission in 1920 were Rupees 31,558, for an average of 0-5-6 per member. In 1950 the offerings had jumped to Rupees 305,017, for an average of 1-4-7 per member. Much of this was accomplished by

361

careful stewardship education and the increased sense of obligation toward the Church. Another large factor is the improved
economic condition of many of the native Christians. This period became one of large Cooperative Societies organized to give
the native Christians an opportunity to help themselves. The
Rev. G. R. Haaf, working with the non-Brahman Madras government
of the 1920s, was able to secure for the Christian communities
in the Guntur District through such Societies some 20,000 acres
of land for cultivation. Most of the land consisted of river
'lankas,' areas of marginal land along the river or on islands in
the wide lower areas of the Kistna River. Other missionaries
were active in this type of effort as well as developing industrial and educational programs for the Christian people.[2]

Cooperation between the Lutheran Missions became even more
apparent, especially in the field of education and literature.
Much Telugu literature is being developed, most of it written by
native leadership. One great Christian College for the whole
Andhra Desa supported by all the Missions became a reality in
Guntur. In 1950 the Andhra Christian College had a student body
of 1,424 of which 427 were Christian, larger than the number of
Christians enrolled in any other college in all India.

In this period, too, the trend toward indigenous architec-
ture, worship and music was most definite. The majority of the
hymns were based on Telugu lyrics and composed by Indian poets.

362

The Lutheran worship service, although still traditional in its words, would not be recognizable to the ordinary Lutheran congregation in America. But to the Indian it is a moment of deep inspiration and joy to be able to glorify God in the peculiar melodies of the Telugu people. And everywhere is heard the Gospel in song, and audiences sit entranced for hours listening to a 'Kalakshepam,' a lyrical dramatization sung by one or more voices.

The United Lutheran Church Mission became the Andhra Evangelical Lutheran Church in April, 1927. In 1944 the first Indian president was elected, the Rev. Dr. E. Prakasam. Much slower because of the many setbacks it experienced, the Hermannsburg-Ohio Synod Mission became the South Andhra Lutheran Church in 1945. But its development was excellent when we consider that the membership grew from 2,268 in 1918 in a very demoralized Mission to a total of 13,564 Christians in 315 village congregations and nearly 9,000 pupils in 115 schools in 1953. It cooperates with the A.E.L.C. in the Rajahmundry Theological Seminary, the Lutheran Theological College at Madras, the Federation of Evangelical Lutheran Churches of India, and the National Christian Council of India.

In closing, we must mention also that in 1940 the Salur-Parvitapur Field of the Breklum Society was given over to the Andhra Evangelical Lutheran Church and became one of its 32 Conferences. Its baptized membership as of the end of 1950 was

5,160, a decided increase over the 934 baptized members in 1914.[3]

When it is realized that there were only 6,359 baptized members in the Lutheran Church in the Andhra Desa after forty years of effort, we can well imagine the surprise that Heyer, Valett, Mylius or Pohl would register if they could see today the fruit of their patient sowing of the Gospel. Over a quarter of a million Christians in 2400 congregations! A noble army of Christ's drawn from every caste and united in one great purpose -- to proclaim the Word of God to the Hindu! And among them men and women who have honored their Lord through dedicated service in many walks of life -- lawyers, professors, physicians, poets, government officials, contractors, farmers, teachers, pastors, evangelists and simple servants of the soil.[4] That such a Church should come from such meager beginnings and mostly out of such seemingly hopeless material as the outcastes of India reminds us of St. Paul's declaration: "I will all the more gladly boast of my weaknesses, that the power of Christ may rest upon me. For the sake of Christ, then, I am content with weaknesses, insults, hardships, persecutions, and calamities; for when I am weak, then I am strong."[5]

"But thanks be to God, who in Christ always leads us in triumph, and through us spreads the fragrance of the knowledge of him everywhere. For we are the aroma of Christ to God among those who are being saved and among those who are perishing, to

one a fragrance from death to death, to the other a fragrance
from life to life. Who is sufficient for these things? For we
are not, like so many, peddlers of God's word; but as men of
sincerity, as commissioned by God, in the sight of God we speak
in Christ."[6]

REFERENCE NOTES

CHAPTER I    The Lutheran Church and the 19th Century Missionary

Movement


1.    The 17th century is included because of Peter Heyling in
Abyssinia, the Swedes in America and among the Lapps, and von
Weltz in South America, efforts largely unsuccessful.

2.    Cf. Warneck, Outline of a History of Protestant Missions, New
York, 1901, p. 57.

3.    Ibid., p. 8.   Also Latourette, A History of the Expansion of
Christianity, 1939, Volume III, pp. 25-26; Singmaster, The
Story of Lutheran Missions, 1917, pp. 16-17; and Rouse-Neill,
A History of the Ecumenical Movement, 1517-1948, Philadelphia,
1954, .p. 84.

4.    Cf. Warneck, op.cit., pp. 8-20; Latourette, op.cit., pp.25-
27; and Warburton, The Making of Modern Missions, 1931, pp.
120-129.

5.    Cf. Warneck, op.cit., pp.43-46; Latourette, op. cit., pp.
303-306; Warburton, op. cit., pp. 131-132; and Rouse-Neill,
op.cit., p. 28.

6.    Cf. Singmaster, op. cit., pp. 18-19; Neve-Allbeck, History of
the Lutheran Church in America, 1934, p.25; and Qualben, The
Lutheran Church in Colonial America, 1940, pp. 141, 153.

7.    Warneck, op. cit., p. 32.

8.    Cf. Warneck, op. cit., pp.32-37; Latourette, op. cit., p. 46;
Singmaster, op. cit., pp. 19-20; and Warburton, op. cit.,
pp. 135-136.

9.    Warneck, op. cit., p. 55.

10.   For further information on Pietism, cf. Warneck, op. cit.,
pp. 51-56; Latourette, op. cit., pp. 14, 46-47; Singmaster,
op. cit., pp. 22-25; Warburton, op. cit., pp. 136-138;
Walker, A History of the Christian Church, 1942, pp. 495-501;
Kurtz, Church History, New York, 1888, Volume III, pp. 41-42,
104-108, 114; and Rouse-Neill, op. cit., pp. 84, 99 ff.

11. Cf. Latourette, op. cit., pp. 47-48; Warneck, op. cit., pp. 58-67; Warburton, op. cit., pp. 138-140; and Rouse-Neill, op. cit., pp. 101ff.

12. Cf. Warneck, op. cit., pp. 70-71; Warburton, op. cit., pp. 140-141.

13. Singmaster, op. cit., p. 57.

14. Cf. pages 22-24, Thesis.

15. The Encyclopedia of Missions, New York, 1904, p. 71. Laury, A History of Lutheran Missions, 1899, p. 94, tells us that the French garrison of Hueningen, in bombarding the city, experienced such a violent east wind that the bombs were spent in the air before reaching the dwellings.

16. Warneck, op. cit., p. 121. Cf. Schreiber, Bausteine zur Geschichte der Norddeutschen Missions-Gesellschaft, 1911, for further details on the organization of the North German Society, pp. 9ff.

17. Cf. pages 54ff., Thesis.

18. Warneck, op. cit., p. 125. Much of the information on the German Societies is taken from Warneck, pp. 116-129; cf. also Latourette, op. cit., Volume IV, pp. 89-92; Singmaster, op. cit., pp. 58-63; and Laury, op. cit., pp. 84-86, 94-95, 155-161, 194-198, 240-241.

19. Cf. Warneck, op. cit., p. 126; Singmaster, op. cit., p.62; Swavely, ed., The Lutheran Enterprise in India, Madras, 1952, pp. 144-145; and Fiensch, Kurze Geschichte der Entstehung und der bisherigen Arbeit der Schleswig-Holsteinischen evang.-luth. Missionsgesellschaft, Breklum, 1890, pp. 25-29. (Noted after this as Kurze Geschichte).

20. Singmaster, op. cit., p. 63.

21. Warneck, op. cit., p. 129.

22. For further details of this early period, see Elsbree, The Rise of the Missionary Spirit in America, 1790-1815, Williamsport, 1928, pp. 8ff.; Latourette, op. cit., Volume III, pp. 216ff.; Warneck, op. cit., pp. 47-50; and Aberly, An Outline of Missions, 1945, pp. 49-50.

23. For further information on this great German immigration, see

Jacobs, The German Emigration to America, 1709-1740, Lancaster, 1898, passim.; Qualben, op. cit., pp. 136ff.; Neve-Allbeck, op. cit., pp. 28-34; Sweet, The Story of Religion in America, °1939, pp. 34, 165ff.; Kreider, Lutheranism in Colonial New York, 1942, pp.34ff.; Clark, The World of Justus Falckner, 1946, pp. 90ff.; Wentz, The Lutheran Church in American History, 1923, pp. 30-32, 45-50; or Wentz, A Basic History of Lutheranism in America, 1955, pp. 9, 15-17 (noted after this as Basic History).

24. Documentary History of the Evangelical Lutheran Ministerium of Pennsylvania and Adjacent States, Proceedings of the Annual Conventions from 1748 to 1821, Philadelphia, 1898, pp. 68, 74, 80 (noted after this as Documentary History, Pa. Min.) Cf. also Qualben, op. cit., p. 198. Note Neve-Allbeck, op. cit., pp. 60-61, on Muhlenberg's unionistic tendencies; also Qualben, op. cit., pp. 214-216.

25. Documentary History, Pa. Min, pp. 28, 103; cf. also Singmaster, op. cit., p. 95; and Laury, op. cit., p. 98.

26. Of special interest in the relation of Lutherans to the American Indians is the success of the Germans from the Palatinate who settled in New York and Pennsylvania in maintaining close harmony with the Indians of the Six Nations. In 1732 John Conrad Weiser, Jr., who had been permitted by his father to live with the Indians as a youth and learn their language, and had been adopted as the son of an Indian tribe, was appointed Head of the Indian Bureau of English Government. It is mainly through his efforts that the Iroquois Indians did not join the French and thus he helped to save the colonies. Cf. Qualben, op. cit., p. 192; Jacobs, op. cit., pp. 91ff. For a good biography of Weiser, read Wallace, Conrad Weiser, 1696-1760, Philadelphia, 1945. Wallace also has a valuable book on The Muhlenbergs of Pennsylvania, 1950.

Muhlenberg's reports to Halle reveal Weiser's attitude about converting the American Indians: "Mr. Weiser thinks that if we desired to make an attempt for their conversion, among many other rules we should have to observe the following: 1. One or several missionaries would have to live among them, seek to become master of their language, adopt as much of their customs, dress, and manner of living, as could be without sin; and as for the rest, rebuke their national vices by a holy walk. 2. They would have to translate the revealed truths into their language, and make things as plain as possible. 3. They would have to learn the Indian tunes and

371

melodies, and present to them the law and the gospel in such tunes, so that it made an impression, and then, under God's blessing and aid, wait for the fruit in patience." Reports of the United German Evangelical Lutheran Congregations in North America, Philadelphia, 1881, Volume 2, p. 113.

27. Jacobs, A History of the Evangelical Lutheran Church in the United States, New York, 1892, pp. 318-319 (noted after this as A History).

28. Ibid., pp. 320ff.

29. Cf. Ibid., pp. 324, 327ff.; also Wentz, Basic History, pp. 73ff.

30. Cf. Elsbree, op. cit., pp. 25ff.; Latourette, op. cit., Volume IV, pp. 77ff. Occasionally there were appeals, such as that of Hellmuth's in 1778. Cf. Bachmann, They Called Him Father, 1942, p. 115.

31. Wentz, Basic History, p. 83.

32. Early efforts, largely ineffective, were Kunze's Seminarium (cf. Haussman, Kunze's Seminarium, passim.) and Hartwick Seminary, established for pastors and missionaries to the American Indians. Jacobs, A History, pp. 332ff. Note also Documentary History, Pa. Min., pp. 537 and 559 for efforts toward a Lutheran and Reformed Seminary.

33. Documentary History, Pa. Min., pp. 528, 538, 541ff., 553-554, 581-582. Cf. also Jacobs, A History, pp. 357ff., and Wentz, Basic History, pp. 78ff.

34. Cf. Jacobs, A History, pp. 358ff., Wentz, Basic History, p. 81; and Neve-Allbeck, op.cit., p. 74.

35. Wentz, Basic History, p. 79.

36. Ibid., p. 83.

37. Aberly, op. cit., p. 65. Cf. Shedd, Two Centuries of Student Christian Movements, 1934, p. 70. Note Bachmann, op. cit., p. 118 for the rebuff given four students in 1832.

38. Shedd, op. cit., p. 83. Shedd adds: "The student chosen was Daniel Alexander Payne, who later became bishop of the African Methodist Episcopal Church and president of Wilberforce

University. His gratitude for this assistance was so great
that when in 1886 he wrote The Semi-Centenary of the African
M. E. Church, he dedicated the book to the faculty, alumni,
and the Society of Inquiry on Missions of Gettysburg College."

39. Cf. especially Evangelisches Magazin, 1812, pp. 137, 139, 142
("Die Tulle der Heiden," p. 137; "Missionen der Lutheraner,"
p. 139; and "Ost Indische Missionsgeschichte," p. 142); also
1813, p. 110; and 1815, pp. 73ff. Quoting from Aberly, op.
cit., p. 67: "The reasons given were that the churches were
too scattered, that the demands of the home fields were too
urgent, and that there was a want of information and of ex-
perimental religion among them."

40. Aberly, op. cit., p. 67.

41. Wentz tells us in his Basic History, p. 108 that "the prevailing distrust of centralized authority delayed the development of Missions for fifteen years." This convention, although called by the General Synod, was a convention of individuals and the membership of the Society formed was individual and not representative.

42. Heyer, Account of first voyage, 1841-46, p. 2. Cf. Wentz,
Basic History, p. 110. That money was being sent to foreign
mission work through the American Board of Commissioners for
Foreign Missions is shown in the Missionary Herald, November,
1838, p. 447; July, 1840, p. 287; July, 1842, p. 303; and
Dec. 1842, p. 504. Also "Our Foreign Missionary Operations",
Evangelical Review, Vol. V, pp. 104-120.

43. Gutzlaff, The Journal of Two Voyages, New York, 1833, passim.
Cf. Also Singmaster, op. cit., pp. 164-165. Gutzlaff's name
was mentioned at the York convention in 1835. Drach-Kuder,
The Telugu Mission, 1914, p. 13. Rhenius and Gutzlaff corres-
ponded with each other, as is seen in Memoir of the Rev. C.
T. E. Rhenius, London, 1841, pp. 258ff., 400, 436, 440ff.

44. Rhenius' Appeal is in the Lutheran Observer, Jan. 13, 1837.
Heyer, Account of first voyage, p. 3, says: "It was admitted
by all, that the Lutheran Church of America owes a great debt
to Foreign Missions. Some of the brethren remarked: We owe
our existence as a Church in this country, under God, to the
labors of Missionaries who were sent from the Fatherland.
Hitherto we have done nothing to cancel this debt. It is
high time that we bring the subject before our Churches and
ask our people for their contributions to this object. We

have been praying for the conversion of the world; but we must also begin to do something, or our prayers can not be heard; they will be a mockery before God." Cf. also Lutheran Observer, February 6, 13, April 17, November 27, and December 25, 1835.

45. See remarks of Bishop Caldwell as quoted in Holcomb, Men of Might in India Missions, 1901, p. 150; and of the Rev. Joseph Wolff, the celebrated missionary to the Jews, Ibid., p. 160. Wolff also is mentioned in Memoir of Rhenius, p. 451. Note also quotations from various periodicals at the time of Rhenius' death, Ibid., pp. 619,622.

46. For discussion of both sides of this tragic break see Pettitt, The Tinnevelly Mission, London, 1851, especially pp. 47ff. and 109ff.; and Memoir of Rhenius, especially pp. 381ff., 427ff., 454ff., 468ff., 475ff., 478ff., and 497ff. Also Heyer, Manuscript of Life, compiled by W. A. Lambert, pp.80ff.

With the establishment of the bishopric in Madras in 1833 and the control of the Societies coming to some extent under the bishop's supervision, the break between Rhenius and the Anglican Church was inevitable. It had been the policy of the English societies ever since the time of Ziegenbalg and Plutschau to employ German missionaries educated at Halle, Basel or Berlin, accepting their Lutheran ordination as valid, allowing them to preach Lutheran doctrine, use Lutheran liturgies and ordain native pastors. Modifications occurred, beginning with 1818, when the missionaries placed themselves under the direction of the "Corresponding Committees" in India, although they had always received their directions previously from Germany. The next step was the use of the Anglican form of service at all stations, to which the Lutherans again complied. Then further developments occurred when the missionaries were required to take Anglican orders or be reordained. Some complied, especially those educated at Basel. "And then came the additional order that the Lutheran missionaries should in their general practice renounce the rights which they actually possessed, rights to confirm and ordain, in favour of the prior rights of the bishops. It is perfectly obvious that for men who were in any sense bound by the traditions of the German Reformation it would be a much more difficult matter to comply with this Anglican demand. A secession like that of Rhenius was only to be expected; and it opened the eyes of many on both sides of the Channel to the fact that the co-operation of Lutheran missionaries in Anglican missions had become, through this development of the

Anglican spirit, impracticable, and that a point had been
arrived at where such a union was harmful to conscience."
Richter, <u>A History of Missions in India</u>, New York, 1908,
p. 160.

47.  Drach-Kuder, <u>op. cit.</u>, p. 15.  Heyer points out that the voluntary contributions to Rhenius helped the congregations in
America realize that they could maintain mission work.  Heyer,
<u>Manuscript of Life</u>, p. 82.

48.  <u>Memoir of Rhenius</u>, p. 600.  Heyer states that $1400 was sent
by the various Lutheran congregations.  Cf. <u>Manuscript of
Life</u>, p. 81.  Apparently the president of the Missionary Society, the Rev. Dr. S. S. Schmucker, wrote to Rhenius rather
than the corresponding secretary, Dr. Krauth.

49.  <u>Memoir of Rhenius</u>, pp. 601ff.

50.  Heyer, <u>Account of first voyage</u>, p. 2, states that in 1835
under the Central Missionary Society he "accepted the appointment and commenced as Domestic Missionary, with the understanding of entering the field of Foreign Missions, as soon
as the necessary arrangements could be made."

51.  Heyer, <u>Manuscript of Life</u>, p. 82.  Whether we can consider
it the hand of God that directed the General Synod away from
Tinnevelly and thus toward its most fruitful work in the Andhra Desa, the Rev. George Pettitt, who had taken over the
Tinnevelly Mission when Rhenius broke with the C. M. S., certainly considered it so.  He tells us in <u>The Tinnevelly
Mission</u>, pp. 210-211: "But I should fail to exhibit the whole
evidence of that wisdom and goodness which we recognize in
the Providence of God towards this Mission, were I to omit
the mention of a circumstance which came to our knowledge
shortly after the division was healed.  Within a month after
the return of Mr. Mueller, with all his catechists and people,
and their reunion with the Church Missionary Society, letters
reached him from parties in America who had become acquainted with the circumstances of the German Evangelical Mission
in Tinnevelly, and felt greatly interested in it.  They offered to Mr. Mueller to take him with all his catechists and
congregations into connection with themselves, to furnish him
with ample means for carrying on the Mission, and to send as
many Missionaries from America as he might wish to have as
fellow-labourers with him in the province.  Had their proposal arrived a few weeks earlier, before Mr. M. had finally
determined upon making his proposals to the Church Missionary

Society, it might possibly have proved an obstacle to our
happy reconciliation, and perpetuated the division." Since
Mueller had been very much up in the air previous to his
decision, and had offered himself even to the London Missionary Society (which had refused), it becomes clear that either
Mr. Mueller did not know of the American Society's previous
offer to Rhenius, or that the Society had not offered any
more than some financial help and missionaries. Note letter
Dr. Krauth was authorized to write Rhenius, p. 23 of Thesis.
See Pettitt, op. cit., pp. 202ff. Aberly, op. cit., p. 67,
footnote, points out that although some $3,000 was contrib-
uted in all to the Palamcotta Mission, it would have required about $12,000 annually to run it at the time of Rhen-
ius' death. Memoir of Rhenius, p. 535, states that the annual need would be between 2000 and 3000 pounds.

52. Drach-Kuder, op. cit., p. 19.

53. After the establishment of the Central and German Foreign
Missionary Societies of the General Synod, similar or auxiliary societies were formed in the various Lutheran Synods,
whether they belonged to the General Synod or not. Thus the
Ministerium of Pennsylvania organized its society on June 1,
1836. For the agreement to be drawn up between the Lutheran
Society and the A. B. C. F. M., see Drach-Kuder, op. cit.,
p. 18.

54. Heyer, Manuscript of Life, p. 85, quoted from Hans Ehrlich's
article in the magazine Lutherische Kirchenzeitung, June,
1841, to add force to his decision. Cf. also Bachmann,
op. cit., p. 120. Letter to Ezra Keller, dated May 15, 1841,
indicates Heyer's willingness to go under the American Board
rather than not at all.

55. See Drach-Kuder, op. cit., pp. 19-20, for letter.

56. Jacobs, A History, pp. 377ff., and Drach-Kuder, op. cit.,
pp. 20ff. Note variation of resolutions in Heyer, Account of
first voyage, p. 6.

57. Bachmann, op. cit., p. 121.

58. A group of conservative Synods, many of whom had broken away
from the General Synod, formed the General Council and held
their first convention at Fort Wayne, Indiana, November 20,
1867. For further details, cf. Thesis, pp. 178ff; Jacobs,
A History, pp. 455ff. and pp.471ff.; also Neve-Allbeck, op. cit.,
pp. 109ff. and pp. 155ff.

59. See p. 187 of Thesis.

60. Swanson, <u>Three Missionary Pioneers</u>, Rock Island, 1945, p. 40.

61. Cf. Burgess, ed., <u>Lutheran World Missions</u>, Minneapolis, 1954, especially statistics on pp. 256-257.

## CHAPTER II     The Beginnings

1.  The Andhra area has been a leader in the effort to divide India on the basis of languages. There has been agitation since 1913, culminating in the formation of the new State in 1953. See Marshall Windmiller: "Linguistic Regionalism in India" in Pacific Affairs, Dec. 1954, pp. 291-318.

2.  Ibid., for the present conflicts in this connection, esp. pp. 305-306. In 1951, 33 million considered Telugu their mother tongue, p. 301. Hyderabad has now been divided and Talengana is part of the present Andhra State.

3.  Hindustan Year Book and Who's Who, 1955, ed. Sarkar, p. 642.

4.  Ibid., p. 642: "Manganese is mined in Visakhapatnam and mica in Gudur (Nellore District)."

5.  Tanks are ponds formed by throwing a mud wall or bund across the valleys of small streams. The majority of these tanks dry up completely in the hot season. Cf. Stamp, A New Geography of India, Burma and Ceylon, 1942, pp. 90ff.

6.  Hindustan Year Book, 1955, pp. 307ff.; 642ff.

7.  Cocanada, eighty miles south of Visakhapatnam and just north of the Godavari River, is next in importance as a port and exports raw cotton, ground nuts, castor seeds and rice. Most of Visakhapatnam's exports come from Madhya Pradesh rather than Andhra State. Cf. Ibid., pp. 302ff.

8.  Chenchiah-Bahadur, A History of Telugu Literature, [n.d.], pp. 14, 20.

9.  Sed, The Pageant of India's History, 1948, Vol. I, p. 178. The Periplus of the Erythraean Sea refers primarily to eastern trade with the Andhra Kingdom. Cf. also Majumdar, An Advanced History of India, 1948, pp. 211ff. For further details on the Andhra Kingdom and its advanced culture, see Sed, op. cit., pp. 176ff., esp. pp. 185-187; Rawlinson, A Concise History of the Indian People, 1950, pp. 94ff.; Aiyangar, Ancient India, 1911, pp. 13, 15-16, 34, 223.

10. Chenchiah, op. cit., p. 10.

11. The historical development is too confused to detail. Cf.
    Majumdar, op. cit., pp. 172ff., 188ff.; Sed, op. cit.,
    pp. 205ff. See also maps in Davies, An Historical Atlas of
    the Indian Peninsula, 1949, pp. 18-29.

12. For a discussion of this see Chenchiah, op. cit., pp. 37ff.;
    and Arden, A Progressive Grammar of the Telugu Language, 1921,
    pp.1ff. Arden points out that there are really three branch-
    es of the Telugu language: "(1) The language of common con-
    versation. (2) The language of prose books. (3) The lan-
    guage of poetry. Each of these three branches differs con-
    siderably from the others not only in the choice of words,
    but also in the grammatical forms of the same words. The
    greatest difference exists between the first and third
    branch, while the second branch holds a middle position be-
    tween the other two, and partakes of the nature and peculiar-
    ities of both." Page 3.

13. There is a difference of opinion as to the source of the
    word 'Telugu'. Some say it comes from 'Trilinga', used to
    signify the land between the three great shrines, lingas, at
    Kalesvaram, Sri Sailam and Draksha Ramam (Bhimesvaram). Others
    state that it comes from 'Tenugu', 'tene' meaning honey, and
    'agu' meaning is. Cf. Arden, op. cit., p. 1, and Chenchiah,
    op. cit., pp. 14-15. Also Caldwell, Comparative Grammar of
    the Dravidian or South Indian Family of Languages, 1875,
    pp. 31ff.

14. Arden, op. cit., p. 11.

15. Ibid. There are 13 vowels in common use and 35 consonants.
    Secondary forms of the vowels are combined with the conson-
    ants to form over 450 distinct compound letters. On the whole,
    however, these are formed upon regular principles and are not
    too difficult to learn. Cf. Chenchiah, op.cit., p. 18.

16. Hibbert-Ware, Christian Missions in the Telugu Country, 1912,
    p.8.

17. Chenchiah, op. cit., p. 69.

18. "The celebrated Vedantist Sankaracharya, though himself a
    Smartha, had Shaiva and Sakta leanings, and he was, in no
    little measure, responsible for the popularity of Shaivism.
    In his attempt to bring Shaivism to the masses and thus drive

out Buddhism from India, Sankara accepted many of the fetishes of the aborigines as manifestations of Shiva, and his followers invented legends to support the theory." Thomas, Hindu Religion, Customs and Manners, [n.d.] , p. 29. It should be pointed out that the predominant power in the Andhra country between the periods of the Chola and Vijayanagar Empires was the Kakatiyas with their capital at Warangal. During this time there arose a 'protestant' reaction to popular Hinduism called Virasaiva, which, though anti-Brahman, had been founded by a Telugu Brahman, Basava. It was these three movements of Sankara, Basava and Ramanuja that dominated Hinduism in the Telugu country. For concise contrast between Shaivism and Vaishnavism, see Griswold, Insights into Modern Hinduism, 1934, pp. 29-35 and Thomas, op. cit., pp. 27-30.

19. Chenchiah, op. cit., p. 99.

20. For examples see Chamberlain, The Cobra's Den, 1900, p. 44; and Chamberlain, The Kingdom in India, 1908, pp. 21-24. From latter book, p. 21, Chamberlain tells us: "Vemana thus rebukes the universal idolatry that he saw prevailing around him:

> 'Not in metal, not in wood and not in stone, nor painted wall,
> Not in picture, nor in image, nor in grosser forms of clay,
> Dwells the great Eternal Spirit, dwells the author of us all;
> 'Tis not thus He shows His person to the race of man today.'"

Cf. The Verses of Vemana, translated by Charles P. Brown, 1911. Some very suggestive passages are as follows: "Sinful creatures are all subject to time; they are intoxicated by the lusts they delight in; ah! what kind of heart is the heart of a drunken man? Vain desire suffers not to attain our end; it only plunges us in troubles, and drags us along; it prevents faith from being born in men. [p. 44] ... Why should you collect stones from the hills and build fine temples to walk about in them? Why torment yourselves so, while the God, as a living being, constantly dwells within you? [p. 112] ... There is but one Lord of the universe who rules the world; is honour due to the rest of the gods? an ape of the woods might as well govern the earth. [p. 113] ... If you consider your possessions as your own, fools alone will agree with you. That alone is yours which you have be-

stowed on others, the rest is not at your disposal. [p. 128]
... If you say 'I know how to conduct myself,' this will
lead to ignorance: if you say 'I am humble,' this is no hum-
ility. If you say 'I can manage the matter,' you will,
through pride, fail of it. [p. 140] ... Those who roam to
other lands in pilgrimage to find the God that dwells within them are like a shepherd who searches in his flock for
the sheep he has under his arm. [p. 167] ... Bald heads!
matted locks! daubing with ashes, harangues, postures, and a
religious garb! No man is a saint who is not pure within.
[p. 173] ... False is the creed of those who hold that it is
profitable to renounce the present life: cannot ye see that
eternal existence commences in this life. [p. 182] ... If a
man meditates adultery with the wife of his neighbour, when
he gazes at her, all the fruits of his former good deeds,
however numerous, shall melt away, as surely as butter in the
heat of fire. [p. 184] ... If we carefully observe and examine the universe, we shall see that all castes equally origin-
ated therein: then all are equal; surely all men are brothers? What matters food, or caste, or country, so as to affect our bodies? Surely the trouble men take about caste is
all ridiculous! [p. 185] ... To what end is all this reading?
what is fruit of a monkish life? why perish entangled in the
six conflicting creeds? worship Him, and know Him who dwells
in your heart. [p. 201] "

21. Chenchiah, op. cit., p. 105.

22. "Pingali Ellanaryudu (1602) is the author of 'Tobhya Charitra,' otherwise known as 'Sarvesvara Mahatya.' ... The book
was written at the instance of Thumma Rayapa Reddi, a petty
prince of Baktavada, in Kondavidu. In the prologue further
details are given as to the circumstances under which he
composed the kavya. Obala Reddi, father of Konda Reddi, received orally from his acharya, Sanjivanadha Swami, an account of the life of Saint Thomas, which was subsequently reduced to writing. This appears to be the basis for the poet's
kavya.

Mangalagiri Anandakavi (1750). About the middle of the
eighteenth century, this poet wrote 'Vendanta Rasayana' and
'Anuruddha Charitra.' 'Vedanta Rasayana' is a kavya in four
cantos dedicated to Nidimamilla Dasayamatya, a member of an
influential family which has adopted the Christian faith.
K. Viresalingam judges the poet to be a writer of very high
eminence, worthy to be placed among the best poets of his
century.

The author approaches the subject in a devotional frame
of mind and gives a clear and succinct account of the life of
Christ. ... The author shows intimate acquaintance with the
scriptures and the rites of the Christian Church. The kavya
is remarkable as the solitary instance in which a Hindu
bhakta, saturated with the thought-forms of his own country,
has reverently undertaken to proclaim the life of Christ to
the world." Chenchiah, op. cit., pp. 105-106. A kavya is
a religious poem, divided into cantos, which emphasizes much
description but not much plot, "the painting of character,
the portrayal of passing moods and moving passions, and the
analysis of emotion." Ibid., p. 70. It is a very decorative
style, full of simile and hyperbole.

23. Paul, History of the Telugu Christians, 1929, p. 3. Most of
the following material on the Roman Catholic work is taken
from Paul.

24. The War of the Austrian Succession, in which the French and
English took opposite sides, spread to India, and even after
the treaty of Aix-la-Chapelle in 1748 continued there through
the intrigues of the French to gain control of the Nawab of
the Carnatic and the Nizam of Hyderabad. Cf. Rawlinson,
op. cit., pp. 254ff.

25. This area was given to the French in 1753 in return for the
services of the Marquis de Bussy to the Nizam in training his
army.

26. The work prospered in certain areas; especially worthy of note
is the effort of Father Bonnand around Phirangipuram in the
Guntur District . In 1827 he reported Christians in 56 villages, 12 church buildings, with two-thirds of the town itself,
or about 400, Christian. Cf. Paul, op. cit., p. 59.

27. Bromley, They Were Men Sent From God, 1937, p. 6, states:
"It is a remarkable circumstance that as early as 1651, fifty-
five years before the landing in Tranquebar of Plutschau and
Ziegenbalg, the first Protestant missionaries to India, the
Dutch East India Company was moved to send the then startling
instructions to its chaplain in Palakol that he was to regard
the teaching of Christianity to the surrounding natives a
part of his duty -- the first recognition recorded of such a
responsibility on the part of a Protestant power in India."

28. Woerrlein, Dreizehn Jahre in Indien, 1885, p. 174. Cf. also

Haccius, Hannoversche Missionsgeschichte, 1914, Section 3, first half, p. 333; Holcomb, Men of Might in India Missions, 1901, pp. 23-24, 29; and Lives of Missionaries, 1st Series, SPCK, [n.d.] ,pp. 41-42. It is likely that he visited Tirupati in 1711, following the completion of the translation of the Tamil New Testament and the training of the newly-arrived missionaries. On this same journey he visited the English Chaplain in Madras with the intention of starting a mission school there. Cf. Hough, The History of Christianity in India, 1845, Volume III, pp. 175-176. He had high hopes of establishing work "through the whole of the Tamil country from Madras in the north right down to Ceylon in the south, preaching the gospel, and of uniting the universities of Germany, Denmark, and Holland in an attempt to accomplish this great work." Richter, A History of Missions in India, 1908, p. 109.

29. Two schools had been started by Ziegenbalg and Grundler in 1716 with the cooperation of the English Chaplain, the Rev. William Stevenson, but these did not last without a resident missionary and were for Portuguese and Tamil children. Westcott, Our Oldest Indian Mission, 1897, p. 2. The Dutch were reaching the natives in their factory at Pulicat, north of Madras. Hough, op. cit., Vol. 3, pp. 217-218, mentions that the Catechist's brother came to Tranquebar to be trained. This, together with what Schultze reports in his diary when he visited Pulicat on a preaching tour, points out that the work was with Tamil and Portuguese rather than any of the Telugu-speaking people. Cf. Notices of Madras and Cuddalore, SPCK, 1858, pp. 16-18, 19, 105-106. Schultze tells of visiting a Telugu school but there is no evidence that it was run by the Christians or that the Christian religion was taught in it.

30. Notices of Madras and Cuddalore, pp. 25-26. He began studying the language October 16, opened the school November 5, and started his translation December 14, 1726. On Schultze's remarks about the similarity between Tamil and Telugu, cf. Ibid., pp. 40ff.

31. Richter, op. cit., p. 113. By August, 1732, Schultze had completed the Bible in Telugu, written on palmyra leaves, but there is no evidence that this was ever printed although he received the authorization to do so at Tranquebar from the Mission College at Copenhagen. Notices of Madras and Cuddalore, p. 113. Apparently he took the translation with him when he returned to Germany in 1742 or sent it to Halle. Cf.

Anstey, Report on Protestant Telugu Christian Literature, CLS, 1917, p. 9; also Note 1, page 389, Volume 3, of Hough, op. cit.. It must be remembered that very little printing in Telugu was done before 1806, and very little progress after that until 1830. Cf. The Principal Nations of India, CLS, 1892, p. 144. From Anstey, op. cit., p. 9: "The earliest version of the Holy Scriptures in Telugu, as far as is known, is that of the New Testament printed at the Serampore Press, under the supervision of Dr. Carey, towards the end of the eighteenth century; though Schultze finished a translation of the New Testament in 1727, but it never appears to have been printed."

32. Notices of Madras and Cuddalore, p. 66.

33. Westcott, op. cit., p. 13.

34. Cf. Woerrlein, op. cit., pp. 56-57; Haccius, op. cit., section 3, first half, p. 316; and Hermannsburger Missionsblatt, 1883, p. 11.

35. Besides the shortage of missionaries, the decline of interest in Europe with the rise of rationalism, and the wars which held up much of the work around Madras, it must be remembered that the missionaries were using four languages already in their service to the Christian constituency -- English, German, Portuguese and Tamil. Cf. Taylor, A Memoir of the First Century of the Earliest Protestant Mission at Madras, 1847, p. 68. Cf. also Gericke's unfulfilled hopes for the Telugu land, Lives of Missionaries, SPCK, First Series, pp. 324ff.

36. The East India Company had failed even to provide chaplains for the military forces in the Northern Circars although they had been in possession of the area since 1765. The Rev. Richard H. Kerr, appointed Senior Chaplain of Madras in 1804 and instrumental in developing a new Christian consciousness among Civil Officials there, had his appointment as chaplain to Ellore turned down by the Court of Directors in 1795. Several years later, in a letter to the Court of Directors he pointed out that there were only three churches to be found in the whole Carnatic and not one in the Circars to serve the civil and military personnel. See Hough, op. cit., Vol. 4, pp. 139ff.

37. The third missionary, William Ringeltaube, decided to stay in the south and began work in South Travancore. It should be pointed out that the cordial reception of these mission-

aries was most unusual on the part of the East India Company officials. _Ibid._, pp. 187-188, 290. And it indicates the changing attitude and the changing personnel of the higher officials, as is shown in the experience of Dr. Richard Kerr. _Ibid._, pp. 150ff.

38. Sherring, The History of Protestant Missions in India, 1706-1881, new edition, 1884, p. 420. For further details see Hough, _op. cit._, Vol. 4, pp. 254ff., Vol. 5, pp.503ff.; Campbell, British India, 1839, pp. 337ff. For the amazing story of this first convert see _Ibid._, pp. 352-355; and Bromley, _op. cit._, pp. 9-11. Bromley says of him, p. 11: "It was the first voice of a Telugu to Telugus -- musical, scholarly, convincing in argument; for the tracts that soon issued from his pen remain today invaluable weapons in the Christian armoury in its warfare with caste and Hinduism; and in the highly gifted Purushottam Chowdhuri was found a great poet whose rich legacy of Christian song of the Telugu has never been matched, as evidenced by the abundance of his beautiful hymns scattered throughout our vernacular hymn-book."

39. Started by the Rev. John Hands in 1809. Cf. Hough, _op. cit._, Vol. 4, pp. 286ff.

40. The Mala caste will be explained later. See pp. 128ff., 131ff. of Thesis. In addition to the 100 converts there were English-speaking and Tamil-speaking members of the congregation. It is difficult to determine the exact number of converts as the reports vary. This is apparently because one writer lists only the communing members, another the baptized and still another includes the inquirers as well in the Christian community. For further details see Campbell, _op. cit._, pp. 360ff.; Sherring, _op. cit._, pp. 403ff.; and Hough, _op. cit._, Vol. V, pp. 526ff.

41. For changes in the charters of 1793, 1813 and 1833, see Latourette, A History of the Expansion of Christianity, Volume VI, 1944, pp. 66-69, 100, 108-109; Richter, _op. cit._, pp. 149-152, 192; Hough, _op. cit._, Vol. 4, pp. 187ff. It is of interest to note that following the charter of 1813 English Chaplains and Officials began to take more interest in reaching the native population; and some of their preliminary efforts in establishing schools and conducting services led to established congregations later taken over by missionaries. See, for example, Hough, _op. cit._, Vol. 5, pp. 406-416; Bromley, _op. cit._, p. 63; Memoir of the Rev. C. T. E. Rhenius, 1841, pp. 126ff. and 175 ff. From these passages in Rhenius it becomes apparent that, as the first C. M. S. miss-

ionary in Madras, 1814-1820, he was making a serious effort
to reach the Telugu-speaking people.  On several occasions
he spoke of establishing work in the Andhra Desa, pp. 128 and
185.  It is appropriate that this same Lutheran missionary
was the one instrumental in leading the American Lutheran
Church to India and finally the Andhra Desa.  See pages 22-
24 of Thesis.

42.  Later, Colonel and then General Sir Arthur Cotton.  For
biography cf. Morris, Heroes of our Indian Empire, Volume II,
1908, pp. 121-164.  Also Lady Hope, General Sir Arthur Cotton,
His Life and Work, 1900, passim.

43.  Latourette, op. cit., vol. VI, p. 122; Bromley, op cit.,
pp. 22ff.  Of interest to Lutherans was Groves' approval of
Rhenius' efforts to establish an independent mission in opposition to ecclesiastical pretensions and sectarianism.  "At
first he was content to support existing enterprise, and
hence his espousal of the cause of Rhenius, his efforts to
obtain workers for various missionary agencies, and the part
he took in the founding of the great Lutheran Mission amongst
the Telugus."  Bromley, op. cit., pp. 24-25; See also p. 64.
By 1836, however, Groves decided to bring his own missionaries, the Darbyites or Plymouth Brethren.

44.  Dr. Claudius Buchanan tells of his travels in the Telugu area
in July, 1806, in his book, Christian Researches, p. 21,
which was so valuable in England and America in arousing the
churches to India's needs.

45.  Baker, Contending the Grade in India, 1947, p. 59.

46.  Also mentioned are "some incidental efforts at Madras, Bellary and other places."

47.  Rhenius took part in its organization in 1818.  Memoir, pp.
163-164.

48.  Missionary Herald, Vol. XXXIII, September 1837, pp. 378-380.
This same article points out that Gordon and Pritchett of
Vizagapatam had completed two good translations of the Tel-
ugu Scriptures, but that only Genesis and 20 chapters of Ex-
odus of the Old Testament had been printed and published.
The rest of the Old Testament had been in the hands of the
Madras Auxiliary Bible Society for eight or ten years.  The
New Testament translation by Pritchett had been in circula-
tion for many years.  Taylor, op. cit., p. 181, mentions
that Pritchett was in Madras in November, 1818, correcting

the Press version of his translation. Cf. also Bromley,
op. cit., p. 7.

49. *Missionary Herald*, Vol. XXXVII, May, 1841, p. 228. It was
at this very time that the German Foreign Missionary Society, after consultation with the ABCFM, was deciding to send
Heyer to the Telugu land. See page 25 of Thesis.

50. Campbell, op. cit., pp. 332 ff. especially.

51. In 1853 the poem of the Rev. S. F. Smith, author of our National Hymn, which he called "Lone Star Mission" saved the
day for what became known as "The Lone Star Mission." See
Downie, The History of the Telugu Mission of the ABMU, 1893,
pp. 46-47 for the poem.

52. For this amazing story, see J. E. Clough, From Darkness to
Light, 1882, passim., and Social Christianity in the Orient,
1914, passim. Nine thousand people were baptized in six
weeks beginning on July 2, 1878, with 2,222 of them baptized
in one day. See also Downie, op. cit., and Baker, op. cit.,
for histories of the work.

53. Gledstone, The C. M. S. Telugu Mission, 1841-1941, pp. 1-2.

54. It should be stated that Fox and his wife arrived in Masulipatam first, hurrying there August 18th before their baby was
born; but Masulipatam was selected as the field of work at a
later date. For further details on the C.M.S., see Gledstone,
op. cit., passim.; Hibbert-Ware, op. cit., pp. 184ff; and
Stock, A History of the Church Missionary Society, 1899, Vol.
I, p. 327; Vol. II, pp. 169, 198-213. Biographies of the
first two men are : Noble, A Memoir of the Rev. Turlington
Noble, 1867, and Fox, A Memoir of the Rev. Watson Fox, 1853.

55. All but the mission work in the Danish-owned town of Tranquebar itself had been incorporated in the Anglican Church when
the SPCK handed over its work to the SPG in 1825. The town
nearly went to the English Society when Tranquebar was sold
to the British Government in 1845; but the Danish King decided it should remain Lutheran and gave the property to the
Dresden (now known as the Leipzig) Mission in 1847. Dresden
had sent a missionary there in 1840, Cordes. Cf. Latourette,
op. cit., Vol. VI, p. 128; and Baierlein, The Land of the
Tamulians and Its Missions, 1875, pp. 142ff.

56. Drach-Kuder, The Telugu Mission, 1914, p. 24; and Bachmann,

*They Called Him Father*, 1942, p. 9.

57. Bachmann, op. cit., p. 14.

58. Helmuth had planned to have Heyer go to the University of Halle which he had attended, but it was closed because of the war.

59. Cf. Bachmann, op. cit., p. 40, for his experience at French Creek.

60. Ibid., p. 43; also pp. 41ff. on handling the revivals. Cf. also Heyer, Manuscript of Life, by W. A. Lambert, p. 2b.

61. Drach-Kuder, op. cit., p. 28. See concerning his appointment in Documentary History of the Evangelical Lutheran Minister-ium of Pennsylvania and Adjacent States, 1748-1821, p. 565. Heyer was given $12 for 1000 tracts that he was to distri-bute. The response of the people in Kentucky and Indiana to Heyer's visit was most cordial, and they urged more traveling preachers be sent. p. 573.

62. See pages 22,24 of Thesis. Interestingly enough, Heyer also was elected the first president of the Society, indicating that he was one of the moving spirits in the missionary move-ment. The corresponding secretary was Professor Samuel S. Schmucker of the Gettysburg Seminary.

63. Drach-Kuder, op. cit., p. 31, quoting his call by the Society.

64. One individual who witnessed the work of Heyer on this trip wrote: "Our much esteemed brother Heyer ... seems to be ex-actly suited for the arduous and self-denying, and yet impor-tant and responsible business in which he is engaged. The church could not have procured a better qualified individual for the task. Much may be expected from his mission." Quoted from Bachmann, op. cit., pp. 93-94.

65. "By his tactful, whole-souled manner Heyer managed to hold the friendship of all three congregations he had founded in 1837. Reviewing the results of his work in Pittsburgh, one marvels how from those three congregations, begun in the same year, three of the major Lutheran church bodies in Amer-ica have reaped the original churches as well as their numer-ous offspring. First English Church is in the United Luth-eran Church; Trinity, in the Missouri Synod; and St. John's, Allegheny, in the American Lutheran Church. Heyer well de-serves the title, 'Father of Lutheranism in Pittsburgh.'" Ibid., p. 112.

66. This had been organized in October, 1829, by a number of
    delegates to the General Synod at Hagerstown, Md., at the
    instigation of the West Pennsylvania Synod of which Heyer was
    secretary at the time. He became president of the Synod in
    1831. The American Sunday School Union, which provided the
    inspiration for this Society in the Lutheran Church, had been
    established in 1824 and by 1831 reported a membership of some
    70,000 teachers and 700,000 pupils. See Ibid., pp. 60ff.,
    for further details.

67. Drach-Kuder, op. cit., p. 29, have added a footnote at this
    point saying: "Experience seems to have cooled his ardor.
    Some years later he wrote: 'Sunday schools are only small
    plasters on large sores. We consider it our duty to recommend
    their establishment most heartily, but they are not to be
    considered as substitutes for Christian day schools'"

68. Ibid., pp. 29-30. By 1831 there were 74 schools connected
    with the Union, 567 teachers and 4,890 pupils, and when he
    resigned in 1832 there were 119 schools, 365 men teachers,
    460 women teachers, 3,624 boys and 3,706 girls. Bachmann,
    op. cit., pp. 68-69. It should be emphasized that the Luth-
    eran Church had more than just the wish to provide addition-
    al Bible instruction in mind when they joined in heartily in
    the Sunday School movement. They also saw in it a way to
    preserve the German language among the children, now that most
    of the parochial schools were disappearing with the rise of
    the public school system.

69. Heyer, Manuscript of Life, by W. A. Lambert, pp. 1b, 5b.

70. Interestingly enough, while in Baltimore Heyer lost none of
    his missionary fervor; for he re-organized a struggling miss-
    ion of six members into an active congregation with its own
    church building. Cf. Bachmann, op. cit., p. 122; Drach-Kuder,
    op. cit., p. 33.

71. Heyer's roving and pioneering spirit is indicated by a letter
    he wrote on board ship after leaving Zanzibar: "If in Zanzi-
    bar, as in Southern India, we could enjoy the protection of
    a Christian Government, I should decidedly be of the opinion
    that we ought to commence our Foreign Missionary operations
    on this Island, with the design of extending them to the in-
    terior and unexplored regions of Africa. It would be a great
    and noble undertaking, to go as the first Evangelist to these
    dark and benighted regions. If I had acted on my own indi-
    vidual responsibility, I should have been willing to risk my

life in the attempt; but being the Agent of an Ev. Luth. Mis. Society, I considered it my duty, to proceed according to previous arrangements." Heyer, Account of His First Voyage to India, p. 16. On one occasion in later years, Father Heyer said: "If I should be drowned near the Cape of Good Hope, you may put this on my tombstone: 'Here lies Christian Frederick Heyer, a Cosmopolite, born in Europe, pastor in America, missionary in Asia, drowned in Africa.'" Heyer, Notes for Life of Father Heyer by W. A. Lambert, comment made to Dr. Schaeffer.

72. Bachmann, op. cit., p. 135. For detailed description see Heyer, Account of First Voyage, pp. 32ff.

73. See reference note 55, chapter II.

74. See pages 22-24 of Thesis.

75. Heyer, Account of First Voyage, p. 38.

76. Ibid., pp. 38-39. This Account proves to be most interesting in the description of villages and temples as well as the mission stations Heyer visited. Of historical interest is this interview Heyer had, told on pages 56-57: "About noon I conversed with Nyanapracasan, a native priest, 93 years of age. This aged disciple embraced the gospel at Tranquebar in 1756, during Rev. Mr. Kohloff's, Sen., time. He was first employed by Mr. Schwartz as teacher in Trichinopoly, afterwards appointed Catechist, and in 1811 was ordained by Rev. Messrs. Pohle, Kohloff and Satianaden. ... The last ordination of native priests by Lutheran Missionaries at Tanjore, took place in 1817."

77. It was in Ongole that the Rev. John E. Clough, leader of the great mass movement among the Madiga outcastes, as mentioned on page 39 of the Thesis and reference note 52, chapter II, made his headquarters in 1866.

78. Heyer, Account of First Voyage, p. 69. Stokes first heard of Heyer when the latter arrived at Bapatla and tied his palanquin between two palmyra trees with the assertion that he would start his work there. Stokes talked him into coming to Guntur; and when he asked Heyer where he intended to live, the palanquin was pointed out to him. "His friend was not slow in recognizing the earnestness of Heyer, but told him that he could not hope to live in that manner, that he came not to die, but to live and work. Stokes accordingly took

him into his own home in Guntur until a house could be arranged for him. 'For six months,' says Heyer, in speaking of his residence with the collector, 'I lived with this servant of God, and whereas I expected nothing but privation and self-denial in India, I soon found that with him and at his table I was to live like a prince. I was never more comfortably situated in my life." Laury, A History of Lutheran Missions, 1899, p. 102. Cf. also Swavely, One Hundred Years in the Andhra Country, 1942, p. 8.

79. Some of the names of these most helpful officials are given by Heyer. In addition to Stokes, they were Mr. Newill, first Assistant Collector, assistant collectors Hutway and Barlow, Judges Walter and Wood, Drs. Evans and Smith, General Buckel and Captain O'Neil. Drach-Kuder, op. cit., p. 51.

80. Letter dated September 17, 1842, quoted in Heyer, Account of First Voyage, p. 70. The expenses of the first year amounted to approximately $1,585, of which $804 came from America and $780 was contributed by the English residents. Of the $804, St. John's Lutheran Church, Philadelphia, contributed $140, the rest coming from the Missionary Society, including $600 for Heyer's salary. Bachmann, op. cit., p. 154, states: "Over against this cautious support given by the Society to its missionary, the liberality of the English residents of Guntur is impressive. These few residents, members of the Church of England, with incomes not large like those of wealthy nabobs, gave the Lutheran mission a total of $780. Deducting the alms they handed Heyer for distribution, they donated over $600. From this it is unmistakable that if the way had not been prepared for Heyer, and if his British friends had not continued to support the new Lutheran mission as though it were their very own, then the first venture of the Lutherans in America on the foreign field might easily have died in infancy."

81. How persistent this custom of Wednesday evening prayer became can be testified to by the author who attended them as late as 1937, with the afternoon previous to it being devoted to a social gathering with tennis and tea being the main features.

82. Although his first effort was unsuccessful with this boy, it shows the "first feeble attempt at a boarding school for the training of native workers in the Mission." Drach-Kuder, op. cit., p. 52.

391

83. One of these schools was 12 miles south of Guntur, another 5
    miles west, and the third in a suburb of Guntur. "At first
    a number of Brahman boys came to the Guntur school and to the
    one in Prattipadu; but when the parents realized that the
    missionary aimed, above all things, to inculcate the truths
    of Christianity, they not only withdrew their sons from the
    schools, but also showed considerable hostility toward the
    missionary and his work." Ibid., p. 53.

84. Ibid., p. 54; also Bachmann, op. cit., pp. 151-152.

85. See page 38 of Thesis.

86. "Before his departure, in 1841, Heyer offered to report reg-
    ularly to the General Synod, provided it would annually con-
    tribute $200 toward his salary. No doubt this offer had the
    consent of the Ministerium's Society. At any rate it left
    the way open for future cooperation. In the meanwhile, the
    General Synod had rescinded its intended collaboration with
    the American Board; a plan which had originally caused Heyer
    to decline the Synod's support. Thus at the annual meeting
    of the General Synod, in 1843, the way was cleared for co-
    operation with the Ministerium. Signalizing this opportun-
    ity was the election of Walter Gunn as missionary of the Gen-
    eral Synod. He was to serve as Heyer's colleague in Guntur."
    Bachmann, op. cit., p. 155; see also Drach-Kuder, op. cit.,
    pp. 59ff., especially footnote 1 on page 59.

87. See page 54 of Thesis.

88. See footnote 26, chapter II.

89. Heyer, Account of First Voyage, pp. 82-83.

90. Ibid., p. 84. Sherring, The History of Protestant Missions
    in India, 1706-1881, London, 1884, is mistaken in his state-
    ment on page 414, that Heyer reaped the benefit of previous
    visits by Baptist and North German Missionaries.

91. Walter Gunn, born June 27, 1815, in Carlisle, Schoharie, N.Y.,
    studied for a time in Schenectedy, N.Y., and in Hartwick
    Seminary, completing his work at the Theological Seminary at
    Gettysburg in 1843. Licensed by the Hartwick Synod, he and
    his wife, the former Lorena Pults, were commissioned in Oct-
    ober and sailed November 18, 1843. During that summer they
    had delivered 56 mission addresses in 44 churches in Pa.,
    N.J. and Md. Gunn's response to the charge at his commission-
    ing was most prophetic. He said, among other things, "If it

is our duty to go to the heathen land, it is yours to uphold
us there. You give your money, we give more: we give our
lives." Bachmann, op. cit., p. 156. See Drach-Kuder, op.
cit., pp. 60ff. for interesting story of how Gunn became a
missionary, the result of the prayers of four women.

92. For further details on this occasion, see Drach-Kuder, op.
cit., p. 64; and Bachmann, op. cit., pp. 161-162.

93. Refer to page 40 of the Thesis and footnote 55 of Chapter II.
This move of the Leipzig missionaries coincides with the
pending sale of Tranquebar to the English. Believing they
were to lose Tranquebar Mission also, evidently they were
looking for a new area of work, until they learned that the
Danish King wanted to keep the Mission for the Leipzig Society. Along with this, Collector Stokes was interested enough
in the situation to buy Mayavaram from the C.M.S. and hand it
to the Leipzigers as a new station. Cf. Swavely, The Lutheran Enterprise in India, 1952, pp. 15-16; and Baierlein, op.
cit., p. 195.

94. See page 37 of Thesis.

95. See page 10 of Thesis. The Stade Society invited the Bremen
and Hamburg groups to an anniversary in 1834; extended the
invitation to others the next year at which time a candidate
offered himself as a missionary. This proved to be the impetus needed to organize the North German Society on April 9,
1836, with six Societies forming a federated group. It was
made up of Lutheran and Reformed who worked out a constitution whereby candidates were to be ordained in the church the
missionary confesses, but were to be trained according to the
Augsburg Confession, 1530. The Mission Institute was opened
in 1837 under Inspector J. H. Brauer and consisted primarily
of students from farms or crafts, educated as in Basel, with
the first missionaries sent out after five years. Two of
the first graduates were selected to go to the Telugu land.
The needs of this area had been brought to the Society from
various sources. Initially considering work in Kanara, the
Basel Society advised otherwise. Brauer then went to England and Holland to discuss the possibility of a mission
field. They all recommended the Telugu area. The Rev. Mr.
Wyneken and other friends of the Society in America also
brought this area to Brauer's attention. The two candidates
selected were very close friends; and when one of them became quite ill, it was considered unsafe to send them to India, but they went to New Zealand instead. It was at this
time that Valett came into the picture; and since the Society

decided it could use an 'academically-trained' man in a cultured land such as India, he was accepted. Cf. Wischan, _Wilhelm Groenning, Missionar Im Telugu-Lande, in Indien,_ 1891, pp. 25ff.; Schreiber, _Bausteine zur Geschichte der Norddeutschen Missionsgesellschaft,_ 1911, pp. 9ff., 31ff.; Petri, _Die Ausbildung der evangelischen Heidenboten in Deutschland,_ 1873, pp. 108ff.; _Monats-Blatt der Norddeutschen Missions Gesellschaft,_ 1876, pp. 51ff.; Drach-Kuder, _op. cit.,_ pp. 83ff.

96. See page 51 of Thesis. There is evidently some question as to Valett's date of arrival in Rajahmundry. Schreiber, _op. cit.,_ p. 31, says December 21, 1844; _Monats-Blatt,_ April, 1876, p. 53, gives December 26, 1844, as the date; others agree on January, 1845. Cf. Swavely, _One Hundred Years,_ pp. 8, 147; Drach-Kuder, _op. cit.,_ p. 84; Bromley, _op. cit.,_ p. 70; Drach, _Our Church Abroad,_ 1926, p. 31; and Dolbeer, _The Andhra Evangelical Lutheran Church,_ 1951, p. 2. Bachmann, _op. cit.,_ is vague, mentioning later that year (1844) on page 158; and 1845 on p. 215. Exact dates would suggest one of the first two; but the number of authorities recommends January, 1845. It is probable that he left Guntur after the Christmas festivities and arrived in Rajahmundry just as the new year began.

97. Schreiber, _op. cit.,_ p. 31, states that Valett moved into the newly erected bungalow July 22, 1845, and welcomed the new missionaries exactly one year later. Other sources state that the building was under construction in 1846-47. Cf. Swavely, _One Hundred Years,_ p. 147; Dolbeer, _op. cit.,_ p. 4; Drach-Kuder, _op. cit.,_ pp. 85-86. It seems unlikely that the building was completed in July when we realize that he did not arrive until January, had to lease the property from the government which takes time, and plan and construct the building which can take even longer in slow Oriental fashion. On the other hand, it may very well be that, owing to the odd construction of the house, Valett had completed the central portion and occupied it by July 22, 1845. The building is described by Drach-Kuder, _op. cit.,_ pp. 85-86: "In the center of the building was a long, wide room, used as a common living room, school room and place of public worship. At each of the four corners of this large, central room there were two small rooms, each suite for the private use of a missionary, so that four missionaries could be accomodated. The completed building cost about $1,000." Several other discrepancies in dates as well as the negligible information available on the life of the Rev. L. P. M. Valett point up that there was little interest in this five-year period from 1845-1850 on the part of the North German Society since they gave

up the work completely at the end of that time; and also on the part of the American Lutherans because they did not have any part in the work until after 1850.

98. Heyer had left for America. Nothing is known of Heise other than his coming from Frankfurt-des-Oder, his studying at the Mission Institute of the North German Society, and his returning to Germany in 1862 because of poor health to live with his family and labor in Kiel, dying Nov. 22, 1895. On his furlough in 1856-57, Heise with his new bride was asked to come to America and make a tour of American congregations for the benefit of missions. The Executive Committee reported: "The visit of Brother Heise to this country was a happy circumstance. The man, his spirit, his modesty, his mental and missionary endowments, his zeal, his unwearied toil, proved him to be the man for his calling. Not unlike Dr. Duff he passed from city to city and from city to country, everywhere enlightening and gratifying crowded audiences and infusing a new missionary spirit. ... His visit would seem to have marked a new era in the history of our foreign mission." Drach-Kuder, op. cit., pp. 110-111.

99. After Valett left for India, the North German Society tried without success to find another university-trained man. Those who were capable were not wanted by the society or did not want to go; those who were acceptable and able to go, were not capable. Louis Harms was approached four times; but he felt he should not use the back door to escape from his problems with the Hanover Church. Theologians proved to be a real problem as far as sending them to the Mission fields. Groenning and Heise were selected finally from the Mission Institute as the best qualified of the group. Cf. Monats-Blatt, p. 53; Drach Kuder, op. cit., p. 90.

100. Inspector Brauer listed the annual cost in Rajahmundry at Rs. 2800 or approximately $1400, including Rs. 1200 for Valett's salary, Rs. 1000 for Heise, incidental expenses Rs. 600. This meant that both schools were supported by the English residents. The Rs. 1000 school fund debt was really an accumulation from which the Society had borrowed. The two houses built so far were valued at Rs. 4,500. Drach-Kuder, op. cit., p. 92.

101. Valett had married at the close of 1847 the widowed sister of Bowden, Plymouth Brethren missionary located at Dowlaishwaram, and for a period of time there was cooperation and "collaboration in Gospel itineration" between the two missions. Mrs. Valett died in less than a year, October 29, 1848, before

the new bungalow was completed. While in Germany on furlough, Valett married Emilie von Hauffstengel, born May 2,
1829. Arriving in Bellary February 10, 1853, he took the
superintendence of the Wardlaw Insitution, a boys' school,
and did Gosepl preaching. He moved to Chicacole in 1857,
but his wife's failing health forced him to resign June 24,
1859. "Later he accepted a pastorate in Hannover, Germany,
became Superintendent with residence at Sandstedt, near
Bremen, and continued in this office until 1887, when he retired on a pension. He died in Bremen on March 23, 1892,
aged seventy-nine years." Drach-Kuder, op. cit., p. 95.
Cf. also Whitehouse, Register of Missionaries, Deputations,
etc., from 1796 to 1896, LMS, 1896, p. 175; Lovett, The History of the London Missionary Society, 1795-1895, London,
1899, Vol. 1, pp. 90, 133; and Bromley, op. cit., pp. 88-89.

102. Heyer took great care in instructing these individuals and
was cautious about admitting them to the Lord' Supper. He
states: "We do not deem it advisable to administer the Lord's
Supper immediately to all who have been baptized." Drach-
Kuder, op. cit., p. 66.

103. The first grade of fourteen pupils had three Mohammedans, one
Rajput, nine Sudras and a pariah. Ibid., p. 66.

104. Cf. Ibid., pp. 36, 67ff. See Lutherische Kirchenzeitung, May
1, 1845, editorial that emphasizes that Heyer should not
think of coming home in four years when $5500 had been spent
on the work in India, $1500 of it on travel alone.

105. Bachmann, op. cit., pp. 164-165.

106. Drach-Kuder, op. cit., p. 74.

107. Heyer, Letters from J. C. F. Heyer, 1847-52, p. 13.

108. It should be emphasized that this defection of much of the
Vepery congregation from the English, as well as others
throughout the old Tranquebar Mission area when it was learned that the Leipzig Society had taken over the Tranquebar
Mission, came about primarily because the English were trying to enforce their policy of no differentiation between
castes. The Leipzig Society, on the other hand, was willing
to continue the lenient policy of the old Danish Mission. See
Sherring, The History of Protestant Missions in India, 1884,
pp. 354ff.; Latourette, op. cit., Vol.VI, p. 128; Swavely,
Lutheran Enterprise, pp. 16ff.; and Baierlain, op. cit.,
pp. 157ff.

109. See pages 52-53 of Thesis.

110. See footnote 101, chapter II, for collaboration between two
missions. Bromley, op. cit., pp. 88-89, states that the
Palnad already was showing "promise of the big ingathering of
the following years.  Gunn and Beer were kindred spirits.
Though the fires of consumption were already sapping his
physical frame, nothing could quench the flame of Gunn's
passion for souls, that they might be truly converted to
God -- only spared seven years, to the end [on July 5th,
1851] he persevered in speaking of Christ to all who visited
him in his sick room.  To Judge Rohde, who visited him the
day before he died he feebly whispered, ' I know in whom I
have believed, and am persuaded that He is able to keep that
which I have committed unto Him against that day.'"  See
Heyer, Letters, p. 43, concerning his funeral which was attended by all the officials in Guntur.  He was very popular.

111. His mode of traveling is worth noting.  He tells that he used
a strong two-wheeled cart, purchased for about $15, with a
box set on top about six feet long, two and a half feet broad
and three feet high.  Over the box hoops are tied, and then a
bamboo mat covered with a coarse cloth painted white on top
and black on the sides is stretched over the hoops.  This
provides protection from heat by day and moisture at night.
On top of the box, under the mat, clothes and provisions are
stored.  Inside the box a bed is arranged to permit lying or
sitting, with a door at the back.  The driver and two bullocks
pull the cart at a cost of five dollars or ten rupees a month.
He takes with him his toasted bread for the whole trip, and
purchases his milk, chicken and eggs along the way.  Heyer,
Letters, p. 19.

112. This was the work of Malapati John, mentioned above and on
pages 52-53, who told Heyer, while pointing to a book he
held in his hand: "The light of the Gospel was first introduced among us, by the instrumentality of this book; you
presented it to me about four years ago, and since that time
the gospel has spread among us, as you see from the number of
persons who desire to be baptized."  Another of the applicants, a young man, when asked when he had first heard about
Christ, replied: "Three years ago, Sir, I was brought to see
the folly of idolatry, and now feel the need of a better
physician for my soul; since that time my parents also have
commenced seeking the right way, and we all desire to become
Christians."  Ibid., pp. 20-21.  Thirty were brought forward
for baptism, from whom Heyer picked 22 who came from three
villages and seven different families.

397

113. <u>The Missionary</u>, 1849, p. 87.

114. These resolutions were as follows:
"Section I. Name. First Christian Congregation in the
    Palnad.
Section II. Rule of Faith and Practice. The only rule of
    faith and practice which this congregation receives is
    the Word of God, as contained in the Old and New Testa-
    ments. Ephes. ii 20
Section III. Members.
    1. It is required that all who are, or wish to become mem-
    bers of this congregation, should at least know the Ten
    Commandments, the Creed, and the Lord's Prayer.
    2. Besides this knowledge, it is expected that all persons
    shall prove the sincerity of their profession by leading
    Christian lives, and then testify against idolatry, and
    help to establish the kingdom of heaven throughout the
    land.
Section IV. Children. The lambs of the flock, the children
    of the congregation, are to be trained in the nurture and
    admonition of the Lord, by the pastor, school teachers
    and parents.
Section V. Council. The Council of the congregation is to
    consist of the minister and two or more elders and
    deacons." <u>Ibid.</u>, p. 87.

115. Of these, four men and two women were Sudras, the other eight
Mala men. Heyer called them 'Malahvandlus.'

116. Heyer, <u>Letters</u>, pp. 32ff., tells of a special gathering in February, 1850, of all the people who had been baptized or asked for baptism, 81 in all, which proved to be an inspiration
to them and the community that witnessed it. He says: "Admitting that most of these people scarcely know the first
principles of Christianity, still is evident, that there is
a remarkable moving among these dry bones; the more remarkable, because it has taken place in India, where hitherto the
progress of the gospel has been so very slow, and where even
the servants, who are employed in European families, can but
seldom be prevailed on, to embrace the gospel. That all
these people will eventually be found among the wheat, is
more than we can calculate on; however, I pray, that the Lord,
who has called them, may also enlighten, regenerate, justify
and sanctify and save them. ... I consider this the most interesting meeting, I have ever attended in India; and it is
certain, that for many miles around, there is not a missionary station, where so many natives could be collected, who

have received, or are willing to receive, the holy ordinance of Baptism.  It must appear the more remarkable when
you consider, that the Palnaud Station was commenced less
than a year ago." Footnote on p. 99, Drach-Kuder, op. cit.,
lists the total number of baptisms up to February, 1853,
and the villages from which they came.

117.  Swavely, One Hundred Years, p. 11.  Cf. also Bachmann, op.
cit., p. 220.

118.  Heyer, Letter to Dr. S, undated but probably 1853.

119.  Ibid.

120.  See footnote 98 of chapter II.

121.  For nearly twenty years after that, there was no resident
missionary in the Palnad, until the Rev. John H. Harpster
came in 1873.

122.  Heyer was afraid to stay in India over one more hot season;
yet his amazing health throughout his years in India and the
fact that within six months he was out in the frontier country of Minnesota establishing new congregations and then organizing the Minnesota Synod and acting as its first President, seem to indicate that his health was not failing seriously.  For Heyer's outstanding work as a Home Missionary
in his later years, see Bachmann, op. cit., pp. 239ff; and
Drach-Kuder, op. cit., pp. 114ff.

123.  Ochs was one of the missionaries who had come to Guntur in
1845; see page 54 of Thesis.  General Synod Convention Proceedings, 1859, pp. 74ff.  Cf. Ochs, Die Kaste in Ostindien,
1860, passim.; Plitt, Geschichte der Lutherischen Mission
nach den Vorträgen, new edition by Hardeland, Part 2, 1895,
pp. 71ff.; Swavely, Lutheran Enterprise, pp. 25, 83; and
Swavely, One Hundred Years, p. 12, for further details on
the caste controversy.  Cf. also Rowe, "Historical Sketch of
our India Mission" in The Lutheran Quarterly, April, 1879,
p. 274.

124.  Schaefer, A History of the Hermannsburg Lutheran Mission in
India, B.D. Thesis, 1946, p. 6.

125.  Also involved was a controversy over caste as well as the
feeling that Mylius was too 'Catholic' and infected by Lutheran pietism.  Born at Bauneize of Lueneburg Province in
1819, he had studied theology along with Theodore Harms.

Ordained September 3, 1846, he arrived in India early in 1847. He is said to have been a powerful preacher who dressed in a long white robe and wore a crucifix -- much like a Catholic priest. As a strict evangelical Lutheran he did not feel he should give up his liturgical forms just for the Calvinistic and English groups in the Tranquebar area, as the Leipzig missionaries evidently had done. Mylius could not go along with the leniency of the Leipzig Mission in regard to caste. So he finally resigned and returned to Germany where he served as a pastoral counsellor for 13 years in the Fredericka Hospital before offering himself to Harms. Outside of his priestly tendency and his attitude toward caste, the Director of the Leipzig Mission is said to have respected him deeply as an excellent evangelist and missionary; and he was spoken of as the "Pearl of the Lutheran Mission." Cf. Harms, Geschichte der Hermannsburger Mission in Indien, 1935, pp. 37ff.; and Plitt-Hardeland, op. cit., p. 62.

126. The letter, written June 21, 1864, reads as follows: "On the last day of May I received a very cheering letter from Pastor Harms, in which he promised to send a man to help as a missionary here. I feel very thankful for this kind offer, and I am sure you will acknowledge herein the hand of Providence. In the month of December ult., I wrote to him to say that on account of the war in America, it seems impossible for my society to send any reinforcements for some time. If he would send a proper man, you would most probably support him by and by. To my surprise he has written that he would. If you feel that it would tax your resources too heavily to carry on this mission station, Pastor Harms, I think, would be willing to take it from you; but if you feel strong enough, his society may look for some other place in this vicinity..." Quoted from Drach-Kuder, op. cit., p. 125.

127. Ibid. In a letter written from Groenning to Harms, the former mentions that he wants to give a section of work near Rajahmundry to Mylius. He has a new house to offer and a tent, bought from an English official at Dowlaishwaram. Hermannsburger Missionsblatt, 1864, p. 179.

128. In 1866 the General Synod split wide open on this issue, and others, with the result that the Pennsylvania Ministerium went together with other Synods to form the General Council the next year. See footnote 58 of chapter I. It should be stated, on the other side, that the General Synod was very suspicious at this time of the Hermannsburg Society's piet-

ism and struggle against the Hanover Church and was not
willing to share any work with them. Moreover, now that the
Civil War was over it was sure that greater support and
man supply would soon be available. Cf. Harms, Geschichte,
p. 43; Plitt-Hardeland, op. cit., p. 221; and Schaefer,
op. cit., p. 6ff. Also Missionsblatt, 1866, p. 27 for Mylius' claim that the General Synod was too high church.

129. Mylius, during this time, had not been idle. When he left
Rajahmundry, Groenning commented on how good his Telugu was
and that he spoke clearly and enunciated well. Harms, Geschichte, p. 43. Groenning shortly after this had to leave
for Germany because of serious illness. His departure
September, 1865, was a great loss to the Mission. Next to
Heyer, he was the best of the early missionaries and a real
builder of the Church. In two years (1861-62) after his
coming to Rajahmundry from the Guntur field, he baptized 54
persons in an area where practically nothing had been accomplished since 1845. Born November 22, 1813, in Denmark,
Charles William Groenning learned the weaving trade and it
was while he was working in a carpet factory at Elberfeld,
near the Rhine, that he came in contact with the Moravians
and decided to become a foreign missionary. He entered the
Mission Institute in March, 1840, and was graduated five
years later. After his return to Germany in 1865 he continued to keep in close contact with the work, helped provide missionaries and sent his own son in 1885, sent contributions while pastor in Ballum, Schleswig, and Apenrade,
Denmark, and proved to be a real friend in time of need. He
died in Denmark February 1, 1898.

130. Schaefer, op. cit., p. 7.

131. Ibid., p. 8, states that this Mr. Jackman and a group of
Brahmans led the opposition against Mylius and tried to prevent the Rajah from selling suitable land; but all other
sources state otherwise. The Hermannsburger Missionsblatt,
1866, reports that Mylius met Jackman as early as October
18, 1865, on a trip from Madras to Naidupet, and that he
asked for baptism, gave a good witness, understood English
and Tamil, and that he would prove of great help if he remained true in his faith. P. 27. Cf. also Ibid., 1871,
pp. 174ff.

132. Mylius considered January, 1867, as the real beginning of
the Mission, when property was bought and men arrived. Up
to then, he did not know whether he would stay there. Cf.
Hermannsburger Missionsblatt, 1876, p. 37.

133. Mylius brought this Brahman teacher and another helper with him from Madras, but they proved to be very unreliable and had to be dismissed. Harms, Chronik des Seminars für Gehilfen in Nayudupeta, manuscript, p. 1. Ravuri Paul served as catechist 1866-72, 1891-94, and helped Mylius on teaching the language to new missionaries as well as translation. Ibid. See interesting letter written by him to Germany in Hermannsburger Missionsblatt, 1870, pp. 243ff.

134. Cf. Schaefer, op. cit., p. 60.

135. Haccius, op. cit., Part 3, first half, pp. 316ff. Even native catechists were not successful on this island; they found the people most decadent in drunkenness, faithlessness, superstition and vices. Travel was extremely difficult by water, hot sand and marsh; elephantiasis was a dread disease rampant there. Cf. Schaefer, op. cit., p. 13, for story of Brunotte being bitten by a snake and treated by native witch doctors while still unconscious. His subsequent recovery made it difficult for him to do any missionary work after that, for it was spread around that he had come to the Hindu religion and its doctors when he was sick unto death.

136. Woerrlein, Die Hermannsburger Mission in Indien, 1899, p. 70, felt that Dahl could have been saved for India if there had been a Council of missionaries working with Mylius instead of his having complete authority as Superintendent. In this way the Rajah could have been kept in a more favorable relationship with the Mission, although his conversion was most unlikely.

137. Hermannsburger Missionsblatt, 1870, p. 216. Cf. Ibid., pp. 160ff for Dahl's method of approach during Hindu religious festivals.

138. Cf. Woerrlein, Dreizehn Jahre, pp. 85ff. Schaefer, op. cit., p. 11.

139. Hermannsburger Missionsblatt, Oct. 1915, p. 286; Cf. also Swavely, Lutheran Enterprise, pp. 100-101.

140. See Thesis, pp. 34-35.

141. Haccius, op. cit., Part 3, first half, p. 288.

142. See page 14 of Thesis.

143. The first teacher and director , Hober, died March 22, 1879.

144. Cf. Gledstone, op. cit., pp. 35ff.

145. The Plymouth Brethren mentioned on pages 37-38 of Thesis.

146. Drach-Kuder, op. cit., pp. 222, 208ff.; Cf. also Fiensch, Kurze Geschichte der Entstehung und der bisherigen Arbeit der Schleswig-Holsteinischen evang.-luth. Missionsgesellschaft, 1890, pp. 34ff.; Drach, Kingdom Pathfinders, pp. 79ff.; Bromley, op. cit., pp. 195ff.; and Dolbeer, op. cit., pp. 28ff. When the British Government heard of this incident and another shortly after this when 100 people were slaughtered by the Rajah, troops were sent to Jagdalpur and the Rajah was deposed.

147. Swavely, Lutheran Enterprise, p. 145.

148. The L.M.S. gave up the whole Vizianagram District because of lack of means and men, giving the coastal area to the Baptists. Cf. Lovett, op. cit., Vol. 2, p. 133; and 95th Report of the L. M. S., 1889, London, p. 95.

149. Most of the preceding material was taken from Fiensch, Kurze Geschichte, pp. 41ff.; Plitt-Hardeland, op. cit., pp. 157ff.; and Swavely, Lutheran Enterprise, pp. 144ff.

CHAPTER III    The Way Prepared

1.  Mayhew, Christianity and the Government of India, London,
    1929, pp. 26ff., 80ff., 90ff.  Cf. also Ibid., pp. 61ff.; and
    Sherring, The History of Protestant Missions in India, Lon-
    don, 1884, pp. 57-77, for the difficulties Carey and other
    missionaries encountered with the Government in Bengal.

2.  Latourette, The Great Century in Northern Africa and Asia,
    Volume VI of A History of the Expansion of Christianity,
    New York, 1944, pp. 100-102; and Mayhew, op. cit., pp. 73ff.

3.  Mayhew, op. cit., pp. 89ff.  Lord Wellesly, who had attempted
    in 1800 to force the Danish Governor of Serampore to expel
    four new Baptist missionary families, reveals his change in
    attitude when he stated: "While I was in India, I never knew
    of any danger arising from the missionaries' proceedings.
    They are a quiet, ordered, discreet and learned body.  I
    thought it my duty to have the Scriptures translated into the
    tongues of the East.  A Christian Governor could not do less
    than this.  A British Governor could not do more."  Ibid.,
    pp. 101-102.  Cf. also "Occasional Papers on India, No. IX"
    in Missionary Papers, etc., Volume XII, London, Church Miss-
    ionary House, 1860, Paper No. 10 entitled "The Policy, as
    established by Law, of the Indian Government, Opposed to the
    Neutral Policy in Respect of Christianity", pp. 7ff.

4.  Kaye, The Administration of the East India Company, London,
    1853, pp. 1ff., 134ff.

5.  Ogilvie, Our Empire's Debt to Missions, London, 1924, pp.
    20ff.

6.  Cf. footnote 41, chapter II, of Thesis.

7.  Memoir of the Rev. C. T. E. Rhenius, London, 1841, pp. 127-
    128, 175-183.

8.  Pages 39-40 of Thesis.  Cf. also Prinsep, Record of Services,
    London, 1885, p. 61.

9.  Pages 47ff. of Thesis and footnote 78, chapter II.  Cf. also
    Prinsep, op. cit., pp. 134-135.

10.  Drach-Kuder, <u>The Telugu Mission</u>, Philadelphia, 1914, p. 75.

11.  <u>Ibid.</u>, p. 104.

12.  Cf. page 37 of Thesis.

13.  Bromley, <u>They Were Men Sent From God</u>, Bangalore, 1937, pp.
     56ff.; cf. also Raghavaiyangar, <u>Memorandum on the Progress
     of the Madras Presidency</u>, Madras, 1893, pp. 27, 30.

14.  Cf. page 54 of Thesis.

15.  Cf. pages 37-38 of Thesis.

16.  Bromley, <u>op. cit.</u>, p. 78.  Cf. also Wischan, <u>Wilhelm Groen-
     ning, Missionar im Telugu-Lande, in Indien</u>, Philadelphia,
     1891, p. 25.  Fiensch, <u>Kurze Geschichte</u>, Breklum, 1890,
     p. 34, mentions Cotton as almost a full-time evangelist.  Cf.
     also Drach-Kuder, <u>op. cit.</u>, p. 248.

17.  Haig performed an amazing feat with the construction of an
     aqueduct which took a canal large enough for transportation
     over a branch of the Godavari river to a large island in the
     delta separated from the main land by the river.  "This aque-
     duct consisted of forty-nine arches, a work of great engin-
     eering skill, and was successfully constructed under special
     difficulties.  It was built in only four months, and it was
     ready for water to pass over it in another four months.  It
     was constructed by the late Major-General Haig, one of Cot-
     ton's ablest officers, and the latter said of it: 'I have
     always looked upon the Gannaram aqueduct as the most extra-
     ordinary result of courage, energy, and skill in the execu-
     tive to be found in any building in the world."  Morris,
     <u>Heroes of our Indian Empire</u>, Vol. II, London, 1908, p. 142.
     Later, Haig opened up 500 miles of the Godavari to commercial
     navigation.  Cf. Bromley, <u>op. cit.</u>, pp. 79ff.

18.  Colonel Cotton's appeal for the evangelization of the Kois
     had this statement: "Two things are wanted, to make this
     country a garden: the natural water and the water of life."
     Stock, <u>The History of the Church Missionary Society</u>, Vol. III,
     London, 1899, p. 191.

19.  <u>Ibid.</u>, p. 195.

20.  Cf. p. 76 of Thesis and footnote 144, chapter II, for Haig's
     interest in opening up Bastar State to Christianity.  As a

young man he is said to have jumped on the great Juggernaut car carrying the idol and preached about Christ. The Brahman priests tried to drive him off, but the people insisted on hearing the young engineer whom they trusted and honored. He helped disperse the crowd. In later years he served on the Home Committee of the Church Missionary Society and made several important suggestions for improving their program, and also took a trip of missionary research in addition to serving for eighteen months full time as a missionary at Dummagudem. Cf. Stock, op. cit., pp. 329ff. Also One Hundred Years, London, 1899, p. 143; and Bromley, op. cit., pp. 79ff.

21. Cf. Thesis, pp. 47ff, 59-60, 69ff., 82. Cf. also Hermanns-burger Missionsblatt, 1877, pp. 11, 232.

22. Cf. Heyer, Letters, 1847-52, page 16, insert p. 2 of letter No. 6, September, 1848; Drach-Kuder, op. cit., p. 78.

23. Ibid., p. 104. Cf. also page 57 of Thesis and also footnote 80 of chapter II for figures for the Guntur Station.

24. Cf. page 65 of Thesis.

25. Cf. page 182 of Thesis. Unangst continued to try to cover the whole field - Palnad, Guntur and Rajahmundry - from his Guntur residence. Cf. also Drach-Kuder, op. cit., pp.126, 144, 151-52, 166, 228; and Drach, Kingdom Pathfinders, Phil-adelphia, 1942, p. 22.

26. Proceedings of the Convention of the General Synod of the Evangelical Lutheran Church in the United States, 20th Con-vention, Lancaster, Pa., May 1-8, 1862, p. 78.

27. Drach-Kuder, op. cit., p. 105.

28. Hermannsburger Missionsblatt, 1875, p. 197.

29. Hough, The History of Christianity in India, Volume 5, Lon-don, 1860, p. 21.

30. The Cambridge History of India, Dodwell, ed., New York, 1932, Volume VI, p. 125. Cf. also Woerrlein, Dreizehn Jahre in Indien, Hermannsburg, 1885, p. 169, for the situation at the temple at Tirupati.

31. Goffin, At Grips, London, 1913, pp. 17ff. The English of-

ficials claimed that they were completely neutral in the
matter. Cf. Heyer, Letters, 1847-52, p. 13; "Occasional
Papers on India," Nos. IV (1859), VIII and IX (1860) in
Missionary Papers, etc., Volume XII, papers 5, 9 and 10 respectively entitled "Religious Neutrality in India," "Recent Policy of the Indian Government in respect of Christianity in India," and "The Policy, as Established by Law,
of the Indian Government, Opposed to the Neutral Policy in
Respect of Christianity"; and also in the same book paper
no. 3 entitled "Speech of John Poynder, Esq. at a General
Court of Proprietors of the East-India Company, on Wednesday, September 22, 1830, containing evidence in proof
of the direct encouragement afforded by the company to the
Licentious and Sanguinary System of Idolatry; and Demon-
strating the Net Amount of Pecuniary Profits derived by the
Company from the Tax imposed on the Worshippers at the
Different Temples," Cf. also Mayhew, op. cit., pp. 144ff.;
Richter, A History of Missions in India, New York, 1908,
pp. 185ff.; and Basle Miss. Mag., 1858, p. 346.

32. Kaye, op. cit., pp. 646ff. Mayhew, op. cit., p. 87, states:
"No trouble would have been excited by a Government that
protected unflinchingly the Christians, so long as their
campaign was inspired by love and directed by tactful sympathy. ... What the Hindu failed to understand and watched
with ever-growing suspicion was a Government that oscillated
between covert acceptance, of even carefully veiled approval,
of evangelists, who were spreading what was presumably their
own religion, and nervous disavowal of them and all their
work. And when in later years this same intriguing Government opened and supported schools which, without open profession of religion, undermined the very foundation of
caste, it is small wonder that they attributed to such myster-
ious rulers the most sinister designs on their institutions.
The Indian Mutiny was the outcome, not of any fear or dis-
like of Christianity, but of genuine misunderstanding of a
Government which had failed to take India into its confidence
or to announce how far it was definitely prepared to go in
the protection of those who were trying morally and spiritually to heal her. There was no perfect love that casteth
out fear, no glorious liberty that is the birthright of the
sons of God." Cf. Ibid., pp. 83ff.

33. Shenston, Teloogoo Mission Scrap Book, Brantford, Ont., 1888
p. 223.

34. Cf. p. 72 of Thesis.

35. Cf. p. 68 of Thesis.

36. Woerrlein, *Dreizehn Jahre*, pp. 72, 86-87.

37. Cf. Thurston, *Castes and Tribes of Southern India*, Madras, 1909, Volume IV, pp. 79ff. for Kshatriya, and Volume VII, pp. 271ff. for Vaisya. Cf. also Caldwell, *Comparative Grammar of the Dravidian or South Indian Family of Languages*, London, 1875, pp. 114ff.; and Elmore, *Dravidian Gods in Modern Hinduism*, Hamilton, N.Y., 1915, p. 10.

38. Hibbert-Ware, *Christian Missions in the Telugu Country*, Westminster, 1912, p. 74. Cf. also pp. 93ff.

39. Graefe, *The Task of a District Missionary in India*, [n.d.], p. 3.

40. *Ibid.*; cf. also Woerrlein, *Die Hermannsburger Mission in Indien*, Hermannsburg, 1899, pp. 137ff.

41. Elmore, *op. cit.*, cites cases where Brahmans take an active part in the village festivals and bloody sacrifices, brought about by their real fear of the power of the demons and malevolent deities worshiped by the Dravidians. Cf. especially pp. 110ff., 118.

42. Graefe, *op. cit.*, p. 5.

43. Curtis, *The New Sudra Mass Movement Among the Telugus in South India*, Hartford M.A. Thesis, 1936, pp. 26ff. Cf. also Hibbert-Ware, *op. cit.*, pp. 36ff.

44. Indian revenue officers, magistrates over the smallest administrative unit in a district, an area from twenty to thirty miles square. These men were notoriously corrupt in the early days of British rule and could be bribed to make a judgment against the Christians and the missionary, especially as many of them were Brahmans. Cf. Kaye, *op. cit.*, p. 227; and Woerrlein, *Die Hermannsburger Mission*, pp. 169ff.

45. Cf. Thesis, pp. 68, 72 and 82. Also, *Hermannsburger Missionsblatt*, 1875, p. 198; Woerrlein, *Dreizehn Jahre*, pp. 87, 156ff., 174, 184ff.; Haccius, *Hannoversche Missionsgeschichte*, Hermannsburg, 1914, pp. 302, 328ff., 334 of section three, first half, and p. 320 of section three, second half; Fiensch, *Kurze Geschichte*, pp. 47ff.; Heyer, *Account of His First Voyage to India*, his experience and return, 1841-1846, p. 81; and *Letters*, pp. 39ff.

46. Drach-Kuder, op. cit., p. 53.

47. Ibid., pp. 107ff. Cf. also Woerrlein, Die Hermannsburger Mission, p. 157; Haccius, op. cit., pp. 336ff., of section three, first half; and pp. 318 and 327 of section three, second half; Fiensch, op. cit., pp. 53ff.; and Schaefer, A. History of the Hermannsburg Lutheran Mission in India, B.D. Thesis, Columbus, 1946, pp. 29, 89ff.

48. Drach-Kuder, op. cit., p. 77.

49. Harms, Das 50 Jährige Jubilaum Der Hermannsburger Mission, [n.d.], p. 6; and Chronik des Seminars für Gehilfen in Nayudupeta, [n.d.], pp. 4ff. Read the interesting story of Gadu, whose father was a priest for the outcastes in 64 villages. He inherited his father's position and found in his home a Christian book which finally led to his conversion. Cf. Hermannsburger Missionsblatt, 1881, p. 225, and note letter written by two former Dasari priests, p. 209.

50. Cf. p. 39 of Thesis and footnote 52.

51. Clough, Social Christianity in the Orient, New York, 1914, pp. 94, 100.

52. Cf. pp. 52-53 of Thesis.

53. Heyer, Letters, p. 20.

54. Only a person who has lived among these people can realize their insatiable curiosity. As late as the 1920's and 1930's the author, in touring with his father, used to get exasperated as a boy by the fact that from dawn to dusk a group, especially of children, would stand and sit at a respectful distance from the missionary tent and just watch -- watch us eat, study, typewrite, converse, rest on the cots when it was too hot to close the tent flaps, etc., not missing a single movement or activity. Wherever we walked in the village, a crowd followed; when we went into a hut, they sat down on their haunches and patiently waited until we came out again, or tried to worm their way into the crowded hut or its doorway to hear and see.

55. Letter dated Rajahmundry, India, April 8, 1949, p. 2.

56. The Foreign Missionary, September, 1946, p. 12. The whole article entitled "The Village Munsiff Calls Off the Boycott,"

beginning on page 10, is interesting as an indication of the struggle the poor, formerly outcaste Christians have to get and hold onto land of their own.

57. Heyer, Letters, pp. 56-57.

58. Woerrlein, Dreizehn Jahre, p. 93. Cf. also Heyer, Letters, pp. 55ff.

59. Haccius, op. cit., p. 304.

60. Cf. Fishman, Culture Change and the Underprivileged, Madras, 1941, pp. 15ff., 188.

61. Cf. especially Heyer, Letters, pp. 35ff. Cf. also p. 22 (insert p. 1 taken from The Missionary, 1849, p. 87).

62. This fact becomes clear to those missionaries who have worked both in Telugu and Tamil areas. Dr. J. E. Graefe, after having taught for some years in Madras at the Lutheran Theological College at Gurukal in the 1930's, remarked: "You can't imagine the difference between the Telugus and Tamils until you've lived among both. I've tried to do some evangelistic preaching in Madras like we do up our way. It is like hammering at a granite wall. These Tamils are absolutely indifferent, completely hardened. The fact that Christian Missions have worked down here longer than anywhere in India, instead of loosening the soil seems merely to have hardened it. Be glad ... that you can preach to the Telugus. They at least are willing to listen." The Foreign Missionary, "Thanks, Friend Buddha!", February, 1947, p. 10.

63. Ibid., pp. 11-12. The author of this article takes this theory from a book issued by the Andhra University entitled Buddhist Remains in Andhra Desa; with a Brief History of the Andhra Kingdoms from 100-500 A.D.

64. "Thanks, Friend Buddha!", The Foreign Missionary, February, 1947, p. 12.

65. Hermannsburger Missionsblatt, 1881, pp. 13ff.

66. Cf. "Letter from C. F. Kuder, Rajahmundry, India, August 15, 1898" in Correspondence of W. A. Lambert in regard to Father Heyer, 1898; Wolf, Missionary Heroes of the Lutheran Church, Philadelphia, 1911, p. 105; and Drach-Kuder, op. cit., p. 67.

67. Bachmann, They Called Him Father, Philadelphia, 1942, p. 318.

68. Cf. Heyer, Manuscript of Life, by W. A. Lambert, Philadelphia
    Seminary Archives, pp. 178-179; also Drach-Kuder, op. cit.,
    p. 123; Swavely, One Hundred Years in the Andhra Country,
    Madras, 1942, pp. 38-39, points out that Heyer's Telugu was
    far from perfect, but the people never smiled because of his
    seriousness and sincerity.

69. Woerrlein, Die Hermannsburger Mission, p. 65; cf. also
    Schaefer, op. cit., p. 61; Fiensch, op. cit., p. 45; and Her-
    mannsburger Missionsblatt, 1866, p. 192 and 1868, p. 63.

70. Heyer, Account, p. 72.

71. Drach-Kuder, op. cit., p. 54.

72. Haccius, op; cit., section three, first half, pp. 294-295;
    cf. also section three, second half, pp. 249-250, 344; Her-
    mannsburger Missionsblatt, 1871, p. 182 and 1877, p. 9;
    Woerrlein, Die Hermannsburger Mission, p. 89; and Schaefer,
    op. cit., pp. 75ff. and 95.

73. Heyer, Letters, p. 28.

74. Heyer, Account, p. 73.

75. Heyer, Letters, p. 16, insert page 1 of letter from The Mis-
    sionary, February, 1849.

76. Heyer, Letters, p. 18.

77. Hermannsburger Missionsblatt, 1874, p. 57.

78. Ibid., 1871, pp. 182ff.; 1876, pp. 30ff.  This bringing of the
    catechumens to a central location was continued for some time;
    in 1892 Harms describes the busy life of Nayudupeta where
    more than 100 people, including entire families, slept in the
    church, school and porches of the two bungalows during the
    period of instruction.  Famine and lack of rain had given
    them an opportunity to come as families.  Material help was
    very likely a big attraction.  Cf. Harms, Geschichte der
    Hermannsbuärger Mission in Indien, 1864-1918, Hermannsburg,
    1935, pp. 191ff.; and Strasser, Die Taufe in der Geschichte
    der Deutschen evangelisch-lutherischen Mission, Leipzig, 1925,
    pp. 79ff.

79. Harms, Chronik, p. 7.

80. *Hermannsburger Missionsblatt*, p. 183, 1871.

81. Cf. p. 68 of Thesis; also *Hermannsburger Missionsblatt*, 1876, p. 238 and 1877, p. 9; and Woerrlein, *Die Hermannsburger Mission*, pp. 89-90.

82. Drach-Kuder, *op. cit.*, p. 78.

83. *Ibid.*, p. 105.

84. Bachmann, *op. cit.*, p. 173.

85. Heyer, *Letters*, p. 18.

86. Cf. pp. 46 and 64 of Thesis.

87. Heyer, *Letters*, p. 33; cf. also Fiensch, *op. cit.*, p. 67, for similar position of the Schleswig-Holstein Mission.

88. Drach-Kuder, *op. cit.*, p. 123.

89. *Ibid.*, p. 123.

90. In all probability the North Arcot Dutch Reformed Mission, neighbors to the south; or the Church of Scotland Mission to the southeast. It was against the latter mission and its school system that the Hermannsburg Mission directed its major criticism. Cf. Woerrlein, *Die Hermannsburger Mission*, p. 112.

91. *Ibid.*, p. 106.

92. Woerrlein, *Die Hermannsburger Mission*, pp. 112-113. Cf. also *Ibid.*, pp. 105-106; Haccius, section three, first half, *op. cit.*, pp. 300-301, 336-337; Schaefer, *op. cit.*, pp. 24, 89; and Devadas, *75 Samvatsaramula Klupta Charitram*, Madras, 1941, pp. 34-35, 39-41. The Guntur Mission had similar problems when the Rev. L. L. Uhl opened a high school in 1874. Cf. *Proceedings, General Synod*, 1875, pp. 55-56; 1877, pp. 51-52; and Swavely, *One Hundred Years*, p. 234.

93. Cf. page 107 of Thesis.

94. *Ibid.*, p. 107.

95. "It included a modified form of the Chief Service of the General Council's Church Book, together with the Communion

Service, the Old Evening Service, The Litany and the Tables
of Gospels and Epistles. The orders for Holy Baptism and
Marriage were taken from the Lueneberg Ordnung as translated by the Hermannsburg missionaries; the orders for Con-
firmation and Burial, from the Liturgy of the Pennsylvania
Ministerium." Drach-Kuder, op. cit., p. 206.

96. Cf. page 90 of Thesis.

97. Cf. footnote 48, Chapter II of Thesis; and footnote on
    page 191 of Drach-Kuder, op. cit.

98. Bromley, op. cit., p. 132; cf. also Drach, Kingdom Path-
    finders, p. 42.

99. Dolbeer, The Andhra Evangelical Lutheran Church, A Brief
    History, Rajahmundry, 1951, p. 16. Cf. also Richter, op.
    cit., p. 293; Anstey, "Report on Protestant Telugu Christ-
    ian Literature" in Surveys and Reports of Christian Liter-
    ature in India, 1918, Madras, p. 9; Drach, Kingdom Path-
    finders, p. 77; Drach-Kuder, op. cit., pp. 166-167, 191
    and 291. Footnote on page 167 of Drach-Kuder tells that
    the original committee in 1873 consisted of four mission-
    aries and two native pastors: "Besides the old Telugu
    versions they used the Hebrew, Septuagint, Vulgate, San-
    scrit, Tamil, Canarese, Mahratti, Hindustani, English,
    German and Danish. The Telugu Missions interested in this
    revision and their relative strength at that time are given
    in the following table:

| Mission | Missionaries | Adherents 1861 | 1871 |
|---|---|---|---|
| 1. American Baptist, Nellore | 5 | 23 | 6418 |
| 2. Hermannsburg Lutheran, Nayudupet | 8 | | 150 |
| 3. General Synod, Lutheran, Guntur | 3 | 338 | 2150 |
| 4. General Council, Lutheran, Rajahmundry | 2 | 29 | 320 |
| 5. Church Missionary Society, Ellore | 13 | 259 | 1882 |
| 6. London Missionary Society | 5 | 299 | ? |
| 7. Plymouth Baptist, Narsapur | 4 | 350 | 1000 " |

100. Woerrlein, Die Hermannsburger Mission, p. 67.

101. Hermannsburger Missionsblatt, 1874, p. 55.

102. Woerrlein, Die Hermannsburger Mission, pp. 65, 67, 68; and
     Haccius, op. cit., section three, first half, pp. 289-290.

103. Haccius, op. cit., section three, first half, p. 290; cf. also Woerrlein, Die Hermannsburger Mission, pp. 105, 167; and Hermannsburger Missionsblatt, 1876, pp. 233-234.

104. Haccius, op. cit., section three, first half, p. 289.

105. Cf. page 162 of Thesis; also Harms, Chronik, p. 11; Harms, Lebensbeschreibung von Missionar Hartwig Harms, American Lutheran Church archives, pp. 27ff.; Hermannsburger Missions-blatt, 1876, p. 236 and 1871, p. 184. Woerrlein, Scriba and Aberly (of Guntur) participated actively in the development of native literature at the close of this period. Cf. the supplemental list, pp. 2ff. of Anstey, op. cit.

106. Harms, Chronik, pp. 1-2.

107. Hermannsburger Missionsblatt, 1871, p. 184.

108. Harms, Geschichte, p. 380.

109. Fiensch, op. cit., p. 59. Dr. John Hay was one of the leaders in the revision and translation of the Telugu Bible from 1852 on. Cf. Lovett, The History of the London Missionary Society, 1795-1895, London, 1899, volume 2, pp. 134ff., 286; and Whitehouse, Register of Missionaries, Deputations, etc. From 1796 to 1896, London, 1896, pp. 127-128.

110. Cf. page 67 of Thesis.

111. Cf. page 66 of Thesis and footnote 125, chapter II.

112. Hermannsburger Missionsblatt, 1872, pp. 161, 192; cf. also Haccius, op. cit., section three, first half, pp. 284ff.; Richter, op. cit., p. 173, points out that the Leipzig Mission stood almost "alone on the side of the sufferance of caste, while on the other side is arrayed the almost unanimous concensus of opinion of all the other societies, and it is just such German societies as those of Basle and of Hermannsburg and such Lutheran societies as the Danish and those of the General Council and General Synod, which advocate the standpoint of opposition to all caste with the greatest firmness." Cf. also Swavely, One Hundred Years, p. 153.

113. Hermannsburger Missionsblatt, 1872, p. 192; cf. also Richter, op. cit., p. 169.

114. Cf. pages 70-71 of Thesis.

115. Cf. Woerrlein, *Dreizehn Jahre*, p. 82.

116. *Hermannsburger Missionsblatt*, 1873, p. 34.

117. Haccius, *op. cit.*, section three, first half, p. 284; and *Hermannsburger Missionsblatt*, 1872, p. 161.

118. Heyer, *Letters*, p. 46.

119. Fiensch, *op. cit.*, pp. 50ff.

120. Haccius, *op. cit.*, section three, first half, p. 285.

121. *Hermannsburger Missionsblatt*, 1874, p. 58.

122. *Ibid.*, 1872, p. 161.

123. This bitterness is increased by an ancient feud. Most castes below the Brahmans are divided into two groups, called the right-hand section and the left-hand. "The higher castes of the Sudras, and all the Malas, are placed in the right-hand section; the merchants, the rest of the Sudras, and the Madigas, in the left-hand section. The class of Sudras from which the village magistrates are almost always derived belongs to the second section. Consequently, whenever the feud breaks out, the Malas are opposed by the village magistrate and his tribe, and by the merchants -- two of the most powerful elements of the village. The occasion of hostilities has often been an absurdly trivial thing, such as the use by one party at a marriage of some ceremony or garment supposed to be the distinctive property of the other party. But by far the commonest thing that leads to a riot is a dance, performed by the Madigas against the Malas, and called the Chindu dance. ... It expresses the triumph of the Madigas over a Mala chief of former times. It is a story of immoral deeds, and the actions which accompany the dance are obscene. It is accompanied by music of a barbarous nature. This dance has invariably a rousing effect on the Malas, even the peculiar beating of the drums, with which it starts, serving violently to excite them. It is sometimes performed before the idol at a great festival, for the goddess is supposed to delight in such spectacles. Very often, when caste feeling runs high, it is used to irritate the Malas. Either the Madigas do it on their own initiative, or the Sudras stir them up to do it." Hibbert-Ware, *op. cit.*, pp. 92-93. Cf. also Thurston, *op. cit.*, Volume 4, pp. 292ff. and 329ff.

Although Hibbert-Ware, page 93; Curtis, op. cit., p. 57; and Fishman, op. cit., pp. 148ff. point out that this feud still carries over between Mala and Madiga Christians, J. W. Pickett, Christ's Way to India's Heart, Lucknow, 1937, pp. 54ff. emphasizes that the bitterness is definitely lessened among the Christians although there is ample evidence it still exists. He states on page 55: "During our search for data the persistence of prejudice came to light frequently, but rarely did we discover such antagonism within the Church as is met at almost every contact with groups of either caste who have not come under the influence of Christ." Cf. also Pickett, Christian Mass Movements in India, New York, 1933, p. 327.

124. Drach-Kuder, op. cit., p. 229.

125. Heyer, Letters, p. 44.

126. Ibid., p. 24.

127. Hermannsburger Missionsblatt, 1876, p. 26; cf. also Bachmann, op. cit., pp. 205ff.

128. Fishman, op. cit., p. 64, reports that even in recent years he was unable to persuade Mala and Madiga Christians to use the same well.

129. Hermannsburger Missionsblatt, 1879, p. 198.

130. Heyer, Letters, p. 43.

131. Albrecht, In Tent and Bungalow, undated manuscript in Gettysburg Seminary archives, reports that these god-pots usually contain the image of Ganesh, the god of wisdom, with an elephant head, four arms, protruding belly and painted red; an image of some female deity; a string of gold and silver pieces, among them a marriage badge; curious utensils ornamented with snakes, bulls, etc., all evidently connected with the worship of the idols. She states: "You cannot imagine, how these people suffer from fear. Many have a sincere though incomplete belief in the truth ... but are kept away from Christ through fear of the terrible gods and still more terrible goddesses who can in a moment of rage kill them or their children or their cattle." Cf. Elmore, op. cit., pp. 26ff., 41ff., concerning a household goddess and the use of earthenware pots in religious ceremonies.

132. Heyer, _Letters_, p. 36.

133. Cf. Hibbert-Ware, _op. cit._, pp. 87ff. for details of buffalo sacrifice; also Elmore, _op. cit._, pp. 23, 28, 40-41, 46-47; and Thurston, _op. cit._, pp. 332ff.

134. Hibbert-Ware, _op. cit._, p. 89. Cf. also Fishman, _op. cit._, p. 184.

135. Heyer, _Letters_, p. 45.

136. _Ibid._, p. 29.

137. Albrecht, _op. cit._, p. 159.

138. Strasser, _op. cit._, p. 113.

139. _Ibid._, p. 99.

140. Heyer, _Letters_, pp. 43,53 and 64.

141. Bachmann, _op. cit._, p. 205; cf. also Wischan, _op. cit._, pp. 243-244.

142. Cf. _Hermannsburger Missionsblatt_, 1870, p. 35; and Fishman, _op. cit._, pp. 132ff.

143. Cf. _Hermannsburger Missionsblatt_, 1870, p. 245; 1874, pp. 59, 62; 1876, p. 195; 1880, pp. 20ff.; 1881, p. 94; Fiensch, _op. cit._, p. 57; and Haccius, _op. cit._, section three, second half, p. 277.

144. _Hermannsburger Missionsblatt_, 1880, pp. 20ff.

145. Swavely, _One Hundred Years_, p. 28; Fiedler, _Then the Light Came_, Philadelphia, 1941, p. 89; and Drach-Kuder, _op. cit._, p. 238.

146. Strasser, _op. cit._, pp. 86, 107ff; cf. also _Hermannsburger Missionsblatt_, 1882, pp. 181ff.; and Schaefer, _op. cit._, p. 57.

147. _Hermannsburger Missionsblatt_, 1882, pp. 186ff.

148. Heyer, _Letters_, p. 40.

149. Fishman, _op. cit._, pp. 15-16.

150. Heyer, *Letters*, pp. 45-46.

151. Albrecht, op. cit., p. 119.

152. Heyer, *Letters*, pp. 47, 36.  Cf. also Bachmann, op. cit., pp. 192ff.

153. Heyer, *Letters*, p. 53; cf. also p. 51.

154. Albrecht, op. cit., p. 167.

155. Hermannsburger Missionsblatt, 1882, pp. 189ff.  Cf. also Schaefer, op. cit., pp. 74ff., 80ff.

156. Fishman, op. cit., p. 112.

157. Cf. Elmore, op. cit., p. 138.

158. Strasser, op. cit., pp. 97-98, 113.

159. Hermannsburger Missionsblatt, 1882, p. 54.

160. Schaefer, op. cit., p. 61.

161. Woerrlein, Dreizehn Jahre, pp. 121, 122 and 125.  Cf. also Rowe's attitude in "The Practical Religion of the Hindus", The Lutheran Quarterly, July 1880, pp. 436ff.

162. Cf. page 60 of Thesis.

163. Cf. page 61 of Thesis.

164. Cf. page 60 of Thesis.

165. Heyer, *Letters*, p. 25.

166. Ibid., p. 66.

167. Ibid., pp. 53ff.

168. Cf. page 62 of Thesis.

169. Drach-Kuder, op. cit., p. 101.  Of these only Tota Joseph became a pastor, ordained December 25, 1878, as one of the first two pastors in the Rajahmundry field.  Cf. pp. 152ff. of Thesis.  W. B. Passavant was drowned in Rajahmundry in 1856; and no further record is found of Ramurdu, other than

that he was a Brahman and married Susanna Lavel, the first Christian female teacher of a Rajahmundry girls' school, who died suddenly September, 1855.

170. Heyer, Letters, p. 42.

171. Cf. Clough, op. cit., pp. 185ff., 189, and 332ff.

172. Rowe, "Historical Sketch of our India Mission" in The Lutheran Quarterly, April, 1879, p. 269, says Cully had "become so much involved in financial difficulties in the Palnad, that it was neither pleasant nor profitable for him to continue his work there."

173. Swavely, One Hundred Years, p. 125.

174. Proceedings, General Synod, 1877, p. 52.

175. Ibid., p. 52.

176. Cf. page 149 of Thesis.

177. Cf. page 61 of Thesis.

178. Drach-Kuder, op. cit., p. 146.

179. Ibid., p. 185, footnote 3.

180. Ibid., p. 189.

181. Ibid., pp. 325-326.  Cf. also p. 197.

182. Dolbeer, op. cit., p. 17.

183. Cf. pages 185-186 of Thesis.

184. Drach-Kuder, op. cit., pp. 206-207.

185. Ibid., p. 238.

186. Cf. page 121 of Thesis and also Drach Kuder- op. cit., p. 170.

187. Cf. page 128 of Thesis.

188. The missionaries in the Guntur field never considered the Rev. R. E. Cully as an equal to them, but rather as a native

pastor. Cf. pages 150-151 of Thesis. When he was a catechist, Groenning paid him Rs. 600 a year in 1863 and 1864.

189. Schmidt, The Strike in the Telugu Mission of the General
Council of the Ev. Luth. Church in America, manuscript,
1899, Rajahmundry, pp. 17ff.; and Jacobs, Unpublished Manuscript of the Memoirs of H. E. Jacobs, p. 617. Schmidt
states that two other brothers of McCready were sent to
America; but the parents regretted having done so when missionary Artman had to drop the English services for officers and the Young Men's Association because of overwork
and they consequently lost interest in the Mission. The
rest of the McCready family had not actually joined the
congregation in Rajahmundry.

190. Cf. page 91 of Thesis.

191. Wischan, op. cit., p. 99. Cf. also Schmidt, op. cit.,
p. 97.

192. Cf. Harms, Das 50 Jährige Jubilaum, p. 6; and Harms, Chronik,
p. 7. Cf. also page 112 of Thesis.

193. Cf. pp. 68 and 122 of Thesis.

194. Harms, Chronik des Seminars für Gehilfen in Nayudupeta, is
an undated manuscript; but internal evidence would indicate
that the first part was written about 1908 and the second
about 1933.

195. Cf. page 160 of Thesis.

196. Haccius, op. cit., section three, first half, pp. 268, 260ff.;
cf. also Harms, Chronik, pp. 20ff., 40; Devadas, op. cit.,
pp. 17-18, 32-34; Harms, Geschichte, p. 229.

197. Harms, Geschichte, p. 308.

198. Hermannsburger Missionsblatt, 1874, p. 60; 1877, pp. 11-12;
Woerrlein, Die Hermannsburger Mission, p. 90.

199. Haccius, op. cit., section three, first half, p. 291.

200. Schaefer, op. cit., p. 78. Scriba's statement is found in
Woerrlein, Vierzig Jahre in Indien, 1913, p. 144.

201. Cf. page 127 of Thesis.

202. Fiensch, op. cit., pp. 50, 70ff.; and Swavely, The Lutheran Enterprise in India, Madras, 1952, p. 150.

203. Fiensch, op. cit., pp. 64ff; Drach-Kuder, op. cit.,p.262; and Swavely, Lutheran Enterprise, p. 145.

204. Strasser, op. cit., pp. 102ff.

205. Swavely, Lutheran Enterprise, p. 152.

206. Cf. Schaefer, op. cit., pp. 80ff.

207. Drach-Kuder, op. cit., pp. 141 and 152. Cf. also pp. 152ff. of Thesis where is indicated that the congregations spread quickly into the villages under Pastors Paulus and Joseph.

208. Heyer, Letters, p. 31.

209. Plitt, Gustav, Kurze Geschichte der lutherischen Mission in Vorträgen, Erlangen, 1871, p. 286.

210. Cf. Haccius, op. cit., section three, second half, pp. 342-343.

211. Hermannsburger Missionsblatt, 1875, p. 59; Haccius, op. cit., section three, first half, p. 305.

212. Hermannsburger Missionsblatt, 1879, p. 8.

213. Haccius, op. cit., section three, first half, p. 266; Woerrlein, Die Hermannsburger Mission, p. 193. Cf. note 78, chapter II, of thesis.

214. Haccius, op. cit., section three, first half, p. 328.

215. Woerrlein, Die Hermannsburger Mission, p. 227.

216. Harms, Geschichte, p. 183.

217. Hermannsburger Missionsblatt, 1876, pp. 30-31.

CHAPTER IV    The Difficult Years

1. Cf. pages 57ff. and 65ff. of Thesis.

2. Although the Ministerium of Pennsylvania had helped to organize the General Synod in 1820, it had withdrawn its connection by 1823 and did not return until 1853.  It was during
   this period that Heyer was called by the Foreign Missionary
   Society of the General Synod to go to India, but went under
   the auspices of the Ministerium of Pennsylvania instead,
   when he learned that the General Synod was planning to work
   through the American Board of Commissioners for Foreign
   Missions.  Cf. pages 25ff. of Thesis.

3. Cf. pages 61ff. of Thesis.  From 1823 the General Synod expanded from three small synods, the large Ministerium of
   Pennsylvania having withdrawn, to 26 synods, 864 ministers
   and 164,000 communicants in 1860.  "The great increase in German immigration began about 1840.  The crest of the wave was
   reached in the decade preceding the Civil War, when nearly a
   million Germans reached American shores."  Wentz, The Lutheran Church in American History, Philadelphia, 1923, p. 149.
   The Scandinavians also were beginning to come in large numbers.  Cf. also Neve-Allbeck, History of the Lutheran Church
   in America, Burlington, 1934, pp. 71, 81-82.

4. Cf. page 65 of Thesis.

5. "The following table is interesting as an index of the foreign
   mission activity of the Lutheran Church in America for the
   twenty years from 1839 to 1859:

| General Synod Meeting | Foreign Mission Receipts | Foreign Mission Expenditures | Supported |
|---|---|---|---|
| 1839 | $2,284.79 | $2,222.79 | Rhenius, Palamcotta |
| 1841 | 1,265.12 | 642.82 | Guetzlaff, Heyer |
| 1843 | 234.17 | | |
| 1845 | 1,137.39 | 1,749.15 | Gunn, Guntur |
| 1848 | 2,790.41 | 3,210.90 | Gunn and Heyer |
| 1850 | 4,230.42 | 4,230.42 | Gunn, Heyer, Martz |
| 1853 | 14,486.10 | 14,478.12 | Guntur, Rajahmundry |
| 1855 | 11,797.00 | 11,485.93 | Guntur, Palnad, Rajah. |
| 1857 | 12,868.33 | 12,434.04 | Guntur, Palnad, Rajah. |
| 1859 | 11,876.18 | 11,697.64 | Guntur, Palnad, Rajah." |

Quoted from Drach-Kuder, <u>The Telugu Mission</u>, Philadelphia, 1914, p. 113. (Writer of Thesis abbreviated 'Rajahmundry' in last column of table.)

6. Cf.pp. 66ff.of Thesis.

7. Ochsenford, <u>Documentary History of the General Council of the Evangelical Lutheran Church in North America</u>, Philadelphia, 1912, p. 66.

8. Schmucker, <u>American Lutheranism Vindicated</u>, Baltimore, 1856, p. 15.

9. Wentz, <u>op. cit.</u>, p. 166. That they were definitely unionistic in attitude is indicated by Schmucker's "Fraternal Appeal to the American Churches," issued in 1838 calling for reunion of all denominations on an apostolic basis; his active participation along with other delegates from the General Synod in the formation of the "Evangelical Alliance" at London in 1846, which promoted religious tolerance and cooperation; and his cooperation in a letter sent to Germany in 1845 declaring: "In most of our church principles we stand on common ground with the Union Church of Germany. The distinctive doctrines which separate the Lutheran and the Reformed Churches we do not consider essential. The tendency of the so-called Lutheran party seems to us to be behind the time. Luther's peculiar views concerning the presence of the Lord's Body in the Communion have long been abandoned by the majority of our ministers." Ochsenford, <u>op. cit.</u>, p. 63. Schmucker was "also the author of an elaborate and comprehensive scheme of an 'Apostolic Protestant Union' with the following features: 'Unity of name, unity in fundamental doctrines, while diversity in non-essentials was conceded; mutual acknowledgement of each other's acts of discipline; sacramental and ministerial intercommunion; convention of the different churches of the land in synod or council for mutual consultation or ecclesiastical regulation.' This was endorsed by the General Synod at its meeting in New York, 1848." Neve-Allbeck, <u>op. cit</u>., p. 85.

10. Jacobs, <u>A History of the Evangelical Lutheran Churches in the United States</u>, New York, 1912, p. 432.

11. Cf. <u>Ibid</u>., p. 449.

12. Cf. <u>Ibid</u>., p. 453.

13. Cf. <u>Ibid</u>., pp. 457-458. An indication of its opposition to

423

the Augsburg Confession is seen in the Charter of the Western Conference of the Franckean Synod, article five, part of
which reads: "Believing as we do with other good men, both
in and out of the Lutheran Church, that the Augsburg Confession does teach Baptismal Regeneration, Christ's Bodily Presence in the Eucharist, Private Auricular Confession and
Priestly Absolution, and sets aside the Divine Institution
and Obligation of the Christian Sabbath, therefore no minister or candidate for the ministry who advocates a subscription to the Augsburg Confession as a test of ministerial office, or church membership, shall be received into our
connection. Neither shall they be employed to teach in our
classical or theological schools of learning and we advise
our churches not to employ such as their pastors." Ochsenford, op. cit., p. 73.

14. Cf. p. 178 of Thesis; also Neve-Allbeck, op. cit., p. 105;
and Jacobs, op. cit., pp. 458-459, who quotes one of the resolutions made in 1853: "Should the General Synod violate its
constitution, and require of our synod, or of any synod, as a
condition of admission or continuance of membership, assent
to anything conflicting with the old and long-established
faith of the Evangelical Lutheran Church, then our delegates
are hereby required to protest against such action, to with-
draw from its sessions and to report to this body."

15. Cf. Jacobs, op. cit., p. 460.

16. Evangelical Review, vol. XX, pp. 122-123, reports that in
1868 the General Synod had 610 pastors, 1,008 churches and
87,123 communicants; the General Council 575 pastors, 1101
churches and 144,716 communicants; and the Southern General
Synod 120 pastors, 214 churches and 17,112 communicants.

17. Proceedings of the Conventions of the General Synod of the
Evangelical Lutheran Church in the United States, 1862,
pp. 77ff.

18. Ibid., 1864, p. 74.

19. Ibid., 1866, pp. 70-71.

20. Drach-Kuder, op. cit., p. 126.

21. Proceedings, General Synod, 1866, pp. 78, 80.

22. Ibid., 1868, p. 74.

23. Drach-Kuder, op. cit., pp. 128-129.

24. Further statistics: 4 stations, 25 outstations, 50 adult
    baptisms in 1867, 46 children. Twenty-two Telugu boys'
    schools, 2 girls' schools. Eight boarding boys, 9 boarding
    girls. Two hundred and four day boy students, 82 day girl
    students, for a total of 24 schools and 303 pupils. Twenty-
    one men teachers and 2 women teachers. One headmaster, 2
    catechists, 4 colporteurs. Thirteen marriages. Proceedings,
    General Synod, 1868, p. 75. Rowe, "Historical Sketch of our
    India Mission" in The Lutheran Quarterly, April, 1879, p.
    272, lists 161 baptisms in 1869 and 685 in 1870 for Guntur
    and the Palnad.

25. Cf. Drach-Kuder, op. cit., p. 126, and Proceedings, General
    Synod, 1869, p. 76.

26. Foreign Mission Board instead of Foreign Mission Society is
    used from this point on because the Society asked and re-
    ceived permission in 1869 to dissolve itself so that a Board
    of management could be appointed by the Synod in accordance
    with the new constitution drawn up in 1868. This began a day
    of increased responsibility and growing interest on the part
    of the General Synod for its mission work. Cf. Proceedings,
    General Synod, p. 30.

27. Drach-Kuder, op. cit., p. 135.

28. Ibid., p. 136.

29. Cf. page 119 of Thesis.

30. Heyer, Manuscript of Life, by W. A. Lambert, p. 167. Heyer
    reported that Morris contributed about $120 and the sub-
    collector $60 annually for the work of the Mission.

31. Ibid., p. 146.

32. Ibid., p. 178.

33. Drach-Kuder, op. cit., pp. 164-165.

34. Cf. pages 150-151 of Thesis.

35. Proceedings, General Synod, 1871, p. 73.

36. Laury, A History of Lutheran Missions, Reading, 1899, p. 117.
    Cf. also Proceedings, General Synod, 1875 pp. 54-55; and

1877, p. 50.

37. Addresses Delivered at the Fortieth Anniversary of Home Missions, Foreign Missions and Church Extension of the General Synod of the Evangelical Lutheran Church, Philadelphia, 1909, p. 141.

38. Drach, Kingdom Pathfinders, Philadelphia, 1942, p. 31.

39. Rowe, op. cit., p. 271.

40. Cf. page 73 of Thesis.

41. Hermannsburger Missionsblatt, 1891, p. 26; Woerrlein, Die Hermannsburger Mission in Indien, 1899, p. 171; and Schaefer, A History of the Hermannsburg Lutheran Mission in India, 1946, pp. 65ff.

42. Harms, Lebensbeschreibung, undated manuscript, p. 13.

43. Haccius, Hannoversche Missionsgeschichte, section three, first half, pp. 291-292.

44. Schaefer, op. cit., p. 50.

45. Cf. page 69 of Thesis.

46. At the last Otto became lackadaisical in his work and lost much of his faith, so that he upbraided the Home Board for sending young missionaries to the field where they would only meet disappointment. Cf. Schaefer, op. cit., p. 46. Woerrlein did not consider him a great missionary as he found it difficult to reach the natives or work with them. Woerrlein, op. cit., p. 67.

47. Harms, Geschichte der Hermannsburger Mission in Indien, 1935, p. 116.

48. Woerrlein, op. cit., pp. 70, 96.

49. Harms, Geschichte, p. 117.

50. In 1866 the province of Hanover was incorporated with the kingdom of Prussia, and the strongly Lutheran center of Hermannsburg looked with disfavor on any effort to introduce Prussian unionism in the church government. When a bill was passed in February, 1874, requiring civil marriage as oblig-

atory and abolishing compulsory baptism, and a new marriage
ordinance was enacted in Hanover as a result of this law,
Harms rebelled from the conviction that civil marriage did
not deserve to be recognized as marriage.  He was suspended,
then deposed from office in 1877, and with most of his congregation he founded a separate Lutheran community to which
other small congregations were added later.  Teachers and
pupils in the seminary, the missionary journals and festivals,
all spoke out in favor of this secession, with the result
that the Hanover Consistory refused to permit the usual Epi-
phany season missionary offerings for Hermannsburg.

Thus was broken the "connection between the state church
and the institution which had hitherto been regarded as 'its
pride, its preserving salt.'  A reaction has since set in
in favour of the seminary and its friends on the assurance
that the interests of the separation would not be furthered
by the seminary, and that several objectionable features,
e.g. the frequent employment in the mission service of artisans without theological training, the sending of them out in
too great numbers without sufficient endowment and salary,
so that the missionaries were obliged to engage in trade
speculations, should be removed as far as possible; but since
the seminary life was always still carried on upon the basis
of ecclesiastical secession, it could lead to no permanent
reconciliation with the state church.  Harms died in 1885.
His son, Egmont, was chosen his successor, and as the consistory refused ordination, he accepted consecration at the
hands of five members of the Immanuel Synod at Magdeburg."
Kurtz, Church History, New York, 1888, Vol. III, p. 287.

1. Hermannsburger Missionsblatt, 1881, pp. 19ff; Harms, Geschichte, p. 116a; and Woerrlein, op. cit., p. 105.

2. Cf. pages 79-80 and 84 of Thesis.

3. Lutherisches Weltmissionsjahrbuch, Leipzig, 1927, p. 51.  Cf.
also Richter, A History of Missions in India, New York, 1908,
p. 221.

4. Cf. page 168 of Thesis.

5. Drach-Kuder, op. cit., p. 317.

6. Swavely, The Lutheran Enterprise in India, Madras, 1952,
pp. 175-176.

57. *Ibid.*, p. 146.

58. A leader in this was Theosophist Mrs. Besant, enemy of all
    mission work according to <u>Jahrbuch der Sächsischen Missions-</u>
    <u>konferenz für das Jahr 1917</u>, Leipzig, p. 43. Military of-
    ficials also proved hard to deal with; and the mission work
    would have been more seriously damaged had not the civil
    government broken or blunted the sharpness of military orders.

59. These stations had been bought from Hermannsburg by the Joint
    Synod of Ohio and other States in 1912, but they had not been
    able to send any missionaries yet. They had supported the
    two stations since 1910.

60. Harms, <u>Geschichte</u>, p. 564, reports that the Bishop of Madras
    was willing to have the German missionaries stay, because of
    their good work, if they would agree to sign a paper that
    they were opposed to the cynical break of the neutrality of
    Belgium, the tribal cruelties to the Belgian people, the
    sinkings of the 'Lusitania'and other peaceful ships, the
    use of poisonous gas, the poisoning of the drinking water,
    and the brutal treatment of English prisoners. The mission-
    aries felt that they could not possibly sign such a 'propa-
    ganda-filled statement.' They were sure the English mission-
    aries did not know the whole truth and were misled by the
    newspapers that they read. For further details concerning
    their life in the internment camps, a review of the fifty
    years of the mission (the 50th anniversary could not be cele-
    brated), and the return of the missionaries to Germany, cf.
    <u>Hermannsburger Missionsblatt</u>, 1915, passim.

61. Cf. pp. 101ff. and 131ff. of Thesis.

62. Goffin, <u>At Grips</u>, London, 1913, pp. 50, 53, 144ff.

63. Craig, <u>Forty Years Among the Telugus</u>, Toronto, 1908, p. 209.

64. Albrecht, <u>In Tent and Bungalow</u>, undated manuscript, p. 131.

65. *Ibid.*, p. 133.

66. <u>Letter</u> to author from Dr. Martin L. Dolbeer, Sr., dated Raj-
    ahmundry, April 8, 1949, p. 1.

67. Cf. pp. 131ff. of Thesis.

68. Phillips, <u>The Outcastes' Hope</u>, London, 1912, pp. 40-41. Cf.
    also Graham, <u>Dornakal, Every Christian a Witness</u>, Westminster,

pp. 16-17.

69. Cf. pp. 139-140 of Thesis where we speak of the "status-feel-
ing" developed among the outcastes by the interest and backing of the missionary.

70. Letter to author from Dr. Martin L. Dolbeer, Sr., dated
Rajahmundry, April 8, 1949, pp. 1-2. Dr. Dolbeer relates in
this letter an experience which occurred in his field of
work in the 1930s: "Even up to our day the Missionary has had
to defend his flock at times against arrogant and self-
willed landlords. I remember about 1930 a Christian in
Chejerla being beaten by a ryot in a fit of anger so that
his leg was broken. It was crudely tied up by someone, and
blood circulation stopped, gangrene set in, and the man was
near death when brought in to Narasaravupet. The leg was
amputated at the Government dispensary by the local surgeon.
We immediately put a charge against the ryot. Of course he
was able to fight the case in court and might have bribed
his way out of it. Fortunately for us, he got cold feet
and sent word that he was willing to compromise. We demanded that he register three acres of land to the Christian as
compensation, which he did. But without the backing of the
missionary in cases like this the poor village Christian
was completely helpless." Page 2. Cf. also Clough, Social
Christianity in the Orient, New York, 1914, pp. 108, 171-
172.

71. The missionaries learned very quickly that they must refuse
most of the innumerable requests for help which came from
the outcastes, or they would have become completely entangled
in a network of petty grievances, real and imagined. Cf.
"Almost Thou Persuadest Me to Be a Christian," in Sowing the
Seed, 1928 Annual Report of the Board of Foreign Missions
of the Evangelical Lutheran Joint Synod of Ohio, 1929,
pp. 5-6.

72. Cf. page 141 of Thesis; Drach-Kuder, op. cit., pp. 176-177,
276, 289, 312-313, 359; Swavely, One Hundred Years, Madras,
1942, pp. 41-42; Schmidt, The Strike in the Telugu Mission,
Rajahmundry, 1899, pp. 99ff.; Report of C. Theodore Benze,
Rajahmundry, 1909, pp. 56ff.; Haccius, op. cit., section
three, second half, p. 325; Harms, Geschichte, pp. 337ff.,
464ff.; and India Conference Minutes, Ev. Luth. Jt. Synod,
Tirupati, April 5-8, 1921, pp. 7ff.; October 11-18, 1921,
pp. 8-9.

73. Cf. page 260 of Thesis.

74. Goffin, op. cit., p. 55. Cf. also Ibid., pp. 28, 130ff.; and Haccius, op. cit., section three, second half, p. 284, where he reported that the catechist Narudu offered land to the natives to persuade them to become Christians.

75. Goffin, op. cit., p. 56.

76. Cf. Pickett, Christian Mass Movements in India, New York, 1933, pp. 155ff. for motives underlying conversion.

77. Richter, A History of Missions in India, New York, 1908, pp. 231-233. The old Danish Tranquebar Mission reported three-fourths of their Christians were Sudras. Of the 91,000 native Christians in 1851, almost two-thirds were Sudras. Cf. also Fiedler, Then the Light Came, Philadelphia, 1941, pp. 20-21.

78. Cf. pages 240ff. of Thesis.

79. Richter, op. cit., p. 233.

80. Schmidt, op. cit., pp. 4-5.

81. Albrecht, op. cit., pp. 75-76.

82. Ibid., p. 82.

83. Ibid., pp. 83-84.

84. Cf. page 155 of Thesis.

85. Drach-Kuder, op. cit., p. 180.

86. Cf. pages 160-161 of Thesis.

87. The Lutheran Standard, Vol. LXIV, September 22, 1906, p. 602, Cf. also Woerrlein, Die Hermannsburger Mission, p. 189; and Haccius, op; cit., section three, second half, pp. 264-265.

88. "Every deed of man has its inevitable effect and the inexorable Law of Karma (cause and effect) is blind, pitiless and impersonal. The man who does evil begets evil and he lives through countless lives of sorrow before he is purified. The Buddha himself, it is said, lived for more than 500 births after he became Bodhisatva (Buddha-elect), his lives prior to

attaining this exalted stage being countless!" Thomas, _Hindu Religion, Customs and Manners_, Bombay, [n.d.] , p. 52.

89.  _Bericht über die Hermannsburger Mission_, 1910, pp. 33-35.

90.  Cf. pages 117, 127 of Thesis.

91.  Harms, _Geschichte_, pp. 288ff.; and Haccius, _op. cit._, section three, second half, p. 318. Cf. Bachmann, _They Called Him Father_, Philadelphia, 1942, pp. 223-224, for similar experience in a girls' school in Guntur.

92.  Albrecht, _op. cit._, p. 116.

93.  Haccius, _op. cit._, section three, first half, p. 313; cf. also _Ibid._, second half, p. 327.

94.  Albrecht, _op. cit._, pp. 116-117.

95.  _Ibid._, p. 35. Cf. also Davis, _The Life Story of a Leper_, Toronto, 1918, pp. 109ff.; and Goffin, _op. cit._, pp. 134ff.

96.  Drach, _Kingdom Pathfinders_, Philadelphia, 1942, p. 43. L. L. Uhl converted quite a number of Yenadis, Sudras and Brahmans between 1878 and 1883. Later there were converts from the Kamma and Goldsmith castes.

97.  Albrecht, _op. cit._, p. 198.

98.  Haccius, _op. cit._, section three, second half, p. 290.

99.  Cf. pages 155-156 of Thesis.

100.  Cf. page 78 of Thesis.

101.  Dolbeer, _The Andhra Evangelical Lutheran Church_, A Brief History, Rajahmundry, 1951, p. 30. As late as 1909 the Rev. C. Theodore Benze mentioned over and over again in his _Report as Special Commissioner to the General Council India Mission_ that townspeople and missionary alike had emphasized to him what a serious mistake the Board had made in again closing the High School (it had been opened once more in 1902 after 16 years and then closed in 1908). He stated, pp. 38-39: "I cannot understand the action in closing the school before our arrival, when we were told to investigate its necessity. So far as I can judge, it was a serious mistake to close it. ... It would still prove most useful

for High School purposes and that in the eyes of the community such a school is required at that place, may be seen from the fact that Veerasalingam Pantulu the great writer and reformer has put in a petition for the lease of this property to house a High School which he is about to establish because we have dropped the work. It is a shame that we have done so and that a non-Christian must show us where our duty lay and still does lie. ... since the High School was closed there is not a single agency operative in Rajahmundry having for its aim the reaching of men, least of all those of the higher classes. It makes me blue to think what splendid opportunities we are passing by without putting forth a single effort to avail ourselves of them. This is the weakest point I have found so far in our Mission."

102. General Council Foreign Missions, Correspondence ..., Letter from F. S. Dietrich, Rajahmundry, October 19, 1883.

103. Graefe, The Task of a District Missionary in India, [n.d.], p. 6.

104. Wischan, Wilhelm Groenning, Missionar im Telugu-Lande, in Indien, Philadelphia, 1891, p. 290. Cf. also Drach-Kuder, op. cit., p. 260.

105. The Lutheran Standard, Vol. LXV, October 19, 1907, p. 663.

106. Ibid., p. 663.

107. Haccius, op. cit., section three, second half, pp. 266-267.

108. Ibid., pp. 270-273.

109. Ibid., pp. 277-278.

110. Cf. page 137 of Thesis.

111. Cf. page 163 of Thesis.

112. Haccius, op. cit., section three, second half, pp. 300-301.

113. Ibid., pp. 274, 320-321.

114. Ibid., pp. 324, 329.

115. Swavely, Lutheran Enterprise, p. 165.

116. Strasser, Die Taufe in der Geschichte der deutschen evangel-
ish-lutherischen Mission, Leipzig, 1925, pp. 106, 114.

117. Drach, Kingdom Pathfinders, pp. 28ff.

118. Ibid., p. 42.

119. Harms, Geschichte, p. 276

120. Proceedings, General Synod, pp. 76-77. J. E. Clough, the
leader of the mass movement in the Telugu Baptist Mission,
located between the Hermannsburg and Guntur Missions, laid
down three requirements for Christian converts: "Do not
work on Sunday; do not eat carrion; do not worship idols."
Clough, op. cit., p. 159.

121. Fiedler, op. cit., p. 89.

122. Craig, op. cit., p. 171.

123. Drach, Kingdom Pathfinders, p. 96.

124. Albrecht, op. cit., p. 156.

125. Craig, op. cit., p. 115. In a conversation with an English
coffee planter Wm. Groenning and other missionaries were
ridiculed. It was no use trying to convert Indians -- they
were rascals, only interested in eating, drinking, sleeping
and whoring. Converts were worse than others. They pre-
tend to be Christian only to get some money from the missionaries. They are rogues. The school work is especially
valueless; the only result is to puff the Hindus up and
make them think they are equal to the white man. But you
can't improve them; they are no better than the cattle of
the field. Groenning pointed out in answer that the
people are sunk in their environment, and cannot quickly be
changed. Even Europe with its long history of Christianity
is filled with evil peoples, some of them much worse than
the Indians. It takes time. Cf. Wischan, op. cit., pp.
152-155.

126. Albrecht, op. cit., pp. 63-64.

127. Drach-Kuder, op. cit., p. 251. Cf. also Pickett, op. cit.,
pp. 97ff.

128. Davis, op. cit., p. 98.

129. Cf. pp. 170ff. of Thesis.

130. Cf. pp. 150-151, 192 of Thesis.

131. Uhl, My First Missionary Tour, Baltimore, [n.d.], p. 2.

132. These are listed and a little told of their beginnings in Dolbeer, A.E.L.C., A Brief History, pp. 7-10.

133. Ibid., p. 12.

134. Cf. pages 150-151 of Thesis.

135. Dolbeer, A.E.L.C., A Brief History, p. 13.

136. Swavely, One Hundred Years, p. 211.

137. Ibid., p. 210. Two of Abraham's sons and one of his grandsons became pastors.

138. Cf. page 188 of Thesis.

139. Cf. pages 187-188 of Thesis.

140. Dolbeer, A.E.L.C., A Brief History, p. 15.

141. Cf. pages 156-157 of Thesis. Pages 155-156 list three men who did yeoman service in the Mission, but who were just getting started in the work in 1880.

142. Cf. pages 185-187 of Thesis.

143. Dolbeer, A.E.L.C., A Brief History, p. 34. It is difficult to determine from the records exactly how many congregations were in existence -- thus the use of the word 'about'.

144. Cf. pages 152-154 of Thesis.

145. They were: Sulurpeta (established in 1866), Gudur (1867), Nayudupeta (1867), Venkatagiri (1869), Sriharikota (1869), Vakadu (1871), Kalahasti (1873), Rapur (1873) and Tirupati (1877).

146. Missionsblatt, 1880, p. 23. A discrepancy is shown in the figure of 871 baptisms when we compare these statistics with those given in Woerrlein, Die Hermannsburger Mission, p. 236, where 848 is the total of baptisms. This is probably because the missionary children's and other European baptisms

are included in the larger figure. The 582 living Christians does not include Europeans.

147. Woerrlein, _Die Hermannsburger Mission_, p. 122.

148. _Ibid._, p. 123. Cf. also _Missionsblatt_, 1881, pp. 23-24.

149. Woerrlein, _Die Hermannsburger Mission_, p. 236. Cf. also pp. 140ff.

150. Petersen was one of the first group of missionaries which arrived in 1866 shortly after Mylius established the work. Cf. page 69 of Thesis. Scriba and Woerrlein came in 1868 and Hartwig Harms in 1882. Harms was the first missionary to come since the five sent out in 1879. Cf. page 201 of Thesis.

151. Harms, _Geschichte_, pp. 228ff.; Haccius, _op. cit._, section three, second half, p. 250; and Woerrlein, _Die Hermannsburger Mission_, pp. 175ff.

152. Woerrlein, _Die Hermannsburger Mission_, pp. 234ff.

153. Haccius, _op. cit._, section three, second half, pp. 342ff.

154. Harms, _Chronik des Seminars für Gehilfen in Nayudupeta_, undated manuscript, p. 43.

155. Haccius, _op. cit._, section three, second half, p. 344.

156. Richter, _op. cit._, p. 218; Clough, _op. cit._, pp. 240ff.

157. Swavely, _One Hundred Years_, p. 14; Dolbeer, _A.E.L.C., A Brief History_, p. 12.

158. Woerrlein, _Dreizehn Jahre in Indien_, Hermannsburg, 1885, pp. 154, 156ff. Cf. also Haccius, _op. cit._, section three, first half, p. 329.

159. Cf. _Missionsblatt_, 1879, pp. 11-12, 196ff.; Woerrlein, _Die Hermannsburger Mission_, pp. 149-150; and Haccius, _op. cit._, section three, first half, pp. 327-328.

160. _Missionsblatt_, 1877, pp. 200, 226-227; 1878, p. 23; 1879, pp. 6-7, 18-32.

161. Cf. pp. 72-73 and 199 of Thesis.

162. Haccius, op. cit., section three, first half, pp. 331-332, 305.

163. Schaefer, op. cit., p. 16.

164. Cf. pages 161-162 of Thesis.

165. Missionsblatt, 1881, pp. 225ff.

166. Richter, op. cit., p. 219.

167. Ibid., p. 218.

168. Cf. page 186 of Thesis.

169. Cf. page 188 of Thesis.

170. Cf. pages 26-27 and 180-181 of Thesis.

171. Cf. page 190 of Thesis.

172. Cf. biography of the Rev. August Carlson in Swanson, Three Missionary Pioneers, Rock Island, 1945, pp. 1-36.

173. Ibid., p. 26. Cf. also pages 157-158 of Thesis.

174. Cf. page 220 of Thesis.

175. Cf. pages 157 and 167-168 of Thesis. For a biography of Wm. Groenning, cf. Wischan, op. cit., passim.

176. Drach-Kuder, op. cit., pp. 258-260.

177. Cf. pages 202-203 of Thesis.

178. Cf. pages 120, 123 and 157 of Thesis.

REFERENCES AND NOTES

CHAPTER V     THE UPSURGE   1880-1920

1.    Cf. pages 62-63 of Thesis. Cf. also Proceedings of the Conventions of the General Synod of the Evangelical Lutheran Church in the United States, 1859, p. 71; and Swavely, One Hundred Years in the Andhra Country, Madras, 1942, pp. 12, 123.

2.    Cf. Swavely, "The Andhra Evangelical Lutheran Church," in The Wittenberg Bulletin, December, 1947, p. 10.

3.    Cf. pages 150-151 and 192 of Thesis.

4.    Cf. page 193 of Thesis.

5.    Proceedings, General Synod, 1877, p. 51.

6.    Miss Kate Boggs could never return to India but served for many years as Editor of the Lutheran Woman's Work, started in 1908. Cf. Swavely, One Hundred Years, p. 15.

7.    Cf. page 192 of Thesis; cf. articles by Rowe in The Lutheran Quarterly, Volumes 9 and 10.

8.    In 1885 there were 175 Christians in 5 villages in Repalle taluk. The 1888 statistics list 6 and not a single worker. Cf. Swavely, One Hundred Years, p. 174.

9.    Cf. Ibid., pp. 16, 27 and 174; Dolbeer, The Andhra Evangelical Lutheran Church, A Brief History, Rajahmundry, 1951, p. 24; Wolf, After Fifty Years, Philadelphia, 1896, pp. 140-142. Not much information is available on this dissension, although it was quite serious. Schnure evidently was broken by the experience. He died in Philadelphia in 1891; and his wife spent some time and effort trying to vindicate him, claiming that her husband had been discriminated against by the other missionaries and not treated with real justice.

10.   Swavely, One Hundred Years, p. 18. For the previous statistics, cf. Ibid., pp. 17-18; and Dolbeer, A.E.L.C., A Brief History, p. 24.

11. Dolbeer, A.E.L.C., A Brief History, p. 25.

12. Cf. Drach, Kingdom Pathfinders, Philadelphia, 1942, pp. 40-41. This is an autobiography of Uhl, pp. 28-47 inclusive. The author had the rare experience of meeting this venerable gentleman in 1942 at Gettysburg, just a year before his death on February 7, 1943, at the age of 95. His mind was still clear and he was full of vivid tales of his experiences in India. At the time we met the Andhra Evangelical Lutheran Church was celebrating its 100th anniversary; and it was a thrill, to say the least, to realize that Dr. Uhl went to India in 1873, the year that the founder Father Heyer died, and thus linked the very beginning with the present in two men. He spoke of the fact that he worked with Dr. Unangst for 23 years and learned about all there was to know from him and the native workers, whose minds were still filled with the close and vital associations made with the Founder of the Lutheran work in the Andhra Desa in 1842.

13. Dolbeer, A.E.L.C., A Brief History, p. 25. Most of this previous material has been taken from Ibid., pp. 21-25; and Swavely, One Hundred Years, pp. 17-18.

14. Swavely, One Hundred Years, p. 222.

15. Dolbeer, A.E.L.C., A Brief History, p. 41. Note the differences in the two quotations as found in Dolbeer and Swavely, One Hundred Years, p. 229. The latter book, written for the 100th Anniversary by many individuals with little historical background, is found to have a great many discrepancies and has to be checked constantly with other sources.

16. Cf. Swavely, The Lutheran Enterprise in India, Madras, 1952, pp. 232ff.

17. As early as 1850 Heyer reports that two men visited him from that area who told him "that they had heard about what was going on in the Palnaud, and they had come on purpose to tell me, that in their region of country many were desirous to hear the gospel, and wished to have their children instructed." Heyer, Letters from J. C. F. Heyer, 1847-1852, p. 36. He sent some men, but distance and intervening hills made the work difficult to maintain at that time. Two families in 1888, after having lived for a time in Narasaravupet taluk, returned to Kanigiri taluk and quietly spread the Gospel message until by 1890 several hundred people professed an interest in Christianity. The work developed so successfully

that a mission station was opened in 1910 at Tarlupad. It was from this Markapur-Cumbum field that the Home Mission field was selected and separated in 1918. Work has gone on steadily. By 1934 St. Thomas' Church was erected as a memorial to his parents by the Rev. C. R. Gopal -- the Rajahgopal - Siromoney Memorial.

18. Swavely, One Hundred Years, p. 133.

19. Strock, Letter to Dr. Wentz, Rentachintala, June 4, 1919, p. 2.

20. Ibid., p. 2.

21. Cf. Dolbeer, A.E.L.C., Brief History, p. 73; and Swavely, One Hundred Years, pp. 19, 21.

22. A separate figure for the number of congregations in the Guntur Mission in 1920 is not available. Together Rajahmundry and Guntur had 1,058 congregations at the time of the merger in 1920.

23. Swavely, One Hundred Years, p. 178; cf. also Dolbeer, A.E.L.C., Brief History, p. 40.

24. Cf. page 255 of Thesis.

25. Cf. footnote 54, Chapter V, also page 280 of Thesis.

26. Cf. pages 308ff., 317ff., 323ff., and 327ff. of Thesis.

27. Dolbeer, A.E.L.C., A Brief History, p. 39. Andhra Evangelical Lutheran Church is the name adopted by the Guntur and Rajahmundry Missions after they united. Cf. page 342 of Thesis.

28. Albrecht, In Tent and Bungalow, undated manuscript, p. 153.

29. Most of the previous material has been taken from Swavely, One Hundred Years, pp. 19-21; and Dolbeer, A.E.L.C., Brief History, pp. 37-41. Uhl in describing the Jubilee celebration mentioned how he had headed the procession of 3,000 in Guntur on a giant steed, "Jumbo." The parade was half a mile long. Eighteen missionaries took part in the tour, covering 1,047 villages. Uhl traveled 143 out of the 149 touring days. He also mentioned that the Guntur Mission had grown from 2,000 Christians in 1872, just before he ar-

rived, to 57,770 in 1917 at the time of the Jubilee. We
might add that it was close to 100,000 at the time of his
retirement in 1923 and 200,000 at the time of his death in
1943. Cf. Drach, Kingdom Pathfinders, p. 34.

30. Cf. page 153 of Thesis.

31. Drach-Kuder, op. cit., p. 198, footnote 1.

32. Ibid., p. 207.

33. At the beginning of 1882 Artman had graded the school into
    three departments: a Lower department of four grades, an
    Upper of four, and a Primary or Sand-writing department.
    In July he added a Senior department of two grades for the
    benefit of married men preparing to be teachers.

    "Although this arrangement for an abbreviated course of
    training was continued for only a few years, and the hope of
    the missionaries really centered on the young men who were
    regularly trained, it is, nevertheless, true that some of
    the best agents the Mission ever had, were secured through
    this temporary arrangement. In September, 1882, five
    teachers besides Artman, 120 enrolled pupils and an average
    attendance of 100 in the school were reported"
    Ibid., p. 210.

34. Cf. pages 155-156 of Thesis.

35. Drach-Kuder, op. cit., p. 219.

36. Cf. page 220 of Thesis.

37. Cf. pages 157-158 of Thesis.

38. The Rev. Adam Long had started work here in 1859 but had
    baptized only two adults in his six years of residence. Cf.
    pages 177 and 182 of Thesis.

39. Cf. page 248 of Thesis.

40. Cf. page 220 of Thesis.

41. Cf. footnote 33 of Chapter V.

42. Drach-Kuder, op. cit., p. 241.

43. These Rules and Regulations had been prepared by the Foreign

Missions Committee in consultation with Dr. Schmidt when he was in America in 1884, were adopted February 23, 1885 and later accepted by the Mission.

44. Drach-Kuder, op. cit., p. 248.

45. Cf. page 248 of Thesis.

46. Cf. Wischan, Wilhelm Groenning, Missionar im Telugu-Lande, in Indien, Philadelphia, 1891, pp. 290-294. The death of Groenning was a serious blow. "Crushed," said Schmidt, "we all stood around the grave. Our Mission had lost a force the like of which we never had before and may not soon have again." And the Foreign Missions Committee paid him tribute when they inserted in the minutes: "In the sudden and un-expected death of our dear brother we experienced the heavi-est blow which our Mission has ever suffered. ... In the few years during which in God's providence he was permitted to work in our Mission, particularly as superintendent of our educational institution, he had done most noble and effect-ive service in all faithfulness and conscientiousness, with a clear insight into the character of the work, with great energy and unselfish devotion to our Mission, the fruits of which we may hope to reap in coming years." Quoted from Drach-Kuder, op. cit., p. 261.

47. Dolbeer, A.E.L.C., Brief History, p. 34.

48. Cf. Paulus' own account of this as given us in Swavely, One Hundred Years, p. 200.

49. Cf. statistics in Ibid., p. 201; and Dolbeer, A.E.L.C., Brief History, pp. 34-35.

50. Cf. pages 168, 202, 248 of Thesis.

51. Cf. Drach-Kuder, op. cit., p. 291, concerning Edman's ex-periences in the interior at Addetigala.

52. Ibid., p. 288.

53. Cf. pages 155-156 of Thesis.

54. McCready was the next oldest missionary, having started work in 1884. Those who were present at the time the dissension broke out and their time of arrival in India are as follows: Pohl (1889 to Rajahmundry), Edman (1890), Kuder (1891),

Arps (1893), Isaacson (1893), Mueller (1896), and Holler (1897); and women missionaries: Miss Agnes Schade (1890), Miss Katherine Sadtler (1890) and Miss Charlotte Swenson (1895).

55. Jacobs, Memoirs of H. E. Jacobs, undated manuscript, p. 624. Cf. Ransom, The Christian Minister in India, London, 1946, pp. 175ff. on problem of national characteristics affecting Mission work.

56. Schmidt, The Strike in the Telugu Mission, manuscript, Rajahmundry, 1899, p. 32.

57. Cf. pages 272-273 of Thesis.

58. Drach-Kuder, op. cit., p. 308.

59. Schmidt, op. cit., p. 27 states: "The Foreign Missionary Societies rightly claim that the administration of Foreign Funds must remain with the Home Boards. But they generally very readily leave the administration of the Income of the Native Church to that body. In India are Native Pastors, brought up at the expense of the Home Boards and educated, some in India but others in America or England, who draw as high salaries as a Missionary, & they hold the opinion that the best thing would be to send all Foreign Missionaries home & divide all Foreign Mission money among Indian born workers."

60. Ibid., p. 28.

61. Schmidt complained that the Board had been too lenient and allowed things to be passed over which should have received closer attention. In regard to the late Pastor T. Joseph, who, although a member of the Ministerium of Pennsylvania, was deposed by the Mission Council without the matter being reported to the Board and the Board's orders considered, Schmidt said: "The Council assumed an authority which it had never before over Native Pastors. It wanted to have the same authority over Missionaries also & when I objected the four raised the question, whether I should be subject to the Council or the Council to me? The experiment with Mr. McCready succeeded. The Council elected him to build the Dormitory for 120 girls. He moved from Tallapudi to Rajahmundry & did the work. The Board wrote that this was not proper, but Council order prevailed.

A fundamental Rule has always been, that each Missionary
stands under the Board & that he is not subject to the
wishes of the other Missionaries individually or in Council.  They can only refertheir wishes to the Board for action.  Another fundamental Rule has been that no building
shall be taken in hand unless the Board has received intelligent information & approved estimate & plan."  Ibid.,
pp. 36-37.  Cf. also pages 51ff., 64ff.

62.  Cf. page 306 of Thesis.

63.  Jacobs, op. cit., p. 625.

64.  A printed sheet entitled "Extracts from Board Circulars" in
the Philadelphia Seminary Archives, evidently written by
Schmidt, has the following information: "Whenever there is
difference of opinion, a brief statement in writing of the
different views is submitted to the Board and a copy circu-
lated among the Missionaries so that the Board can come to
a conclusion and act in the matter.  This was also done in
J. William's case. ... [Kuder concluded] that there is a
great need for the services of some Native Christian, who
is able to travel in all sorts of weather and in all seasons
of the year, is qualified to perform marriages among native
christians, can scarcely be doubted, and was in fact admitted by all. ... We owe it to our christians to attend to
their churchly needs; that if we gather them into the Church
and instruct them under penalty of excommunication they must
be married in a christian way only, we have no right to
withhold from them men qualified to perform the weddings
among them. ... [McCready wrote:] Ordination first -- Marriage License to follow.  This proper order.  Unordained men
not permitted to distribute church blessings -- nor to officiate before a Lutheran Altar at marriages. ... [Isaacson
wrote:] According to my opinion only ordination qualifies a
man to administer the Sacraments and perform the benedictive
Acts. ... Most of all I wish that the Board would take such
steps that would speedily lead to the ordination of J. William and thus all the difficulties on that question would
be removed and great help rendered to our Mission."  Arps
also felt ordination was necessary unless the Lutheran church
changed her 'praxis and theory.'  Mueller felt only the
Ministerium of Pa. had the authority as the authorized
Board to install William as a 'candidatus.'  Schmidt left
the decision to the Board.  Cf. General Council.  Foreign
Missions, Case of Rev. J. William, 1901.

443

65. Jacobs, op. cit., pp. 618, 625, 629.

66. Cf. pages 155-156 of Thesis.

67. Harpster was the brother-in-law of the Rev. Prof. Henry E. Jacobs, new president of the Board of Foreign Missions. No one in the field was able to take over the leadership of the Mission. Jacobs comments that Edman lacked administrative ability; Isaacson was well-meaning but not very efficient as a leader; Neudoerffer had just arrived and did not know enough Telugu; Dr. Lydia Woerner, medical missionary, was just two years in the service; Miss Emilie Weiskotten, who came with her father in 1900, was in doubtful health mostly from the shock of her father's death; and Miss Strempfer, seriously ill, stayed only three years. Others were on furlough. Jacobs, op. cit., p. 627.

68. Drach-Kuder, op. cit., p. 373; cf. also Drach, Kingdom Pathfinders, p. 81.

69. Cf. Swavely, Lutheran Enterprise, p. 45; and Dolbeer, A.E.L.C., A Brief History, pp. 45-46, 55.

70. Cf. pages 155 and 318 of Thesis.

71. Drach-Kuder, op. cit., p. 375.

72. Cf. pages 189-190 of Thesis.

73. Dolbeer, A.E.L.C., A Brief History, p. 56.

74. Cf. Report of C. Theodore Benze as Special Commissioner to the General Council India Mission, Rajahmundry, 1909, passim.

75. Cf. pages 263-264 of Thesis.

76. Cf. page 320 of Thesis.

77. Cf. page 238 of Thesis.

78. Cf. page 163 of Thesis.

79. Devadas, 75 Samvatsaramula Klupta Charitram, Madras, 1941, pp. 32-33.

80. Ibid., p. 42.

81. Harms, _Geschichte der Hermannsburg Mission in Indien_, manu-
    script, 1935, p. 349.

82. _Ibid._, p. 513.

83. Cf. page 67 of Thesis.

84. Cf. page 217 of Thesis.

85. Cf. Haccius, _Hannoversche Missionsgeschichte_, Hermannsburg,
    1914, second half, p. 318.

86. Cf. page 226 of Thesis.

87. Cf. pages 333-334 of Thesis.

88. Devadas, _op. cit._, pp. 52-54. Cf. also Swavely, _One Hun-
    dred Years_, p. 241, and Dolbeer, _A.E.L.C., A Brief History_,
    p. 119.

89. Harms, _Geschichte_, pp. 442-443.

90. Haccius, _op. cit._, second half, pp. 251-252; and _Hermanns-
    burger Missionsblatt_, 1910, pp. 69-79. See pages 201-204 of
    Thesis for the little information available about the Brek-
    lum Mission in this period.

91. Cf. pages 240ff. of Thesis.

92. J. E. Clough tells of being forced into action finally by
    the warning from two Roman Catholic priests that they would
    baptize the Madigas clamoring for baptism in the Ongole area,
    if he did not. He reports their meeting: "In a straight-
    forward way they told me that their bishop considered it an
    anomaly that thousands of converts should be kept waiting,
    asking repeatedly for admission into the church, only to be
    met with a continued refusal. Their church was having
    large accessions in other parts of the famine area. They
    intimated to me that if the religious body to which I be-
    longed could not , on principle, allow me to cope with this
    situation, their church had no such restrictions." Clough,
    _Social Christianity in the Orient_, New York, 1914, p. 273.

93. Cf. Pickett, _Christ's Way to India's Heart_, Lucknow, 1937,
    pp. 33ff.; cf. also Haccius, _op. cit._, first half, p. 305.

94. Cf. pages 229-230 of Thesis.

95. Cf. Pickett, Christ's Way, pp. 50ff.

96. Ibid., p. 40.

97. Pickett, Christian Mass Movements in India, New York, 1933, p.332.

98. Ibid., p. 334.

99. Albrecht, op. cit., pp. 75, 82, 94, 131 and 198.

100. Cf. page 260 of Thesis. This continued in the Palnad. "On Thanksgiving Day, 1931, 261 were baptised in the village of Adigoppula." Swavely, One Hundred Years, p. 131. Cf. also Curtis, The New Sudra Mass Movement Among the Telugus in South India, Hartford, 1936, passim., especially pp. 45-46.

101. Dolbeer, A.E.L.C., A Brief History, p. 57.

102. Albrecht, op. cit., pp. 182-184.

103. Strasser, Die Taufe in der Geschichte der deutschen evangelisch-lutherischen Mission, Leipzig, 1925, p. 106. Cf. also Davis, The Life Story of a Leper, Toronto, 1918, p.180.

104. Harms, Geschichte, p. 266.

105. Lutherisches Weltmissionsjahrbuch, Leipzig, 1927, p. 25. Cf. also Haccius, op. cit., second half, p. 252.

106. Fiensch, Kurze Geschichte der Entstehung und der bisherigen Arbeit der Schleswig-Holsteinischen evang.-luth. Missionsgesellschaft, Breklum, 1890, p. 67.

107. Fiedler, Then the Light Came, Philadelphia, 1941, pp. 29-35.

108. Strasser, op. cit., p. 86.

109. Harms, Geschichte, pp. 191-193.

110. Ibid., pp. 175-176, 230-231.

111. Haccius, op. cit., second half, p. 274.

112. Cf. Davis, op. cit., p. 106, and Sowing the Seed, Foreign Missionary Annual, Evangelical Lutheran Joint Synod of Ohio, 1930, p. 8.

113. Harms reports that the greatest famine in that area, outside of 1876-1878, came in 1903-1905. There was less rain in 1904 than for 90 years previous. Many had sown seed five times and received nothing. Worst hit were the coolies, who could find neither labor nor food. The Mission was able to help many through gifts from Germany, America and Africa, and also through employment on construction projects. Harms, Geschichte, pp. 318ff.

114. Schaefer, A History of the Hermannsburg Lutheran Mission in India, Columbus, 1946, p. 75. Cf. also India Conference Minutes of Ev. Luth. Missionaries in India, Tirupati, April 5-8, 1921, pp. 7-10.

115. Schaefer, op. cit., pp. 88-89. Cf. also Devadas, op. cit., p. 44.

116. Cf. page 285 of Thesis.

117. Benze, op. cit., p. 26. Information about the Industrial School is taken from Devadas, op. cit., p. 44; Haccius, op. cit., second half, pp. 269-270; Harms, Lebensbeschreibung von Missionar Hartwig Harms, manuscript, p. 16-17; and Woerrlein, Die Hermannsburger Mission in Indien, Hermannsburg, 1899, p. 229.

118. Proceedings, General Synod, 1879, p. 55.

119. Richter, A History of Missions in India, New York, 1908, p. 239.

120. Drach, Kingdom Pathfinders, pp. 41-42; and Harpster, Among the Telugoos, Philadelphia, 1902, p. 80.

121. Drach, Kingdom Pathfinders, p. 45. Cf. Albrecht, op. cit., p. 92.

122. Cf. page 190 of Thesis.

123. See footnote 101, Chapter II.

124. Dolbeer, A.E.L.C., A Brief History, pp. 31-32.

125. Drach-Kuder, op. cit., p. 177.

126. Cf. pages 277-278 of Thesis.

127. Benze, op. cit., p. 57.

128. Cf. pages 277-278, and 281 of Thesis. Schmidt, in defending his position, declared: "I do not believe in a Christian church consisting of immortal souls only, with bodies underfed & without clothing & shelter. I believe in a church which has market value. Most Hindus are cultivators & if the Christians do not get possession of the soil, they can never support their church. The history of a missionary may be to 'come, eat and go' -- but the history of the native Christians must be 'replenish the earth & subdue it.'" Schmidt, op. cit., p. 99.

129. Dolbeer, Letter to Author, Rajahmundry, dated April 8, 1949, p. 3.

130. Benze, op. cit., p. 82.

131. Cf. page 50 of Thesis.

132. Cf. page 53 of Thesis.

133. Wolf, After Fifty Years, Philadelphia, 1896, p. 200.

134. Proceedings, General Synod, 1871, p. 75.

135. Ibid., 1877, p. 50; and 1879, pp. 51-52, 55.

136. Cf. page 252 of Thesis.

137. The author remembers "Aunt" Minnie as his favorite friend as a boy in Narasaravupet. Connected with the Guntur field for 64 years, she still lives there in quiet retirement, a great influence among the single missionaries and the Bible women.

138. The preceding material primarily taken from Wolf, After Fifty Years, pp. 196ff., Swavely, One Hundred Years, pp. 254ff., and Dolbeer, A.E.L.C., A Brief History, pp. 20-21, 43-44.

139. Benze, op. cit., p. 79.

140. Previous material taken primarily from Drach, Kingdom Path-Finders, pp. 89-103 (biography of Miss Agnes Schade); Fiedler, op. cit., pp. 29-35; Swavely, One Hundred Years,

pp. 269ff.; Dolbeer, A.E.L.C., A Brief History, pp. 33, 50-52, 53; and Drach-Kuder, op. cit., pp. 98ff., 205, 304ff., 310ff.

141. Previous material taken primarily from Devadas, op. cit., pp. 30, 37-39, 52, 55; Haccius, op. cit., second half, pp. 333-340; Harms, Geschichte, pp. 277-279, 348, 460-463, 541-542.

142. Cf. Dolbeer, A.E.L.C., A Brief History, p. 53.

143. Under Neudoerffer's aggressive leadership, the Christians in the Bhimawaram-Narsapur field increased from 4,000 in 1909 when he moved there to about 9,000 in 1920.

144. Cf. pages 220, 268 of Thesis and footnote 101 of Chapter IV.

145. Cf. page 280 of Thesis. While still a missionary of the Rajahmundry Mission, McCready had become quite interested in tile manufacturing and took a leave of absence in 1893 to learn about it so that he could establish a factory at Tallapudi, where Christians could secure work. Cf. Drach-Kuder, op. cit., p. 290.

146. Cf. pages 285-286 of Thesis. The six men were P. Benjamin, J. M. Franklin, N. I. Jacob, V. Prakasam, G. T. Paulus, and T. Shadrach.

147. Cf. page 256 of Thesis.

148. Cf. page 193 of Thesis.

149. A large portion of the money raised had come from the Watts family.

150. Swavely, One Hundred Years, p. 235.

151. Cf. Strock, Copy of Resolutions in regard to United Christian College, May 14, 1920.

152. Strock, Letter to Dr. Wentz, Guntur, May 12, 1920, passim. Most of the preceding information taken from Dolbeer, A.E.L.C., A Brief History, pp. 23, 43, 52-54; Swavely, One Hundred Years, pp. 47ff., 56ff., 93ff., 139ff., 165ff., and 234ff.

153. For statistics, cf. Haccius, op. cit., second half, pp. 342-
343. For information on the schools, cf. Devadas, op. cit.,
pp. 34-36.

154. We have already mentioned Heyer. Cf. page 58 of Thesis.
Cf. also Wischan, op. cit., p. 62; Woerrlein, Dreizehn
Jahre in Indien, Hermannsburg, 1885, p. 117; and Albrecht,
op. cit., pp. 219-220.

155. Drach, Kingdom Pathfinders, p. 56.

156. Cf. page 234 of Thesis.

157. Polack, Into All the World, St. Louis, 1930, p. 115.
Kretzmann, Glimpses of the Lives of Great Missionary Women,
St. Louis, 1930, p. 85, states that this Rajah was M. Bhu-
janga Rao Bahadur of Ellore. Dr. Kugler had restored his
wife and saved the life of his son and heir. He built a
rest home for relatives of the patients out of gratitude
to her. He was interested in the secret of Dr. Kugler's
power, so she gave him a New Testament, which he translated
into Telugu poetry "which Brahmans and all educated Telugus
would delight to read. When the new rest home was dedicated, he gave away five hundred copies of his translation to
the guests. His youngest child is named Annamma in honor
of the doctor. On his very letter-head this Brahman Rajah
has printed a picture of the Christ which he now regards as
the hope of India and whom, as he says in the preface to
his translation, he first saw reflected in the pure and
beautiful life of this American doctor." Wiles, A Pioneer
Medical Missionary, Anna S. Kugler, M.D., Philadelphia,
[n.d.], p. 3 states that the Madras papers announced on Dr.
Kugler's arrival in India that there was 'no other woman
physician in the Presidency.'

158. Kretzmann, op. cit., p. 48.

159. Woerrlein, Dreizehn Jahre, p. 117; also Haccius, op. cit.,
second half, p. 343.

160. Harms, Geschichte, p. 230.

161. Cf. Haccius, op. cit., second half, pp. 330-331; Harms,
Geschichte, pp. 400-403; and Devadas, op. cit., pp. 50-51.

162. Dolbeer, A.E.L.C., A Brief History, p. 132. Although statistics are not available for 1920, the present capacity

of the Home is 150. Dr. R. Sudarsanarao served the institution for more than 15 years; the present medical superintendent is Dr. Y. J. Paul.

163. Cf. page 313 of Thesis.

164. Cf. Dolbeer, A.E.L.C., A Brief History, pp. 134-135.

165. Cf. Albrecht, op. cit., pp. 214ff.; Dolbeer, A.E.L.C., A Brief History, pp. 138-139; and Swavely, One Hundred Years, pp. 128-129.

166. Cf. Woerrlein, Die Hermannsburger Mission, p. 198.

167. Those who took part in the program were Unangst, Uhl, Wolf, Harpster, Aberly, Dr. Anna Kugler and Miss A. L. Sadtler of the Guntur Mission; Kuder, Pohl and Miss Agnes Schade of the Rajahmundry Mission; Schultze and Harless of the Breklum Mission; and Woerrlein and Maneke of the Hermannsburg Mission.

168. Cf. page 290 of Thesis.

169. Harms, Geschichte, pp. 380-381.

170. Other Missions were Swedish, Leipzig, Danish, Hermannsburg, Guntur, Rajahmundry, Breklum and Gossner.

171. Harms, Geschichte, pp. 383-394. Statistics for all Lutheran Missions in India for 1907 were: ordained missionaries 169, unordained missionaries 5, missionary wives 107, single women missionaries 51, evangelists and catechists 1,034, school teachers 1,763, Bible women 194, total baptisms in 1906--1,161, schools 681, pupils 36,904, and total number of Christians 168,329. Ibid., p. 397.

172. Swavely, Lutheran Enterprise, p. 244.

173. Ibid., p. 244. This led to the establishment of the Federation of the Evangelical Lutheran Churches in India in February, 1928. By 1950 the Federation represented 543,225 Christians in India.

174. Cf. page 258 of Thesis. The Rev. B. J. Krupadanam, who had been working among the Kois and Reddis of the Agency hill tribes north of Rajahmundry, was selected as a missionary of the L.N.M.S. in 1941. Cf. pp. 189-190, 284 of Thesis.

451

175. Cf. Swavely, <u>Lutheran Enterprise</u>, pp. 232ff. and <u>Luther-isches Weltmissionsjahrbuch</u>, 1927, pp. 13ff. for further details.

176. Haccius, <u>op. cit.</u>, second half, p. 387. Many of the Ohio pastors had been trained at Hermannsburg and their interest in its Missions was natural.

177. <u>Lutheran Standard</u>, September 22, 1906, p. 666.

178. <u>Hermannsburger Missionsblatt</u>, 1904, p. 327, states that the Mission Council of Hermannsburg could not make any binding promises as to handing over the stations permanently. This would have to be left to later agreements, if the desire to become independent still remains.

179. <u>Lutheran Standard</u>, September 10, 1910, p. 584.

180. <u>Letter from Dr. E. Harms to Dr. Pfeiffer</u>, Ennersdale, Natal, May 2, 1911.

181. Cf. pages 204-205 of Thesis.

182. Burgess, <u>Lutheran World Missions</u>, Minneapolis, 1954, pp. 27-28.

183. <u>Ibid.</u>, p. 29.

184. <u>Ibid.</u>, p. 29.

185. Sheatsley, <u>Our Mission Field in India</u>, Columbus, 1921, p. 138.

186. Swavely, <u>Lutheran Enterprise</u>, p. 156.

187. <u>Ibid.</u>, p. 157. (Missionaries from the United Lutheran Church Mission also helped the autonomous Gossner Church from 1920 to 1928.)

188. Cf. pages 179-181 of Thesis.

189. Cf. pages 257-258 of Thesis.

REFERENCES AND NOTES

CHAPTER VI     THE CONCLUSION

1.     There were 799 schools in 1920, 801 in 1950; pupils were
       30,200 in 1920 and 69,153 in 1950; teachers were 1,216 in
       1920 and 2,732 in 1950.  These statistics are from Dolbeer,
       The Andhra Evangelical Lutheran Church; A Brief History,
       Rajahmundry, 1951, pp. 60-61.

2.     Ibid., p. 78.

3.     Burgess, Lutheran World Missions, Minneapolis, 1954, p. 34;
       and Dolbeer, A.E.L.C., A Brief History, p. 75 for statis-
       tics.

4.     Cf. Dolbeer, A.E.L.C., A Brief History, pp. 140ff., and
       147ff. for a list of some of the most prominent clergy and
       laymen of the Andhra Evangelical Lutheran Church.

5.     2 Cor. 12:9-10.

6.     2 Cor. 2:14-17.